OUT OF THE RED SHADOWS

RUSSIAN STUDIES SERIES

Valery Kuvakin, General Editor

GENERAL INTEREST

History of Russian Philosophy, 2 volumes, edited by Valery Kuvakin

The Basic Bakunin: Writings 1869–1871, translated and edited by Robert M. Cutler

Anton Chekhov: Stories of Women, edited and translated by Paula Ross

FROM THE SECRET ARCHIVES OF THE FORMER SOVIET UNION

Out of the Red Shadows: Anti-Semitism in Stalin's Russia, by Gennadi V. Kostyrchenko

Lenin's Will: Falsified and Forbidden, by Yuri Buranov

The Red Army and the Wehrmacht: How the Soviets Militarized Germany in 1922–1933 and Paved the Way for Fascism, by Yuri L. Dyakov and Tatyana S. Bushuyeva

The Struggle for Power in Russia in 1923, by Valentina P. Vilkova (Fall 1995)

OUT OF THE RED SHADOWS

Anti-Semitism in Stalin's Russia

GENNADI KOSTYRCHENKO

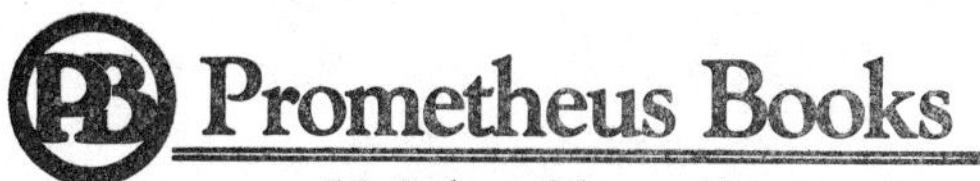

Prometheus Books
59 John Glenn Drive
Amherst, New York 14228-2197

 Inquiries should be addressed to Prometheus Books, 59 John Glenn Drive, Amherst, New York 14228-2197; 716-691-0133 / FAX: 716-691-0137.

99 98 97 96 95 5 4 3 2 1

Library of Congress Cataloging-in-Publication Data

Kostyrchenko, Gennadi V., 1954–

Out of the red shadows : anti-Semitism in Stalin's Russia : from the secret archives of the former Soviet Union / by Gennadi V. Kostyrchenko.

p. cm.

Translated from Russian.

Includes bibliographical references.

ISBN 0-87975-930-5 (alk. paper)

1. Antisemitism—Soviet Union—History. 2. Jews—Persecutions—Soviet Union. 3. Jews—Soviet Union—Intellectual life. 4. Stalin, Joseph, 1879–1953—Views on Jews. 5. Soviet Union—government—1936–1953. I. Title.

DS146.S65K68 1995

q47' .004924—dc20

94-39151

CIP

Printed on acid-free paper in the United States of America.

Table of Contents

Key to Abbreviations

ACP(b) / VKP(b)—(1925–1952), All-Union Communist Party (Bolshevik) / Vsesoyuznaya Kommunisticheskaya Partiya (bol'shevikov)

Agitprop—Propaganda and Agitation Department of the CC of the ACP(b) / Otdel propagandy i agitatsii TsK VKP(b)

ALCUY / VLKSM—All-Union Leninist Communist Union of Youth / Vsesoyuznyí Kommunisticheskií Soyuz Molodezhi

CAA—Committee of Arts Affairs at the Council of Ministers of the USSR / Komitet Po Delam Iskusstv Pri Sovyete Ministrov SSSR

CC / TsK—Central Committee / Tsentral'nyí komitet

CCC / TsKK—Central Control Commission at the Central Committee of the Communist Party of the Soviet Union / Tsentral'naya Komtrol'naya Komissiya pri Tsentral'nom Komitete Kommunisticheskoí Partii Sovyetskogo Soyuza

CP / KP—Communist Party / Kommunisticheskaya Partiya

CPC USSR / SNK SSSR—Council of People's Commissars of the USSR / Sovyet Narodnykh Komissarov SSSR (Sovnarkom)

CPSU / KPSS—(1952–1991), Communist Party of the Soviet Union / Kommunisticheskaya Partiya Sovyetskogo Soyuza, formerly the ACP(b)

GARF—State Archives of the Russian Federation / Gosudarstvennyi Arkhiv Rossiískoí Federatsii

JAC / YeAK—Jewish Antifascist Committee / Yevreískií Antifashistskií Komitet

LSUK—Medical and Sanitary Directorate of the Kremlin / Lechebno-Sanitarnoye Upravleniye Kremlya

MCSC—Military Collegium of the Supreme Court / Voennaya Kollegiya Verkhovnogo Suda

MGB—Ministry of State Security / Ministerstvo Gosudarstvennoí Bezopasnosti, formerly the NKVD

MSU / MGU—Moscow State University / Moskovskií Gosudarstvennyí Universitet

NKVD—People's Commissariat of Internal Affairs / Narodnyí Kommissariat Vnutrennikh Del, later the MGB

RSFSR—Russian Soviet Federative Socialist Republic / Rossiískaya Sovyetskaya Federativnaya Sotsialisticheskaya Respublika

RTsKhIDNI—Russian Center for the Preservation and Study of Documents of Modern History / Rossiískií Tsentr Khraneniya i Izucheniya Dokumentov Noveísheí Istorii

Sovinformburo—Soviet Information Bureau / Sovyetskoye Informatsionnoye Byuro

USC / SSK—Union of Soviet Composers / Soyuz Sovyetskikh Kompozitorov

USW / SSP—Union of Soviet Writers / Soyuz Sovyetskikh Pisateleí

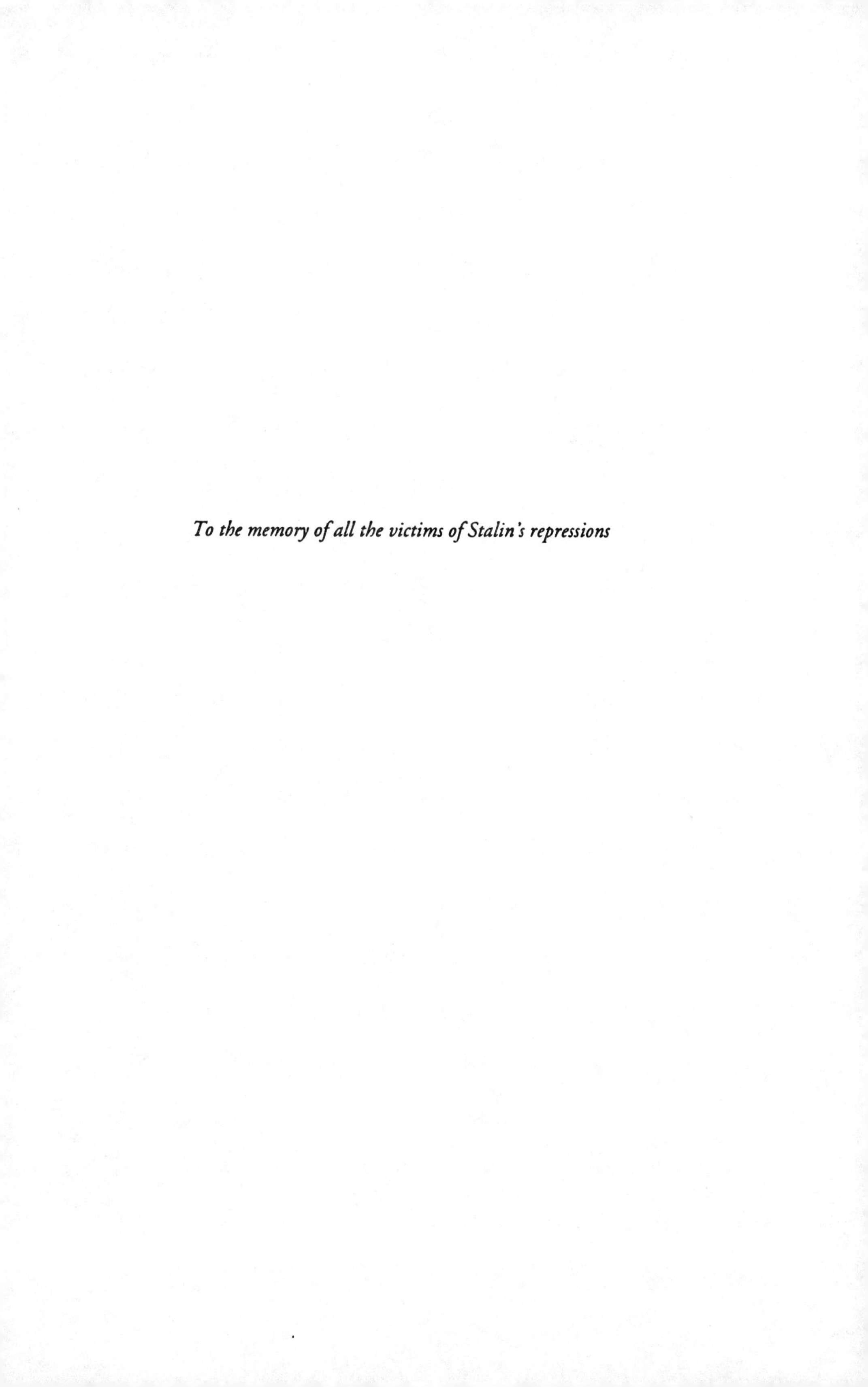

To the memory of all the victims of Stalin's repressions

Introduction

The Stalinist policy toward the Soviet Jews has been a taboo topic in official Soviet historiography. There are several reasons for this, the main one being that anti-Semitism had for many years remained a major ideological and psychological component of the ruling Communist regime. At the same time, it was assumed that the Jewish problem was, as it were, nonexistent, and that any talk about it was hostile Western propaganda designed to interfere in the internal affairs of the Soviet Union. Whatever contradicted the guidelines of the authorities was concealed from public consciousness, and the principle of "if the facts are against us, so much the worse for the facts" prevailed. The archives of the Party and state, which contained documents about the Stalinist policies of suppressing and eliminating all free manifestations of Jewish life and of forcibly assimilating the Jews, were secret and inaccessible to researchers even during the years of perestroika.

Western historians have attempted to overcome this information vacuum. In the late 1940s studies of postwar Stalinism in general, and its innate anti-Semitism in particular, began to appear in the West, mainly in the English-speaking countries and in Israel.[1]

It is to the credit of Western historians that, though they were forced to rely on very limited resources (e.g., Soviet periodicals, published documents of the Communist Party and government bodies of the USSR, and eyewitness accounts of repatriated Jews), they nevertheless succeeded in correctly discerning the main

---

1. For example, see Robert Conquest, *Power and Policy in the U.S.S.R.: The Struggle for Stalin's Succession, 1945–1960* (New York: Harper & Row, 1967); Milovan Djilas, *Conversations with Stalin* (New York: Harcourt, Brace & World, 1962); Shimon Redlich, *Propaganda and Nationalism in Wartime Russia: The Jewish Antifascist Committee in the USSR, 1941–1948* (Boulder, Colorado: East European Quarterly, 1982); Yehoshua A. Gilboa, *The Black Years of Soviet Jewry, 1939–1953* (Boston: Little, Brown and Company, 1971); and Benjamin Pinkus, *The Jews of the Soviet Union: The History of a National Minority* (Cambridgeshire: Cambridge University Press, 1988).

trends in the life of Soviet Jewry in the Stalinist and post-Stalinist periods. However, due to the inaccessibility of archive documents, Western scholars have failed to recreate the specific historical dynamic of events that determined the destinies of Jews in the USSR. Nonsystematic attempts by scholars abroad and by their colleagues in Russia to break through the Kremlin's wall of secrecy were as a rule fruitless, and sometimes their search for a scoop led them too far from historical objectivity. It is sufficient to recall in this context Stuart Kahan's book about Lazar M. Kaganovich, which could be only conditionally regarded as accurately depicting his real life story.[2]

The books by A. Borshchagovskií,[3] M. Aleksandrovich,[4] Z. Sheínis,[5] and Ester Markish[6] were written in the style of emotional journalism, as were other books by eyewitnesses and active participants in the events of the 1940s and early 1950s, who had to some extent firsthand experiences of the consequences of the anti-Semitic political campaigns. No matter how valuable the recollections of eyewitness and victims of the Stalinist anti-Semitic repression may be, they reflect their personal biases about the Stalinist epoch, which not only crippled the mentality of each individual, but also distorted the social consciousness of "real" socialism. The decades of lies spread by official propaganda in the period of mass ideological, psychological, and overt terror, which the Iron Curtain imposed in all spheres of information, have left their indelible imprint. Now that Russia has finally gained some opportunity objectively to study and freely to assess and criticize its past, this opportunity is not always adequately realized; sometimes people use it to settle personal accounts with the past or to vent their pent-up negative emotions, rather than to establish the historical record. This may well be understood and even justified psychologically. However, a scholar should, I submit, follow Spinoza's wise advice "not to weep, not to laugh, not to curse, but to understand."

Fortunately, there is in today's post-Soviet world an obvious trend toward a more objective approach to understanding the past—amidst the fanciful layers of rumors and legends described in memoirs. A more careful approach to the historical facts is a feature, for example, of Ya. Rapoport's book, *At the Boundary of Two Epochs: The Doctors' Case in 1953.*[7]

A great number of recent articles in Russian newspapers and magazines, based on archival materials, have also contributed to some restoration of the true picture

2. Stuart Kahan, *The Wolf of the Kremlin* (New York: W. Morrow, 1987).

3. A. Borshchagovskií, *Zapiski balovniya sud'by* [*Notes of a Favorite of Fortune*] (Moscow, 1991).

4. M. Aleksandrovich, *Ya pomniu . . .* [*I Remember . . .*] (Moscow, 1992).

5. Z. Sheínis, *Provokatsiya veka* [*Provocation of the Century*] (Moscow, 1992).

6. Ester Markish, *Stol' dolgoye vozvrascheniye . . . : vospominaniya* [*A Long Way Back . . . : A Memoir*] (Tel Aviv: Izd. Avtora, 1989).

7. Ya. Rapoport, *Na rubesze dvuh epoh. Delo vracheií 1953 goda* (Moscow, 1988).

of past events. Arkadiĭ Vaksberg's undoubtedly interesting—although not always indisputably accurate—essays certainly enjoy the greatest popularity.[8] In early 1994 A. Borshchagovskiĭ published an interesting book, *Blood on Trial*,[9] based largely on an extensive number of documents of proceedings and investigations on the JAC case, documents that until now had been classified.

No clear answer, however, has as yet been provided by researchers to the key question: What was the predominant factor in Stalin's anti-Semitism; was it pathological paranoid Judeophobia, or was it Machiavellian pragmatism? Some authors maintain that the answer was merely Stalin's personal hostility toward the Jews; and by absolutizing this idea, they interpret it as the main factor behind the anti-Semitic campaigns of the 1940s and early 50s. Others assert that those events were the logical result of the development of totalitarianism in the USSR; and that, consequently, the subjective factor was of little significance. The correct answer to this question is probably to be found midway between these two accounts.

The objective of the present study is not primarily Stalin's personal anti-Semitism per se. Rather, I wish to focus on the socio-political and concrete historical aspects of the problem. That is why I have stressed the actual documents and decisions approved at the highest Party and State levels that initiated and promoted anti-Semitism in all spheres of public life in the USSR.

I have set for myself the task of documenting and reconstructing the events that formed the basis of Stalin's anti-Semitism and that proved so disastrous for the Jewish people. This research is based on hundreds of previously unpublished and recently declassified documents that I have discovered mainly in the former secret archives of the Central Committee of the Communist Party of the Soviet Union, of the KGB, and of the archives of the Federal Counterintelligence Service. Together with the original archive files, I was also given access mainly to the photostatic copies (identical to the originals) of documents from the Central Archives of the Federal Counterintelligence Service of the Russian Federation, which lacked any archival cataloging codes (the documents of the State Security Office have not yet been catalogued and processed in accordance with the archives' regulations). For this reason I refer, in the footnotes, to these documents by the general term "Document from the archives of the former KGB." I use a similar term for photocopies of documents from the archives of the president of the Russian Federation.

The present study is the first of its kind. It places a substantial number of new archival materials into scientific circulation. I do not claim to provide a

8. For example, see his article, "Stalin protiv yevreev" ("Stalin vs. the Jews"), *Detektiv i Politika (Detective Stories and Politics)*, 1992, no. 3, pp. 150–208.

9. A.A. Borshchagovskiĭ, *Obvinyaetsya krov* (Moscow, 1994).

detailed analysis and all-around assessment, and I have certainly not set myself the task of drawing final conclusions. That would hardly be justified, as not all of the documents bearing on this subject have yet been uncovered and studied. However, the somewhat incomplete nature of the sources did not induce me to renounce the attempt to make a documented reconstruction of past events and of drawing some generalizations about them. Whether or not I have succeeded is for the reader to decide.

It should be noted that this research was conducted under a steadily growing stream of information. As new facts were discovered in the archival record, they had to be worked into the manuscript after it had already been accepted for publication—even up to the last moment of the dispatch of this book to the printer. This should help explain the over-saturation of documents on the one hand, and the impossibility of evaluating all of them in detail on the other. What this study will reveal is a systematic and sinister attempt by the Stalinist regime to suppress Soviet Jewry in all aspects of public life.

I express my gratitude toward and acknowledge the cooperation of the following organizations: RTsKhIDNI, the State Archives of the Russian Federation, the Central Archives of the Federal Counterintelligence Service, and others. I also thank my translator, A. Riazantseva, my colleagues I.A. Altman, A.I. Barkovets, V.A. Kuvakin, L.L. Mininberg, B.Ya. Khazanov, as well as the direct participants of the events described in the book and their relatives: A.M. Borshchagovskiĭ, L.M. Vovsi, I.B. Zbarskiĭ, L.B. Kogan, N.M. Kogan, S.M. Sandler, I.S. Sobol, V.Ya. Temkina, D.I. Fefer, Ya.Ya. Etinger, and others who helped in the preparation of this book, provided documents and illustrated materials, and shared their thoughts and memories. I express my special gratitude to Professors Paul Kurtz and Viktor Mushinskiĭ, on whose initiative and with whose help the publication of this book in English and in Russian was possible.

One

The Tangle of National Contradictions

The victory over fascism did not put an end to the Jewish national tragedy, whose most ominous and terrible pages had just been opened. The postwar years brought new trials to the life of the Jewish people, and however paradoxical it may seem, the Soviet Union, the country that had contributed more than any other to the military termination of the Holocaust, also had its own cruel blows to strike at its Jews. To understand why this happened, we need to take an excursion into the question of nationalities in the USSR.

It is well known that in the mid-1930s Stalin promoted the ideology of Russian chauvinism in order to counteract aggressive German totalitarianism, whose confrontation with Communist Russia had then become acute. This ideology to a certain extent replaced the slogans "world revolution" and "proletarian internationalism," which had become tarnished by intra-Party discords with the followers of Bukharin, with the Trotskyites, and with other members of the opposition.

Stalin thought this revival of traditional imperial Russian nationalism would support his foreign policy. This chauvinism also became a cornerstone of his newly elaborated national-state doctrine, "the theory of the elder brother," which was written into the Constitution of 1936. This doctrine curtailed the rights of the Soviet republics and almost completely eliminated the rights of national minorities.

As the "leader of the peoples," Stalin needed this theory to disguise his policy of concentrating absolute power in his own hands and of placing himself above the Party and above the state administrative machinery. He justified his policies, saying, "Owing to the historical development we inherited from the past (and by right of succession), one nationality, namely the Great Russian one, turned out to be more politically and industrially developed than the other nationalities."[1]

On March 13, 1938 the USSR Council of People's Commissars (CPC) and the CC of the All-Union Communist Party (Bolshevik) approved a resolution about "the compulsory learning of the Russian language in the schools of the national republics and regions." In one of her letters to Stalin, Nadezhda Krupskaya[2] wrote about some of the consequences of such a decision.

> Dear Iosif Vissarionovich,
>
> We're implementing the compulsory teaching of the Russian language throughout the USSR. It is nice . . . . But I'm anxious about *how* we will carry out this teaching. Sometimes it seems to me that great-power chauvinism begins to show its horns . . . . Such a curse-word as "Zhid" has emerged among children . . . . [3]

It was at this time that national minorities, including the Jews, began to suffer the forcible closures of their newspapers, magazines, and sociopolitical, cultural, and educational organizations.[4] The intensive program of Russification and assimilation began first among minorities who did not have their own states. In order to justify this aspect of this policy to the Jews, the Stalinist regime resorted to the appropriate quotations from Lenin's voluminous works, and in particular to his statement that "only a Jewish reactionary middle class strongly interested in turning back the wheel of history can rail against 'assimilation activities'. . . . "[5]

World War II had already been a heavy burden to the Russians. Now Stalin wished to take advantage of this situation to add more features to his national-hierarchical conception. On the one hand, the decrees of the Presidium of the USSR Supreme Soviet pompously instituted military orders in honor of such famous Russian military leaders as Suvorov, Kutuzov, and Aleksandr Nevskií. On the other hand, the Party and state machinery began secretly, and with bureaucratic awkwardness and rigidity, to launch a campaign of so-called "national-personnel" control. This policy was supposedly intended to give

---

1. I.V. Stalin, Marksizm i natsional'no-kolonial'nyí vopros: sbornik izbrannykh stateí u recheí [Marxism and the National-Colonial Problem: Selected Articles and Speeches] (Moscow, 1939), p. 98.

2. *Editor's note:* Krupskaya was Lenin's widow.

3. *Izvestiya TsK KPSS*, 1989, no. 3, p. 179. *Translator's note:* "Zhid" is equivalent to the English "Yid." *Izvestiya TsK KPSS* is an official Party journal, not to be confused with the newspaper *Izvestiya*.

4. RTsKhIDNI, f. 17, op. 114, d. 635, l. 13; d. 644, l. 52; d. 833, l. 248. *Translator's note:* f = fond, meaning "collection"; op = opis, meaning "list"; d = delo, meaning "file"; and l = list, meaning "page."

5. V.I. Lenin, "Kriticheskiye zametki po natsional'nomu voprosu" ["Critical Notes on the National Problem"], in *Polnoye sobracheniye, tom. 24* [*Complete Works, vol. 24*] (Moscow: Institute of Marxism-Leninism, 1961), p. 126.

Russians priority in the key spheres of social life, but in essence it was highly chauvinistic and had a substantial anti-Semitic taint. Not surprisingly, it brought about friction and estrangement among the nationalities.

Many complied with this new "purge" of nationalities, and representatives of the Party and ideology elite turned out to be its most zealous supporters. Particularly during the dramatic days of the Battle of Stalingrad, and especially in Stalin's immediate environment, these elite passionately supported "the selection and promotion of personnel in the arts," most notably of Russians. "The Selection and Promotion of Personnel in the Arts" was in fact the title of a report by the Propaganda and Agitation Directorate (Agitprop) of the CC ACP(b), which was headed at that time by Party philosopher G.F. Aleksandrov. On August 17, 1942 the technical secretariat of the Orgburo of the CC registered this report and sent it to CC ACP(b) secretaries G.M. Malenkov, A.S. Shcherbakov, and A.A. Andreyev. The report stated that:

> . . . the absence of a correct and firm Party line in the field of the development of Soviet art in the Committee of Art Affairs at the CPC of the USSR, and the existence of a process of deviation in the work of art institutions led to a distortion of Party policy in the cause of the selection, promotion, and education of art institutions' ruling staff, including vocalists, musicians, film directors, and critics. This placed theaters and musical organizations in an extremely difficult situation.[6]

The report went on to say that within a few years the national policy of the Party had been distorted in all branches of art. Directorates of the Committee of Art Affairs (under the CAA) and of many Russian institutions of art "turned out to be filled by non-Russian people (mainly by Jews)." Moreover, the report mentioned such names as Falkovskiĭ, Goltsman, Vladimirskiĭ, Plotkin, and Shlifshteĭn, and ominously concluded: "As a result, in many Russian art institutions Russian people turn out to be a national minority."[7]

Having characterized the general artistic environment, the authors of the report then dwelt on the situations in specific art institutions. They began with the Bolshoĭ Theater as "the center and top"[8] of Russian culture and operatic art of the USSR, whose "governing body consisted entirely of non-Russians." They provided the following table in order to support this drastic conclusion:

---

6. RTsKhIDNI, f. 17, op. 125, d. 123, l. 21.

7. Ibid.

8. *Translator's note:* What we translate here as "top" is actually *vyshka*, the principle guard tower of a Soviet concentration camp. Ironically, the word is here used metaphorically, signifying something praiseworthy.

Position	Name	Nationality	Party status
• Bolshoí Theater Acting Director	Leontyev	Jew	non-Party
• Chief Stage Manager and Conductor	Samosud	Jew	non-Party
• Conductor	Faíer	Jew	ACP(b) member
• Conductor	Melik-Pashayev	Armenian	non-Party
• Conductor	Shteínberg	Jew	non-Party
• Conductor	Nebolsin	Russian	non-Party
• Bolshoí Theater Branch Director (until recently)	Gabovich	Jew	ACP(b) member
• Ballet Artistic Manager	Messerer	Jew	non-Party
• Chorus Executive	Kuper	Jew	non-Party
• Chorus Executive	Kaufman	Jew	non-Party
• Chief Orchestra Leader	Zhuk	Jew	ACP(b) member
• Chief Theater Administrator	Sadovnikov	Jew	non-Party[9]

The report maintained that the situation was not much better in the Moscow State Conservatory, "where almost everything was in non-Russian hands": the director of the conservatory "Goldenveízer is a Jew, his deputy Stolyarov is a Jew . . . . The main departments of the conservatory (piano, violin, singing, music history) are in the hands of Jews[:] . . . Faínberg, Tseítlin, Yampolskií, Mostras, Dorliak, Gedike, Pekelis, and others."[10]

The Agitprop report also examined the Leningrad State Conservatory, and mentioned the names of its leaders: Ostrovskií, Shteínberg, Eídlin, and Ginzburg. The report maintained that the conservatory's students were not infused with a love for Russian music or Russian popular songs, and that the majority of well-known musicians and vocalists (D. Oístrakh, E. Gilels, Ya. Fliyer, M. Fikhtengolts, G. Ginzburg, D. Pantofel-Nechetskaya, and others) concentrated chiefly on the compositions of Western European composers.

The report also revealed "glaring distortions of national policy" in the

---

9. RTsKhIDNI, f. 17, op. 125, d. 123, l. 22.

10. Ibid.

Moscow Philharmonic Society, where "all affairs are run by a businessman[11] who has nothing to do with music, i.e., a non-Party member, Lokshin, a Jew, and a group of his close administrators, also Jews: Ginzburg, Veksler, Arkanov, and others. . . . As a result . . . almost all Russians have been dismissed from the Philharmonic Society staff: international competition prize-winners Bryushkov, Kozolupova, Yemelyanova; gifted performers and vocalists Sakharov, Korolyov, Vyspreva, Yaroslavtsev, Yelchaninova; and others. And almost only Jews remained on the staff: Fikhtengolts, Liza Gilels, Goldshteín, Fliyer, Emil Gilels, Tamarkina, Zak, M. Grinberg, Yampolskií, and others."[12]

The Agitprop reporters also had a negative view of music critics, and pointed to "the prevalence of non-Russians," among them S. Shlifshteín, D. Rabinovich, D. Zhitomirskií, L. Mazel, V. Tsukerman, and others. According to these Party ideologists, such critics kept particularly quiet about the creative work of "the best Soviet pianist Sofronitskií (a Russian)" and gave "extensive reviews to concerts by E. Gilels, Oístrakh, Fikhtengolts, and other [Jewish performers]."[13]

Having exposed a "Jewish conspiracy" in art, the Agitprop functionaries claimed that "the incorrect, biased, and one-sided treatment of musical questions in the press . . . is conditioned by the central newspapers' literature and art departments being headed by non-Russians as well." They presented another chart:

Pravda[14]	Literature and Art Section Executive	Yunovich	Jewess
Izvestiya[15]	" " " " "	Voítinskaya	Jewess
Vechernyaya Moskva[16]	" " " " "	Orlikova	Jewess
Literatura i iskusstvo[17]	Music Section	Rabinovich	Jew
"	Executive Theater Section	Bassokhes	Jew
"	Executive Editorial Office Secretary	Gorelik	Jew
Muzgiz[18]	Publishing House Director	Grinberg	Jew[19]

11. *Translator's note:* The Russian here for "businessman" is *delets*, which can also mean or "dealer." *Delets* had a negative connotation.

12. RTsKhIDNI, f. 17, op. 125, d. 123, l. 23.

13. Ibid.

14. *Truth.*

15. *News.*

16. *Evening Moscow.*

The Agitprop authors concluded with a request "to impose upon the Art Affairs Committee at the USSR CPC the duty of pursuing, consistently and steadily, the correct national policy in the field of art"; and for this reason they proposed that "measures aimed at training and promoting Russian personnel" be taken immediately "to partially renew the guiding staff in a number of art establishments."[20]

Such detailed citations from this document allow the reader to get some impression of the mentality of the Stalinist Party ideologues. The serious political aftermath of the apparatus's work was that anti-Semitism was interjected into the cultural sphere. For example, on November 19, 1942 the chairman of the CAA, M. Khrapchenko, reported to the CC ACP(b) that composer V.Ya. Shebalin had been appointed director of the Moscow State Conservatory, replacing Aleksandr Borisovich Goldenveízer, for reasons "of old age."[21]

The scale of the purge at the Moscow Conservatory would undoubtedly have been much greater had not the country's musical elite—among them the greatest Russian musicians and composers—supported the persecuted. For example, in September 1943, when a professor at the conservatory, Ye.M. Guzikov, was threatened with dismissal because of his nationality, N.Ya. Myaskovskií, D.D. Shostakovich, Yu.A. Shaporin, and others signed a petition in his support.[22]

Perceiving the winds that began to blow from the Soviet Olympus, I. Bolshakov, the head of another cultural institution, the Film Affairs Committee at the CPC, decided to do his own bit for the cause of national "purification" of art and personnel. On October 24 he submitted a report to the secretary of the

---

17. *Literature and Art.*

18. The full name is Gosudarsovennoye musykal'noye izfatel'stvo, or State Music Publishing House.

19. RTsKhIDNI, f. 17, op. 125, d. 123, l. 23.

20. RTsKhIDNI, f. 17, op. 125, d. 123, l. 24

21. Strange as it may seem, Goldenveízer was never again persecuted to an appreciable degree. After he had been dismissed from his administrative position, Agitprop no longer saw him as a potential "saboteur" in the conservatory personnel. In 1946 he was even conferred with the title of "People's Artist of the USSR," and in 1947 he was awarded the Stalin Prize. Nonetheless, the games related to his "fifth point" were not over. [*Translator's note:* "The fifth point" is Russian slang; it refers to the fifth item on personnel record forms, which required information on nationality.] Goldenveízer was one of the representatives of the classic academic school, and his creative work was more highly thought of than ever before. Ironically, at the same time V.Ya. Shebalin was accused of formalism, and a Politburo resolution of July 30, 1948 dismissed him as director of the Moscow Conservatory. This followed the February 10, 1948 CC ACP(b) resolution regarding V. Muradeli's opera, *The Great Friendship* (*Velikaya druzhba*). In 1950, when Goldenveízer turned 75, the Politburo adopted a resolution to award him with the order of the Red Banner of Labor. But for this to happen, the CAA had to resort to cunning. Aleksandr Borisovich Goldenveízer had provided documents to the CC stating that he was Russian; but to avoid any possible questions, it was mentioned in brackets that: "Father is of Jewish origin." RTsKhIDNI, f. 17, op. 118, d. 839, l. 149, 153.

22. RTsKhIDNI, f. 17, op. 119, d. 12, l. 126–133.

Central Committee, A. Shcherbakov, in which he explained that he had refused S.M. Eízenshteín's[23] proposal to have F. Ranevskaya play the role of the Russian princess Yefrosinya Staritskaya in his new film, *Ivan the Terrible*,[24] because "Ranevskaya's Semitic features are clearly visible, especially in close-up."[25] To remove any doubt that the CC secretary might have concerning his truthfulness, he included several portrait and profile snapshots of her try-outs.[26] Later, on April 5, 1943, evidently proud of the authority entrusted to him, Bolshakov reported to G. Malenkov that among the young film directors, cameramen, and script writers that the All-Union Institute of Filmmaking had trained in the past year, the Film Committee "had selected the most gifted and capable comrades, mainly Russians . . . which would be of great significance in refreshing the film cadres . . . ."[27] Bolshakov requested that these specialists be exempted from military service, and attached a list of people that included 32 Russians, 2 Lithuanians, 2 Azerbaijanians, 1 Armenian, 1 Latvian, 1 Turkoman, and 1 Kazakh."[28]

Anti-Semitic staff changes subsequently spread to other cultural institutions—art groups, the editorial staffs of various newspapers, and so on. Jewish intellectuals grew anxious over the growing chauvinistic campaign. Many people wondered if these changes were the result of a coordinated official policy, or if they were the result of independent actions of minor functionaries? A letter dated May 13, 1943, from the Russian intelligence veteran Ya. Grinberg to Iosif Stalin, reflected the Jewish opinion on the situation, for Grinberg "expressed the aspirations of a large group of art intellectuals":

> Dear leader and teacher, I.V. Stalin.
>
> How can one explain that at such a grim time for the Soviet country a muddy wave of disgusting anti-Semitism has risen again and penetrated some Soviet institutions and even Party organizations? What is this? Is it a criminal stupidity of excessively zealous people who unintentionally assist fascist agents, or is it something else?
>
> . . . There are rumors and conjectures that a directive might have been given from above to develop Russian national culture, perhaps even to promote national regulations for personnel. In bodies that manage art organizations this is mentioned with a secretive look and a whisper in one's ear. This resulted in hostile attitudes toward Jews who

---

23. *Editor's note:* Known to the West as Sergei M. Eisenstein.

24. *Ivan Groznyi.*

25. RTsKhIDNI, f. 17, op. 125, d. 124, l. 66.

26. RTsKhIDNI, f. 17, op. 125, d. 124, l. 67–71.

27. RTsKhIDNI, f. 17, op. 125, d. 126, l. 11.

28. RTsKhIDNI, f. 17, op. 125, d. 126, l. 12.

> are engaged in this field. In practice, the personnel departments of the Art Affairs Committee and of the other bodies dependent upon it select only Russian employees or officers even for [a position as insignificant as] a manager of a traveling theater. Today Jews of any qualification cannot count on getting an independent job, even of a modest rank. This policy has loosened the tongue of many ignorant and unstable elements, and many Communists are in a very gloomy mood. . . . I know that People's Artist Comrade Mikhoels and People's Artist A.Ya. Tairov speak of this phenomenon with great alarm. . . . It is known that a number of representatives of the art intelligentsia (Jews) appeal to the writer I. Erenburg, asking him to raise this question. The writer Boris Gorbatov talked to me about this phenomenon. It has already come about that some Communists (Russians) and even secretaries of local Party organizations (for instance, of the Directorate of Art Affairs at the Moscow City Executive Committee, of the Art Department of the [Moscow] Region Executive Committee), in a perfectly official way raise the question about [official] bodies being "choked up" apparently with Jews, [and] bring accusations of "pushing Jews through." At the Directorate of Art Affairs they have had to count to determine whether the Jewish quota was violated, i.e., 4 Jews per 30 staff members![29]

In concluding his letter, Grinberg claimed that the emergence of the "Jewish question" yet again[30] was not at all coincidental, because "leading Party bodies are rather well informed." Grinberg implored Stalin personally to investigate this affair.[31]

Stalin most likely never saw this letter. Judging by the notations that Stalin's secretary, Aleksandr Nikolayevich Poskrebyshev, made on it, it was sent to A. Shcherbakov, who forwarded it to Andreyev, who in his turn sent it to Agitprop—that is, to the initiator of the anti-Semitic campaign. This letter was simply filed in the archives.

As early as February 1943, I. Erenburg, speaking at the second Jewish Antifascist Committee (JAC)[32] Plenum, demanded that a stop be put to the anti-Semitism that was "creeping" through the country. Actually, he did not mean the official anti-Semitism of Stalin's "upper strata"; if he had known of that he would

---

29. RTsKhIDNI, f. 17, op. 125, d. 136, l. 123–124.

30. The "Jewish question" had been raised periodically ever since the early twentieth century, during the time of the "Union of Russian People," a chauvinistic monarchist party.

31. RTsKhIDNI, f. 17, op. 125, d. 136, l. 124–125.

32. The Jewish Antifascist Committee was set up in April 1942 as one of the sections of the Soviet Information Bureau (Sovinformburo) on the initiative of S.A. Lozovskií, who was the Sovinformburo's vice-chairman as well as vice chairman of the People's Commissariat of Foreign Affairs,.

had to have kept silent. Rather, he was referring to the anti-Semitism at lower levels, which by that time had spread to front-line units and distant logistical areas.[33] One of the so-called special reports, sent from Third Directorate of the NKVD to Beria in late August 1942, stated that due to the arrival in Uzbekistan

> . . . of a considerable number of evacuated Soviet citizens of Jewish nationality, anti-Soviet elements, exploiting the discontent of the local dwellers (which is on the rise as a result of a reduction of living space, an increase of market prices, and the Jews' aspirations to get jobs within the trade, supply, and storage organizations), have activated the counterrevolutionary propaganda of anti-Semitism. As a result, in Uzbekistan there were three cases of Jews being beaten and taunted with anti-Semitic shouting.

Despite the measures taken to restrain nationalistic passions, and despite the arrests of those who had instigated the pogroms, the Jewish populations of Samarkand, Tashkent, and other Middle Asian cities were seriously concerned about their security.

Something similar took place in Kazakhstan. On October 15, 1942 V.M. Bochkov (the prosecutor of the USSR) informed A.Ya. Vyshinskií (the deputy chairman of the CPC) by secret mail that 20 people had been convicted in the first half of 1942 throughout Kazakhstan for pogrom agitation and for acts of vandalism against evacuated Jews. Bochkov went on to write that 42 people had been prosecuted from August 1 through September 4 in the Alma-Ata and Semipalatinsk regions alone.[34] Jews who resided in areas where the authorities tried "not to notice" the increasing Judeophobic moods were most anxious. For example, at the end of May 1943 the writer A. Stepanov, who at that time had been an evacuee in Frunze (capital of Kirghizia), wrote to D. Ortenberg, the editor of *The Red Star*[35] newspaper:

> About anti-Semitism. Those who chiefly disseminate it are wounded ex-servicemen. They openly say that Jews avoid the war, get cushy jobs at the home front, and carry on truly thug-like propaganda. I saw Jews being turned out of lines, being bitten (even women) by the same legless cripples. It is often wounded people on sick leave who instigate such contemptible pranks on Jews. Militiamen show a criminal mildness toward such delinquencies that borders on

---

33. RTsKhIDNI, f. 17, op. 125, d. 158, l. 31.
34. RTsKhIDNI, f. 17, op. 125, d. 136, l. 121–122; GARF, f. 8131, op. 27, d. 973, l. 123.
35. *Krasnaya zvezda*.

> direct connivance.[36]

Did Ortenberg show this letter to anybody in the CC, asking that measures be taken to fight anti-Semitism? Perhaps. Nevertheless, on July 30 he was summoned to Old Square,[37] to the office of A. Shcherbakov, secretary of the CC ACP(b) propaganda unit. Shcherbakov informed him that the CC had decided to appoint a new editor-in-chief to *The Red Star.* Ortenberg asked how he could explain the motive behind his dismissal to his staff, and Shcherbakov replied, "Tell them that there was no motive."[38] Later, reflecting on possible reasons for his dismissal, Ortenberg remembered that several months earlier Shcherbakov had unexpectedly called for him and, without beating around the bush, demanded that the newspaper's editorial staff be cleansed of Jews.[39] Six years later, in May 1949, when the campaign against "stateless cosmopolitans" had reached its highest point, Ortenberg wrote a letter to Stalin asking him "to take a load off [his] mind" and tell him why he had been dismissed. As with all mail addressed to Stalin, this letter was received by Poskrebyshev, for whom Ortenberg added a postscript:

> You will make me happy for the rest of my life if you will give this letter to Comrade Stalin. I leave the letter's destiny in your own hands. Dear Aleksandr Nikolayevich, I ask you to be as indulgent as my own sensitive and responsive father, and if the letter is poorly written, return it to me so that we may never again refer to it.[40]

Poskrebyshev apparently did not show this letter to Stalin. The "leader of the people" did not see many of the letters sent to him, which was probably for the better. In April 1950 Ortenberg was dismissed as deputy director of the Political Directorate of Air Defense of the Moscow Military District, and on July 29, 1950 he was released from the army. No reason was given.[41]

This growing anti-Semitism was apparent not only in the "purification" of personnel; it also—and quite often—appeared in a veiled form in the sphere of propaganda. For instance, in January 1942 *Bolshevik*,[42] a Party magazine,

---

36. RTsKhIDNI, f. 17, op. 125, d. 190, l. 16–17.

37. *Translator's note:* Old Square (Staraya Ploshchad') was the headquarters of the CC of the ACP(b), later the CPSU.

38. RTsKhIDNI, f. 17, op. 132, d. 118, l. 8–10.

39. D.I. Ortenberg, *Sorok tretil: rasskaz khronika* [*Forty-Third: A Chronicle*] (Moscow, 1991), p. 399.

40. RTsKhIDNI, f. 17, op. 132, d. 118, l. 9.

41. RTsKhIDNI, f. 17, op. 118, d. 925, l. 71–72; op. 119, d. 211, l. 196.

42. *Bolshevik*, no. 2, 1942.

published an article by A.Ye. Badayev, the vice chairman of the Presidium of the Supreme Soviet of the USSR. In his article this old Bolshevik, having previously cited Stalin's words that "the friendship of the peoples of the USSR is a great and serious achievement," gave statistical data on the nationalities of those rewarded with military orders and medals. First he separately listed the numbers of Russians, Ukrainians, Belorussians, and so forth. At the end of this long list he then mentioned in a jumble and without reference to numerical data all other nationalities that were rewarded for their half-year participation in the war, with Jews coming after Buryats, Circassians, Khakases, Avars, Kumyks, and Yakuts. His intention to depreciate the Jewish contribution to the armed struggle against the enemy was obvious. According to data from the Central Personnel Directorate of the People's Commissariat of Defense, as of January 15, 1943 Jews were fourth by the number of rewarded (6 767) after Russians (187 178), Ukrainians (44 344) and Belorussians (7 210). Moreover, in half a year, as of June 1, the Jews left the Belorussians behind and took the third place.[43]

Solomon Mikhoels and Shakhno Epshteín, the heads of the Jewish Antifascist Committee, were indignant at such a scornful attitude toward the service of the whole Jewish population. On April 2, 1942 they sent a note to Shcherbakov, stating that, in their opinion, such distorted information could be taken up "by Hitler's agents, who spread the malicious slander that the Jews did not fight." However, as could be expected, this démarche from the offended leaders of Soviet Jewry was in vain. As with other similar messages, Shcherbakov sent it to the archives, and so it never reached the Central Committee.[44]

Meanwhile, the anti-Jewish purge among art intellectuals intensified. On July 15, 1943, G. Aleksandrov and his deputy, T.M. Zuyeva,[45] sent a new note entitled "On the Activity of the State Academy Bolshoí Theater of the USSR" to the CC secretaries A. Andreyev, G. Malenkov, and A. Shcherbakov. Aleksandrov and Zuyeva wrote this note with characteristically awkward pseudo-patriotic enthusiasm, full of absurd tables showing that the "leading staff had been selected only because of their national origins, and with a prevalence of Jewish names." The two authors ominously concluded that "the Bolshoí Theater was under the threat of a serious crisis and it needed to be strengthened by leading workers."[46]

In reading these documents one may wonder who in the highest Party levels

---

43. RTsKhIDNI, f. 17, op. 125, d. 127, l. 145, 220.

44. RTsKhIDNI, f. 17, op. 125, d. 127, l. 175–175 obverse.

45. From 1940 to 1945 T.M. Zuyeva was the vice chairperson of the Department of Cultural and Educational Institutions of Agitprop. She later became head of the Committee on Cultural and Educational Institutions at the Council of Ministers of the Russian Soviet Federal Socialist Republic (RSFSR). In 1949 she was appointed deputy prime minister of the Council of Ministers of the RSFSR. She also was a member of the Board of the Committee of Soviet Women.

46. RTsKhIDNI, f. 17, op. 125, d. 216, l. 101–104.

needed such chauvinistic hysteria. Who was, if not its inspiration (Stalin's authority here is indisputable), at least its engineer and organizer? According to archival documents the answer is quite clear: it was Shcherbakov (the secretary of the CC ACP(b), the first secretary of the Moscow Regional Committee and of the Moscow City Committee of the ACP(b), the head of the Chief Political Directorate of the Red Army, and the head of Sovinformburo), along with the propaganda machinery under his authority, in which Aleksandrov, the head of Agitprop, played the main role. It was Aleksandrov's signature that was most likely to appear on anti-Semitic documents. This alone makes it necessary to look more closely at the lives of these persons.

In 1940, the 32-year-old G.F. Aleksandrov inherited from A.A. Zhdanov[47] the leadership of Agitprop. A young and ambitious Marxist philosopher, Aleksandrov saw this as an opportunity to become the leading Party theoretician. Full of energy and comparatively better educated than other Party bureaucrats, he decided to test his fortune. He had graduated in 1932 from the Moscow Institute of History and Philosophy, had been engaged in teaching, and before coming to the Central Committee had had a chance to work in the Comintern[48] Executive Committee. In 1943 he received the Stalin Prize for his editorship of the third volume of the *History of Philosophy*.[49] Catering to Stalin's imperial arrogance, Aleksandrov not only strove for "national purity" in Russian art, but also always rigidly opposed even the weakness of the increase of national consciousness after the war. For instance, on November 29, 1943, after a city-wide rally in honor of the liberation of Kiev, Aleksandrov received for his approval a letter from the "Ukrainian people to the great Russian people," but prohibited its publication only because it recognized Russians and Ukrainians as equals. In Aleksandrov's (or, more exactly, Stalin's) opinion, "everyone acknowledged that the Russian people are the elder brothers in the family of peoples of the USSR."[50]

Aleksandrov attempted to strengthen his nationalistic position by patronizing history professors Ye.V. Tarle, A.Ye. Yefimov, A.I. Yakovlev, B.I. Syromyatnikov, S.K. Bushuyev, P.P. Smirnov, and the Armenian writer and publicist Kh.G. Adzhemyan, all of whom, beginning in 1942, wished to rehabilitate the tsars, statesmen, and military figures who had been branded as oppressors and reactionaries after the October 1917 revolution.[51] These scholars were opposed by

---

47. Until May 1941 Zhdanov was the secretary of the Leningrad Regional Committee of the ACP(b) and was formally the CC secretary of ideology. Malenkov and Aleksandrov carried out intrigues that enabled Shcherbakov, who was then secretary of the Moscow Committee and of the Moscow City Committee of the ACP(b), to replace Zhdanov as secretary of ideology.

48. *Translator's note:* "Comintern" was the Third Communist International (1919–1943).

49. *Istoriya filosofii.*

50. RTsKhIDNI, f. 17, op. 125, d. 190, l. 25–42.

51. On July 21, 1942, the Politburo of the CC ACP(b) approved the institution of new military

a group of dogmatic Marxists who united around A.M. Pankratova, the deputy head of the Institute of History at the Academy of Sciences. Pankratova was a disciple of M.N. Pokrovskií, a historian who maintained that "Russian history" was a counterrevolutionary term, of the same nature as the three-colored Russian flag and the slogan "united and indivisible [Russia]."[52] (Incidentally, Stalin had condemned Pokrovskií in 1936.) Among Pankratova's sympathizers were the historians M.V. Nechkina, V.I. Lebedev, S.V. Bakhrushin, I.I. Mints, and N.L. Rubinshteín, who accused their opponents of having an "anti-Marxist attitude" toward science and of "removing class content from the historical process." In particular, they reproached Ye. Tarle, who had called for an end to the characterization of tsarist Russia as the historic "Gendarme of Europe" and "Peoples' Prison."[53] They also criticized Professor S. Bushuyev, director of the Diplomatic Academy, for his slogan, "Deal the final blow to national nihilism," and for his demand that such pillars of Russian autocracy as Count A.A. Arakcheyev; publisher M.N. Katkov; and chief public prosecutor of the Synod, K.P. Pobedonostsev be exonerated.[54]

Passions became heated in the summer of 1943 upon the publication of two school texts edited by Pankratova: *The History of the USSR*[55] and *The History of the Kazakh Soviet Socialist Republic from Ancient Times to the Present.*[56] This second book contradicted Stalin's concept that the aggressive policy of tsarism should be considered a "lesser evil" than the separatist nationalism of the outlying districts of the empire. Aleksandrov was especially displeased and labeled the book "anti-Russian."[57] He organized the "great power" historians to give it a negative review. Others at Agitprop, such as *Pravda*'s editor-in-chief P.N. Pospelov and Aleksandrov's deputy P.N. Fedoseyev, also took an active part in badgering Pankratova. They accused her and her coeditor, M. Abdykalykov (the secretary of ideology of the Kazakhstan CP), of playing into the hands of Kazakh nationalists and showing "ill will not only toward the policies of Russian imperial power, but toward the Russian people as well."[58]

---

awards, i.e., the orders of Suvorov, Kutuzov, and Aleksandr Nevskií. The linkage of this event with the tide of chauvinistic moods in historical circles was obvious.

52. This was the monarchist slogan at the turn of the century. See M.N. Pokrovskií, *Istoricheskaya nauka i bor'ba klassov: istoriograficheskiye ocherki, kriticheskiye stat'i, zametki* [*Historical Science and Class Struggle: Historiographical Essays, Critical Articles, Notes*], Part 2 (Moscow/Leningrad, 1933), p. 344.

53. RTsKhIDNI, f. 17, op. 125, d. 222, l. 116.

54. RTsKhIDNI, f. 17, op. 125, d. 224, l. 3. Synod is from the Greek *synodos*, meaning "assembly." The Synod was one of the supreme government organs of the Russian empire, lasting from 1721 through 1917. Its head, the chief procurator, was appointed by the tsar.

55. *Istoriya SSSR.*

56. *Istoriya Kazakhskoí SSSR s drevneíshikh vremyon do nashikh dneí.*

57. RTsKhIDNI, f. 17, op. 125, d. 224, Ibid., l. 74.

58. These are the words of historian A.I. Yakovlev. RTsKhIDNI, f. 17, op. 125, d. 222, l. 100; d.

Early in 1944 the revolutionary song *International* made its way into the national anthem. It began: "Great Russia has permanently united the free Republics into an indivisible union." This was Stalin's next major step after the dissolution of the Third International [Comintern] in the spring of 1943. The framework of this new policy was developed in the 1930s when, as exiled Russian philosopher G.P. Fedotov put it, "Soviet policy and ideology entered a stage of extreme nationalism."[59] It is notable in this regard that a variant of poet Osip Kolychev's hymn was heralded as one of the most successful variants:

> Be famous, Russia, our state!
> Be famous, the peoples of the Russian land!
> Our state's stately banner
> we carried through trials.
> Glory to the peoples living a friendly life!
> Be famous, Russia—stronghold of friendship!
> Be famous forever, our all-powerful
> and invincible Russian people.[60]

In the midst of this popular surge of great-power chauvinism, Pankratova was attacked even more intensively. Trying to find some protection from her opponents and, more importantly, from Aleksandrov who backed them, she wrote directly to A. Zhdanov in Leningrad in March 1944, asking him to grant her an audience "to explain everything personally and in the smallest detail."[61]

The situation changed considerably in April 1944, when the Politburo unexpectedly passed a resolution sharply criticizing Aleksandrov for having edited the third volume of *History of Philosophy*, which had earlier received great acclaim. Apparently Stalin had become annoyed with Aleksandrov's chauvinism, perhaps because of his thinly disguised Germanophilism and his adoption of the latest Nazi propaganda. The resolution attacked Aleksandrov for being a philosopher with an uncritical approach toward the "reactionary views" of Hegel, Fichte, and other German philosophers who, according to some Soviet theoreticians, were forerunners of Nazism.[62]

Taking cheer in this new development, Pankratova wrote to Stalin, Zhdanov, Malenkov, and Shcherbakov that she blamed Aleksandrov and his staff for neglect

---

224, l. 24 obverse.

59. G.P. Fedotov, *Tyazhba po Rossii* [*Competition Over Russia*] (Paris: YMCA Press, 1982), vol. 3, p. 182.

60. RTsKhIDNI, f. 17, op. 125, d. 217, l. 92.

61. RTsKhIDNI, f. 17, op. 125, d. 224, l. 9.

62. RTsKhIDNI, f. 17, op. 125, d. 254, l. 62–71.

on the "historical front."[63] But Aleksandrov stood his ground and Pankratova shortly came to regret her precipitous initiative.

Zhdanov had meanwhile, in the summer of 1944, moved from Leningrad to Moscow and had begun an intrigue against Aleksandrov. By referring to Pankratova's letters and to documents of historical debates,[64] he attempted to stifle Aleksandrov's career; to undermine his main rival, Shcherbakov;[65] and thereby to strengthen his own position in the struggle for Party ideological leadership. In August and September he prepared several draft theses that dealt with historical problems. Since his position in Moscow was still somewhat unsteady, he wrote very cautiously, but nonetheless quite openly attacked Aleksandrov. He condemned the attempts to "idealize" the tsarist regime, which, he said, had been based on "humiliation, brutal oppression of all non-Russian peoples, propagation of hatred to all non-Russians . . . the spreading of slaughter and pogroms."[66] For the appearance of good form, Zhdanov also mildly reproved Pankratova for repeating the historical errors of the "Pokrovskií school" and for transforming internationalism into "stateless cosmopolitanism."[67] To strengthen the ideological foundations of unity in the country, Zhdanov proposed an increase in the propagandizing of "Soviet patriotism," based "on the love of all Soviet peoples for their socialist fatherland, the USSR."[68]

Stalin found Zhdanov's maneuver to his liking, since he also began to sense that the further dissemination of great-power Russian nationalism might provoke an equal but opposite reaction among other ethnic groups, a reaction that would threaten the integrity of the Bolshevik empire. The political influence of Zhdanov, who was later to be the chief interpreter of Stalin's ideas, increased sharply. But he could not protect Pankratova—or perhaps he did not wish to. On August 30, 1944 Aleksandrov reported to Zhdanov, Malenkov, and Shcherbakov (in that deliberate order) his criticisms of Pankratova's anti-Party factionalism against the CC staff. He also observed that Pankratova had been among the "left Socialist Revolutionaries and Trotskyite groups of Fridlyand-Vanag."[69] This was a strike below the belt, and Pankratova was soon dismissed as deputy director of the Institute of History at the USSR Academy of Sciences.[70]

---

63. RTsKhIDNI, f. 17, op. 125, d. 224, l. 66–75 obverse.

64. RTsKhIDNI, f. 17, op. 125, d. 224, l. 110–131. These debates were summarized at several CC ACP(b) conferences between May 25 and July 8.

65. In the 1930s Shcherbakov had worked under Zhdanov as the first secretary of the Gorkií Regional Party Committee and later of the Leningrad Regional Party Committees.

66. RTsKhIDNI, f. 17, op. 125, d. 222, l. 28.

67. RTsKhIDNI, f. 17, op. 125, d. 222, l. 33

68. RTsKhIDNI, f. 17, op. 125, d. 222, l. 35.

69. RTsKhIDNI, f. 17, op. 125, d. 224, l. 138–140.

70. RTsKhIDNI, f. 17, op. 125, d. 224, l. 146.

Pankratova's fate reflected the games of intrigue at the Party's Olympus, and it is difficult for us to understand the reasons for the persecutions against nationalities unless we get a sense of these games. The Party functionaries were not an amorphous impersonal mass, blind weapons in the hands of the leader. Under the superficial unanimity of the upper echelons of the Party bureaucracy there were a large number of opposing groups, each with its own specific interests. Stalin could not care less about these inter-nomenclatura squabbles. On the contrary, interested in strengthening his autocracy, he periodically compared his courtiers with one another and, with the help of a third person, removed those he thought were most eager to become his heir. Like those in his immediate circle, he was much more worried about the national self-consciousness of the peoples of the USSR, or, in other words, about the nationalisms awakened by the war, whether it be Kazakh, Ukrainian, Bashkir, Jewish, or any other. He saw these nationalisms as the main threat of the eventual dissolution of the Red Empire.

For Stalin, the ideological panacea to these dangerous centripetal trends within the Soviet state was first of all the strengthening of the propaganda that Russians were "the elder brother in the family of the equal Soviet peoples," a doctrine he had preached after Lenin's time. This doctrine was based on the hierarchical principle so characteristic of Stalin's mentality. He proposed his famous toast to the Russian people as "the ruling force of the Soviet Union" in wartime on May 24, 1945; this was the harbinger to all postwar propaganda, which up to his death retained its hard-core chauvinistic nature.[71]

However, Stalin by no means saw the Russian people as valuable in themselves, worthy of special honor and prosperity at the cost of other peoples. Although he placed Russians first as constituting one of the greatest and most populous nations in the world, he only used them as a cementing material that held together and absorbed other peoples of the empire.[72] Any different approaches to the historical mission and destiny of Russians and the upholding of their rights for national, cultural and religious originality, as well as any considerations

---

71. As strange as it may or may not seem, the most zealous advocates of the Stalinist chauvinistic doctrine were two representatives of the Party nomenclatura—L.M. Kaganovich and the first secretary of the CC of the Azerbaijan CP(b), M.D. Bagirov—neither of whom was Russian. In February 1953, not long before "the leader of the peoples" passed away, Bagirov published his article on "The Elder Brother in the Family of Soviet Peoples" in Kommunist magazine (no. 3). Many dogmatic Leninists were bewildered: "Up to now everybody was talking about the leading role of the working class, and now for some reason the question is about the leading role of the Russian people." [Editor's note: Stalin himself was Georgian, not Russian.]

72. According to the Stalinist national-hierarchical scheme, Russians were followed by Ukrainians and Belorussians. Next came the nations who had their own states in the form of Union Republics, followed by the nations who created their own autonomous republics, all in descending order down to the least populous national minorities.

of this nation as "a thing in itself" (or for itself), Stalin categorically and ruthlessly suppressed. This may be the reason underlying the criticism of G.F. Aleksandrov, who in his historiographical debate with A.M. Pankratova got too carried away by the "Russian idea."

The romanticism of Russophilia happened to be so contagious that even the staunch dogmatic communist Zhdanov, who after Shcherbakov's death in 1945 resumed his position as CC secretary of ideology, could not hold his ground. According to N.S. Khrushchev's memoirs,[73] Zhdanov, shortly before his strange and unexpected death, became interested in creating a Bureau of the CC of the ACP(b) for the Russian Federation. And even before that, the chairman of the Council of Ministers of the RSFSR, M.I. Rodionov, who was known to be Zhdanov's man,[74] submitted to his chief a Russian hymn, with music my Dmitriĭ Shostakovich and lyrics by S. Shchipachev. Here is its final verse:

> Be famous, Russia, Fatherland of freedom.
> We'll go forward to new victories,
> in the fraternal unity of free peoples.
> Be famous, our great Russian people.[75]

In July 1948, at a Politburo meeting, Stalin criticized Zhdanov and removed him as second secretary of the CC ACP(b). Shortly afterwards, when Zhdanov died, his adherents, who were blamed for stirring up "Russian nationalism," were punished and the "Leningrad case" was developed, as we shall see later.

As for the "elder brother" doctrine, it died with its creator. It was replaced by a new slogan based on the gradual melding of all the peoples of the empire into some kind of nationless ideological conglomeration called the Soviet people, and later labeled as "a new historical community of people." One of the most consistent theoreticians and champions of this idea, who secured its "steady position" during the epochs of Khrushchev and Brezhnev, was M.A. Suslov. In 1946 Zhdanov promoted Suslov from the peripheral regions of the Soviet Union to the "high ideology" apparatus of the CC ACP(b).

Now that we have digressed to the sphere of, as Bolshevik terminology had it, the "national question," let us come back to 1943 and see how Stalin's regime played the Jewish national card.

---

73. N.S. Khrushchev, "Vospominaniya" ("Memoirs"), *Voprosy istorii* (*Issues in History*), 191, no. 11, p. 47.

74. M.I. Rodionov began his career in Nizhniĭ Novgorod, where Zhdanov was secretary of the Regional Party Committee from 1924 to 1934.

75. RTsKhIDNI, f. 17, op. 121, d. 453, l. 23.

Two

The Tragedy of the Jewish Committee

The campaign for "the purity of Russian art," which was developed in 1942, was an obvious symptom of a lurking and quickly advancing social malady—state anti-Semitism. In reality, this campaign was a result of the worsening defects of Stalin's regime, such as xenophobia, great-power chauvinism, and intellectual conformity. Among the specific causes of anti-Semitism was the aggravation of competition inherent among artistic intelligentsia. The Molotov-Ribbentrop pact furthered the influence of Nazi anti-Jewish propaganda. This influence grew even greater upon Germany's invasion and annexation of enormous territories within the USSR, which subjected the occupied populations to such brainwashing works as Hitler's *Mein Kampf* and Goebbels's *International Jew*. From Soviet front-line areas to the army in the fields, this influence was appreciable. It had seemed that anti-Semitism had vanished through sheer lethargy after the civil war; but now, against a background of general deprivation, disruption, and other burdens brought about by war, anti-Semitism was reawakened by Nazi propaganda. Scapegoats are always found in such critical times.

Luckily, what was most dreaded did not happen: the undercurrent of state anti-Semitism was not legalized and did not become official policy, and so did not further aggravate Judeophobia among a people burdened by a war. During the war Stalin and those in his inner circle could not opt for an openly anti-Jewish campaign, as this would have been fraught with dilemmas such as a loss of credibility in the eyes of the Allies and consequent complications in relations with them. There would also have been an increase in national tensions within the Soviet Union, undermining its unity and solidarity. Finally, such a policy would have led to an identification of Soviet anti-Semitism with the policies of Hitlerism. So Stalin, who was more pragmatic than anti-Semitic, found such a course of action unacceptable. For the sake of maintaining his power, he reluctantly decided to allow the activity of the Jewish Antifascist Committee.[1] He

---

1. The idea of creating a Jewish propagandistic organization originated during the first months of the war. At that time the moral pressure of the broadcasts about Nazi atrocities in the occupied territories convinced a group of Jews to gather around A.S. Lozovskií (the vice minister of foreign affairs and deputy chairman of Sovinformburo) and S.M. Mikhoels (the director of the Moscow Jewish Theater). Members of this group for the most part were literati, and Agitprop at first used them for one-time ideological actions. The first meeting of these "representatives of the Jewish people" took place in Moscow on August 24, 1941, was broadcast by radio, and served to bring the Jews together. Mikhoels, the poet Perets Markish, the writer David Bergelson, literary critic/journalist Shakhno Epshteín, writer Ilya Erenburg, and others took the floor. All this occurred some time after the Moscow Jewry had begun to request permission from the CC to resume publication of the central Jewish newspaper *Einikeit* (*Unity*). All in all, this testified to the growing social activity of the Jewish population.

However, A.S. Shcherbakov, the head of Agitprop, was not especially sympathetic to the Jews. Thus Agitprop would not support their patriotic initiative, and even restrained it at first. The Soviet special services (then headed by Beria) took a more active position on this matter. Quick and energetic, Beria (in contrast to the dull-witted Shcherbakov) immediately saw this as a way of increasing the help rendered to the USSR by the Western allies—especially rich American Jews. The central place in Beria's plan was occupied by two Polish men of Jewish origin, Henryk Erlich and Wiktor Alter, who were monitored by Beria's office. These two were Bund leaders, and for this reason Soviet counterintelligence had arrested them soon after the Western parts of the Ukraine and Belorussia had merged with the USSR in 1939. Erlich had been taken into custody on October 4 in Brest-Litovsk, and Alter was arrested a week later in Kovel. As they were important personages, they were brought to Moscow and accused of having connections with Polish counterintelligence, of having contacts with illegal Bund organizations, and of criticizing the Soviet Union, particularly for the "Molotov-Ribbentrop" pact. None of these accusations was revised even after the war with Germany began in June 1941. In late July and early August 1941 Erlich and Alter were sentenced to death. However, on August 27 they were informed that the death sentence would be replaced by a sentence of ten years of camp. While in camp the prisoners were told about their upcoming release and Beria, who had attended their interrogations, asked them if they might head a Jewish Anti-Nazi organization that was being created in the USSR.

Erlich and Alter agreed to cooperate with the NKVD. However, the NKVD leaders were at the time so occupied with planning Erlich's and Alter's connections with world Jewry that it was not until mid-September that the two prisoners were released. (An August 12, 1941 decree of the Presidium of the Supreme Soviet, on the amnesty of Polish citizens who had been arrested on Soviet territory, stipulated that they were to have been released long before that time.)

From being prisoners without any rights, Erlich and Alter were immediately transformed into highly respected foreigners, and were provided with luxury rooms at the Metropol Hotel. An NKVD captain, V.A. Volkovysskií, was a counterintelligence officer in charge of the Polish section, and had been appointed communications officer between the Soviet authorities and the leaders of General Wladyslaw Anders's Polish Army, which had formed on Soviet territory. It was Volkovysskií who was introduced to Poles as Colonel Arkadií (Aron) Volkovysskií. He had investigated Erlich's and Alter's "case"; but now he went to visit them, and discussed with them issues concerning the creation of a Jewish Committee. Volkovysskií's assistant captain, Khazanovich, was sent to help them, and organized their meeting with Mikhoels, Markish, and other leaders of Soviet Jewry. Acting on Beria's advice, in early October Alter and Erlich sent a letter to Stalin detailing a plan for creating a Jewish Anti-Hitlerite Committee in the USSR. Erlich was proposed for the post of the chair of the committee, Mikhoels as his deputy, and Alter as

was riddled with agonizing doubts about this decision, but he derived great

---

executive secretary.

These two Polish ex-members of the Bund, who had not long ago been outlaws, rapidly overcame their fears and manifested a surprising activism. Their project included, in particular, the creation in the US of a Jewish Legion, which was to be sent to the Soviet-German front, as well as the creation of antifascist committees in the countries of the anti-German coalition. In developing their plans, Alter and Erlich were naïve enough to believe that they could "soften" Stalin's regime and guide it toward democratization. At the same time, Alter and Erlich established permanent contacts with Sir Stafford Cripps, the British ambassador, and Stanislaw Kott, the Polish ambassador, who transmitted to them the tasks of General Wladyslaw Sikorski's London-based government in exile. One such task was to participate in the search for Polish officers who had been scattered throughout Russia, many of whom had been shot in 1940 in the Katyn forest (near Smolensk), Kharkov, and Kalinin-Tver (in the town of Mednoye). In October 1941 Soviet institutions and foreign embassies were evacuated from Moscow to the city of Kuĭbyshev, and it was there that Erlich's and Alter's cooperation with diplomatic missions of the Allies grew stronger.

While disseminating the idea of strengthening Jewish international relations, Alter prepared his journey to England (where he aspired to become a representative of the Bund for the Polish government), and Erlich wanted to go to the US. However, their plans were not to be realized. Though Stalin had hoped to use the compliant Bund leaders to increase considerably Western aid, he could not waive his Bolshevist principles by concluding an alliance with European "social-reformists" who, as he was informed, were protected by foreign special services.

The arrest of Erlich and Alter was a typical NKVD action. On December 3, 1941 Captain Khazanovich called them to say that the NKVD had received Stalin's reply to their letter, and asked them to come to the NKVD offices to read it. Erlich and Alter visited the offices the next day and never came back. It turned out that when the NKVD colonel L.F. Raĭkhman arrived from Moscow he did not show them Stalin's reply, but instead brought an arrest warrant signed by Beria. As Erlich and Alter were considered especially important prisoners, they were put in solitary cells at the NKVD internal prison in Kuĭbyshev under the secret numbers "41" and "42."

On December 5 A.Ya. Vyshinskiĭ informed Ambassador Kott that Erlich and Alter had been arrested for their connections with German intelligence, and went on to call them German agents similar to L.D. Trotskiĭ. They had allegedly agitated for Soviet troops to make peace immediately with fascist Germany. Both Polish men were sentenced to death. Erlich fell into despair and committed suicide by hanging himself from the window bars of his cell on May 14, 1942. Alter was shot in February 17, 1943.

Having rejected this risky experiment with foreigners, Stalin decided to gamble on the Soviet Jewry, which was entirely under his authority, and utilized the plan long ago prepared by Agitprop. At Shcherbakov's and Lozovskiĭ's proposal, on December 15, 1941 Mikhoels was appointed the chairman of the as yet nonexistent JAC, and Sh. Epshteĭn was appointed his deputy and executive secretary. The creation of the JAC took place over the next few months. On February 5, 1942 Lozovskiĭ sent Shcherbakov a proposal for the functions of this new propagandistic organ, which was to become a part of the Sovinformburo, along with the Pan-Slavic, Youth, Women's and other antifascist committees.

In April and May 1942 the organization of the JAC was completed, and its members and presidium were elected. The presidium included, together with Mikhoels and Epshteĭn, the poets I.S. Fefer, S.Z. Galkin, and P.D. Markish; the academician L.S. Shtern; the medical doctor B.A. Shimeliovich; the writer D.R. Bergelson; L.M. Kvitko; and others. The CC then approved the Yiddish newspaper *Einikeit*, which at first was to be published every ten days, but later became a weekly. RTsKhIDNI, f. 17, op. 125, d. 59, l. 29; d. 35, l. 62–63; d. 106, l. 1–3; d. 112, l. 126; *East European Jewish Affairs*, 1992, vol. 22, no. 2, pp. 65–85.

political benefits from it. Nonetheless, fearing that the JAC might foment Jewish nationalism within the Soviet Union, he initially had arranged to have it direct its work exclusively to the outside world. The JAC was given the tasks of favorably influencing world opinion on the Soviet Union through propaganda and through contacts with international Jewish organizations, and of initiating an extensive flow of Western aid to Russia.

The Soviet leadership intended to use the JAC as a master key to American wealth. Since two million Jews lived in New York alone this idea was so tempting that steps to undertake it were made very quickly. In early 1943 contacts were established through the Comintern with Reuben Saltzman, the head of the Jewish section of International Workers Order, an American pro-Communist trade union. On behalf of the American Committee of Jewish Writers, Artists and Scientists and the Jewish Council for Russian War Relief, Saltzman arranged an official invitation to have the JAC leaders, Solomon Mikhoels and Itsik Fefer, visit New York, Philadelphia, Pittsburgh, Chicago, Detroit, Boston, and other North American cities. This tour, prepared by the famous American journalist Ben Zion Goldberg, was intended to be a clamorous propagandistic event. Goldberg had been born in Russia and was the son-in-law of Sholem Aleichem. Since the late 1920s he had cooperated closely with the Soviet leadership—and not only to publicize the works of his famous relative. (Despite this close cooperation, the Soviet security service would later accuse him of having connections with American special services and would incriminate the JAC leaders for their contacts with him. But that came later. For the present, Goldberg remained a "best friend" of the Soviet Union.)

In mid-June Goldberg met Mikhoels and Fefer upon their arrival in the USA. There immediately followed numerous receptions, banquets, and meetings by various American and international Jewish political, cultural, and charitable organizations.[2] Mikhoels and Fefer met with Albert Einstein in Princeton; and

---

2. Mikhoels and Fefer visited not only the USA, but also Mexico, Canada, and Great Britain. Their visit to Mexico was organized by the local writer and journalist Mordecai (Marcos) Corona, who adhered to leftist Zionist views and headed the League for the Soviet Union, together with the Soviet ambassador in Mexico, K.A. Umanskií. In mid-August 1943 Mikhoels and Fefer arrived in Mexico City and were greeted by an airport decorated in Soviet, Mexican, and white-blue Jewish flags.

Mikhoels and Umanskií had known each other quite well in the USSR. Umanskií was an outstanding person with a tragic life. He was an expert on the Russian avant-garde, a friend of the famous Soviet journalist Mikhail Koltsov, had worked as a Western European correspondent for TASS in the 1930s, and later became head of the Press Department of the People's Commissariat of Foreign Affairs. In 1939 this latter post was assumed by E.A. Gnedin (Gelfand), when Umanskií was appointed ambassador to the USA. This new appointment was timely, as Stalin had just ordered an anti-Jewish purge of the Ministry of Foreign Affairs. The minister, M.M. Litvinov, was replaced by V.M. Molotov, and many diplomats of Jewish nationality were taken to Lubyanka, among them Gnedin, the son of the notorious A.L. Parvus who had been implicated in the German financing of Lenin's Party during World War I,

Thomas Mann, Lion Feuchtwanger, Theodore Dreiser, Charles Chaplin, and other cultural figures in Hollywood. Mikhoels also met with Marc Chagall, whom he had met previously in Russia before his emigration.

The Soviet guests were also received by Zionist leaders Chaim Weizmann,[3] president of the World Zionist Organization and later first president of Israel; and Nahum Goldmann and Stephen Wise, the heads of the World Jewish Congress. The leaders of the American Jewish community, led by Rabbi Epstein, asked Mikhoels and Fefer for assistance in establishing relations with chief Rabbi Solomon Shlifer and the chairman of the Jewish community in Moscow, Samuil Chobrutskiĭ.

The Crimean Syndrome

Mysteriously arranged conversations took place in New York between the two Soviet guests and James Rosenberg.[4] Rosenberg was one of the leaders of the

---

[*Translator's note:* Lubyanka was the location of the MGB headquarters in Moscow.]

When the war started, Stalin, to please the Allies, appointed Litvinov as the new ambassador to the USA, and Umanskiĭ returned to Moscow, where a tragedy befell him. His daughter Nina, while studying at the school for the higher nomenclatura children, met Vladimir Shakhurin, son of the minister for the aircraft industry. They soon fell in love. When they learned, in June 1943, that Nina would go to Mexico with her father, they had a farewell date on the Kamennyĭ bridge in Moscow, where they pronounced a passionate declaration of love. Driven to despair by her imminent departure, Vladimir shot Nina and then himself.

The investigation of this case was given to Lev Sheĭnin, the head of the Department of Investigations at the Office of the Prosecutor of the USSR. Sheĭnin did not establish the corpus delicti, but Shakhurin's mother, Sofya Mironovna Lurye, claimed that it was an act of sabotage perpetrated by the Nazis. Despite the prosecutor's conclusion, Stalin could not help but be put on his guard when he learned that the gun used in the murder/suicide belonged to one of the sons of Anastas Ivanovich Mikoyan (the minister of external trade). Thus the case was handed over to the State Security Office for further inquiry. It was later discovered that "Kremlin children" played adult politics: they appointed themselves ministers, elected heads of government, and so forth. The result of this sad story was that Stalin, in order to put children's minds on their studies rather than on love, ordered separate education for girls and boys. Further, the younger sons of Mikoyan were for some time sent out of Moscow.

Umanskiĭ's life also had a tragic finale. Since he was Jewish, he had close contact with Mexican Jewish organizations. Then in 1945 he died in an airplane crash under rather mysterious circumstances. Whether this death was accidental or arranged, one must wonder, as I. Erenburg wrote, "Should we perhaps say that Umanskiĭ also died on time?" (I.G. Erenburg, *Lyudi, gody, zhizn'*, [*People, Years, Life*], in *Sobr. soch.* [*Collected Works*], Moscow, 1967, vol. 9, p. 362). There is evidence that Lev Vasilevskiĭ (deputy to P.A. Sudoplatov, the chairman of the Fourth Directorate of the NKVD—the directorate on acts of sabotage and terrorism), who in 1940 had conducted the operation to kill Trotskiĭ, planned Umanskiĭ's death.

3. The meeting took place at Weizmann's residence at the Regent Hotel on Fifth Avenue.

4. The meetings with Rosenberg, Weizmann, and other high-ranking Americans took place according to the sanction given by V.M. Molotov. Later, during the investigations of 1952 and in the

American Jewish Joint Distribution Committee (popularly known as Joint).[5] As far back as 1926, he visited Russia on business related to a subsidiary company called Agro-Joint, and considered the Soviet Union a possible place for settling European Jewish refugees after the First World War. He was especially attracted to the blessed lands of the Crimea, in the northern part of which three Jewish national districts had existed before the war.

At his first meeting with the JAC leaders (which took place in 1943 at his suburban New York residence), the conversation touched first upon the future of the Crimea and the creation of a large autonomous Jewish settlement there.[6] Joint undertook, to a certain extent, the partial financing of this project.[7]

After their return to Russia in early November 1943, Mikhoels and Fefer informed S.A. Lozovskií of the results of their tour, including Rosenberg's offers. Lozovskií supported the idea of Jewish autonomy in the Crimea, yet some of the JAC presidium members opposed the idea. For example, the well-known Jewish poet, Perets Markish, suggested creating a national Jewish center in the former German republic of Volga, an act he thought would be of "the greatest historical

---

court proceedings, the authorities ignored this detail.

5. In 1944 Joint donated $500 000 to the Soviet Union Relief Fund. GARF, f. 8114, op. 1, d. 16, l. 2.

6. The idea of creating Jewish autonomy in the Crimea first arose in the early 1920s when a project to move 280 000 Jews there was worked out under the leadership of Soviet Party activist Yu. Larin (M.A. Lurye). On February 20, 1924 the Jewish Telegraphic Agency announced that Soviet leaders Lev Trotskií, Lev Kamenev, Nikolaí Bukharin, and A. Tsyurupa approved this plan. However, the people's commissar of agriculture, A. Smirnov, opposed this project, fearing possible frictions among the nationalities. Thus the idea of creating a Jewish republic in the Crimea was thwarted. Nonetheless the Jewish emigration to the peninsula, which started in 1922, continued. In 1936 five Jewish national districts were formed in the Crimea and the southern part of the Ukraine, with 213 Jewish collective farms and 11 035 lots. See N.F. Bugaí, "20—50–ye gody: pereseleniya i deportatsii yevreískogo naseleniya v SSSR" ("From the 20s Through the 50s: Migrations and Deportations of the Jewish Population in the USSR"), *Otechestvennaya istoriya* (*History of the Native Land*), 1993, no. 3, p. 176.

7. Later, after he had been arrested, Fefer, under torture, told his investigator that at the beginning of the conversation Rosenberg complained to his guests that in the 1920s and 30s he had wasted thirty million dollars on creating a Jewish colony in the Crimea that had never become Jewish. As a result of that interrogation, Fefer was forced to "confess" that Rosenberg, who had dreamt of transforming the Crimea into a "Jewish California," was in fact driven by the interests of the US government, which was ready to further the transformation of the Crimea first into a union republic and then into an independent state that would be used as a military base against the USSR. However, in court Fefer retracted his previous "confession" and declared that "there was no conversation about American government support of this plan [of Jewish autonomy in the Crimea], nor of the creation of a base in the Crimea." In the court record, Fefer asserted that Rosenberg declared only that "the Crimea interests us not only as Jews, but also as Americans; since the Crimea is the Black Sea, the Balkan peninsula, and Turkey." This assertion also was obtained from Fefer under pressure. The Records of the Judicial Investigation of the JAC Case, vol. 1, p. 21.

justice."[8] Other JAC members, such as the writers David Bergelson and Der Nister (P.M. Kaganovich), and the critic Ǐ. Dobrushin, supported the development of Jewish autonomy in the Far East region of the Soviet Union, and in particular the idea of having it become a republic.

Unable to come to an agreement, the JAC leaders attempted to obtain a principle decision on this project at the government level. To this end, Lozovskiǐ, deputy to Molotov (the people's commissar of foreign affairs), arranged for a meeting between Molotov on the one hand, and Mikhoels, Fefer, and JAC secretary Shakhno Epshteǐn on the other. Later, in court, Fefer described the meeting with Molotov:

> . . . we raised the question about the creation of a Jewish republic in the Crimea or in the former German republic of Volga. We liked that; it had a beautiful ring to it: "Where once was the republic of the Germans; there shall the Jewish republic be." Molotov said that it had a nice demagogic tone, but that this question should not be raised and that a Jewish republic should not be created in this territory; for the Jews are an urban people and it is impossible to seat a Jew on a tractor. Then Molotov said, "As for the Crimea: write a letter and we'll look into it."[9]

Despite this vague response, the JAC leaders decided to speed things up, as the government's decision on the Crimean question, which was expected shortly, was scheduled to be raised for consideration at the third plenum of the JAC, which would begin on February 27, 1944, a date that was fast approaching. Mikhoels charged Fefer and Epshteǐn to submit a report to the "Instantsiya" (meaning the CC or Stalin personally). He also asked Boris Shimeliovich, the chief physician at Moscow's Botkin Hospital, to do the same. Both reports were shown to Lozovskiǐ, who rejected Shimeliovich's report because of its overly sharp and radical tone. Lozovskiǐ instead used Fefer's and Epshteǐn's report as a guideline, subjecting it to considerable editing.

Lozovskiǐ was later to pay dearly for his participation in the preparation of the "Crimean report." On January 13, 1949, after the JAC had been dissolved, he was summoned to appear before Malenkov and M.F. Shkiryatov, the deputy chairman of the CC CCC of the ACP(b), where he was interrogated. Following is an excerpt from "The Record of Malenkov's and Shkiryatov's Discussion with Lozovskiǐ at the Central Committee of the ACP(b)."

---

8. Ester Markish, *Stol' dolgoye vozvrashcheniye: vospominaniya* [*A Long Way Back: A Memoir*] (Tel Aviv: Izd. Avtora, 1989), p. 172.

9. The Records of the Judicial Investigation of the JAC Case, vol. 1, pp. 22, 23, 75.

Question: Did you participate in drawing up the report?

Answer: I didn't participate at all. Mikhoels and Fefer came in, and since I was in charge of the Antifascist Committee, they asked me. I said that it is doubtful, but if you are drawing it up, I do not know what can come of it. Let them appeal.

Question: Did [they] show you the letter?

Answer: I do not remember; possibly; it was in 1943.

Question: Did [they] consult [you]?

Answer: I said that it is doubtful, but if they want to appeal [to the government], let them appeal. They possibly showed [me] the letter.

Question: Did you correct the letter?

Answer: I don't remember. Possibly. As a matter of fact, I didn't believe. The Antifascist Committee had no right to appeal to the government with a political document.

Question: If this was your opinion, why didn't you explain [this to Mikhoels and Fefer]?

Answer: Apparently, [I] corrected.

Question: Meaning [you] were for it?

Answer: No; but apparently there was nonsense that I corrected.

Question: Does that mean you had a positive attitude?

Answer: No.

Question: It should be logical: if you were against it, they would have followed [your advice]; but if you corrected it, that means [you] agreed.

Answer: [I] don't remember exactly, but most likely I did. Mikhoels, Fefer, and Epshteín came in . . . I was wrong for not having turned them out and informed [on them]. If I didn't inform, I would not have corrected [it]. I think I didn't correct it in an essential way. But mainly, I didn't inform the CC.

Question: You have to answer about the Crimea: you corrected [it] instead of cutting off—

Answer: It's my fault that as a member of the CC I didn't inform.

Question: But you did correct it, keeping in mind that [the government] will refuse—

Answer: As far as I remember, I didn't sympathize: [I] am speaking consciously, that if I did it deliberately, it is one thing; but if [this] Party member, who gave his entire life to the revolutionary movement, has made a mistake, that is another thing.

Question: But you sympathized with their endeavors; you didn't dissuade [them], but participated—and the idea was vicious.

Answer: Yes, it was not clear to me; but now [it is] clear—

Question: You corrected that document to make it look better.

Answer: No, I didn't sympathize; but logically it looks as though

I did.[10]

Lozovskiĭ was in a life-or-death situation, and he knew it. He attempted not to deny but to minimize his participation in preparing the report on the Crimea. Nonetheless, under Malenkov's and Shkiryatov's pressure, he was forced to admit that he not only supported the formation of a Jewish republic in the Crimea, but that he indeed participated in preparing the letter to the government.

There is no doubt that Malenkov and Shkiryatov conducted this interrogation on Stalin's initiative, not their own. Therefore they quickly sent Stalin the report that the former Sovinformburo chief had been accused of political mistakes:

> As can be seen from his answers, Lozovskiĭ often met with Mikhoels, Fefer, Yuzefovich, and other Jewish nationalists. They asked him for aid in performing their nationalistic activity, and he was their permanent advisor. Lozovskiĭ confessed that he knew that the leaders of the Jewish Antifascist Committee—Mikhoels, Fefer, and others—were influenced by nationalism; but, [although] he was an ACP(b) CC member, he hid this from the ACP(b) CC. Lozovskiĭ also confessed that, after their return from America, Mikhoels and Fefer came to him and told him about the relations they had established with Rosenberg, Levine,[11] Goldberg, and other Jewish nationalists in America; and that the American anti-Soviet circles deem it necessary for Mikhoels and Fefer to raise the question in Moscow of creating a Jewish republic in the Crimea. Mikhoels and Fefer asked Lozovskiĭ's advice and appealed for aid to have the government decide this question. From these talks about the plan for creating a Jewish republic in the Crimea along the lines of the Americans' instructions, Lozovskiĭ had to have seen Mikhoels's and Fefer's anti-Soviet face and inform the Central Committee of the ACP(b) about it. But Lozovskiĭ did not do this; on the contrary, he advised Mikhoels and Fefer to send the government their report on the creation of a Jewish republic in Crimea, and [he] himself participated in editing the report.[12]

If Lozovskiĭ had realized what the future had in store for him, he would have acted differently back in early 1944; but he was not so farsighted. Besides, the tide of Jewish (and Russian and Ukrainian and Tatar, etc.) national self-awareness was then so strong that many events were perceived differently. All who had suffered during the Second World War—and especially the Jews, who had endured

10. RTsKhIDNI, f. 589, op. 3, d. 15624, l. 315–316.

11. Louis Levine, chairman of the Jewish Council of Russian War Relief.

12. RTsKhIDNI, f. 589, op. 3, d. 15624, l. 341.

Hitler's unprecedented genocide—wanted to believe that their sufferings had not been in vain. The survivors had a right to hope for a better life. Thus in 1952 Fefer described in court his emotions during the war:

> I spoke that I love my people. But who doesn't love one's own people? . . . My interests in regard to the Crimea and Birobidzhan had been dictated by this. It seemed to me that only Stalin could rectify that historical injustice, which had been created by the Roman emperors. It seemed to me that only the Soviet government could rectify this injustice, by creating a Jewish nation. And I did nothing against Soviet power. I am the son of a poor teacher; Soviet power made me a man and a quite well-known poet.[13]

The lieutenant general of justice, A.A. Cheptsov, who was then also chairman of the Military Board of the Supreme Court of the USSR, noted that Fefer was propagating "exclusively nationalistic"[14] ideas when saying "that the Jews suffered most." Fefer answered with pride: "Yes, you will not find a people who have suffered so much as the Jewish people. Of eighteen million Jews, six million have been exterminated—one-third. These are great sacrifices. We have the right to drop a tear, and we have struggled against fascism."[15]

Reading these bold, sincere, tormented words, it is difficult to believe that the man who spoke them was a dogmatic Communist, a fanatic fighter for the Party, who accused his friends in the JAC of the heresy of nationalism. It is difficult to believe that this man was a secret agent, recruited by State Security in 1944 and conferred with the pseudonym Zorin. Nonetheless, the documents prepared in late 1955, in connection with the rehabilitation of convicted JAC members, do not leave any room for doubt.

Let us consider a very dry, business-like document:

> At the preliminary inquiry, all the defendants except for Shimeliovich pled guilty and gave detailed testimony about criminal anti-Soviet activity ostensibly committed by JAC leaders. However, at the court hearings of the Military Board, which were conducted from May 5 through July 18, 1952, only Fefer initially pled guilty and blamed others. But at the end of the court session Fefer asked for a closed session without the other defendants, at which he denied his testimonies and declared that he was a secret agent of the MGB[16]

13. The Records of the Judicial Investigation of the JAC Case, vol. 1, p. 26.

14. *Translator's note:* In the USSR the words *nationalistic* and *nationalism*, as opposed to *national* or *nation*, were considered negative and felonious.

15. The Records of the Judicial Investigation of the JAC Case, vol. 1, p 43.

16. *Translator's note:* Ministerstvo Gosudarstvennei Bezopasnosti, or Ministry of State Security,

> organs under the pseudonym of Zorin, and that he had been working under their instructions. Further, at this same closed session, Fefer declared: " . . . as far back as the night of my arrest, Abakumov[17] told me that if I did not confess I would be beaten. Therefore I was frightened, and that was the reason I gave incorrect testimonies at the preliminary inquiry." It was established by an additional examination that Fefer indeed cooperated with the MGB.[18]

Though everything seems clear, it is impossible to conclude definitively, as some journalists and literati do, that Fefer was a shady and treacherous character. It is easy to blacken a person's reputation; it is far more difficult to get a good understanding of that person's circumstances. Itsik (or Isaak) Fefer was a contradictory and multifaceted figure. This poet and author might have had a promising life had he not been born in such a terrible and unjust epoch.

Isaak Solomonovich Fefer was born in Shpola, near Kiev, on September 23, 1900. His father was a Jewish teacher, and his mother was a stocking-maker. In his official autobiography,[19] he writes:

> In 1909 I was admitted to the preliminary class of the Shpola secondary school, but since my father did not possess the 25 rubles for my studies, I had to switch to self-education. . . . In 1912, in connection with my maternal aunt's and uncle's emigration to America, our family's economic situation worsened. I was forced to find a job. I was a carpenter, watch-maker, bookkeeper. Finally I entered a printing house as an apprentice typesetter.[20]

The October revolution opened for Fefer doors into politics and literature. He assumed the leadership of the blue- and white-collar trade unions in Shpola, and he was a member of the local chapter of the Bund.[21] In July 1919 he became a Communist. In 1920, in Kiev, he was introduced to the Jewish writers D. Bergelson, D. Gofshteín, and L. Kvitko; and it was there that he published his first poems.

---

formerly the NKVD, and later the KGB.

17. V.S. Abakumov was the minister of state security from 1946 through 1951. In June 1951 he was expelled from the Party, and on December 19, 1954 the Military Board of the Supreme Court sentenced him to death.

18. RTsKhIDNI, f. 589, op. 3, d. 15624, l. 341.

19. *Translator's note:* An "official autobiography" was required of a job applicant in the Soviet Union.

20. RTsKhIDNI, biographical material on I.S. Fefer.

21. The Bund was the General Jewish Labor Union in Lithuania, Poland, and Russia. It was founded in 1897 and dissolved itself in 1921 in Soviet Russia.

Fefer's conflicts with the regime began in the 1930s with the mass closings of Jewish schools, Jewish technical secondary schools, Jewish newspapers, and Jewish social and cultural institutions. The first congress of the Union of Soviet Writers had elected him as a board member in 1934; yet in 1938 he was discharged from the editorship of the Yiddish literary miscellany *Sovyetische literatur* "for displaying nationalistic tendencies." In court he openly declared: "I very much love the Jewish traditions . . . . I can't say that I have regularly attended synagogue, but we [the JAC] were connected with the Jewish religious community."[22]

During the Second World War Fefer wrote his famous poem, "I—a Jew,"[23] on behalf of the "eternal Jew," in which he praised the idea of a "continuous chain" from the prophet Isaiah, the "wise" Solomon, the Maccabees, Rabbi Akiva ben Joseph, Spinoza, and Heine, to Marx, Yakov Sverdlov, and Stalin's "friend" Kaganovich. He enthusiastically welcomed the creation of Israel in 1948. When he was asked during his trial, "You said that the creation of a Jewish state was a joyful event for you. Is this correct?" he answered, "Yes, that is correct. It pleased me that the Jews, driven out of Palestine by Mussolini's ancestors, had again organized a Jewish state."[24]

Contradictory times produce contradictory people. Contradictory times produce much that is mythical and irrational. Rather than simply condemn, it would be more reasonable to judge people by taking into account their circumstances and by comparing their actions with the actions of others around them. So let us compare Fefer's behavior at court with the behavior of his antagonist and fellow man of letters, Perets Markish. They spoke with the judge about the personality and activity of Solomon Mikhoels, who had led the Moscow Jewish Theater until his tragic death in 1948. Fefer was the first to reply to the judge's questions:

> Question: Let us return again to the Jewish Theater. You said at the inquiry that this place was also a center for nationalistic activity.
>
> Answer: Yesterday I spoke about the nationalistic repertoire of the theater when they staged the plays *Holiday Eve*,[25] *Zorye Belenkovich*, *Lampedusa's King*,[26] and so forth. Mikhoels played a great role in all this; he was not only an actor and artistic leader of the theater, but was also a man who worked much for the development of Jewish culture. The Jewish Theater was a very important lever for drawing Jews into Jewish culture.

---

22. The Records of the Judicial Investigation of the JAC Case, vol. 1, pp. 17–18.
23. This was first published in *Einikeit*, December 27, 1944.
24. The Records of the Judicial Investigation of the JAC Case, vol. 1, p. 80.
25. *Kanun prazdnika*.
26. *Korol' Lampeduzy*.

Question: Apparently Mikhoels staged many nationalistic plays during his last years.

Answer: He staged a number of plays.

Question: Did he say to you that the theater is our daily platform for nationalistic propaganda? Was there such talk?

Answer: Yes. He said that the theater is one of the basic levers for drawing Jews into Jewish culture.[27]

Then Perets Markish took the stand.

Question: So, in 1937 the Theater's activity acquired a nationalistic character?

Answer: It was getting rotten because it turned "its face" to the past. In 1937 L.M. Kaganovich visited the theater and called Mikhoels and asked, "Why do you disparage the people?"

Question: From this one can conclude that Mikhoels led the theater to nationalism.

Answer: Mikhoels was a great actor; I can't compare him to first-class artists, but he was well known in Jewish drama circles. He thought the main asset of the Theater was *The Journey of Veniamin III*,[28] and that all the bad inheritance was associated with Granovskiĭ[29] and his relation to the people. He [Granovskiĭ] was a strange man who didn't want to understand that the people were getting freed from the filth and that they are longing to move forward. He was not interested in showing the artistic propaganda of the socialist society. In 1937 the theater reached a state of unbearable deterioration.

Question: But he kept leading the committee [JAC]. How did he allow you to enter the committee?

Answer: He was a "two-faced Janus." He could be tempted when talking with people. When he was actually made chairman of the Antifascist Committee I said that he will be a fool on the throne. But since the government thought it necessary to appoint him for leading such an important section during the war, then it was necessary.[30]

There is no point in examining whose answers were better and whose were worse. Both these literary men were at first treated with kindness by the regime, but later became its victims. Though we may be tempted to judge their behavior harshly, perhaps we should resist.

---

27. The Records of the Judicial Investigation of the JAC Case, vol. 1, p. 62.

28. *Puteshestviye Veniamina III.*

29. A.M. Granovskiĭ was the founder and first director of the State Jewish Theater in Moscow. In the summer of 1927 he defected while on tour abroad.

30. The Records of the Judicial Investigation of the JAC Case, vol. 1, pp. 175, 177.

The same applies to Fefer's cooperation with state security. What kind of cooperation was it? In what forms was it carried out? It is no secret that in public organizations, and especially in creative organizations, people in certain management positions inevitably came to work for the MGB. The secretarial post of the JAC, held by Fefer, was one of these positions. Similarly, Fefer's predecessor, Shakhno Epshteín, had been a state security agent, as had his deputy, Grigorií Kheífets, who had worked for the JAC since July 1947. They had both been agents of state security "according to their position." Kheífets was experienced in Party business. Before his appointment to the JAC he had worked as secretary to Lenin's widow, Nadezhda Krupskaya; and during the war he had been sent to the USA as vice-consul in San Francisco, where he combined his diplomatic duties with intelligence duties.[31] He signed his secret reports to Moscow with the nickname Kharon. Once in the JAC, Kheífets openly declared that he had been appointed by the "organs of the directorate in order to strengthen the Committee's political line." At the same time Kheífets, according to the testimony Fefer gave in court, plainly showed his indignation when, after the war, the Ministry of Foreign Affairs expelled all the Jews in its employ, such as the former vice minister M.M. Litvinov (Max Vallakh),[32] ambassador to Brazil Ya.Z. Surits, and others. He was also indignant that Jews were now prohibited from enrolling at the Superior School of Diplomacy. In 1948 Kheífets accepted into the JAC and registered many "volunteers" who wanted to fight in Israel. Because of all this he was later taken to Lubyanka.[33]

Let us look at another notable person, Iosif Sigizmundovich Yuzefovich (Shpinak). He was born in 1890 in Warsaw, son of a tanner. He had been a member of the Bund, but then in 1917 joined the social-democratic faction of internationalist-solidarists. Later, in the autumn of 1919, he went over to the RCP(b) as a member of Lozovskií's group. For decades Yuzefovich was Lozovskií's right-hand man. The two of them worked together in Profintern[34] and then in the Sovinformburo. They worked apart only from 1931 until 1933, during which time, as he answered in his Party questionnaire, Yuzefovich "carried out underground activities in the USA." During the war he adopted an orphan whose parents had been shot by the Germans. Before his arrest he worked at the Institute of History, a branch of the USSR Academy of Sciences.[35] To complete his portrait, we need to know that there is a document stating that he had been "a

31. The Records of the Preliminary Investigation of the JAC Case, vol. 5, pp. 41–50.

32. Litvinov was fired even though he favored assimilation and officially reported his nationality as "Russian."

33. Document from the archives of the former KGB.

34. *Translator's note:* Profintern was the Red International at the Trade Unions (1921–1937), an international union of the left-wing trade unions.

35. RTsKhIDNI. Biographical materials on I.S. Yuzefovich.

secret employee of the MGB since 1938."[36]

Two JAC members, Ilya Vatenberg and his wife Chaíka (Khaíka) Vatenberg-Ostrovskaya, upon their arrival to the USSR from the USA in 1934, had been recruited by two security officers, Ya.K. Berezin and D.K. Murzin, to act as informants. In 1937 and 1938, when the two security officers were arrested, the couple discontinued their relation with state security. However, in 1947 the MGB again insisted upon being informed about the Vatenberg's acquaintances. But the Vatenbergs double-crossed the MGB by providing only useless information.

Valentin V. Mochalov, the executive secretary of the All-Slavonic Committee (which was allied with Sovinformburo) was also an MGB agent.[37]

On the whole, such cooperation with the MGB was routine work related to collecting and transmitting whatever information the secret service found interesting. This sort of activity was ordinary in a totalitarian state; it was the honorable duty of any Party member or citizen. Such ordinary informants during Stalin's reign should not be compared with, say, the *agents provocateurs* of the tsar's protection service. The lurid but superficial legend that the "Crimean brief" was an act of provocation by MGB agents in the JAC has been exaggerated by some authors.

Actually, the "Crimean brief" was an inevitable consequence of excessive Jewish nationalist feelings, which in turn were an inevitable consequence of the extermination of European Jews. Indeed, it is not at all surprising that the terrors of the war pushed the JAC leaders to take such a hasty step with a touch of national conceit. At the same time, it is unlikely that the "Crimean brief" was inspired by Stalin as a pretext for future repressions. A provocation cannot last so long; it is a perishable and momentary good. In the spring of 1991 I discovered, in the former Central Party Archives in Moscow, a copy of the "Crimean brief" addressed to V. Molotov, which the CC had filed and forgotten a mere week later. It was not for another several years that the MGB dredged it up to begin the falsification of the "Zionist case." A likely scenario of events is that the JAC leaders abandoned their plans; and that later, when compromising material was needed, the MGB used this blunder to their own advantage, exaggerating the scale of the sin to the maximum, thus distorting its meaning. That is why the "Crimean brief" was now considered the main document "exposing the criminal character of the JAC activities."

It is time now to give the floor to the document itself. And let the reader decide as to the sincere but politically naïve aspiration of those who composed the "Crimean brief."

---

36. A. Vaksberg, "Stalin protiv yevreyev" ("Stalin Against the Jews"), *Detektiv i politika* (*Detective Stories and Politics*), 1992, no. 3, p. 198.

37. Milovan Djilas, *Litso totalitarizma* [*The Face of Totalitarianism*] (Moscow, 1992), p. 25.

Deputy Chairman of the Council of People's Commissars
of the USSR
Comrade V.M. Molotov

Dear Vyacheslav Mikhaílovich!

During the patriotic war a number of problems arose concerning the life and the arrangement of the Jewish masses of the Soviet Union. Before the war there were approximately 5 million Jews in the USSR, including approximately one and one-half million Jews in the western regions of the Ukraine, Belorussia, the Baltic region, Bessarabiya, Bukovina, and also those from Poland. It may be presumed that not less than 1.5 million Jews were exterminated in the Soviet regions that had been temporarily annexed by the fascists.

Apart from the hundreds of thousands of soldiers who are fighting with dedication in the Red Army, all the rest of the Jewish population of the USSR has been dispersed over the Central Asiatic republics: Siberia, along the banks of the Volga, and in some central regions of the RSFSR.

Naturally, the first question to be raised for the evacuated Jewish masses concerns their return to their native lands. However, in light of the tragedy that the Jewish people are experiencing today, this would not entirely resolve the problems of the Jewish population in the USSR.

First, owing to the unprecedented fascist atrocities, especially in regard to the Jewish population—such as its general extermination in the temporarily occupied Soviet regions—these native lands have lost their economic and psychological importance for the majority of Jewish evacuees. This is not only a matter of ruined homes; this refers to all the people returning to their native lands. An enormous part of the Jewish population had family members who were late for evacuation; and for them their native lands have been converted by the fascists into a mass cemetery for their families, for their relatives and dear ones who will never return alive again. For the Jews from Poland and Romania the question of returning is not raised at all, for they are Soviet citizens. The rest of their relatives have been exterminated, and all traces of Jewish culture have been wiped from the face of the earth.

Second, owing to an extraordinary growth of national cadres among the fraternal peoples[38] who are [now] creating their own cultures, the considerable part of the Jewish intelligentsia who had earlier worked in different areas of the national cultures of the fraternal

38. *Translator's note:* "Fraternal peoples" = Soviet nationalities.

peoples find a declining demand for their work force, which leads to a loss of professional skills among large circles of the Jewish intelligentsia.

The intelligentsia of Jewish nationality could put their cultural power, which they have accumulated over the centuries and which has made great achievements, to enormous use in creating a Jewish-Soviet culture. But the dispersal of the Jewish population, who constitute inconsiderable minorities in all the republics, does not give the opportunity for realizing this. The educational work in political and cultural matters among the Jewish masses in their native language has actually been terminated. The few available Jewish cultural institutions (several theaters, one publishing house, and one single weekly newspaper) are not capable of satisfying the cultural needs and requirements of the Jewish population, which numbers over 3 million.

. . . During the war, some capitalist vestiges intensified in the psychology of some strata of different nationalities, including their intelligentsia. The new outbursts of anti-Semitism constitute one of the most vivid expressions of these vestiges. These outbursts are stirred up in every way by fascist agents and hidden hostile elements for the purpose of undermining the most important achievement of Soviet power, which is the people's friendship.

These unhealthy phenomena are perceived very keenly by all the strata of the Soviet Jewish population, who have proved themselves to be true patriots of their motherland through the heroism of their best sons and daughters at the fronts of the patriotic war and in the rear. The display of anti-Semitism evokes an acute reaction in the soul of each Jew without exception, all the more since the Jewish people suffered the greatest tragedy in their history, having lost approximately four million people, i.e., one-quarter of their number, as a result of the fascist atrocities in Europe. The Soviet Union is the only country that protected the lives of almost half of the European Jewish population. On the other hand, the existence of anti-Semitism, in combination with the fascist atrocities, promotes the growth of nationalistic and chauvinistic moods among some layers of the Jewish population.

For the purpose of normalizing the economic situation of all strata of the Jewish population and of furthering the growth and development of Soviet Jewish culture; for the purpose of maximum mobilization of all the forces of the Jewish population for the benefit of the Soviet native land; for the purpose of total equalization of the position of the Jewish masses among fraternal peoples; we consider it timely and expedient, regarding the matter of solving postwar problems, to raise the question of creating a Jewish Soviet Socialist Republic.

> Some time ago a Jewish autonomous region in Birobidzhan was created, with a view to transforming it into a Jewish Soviet Republic, and in this way to resolve the state and juridical problem for the Jewish people as well. It is necessary to admit that, for many reasons, the Birobidzhan experience did not have a proper effect; first due to insufficient mobilization of all possibilities, and also due to its extreme remoteness from the location of the main Jewish labor masses. But regardless of all difficulties, the Jewish autonomous region became one of the most advanced regions in the Far East region [of the USSR], which proves the ability of the Jewish masses to build their own Soviet state. This ability has been displayed even more in the development of the Jewish national regions created in the Crimea.
>
> Owing to the above, we would consider it expedient to create a Jewish Soviet republic in one of the regions where it is possible to do so for political reasons. It seems to us that one of the most suitable regions is the territory of the Crimea, which is the best suited, both in terms of its capacity for migration and in terms of the successful experience in developing Jewish national regions there.
>
> . . . The idea of creating a Jewish Soviet Republic is the only one to enjoy popularity among the broadest sector of the Jewish masses of the Soviet Union and among the best representatives of the fraternal peoples. All Jewish peoples, wherever they are, would render their considerable help in the building of a Jewish Soviet Republic. Proceeding from all of the above, we propose:
>
> 1. To create a Jewish Soviet Socialist Republic in the Crimean territory.
>
> 2. In good time, before the Crimea's liberation, to appoint a government commission to study this matter.
>
> We hope that you will give proper attention to our proposal, as the fate of a whole people depends upon its realization.
>
> S.M. Mikhoels
Shakhno Epshteín
Itsik Fefer
>
> Moscow, 21.02.1944[39]

Some six days earlier Mikhoels, Epshteín, and Fefer sent a shorter draft of this same letter to Stalin, which contained a notable paragraph that was deleted from the final version:

> These [nationalistic] moods nourish the various Zionist illusions that the resolution of the "Jewish problem" is possible only in Palestine, which is the only historically suitable country for

39. RTsKhIDNI, f. 17, op. 125, d. 246, l. 169–172.

> Jewish statehood.[40]

It is uncertain why this proposal was not included in the final text of the letter. Possibly the authors were afraid that such an argument could be interpreted as a threat of blackmail by Soviet Jews who would possibly leave for Palestine. But it is apparent that the JAC leaders wished to emphasize the significance of the Crimean project in the context of world policy; yet at the same time they wished to avoid any accusations that they were sympathetic to Zionism. That this latter idea was their wish is confirmed by Fefer's court testimony:

> It is difficult to say that the committee has been close to the Zionists, for the plan to create a Jewish republic in the USSR was anti-Zionist, at least insofar as the Zionists were in favor of creating a Jewish republic in Palestine. Ambidzhan[41] and Joint are anti-Zionist organizations, and they didn't want to support the Zionists; therefore we met with them as well as with representatives of some other organizations.[42]

The "Crimean brief," which was a precursor of postwar Jewish activity in the USSR, did not lessen the Jewish problem, but aggravated it even more by associating Jewish activities with an international character. The JAC leaders lost their sense of reality, especially after Mikhoels and Fefer returned from the West. They thought that, as the elite of the American Jewry had done, they too could influence government circles by participating in the formulation of a state policy favorable to the Soviet Jews. It was naïve for them to believe that Stalin, who took no account even of his close relatives' and fellow comrades' interests, would allow such an influence—especially now that an alternative to the Zionist idea of creating Jewish hearth in Palestine had been put on the agenda. Influential external forces were gradually getting involved in the problem, and Stalin could not but fear such a development. He, one would suppose, planned to send the surviving European Jews to the Near East and thereby weaken considerably the British position in that region. To exist alongside a "Crimean Palestine," to which uprooted European Jewry would rush, was for him surely an unattractive prospect.

---

40. GARF, f. 8114, op. 1, d. 910, l. 34.

41. Ambidzhan was the American Committee for the Settlement of Jews in Birobidzhan, a public organization of both Jewish and non-Jewish Americans that promoted developing relations with the USSR and rendering material aid to the USSR, especially to a Jewish autonomous region. A similar group, the Organization for Jewish Colonization in Russia (ICOR) had been rendering economic help to migrants to Birobidzhan since the 1920s. During the war Ambidzhan and ICOR jointly launched a campaign to collect resources for the migration to Birobidzhan of 30 000 Jewish orphans, and after the war the two organizations merged.

42. The Records of the Judicial Investigation of the JAC Case, vol. 1, p. 32.

Besides, Stalin could not but evaluate this letter as an impertinent request to himself personally and to the system he had created, with its strictly regulated though unwritten rules of conduct.

The JAC was created solely for propaganda work and to pump the West for aid to the Soviet Union. To stimulate such activity, much was permitted to the JAC leaders: they would have the best salaries, they could write for foreign publishers and receive foreign royalties, they could give and accept presents from abroad, and they could travel abroad. And this is not to take into consideration their comfortable apartments, dachas, orders, deputy memberships, honors, and popularity. All this could be gotten in exchange for obedience and strict observance of the system's established game rules.

The authors of the "Crimean brief," knowingly or unknowingly, overstepped their bounds. The brief testified to the JAC leaders' wish not to be formal representatives of the Soviet Jews, but to act as a political force expressing Jewish hopes and national interests. This encroached upon the monopoly of Stalin's state apparatus, and this was a crying insolence that could not remain unpunished. So now any attempts to speak in the name of all Jews, or to reorganize the JAC into a "Department of Jewish Affairs," were imputed to the JAC leaders.

Further, the "Crimean brief" let Stalin know that the JAC wished no longer merely to play its propagandistic role, but aspired legitimately to represent the Soviet Jews. And the JAC wished to do this not only within the USSR, but in the international arena as well. Stalin's apparatus perceived this as especially threatening, and its xenophobia increased. The JAC had signed its own death warrant; it was only a matter of time before the execution would be carried out.

The authors of that letter naïvely felt no sense of doom; but, filled with glowing hopes and euphoria, looked forward to a positive response from Stalin. They continued their activities, unaware of their lethal effects. If we can trust the testimony of the JAC leaders when they were on trial, they now began to distribute portfolios of the future government of the Jewish Republic of Crimea. They called Mikhoels "our president," Shakhno Epshteín would be prime minister, and Fefer would be the minister of foreign affairs. (According to other data, Fefer wished to be chairman of the Arts Committee.) Berl Shimeliovich would be the minister of public health, Leíba Kvitko would be the minister of education, and the literary man Samuil Galkin would be Kvitko's deputy. The lawyer academician[43] A.N. Traínin was expected to be the minister of justice, Iosif Yuzefovich would be the leader of the republican trade-unions, Perets Markish would be the chairman of the Union of Jewish Writers, and so on. It is possible that this strange government game, that so resembled a tasteless musical comedy, was largely invented later by the MGB leadership, who were ever on the

43. *Translator's note:* An academician was a member of the USSR Academy of Sciences.

alert for the activation of Jewish social life.

V. Abakumov, the minister of state security, later reported to Stalin:

> In connection with the dispatch of this [Crimean] brief to the government, propaganda in its support had been spread among the Jewish population. Bergelson, the writer, declared: "It is necessary to act with determination; afterwards it will be too late. It is necessary to have the courage to take responsibility and to pave the way. Such a moment will not be repeated, and so Mikhoels is right to put forth the question about creating a republic. [I] don't doubt that we will convert the Crimea into a pearl. Friends wish this good for the Jews, but enemies want them to concentrate and not to occupy good places in other parts of the USSR owing to their abilities."

In this same message, Abakumov noted:

> Soon after sending the letter to the government, Perets Markish, the writer, gathered together in his apartment the writers Dobrushin, Grubiyan, Gofshteín, and Professor Nusinov, and suggested they develop their project of writing the letter based on the thesis: "It is necessary to create a republic for preserving Jewish culture in order for this republic to be a spiritual center of world Jewry." In this regard, Nusinov declared: "The fate of the Jewish people in all countries is identical. We shall greet the creation of the Jewish state in Palestine; and if we have our own republic, the closest spiritual connection will be established between them."[44]

Months went by, but there was no answer. In mid-May 1944, when the Crimea was liberated from the Germans, Beria's department began to evict the Crimean Tatars, Bulgarians, Greeks, Armenians, Germans, and others (over 225 000 people in all).[45] A confidence then arose that the question of a Jewish republic would be favorably resolved, since it would be necessary for someone to fill in this newly created ethnic vacuum! Anticipating such an outcome, the JAC decided to send the popular writer Leíba Kvitko to the Crimea. He was to collect information about the situation of the Jewish population there, and this information would be used to compose new letters to the government. The JAC emissary beheld a joyless picture. Although 67 000 Jews, Karaites,[46] and

---

44. Document from the archives of the former KGB.

45. *Kommunist*, 1991, no. 3, p. 109; *Istoriya SSSR* (*USSR History*), 1990, no. 6, p. 138.

46. This is what the document says. Another version has it that the Germans did not bother to kill the Karaites, whom they did not consider ethnic Jews.

Krimchaks had perished under the German occupation,[47] this did not alarm the Soviet administration that had just been appointed after the liberation of the peninsula. The local authorities hampered the repatriation of the Jews, refusing them residence and work permits, to say nothing of the necessary economic help. American and Western aid to the Soviet Jews was, as a rule, either stolen or used to help others. All these unlawful actions were reflected in the JAC notes to Molotov, Beria, and Andreyev (people's commissar of agriculture and chairman of the Party Control Commission).[48]

To calm the excitement, the People's State Inspection Commissariat formally examined the matter, and, as could be expected, concluded that the claims made in the letters did not correspond to reality. Mikhoels reacted angrily: "This is not an answer; this is a formal reply that will not change anything. After such an answer things will only be worse. The anti-Semitic bureaucrats will see that they can get away with anything."[49]

Information concerning Stalin's negative reaction to the Crimean proposal now reached the initiators of the project. As Fefer later declared at the trial, Kaganovich had summoned him along with Mikhoels and Epshteín to his office for an extensive conversation. Kaganovich declared that the Crimean brief was worth nothing "in practice" as "the Jews will not go to the Crimea," and that "only artists and poets could have come up with such a project." They nonetheless continued, together with broad circles of the Soviet Jewish population, to hope for the prospect of obtaining their own political system.

Beginning in the autumn of 1944 migrant Slavs from the Ukraine, Voronezh, Bryansk, Tambov, Kursk, and Rostov regions of the RSFSR began to populate the Crimea. This did not dispel the JAC's illusions, however, but only weakened them. Mikhoels's and Fefer's August 25, 1945 note to Malenkov clearly indicates

---

47. *Kommunist*, 1991, no. 3, p. 106.

48. RTsKhIDNI, f. 17, op. 127, d. 478, l. 44–45. Attached to the May 26, 1944 note from the JAC to L.P. Beria (the minister of internal affairs) were letters from Jews who had been repatriated from the eastern part of the country to the liberated areas. These letters complained of the unlawful acts of the local authorities, of their anti-Semitism and discrimination. Beria ordered an investigation, which soon ended up in nothing.

In 1944 the JAC sent two letters (in addition to the "Crimean brief") to V.M. Molotov. Molotov gave the first letter, dated May 18, to the CC and to Beria for examination of the facts stated in it. The second letter was sent on October 28. Mikhoels delivered one of the letters to Molotov through Molotov's wife, P. Zhemchuzhina.

Just as Kvitko had gone to the Crimea, I.M. Nusinov, a professor of literature, was in the summer of 1944 sent to Ukraine to investigate the alarming information that the JAC had received from those regions. On his return to Moscow, Kvitko told the JAC leaders of the raging anti-Semitism in Crimean schools, where Jews were given scornful nicknames by their classmates and sometimes even beaten. Later, Kvitko would be charged with anti-Soviet propaganda for relating this information.

49. Document from the archives of the former KGB.

the JAC's prospective cooperation with Western Jewish charitable organizations; for in this note they write of the idea of having Joint seek permission for the "rendering of help to the Jewish collective farms of the Crimea."[50]

After the war the idea of creating a solid Jewish hearth on Soviet territory was by no means any less real. With the economic dislocation and the enormous problems that resulted from the repatriation of Jews to their former places of residence where the occupied population had been hostile to them, and for other important reasons as well, the importance attached to this idea grew even greater. Unfortunately, local and central authorities did not take any decisive action against the anti-Semitism that flourished after the war; sometimes they even showed an indulgence toward it. The following little-known episodes in particular testify to this.

In early October 1945 the CC received a letter from a group of Kievan Jews addressed to Stalin, Beria, and *Pravda*'s editor-in-chief P. Pospelov. This letter stated that not long before in their still ruined town, where "there was a strong German influence in the air," there was a bloody international clash, described in the letter as "the first Jewish pogrom during the time of Soviet power."

> The words *Zhid* or *beat the Zhids*, spoken with relish, are being heard in the streets of the Ukrainian capital—in the trams, trolleys, shops, markets and even in some Soviet institutions. This took a rather veiled form in the Party apparatus up to the CC of the CP(b).

It became obvious that in this atmosphere of unbridled anti-Semitism, one little spark would be enough to ignite a tragedy—and this is exactly what happened.

> In early September this year, a Jew, a Ukrainian NKVD major, was attacked in the middle of the street by two anti-Semites dressed in military garb who, after having insulted him, forcefully beat him. Unable to stand the humiliation, and apparently psychologically suffering all that the Jews of Kiev—and together with them all the democratic elements of other nations—were experiencing in connection with the wild outburst of anti-Semitism, the major, in temporary insanity, shot those two anti-Semites. That shot marked the beginning of the Jewish pogrom. Some special arrangements were made for the funeral of the two anti-Semites. Their coffins were carried through the most crowded streets, and then the procession

50. RTsKhIDNI, f. 17, op. 125, d. 317, l. 283. G.Z. Sorkin, a Sovinformburo employee, testified at the trial to the "vitality" of the "Crimean project." He remembered that in June 1945, after his return to Moscow from Romania, he went to Lozovskii's reception room while at work, and there found Mikhoels, Fefer, and Epshtein, who were trying, through Lozovskii, to meet Molotov in order to raise the Crimean problem once again.

> made its way to the Jewish market. This procession turned into a demonstration. Then the beating of the Jews started. In one day a hundred Jews were beaten up, 36 of whom, in very serious condition, were rushed to Kievan hospitals, where five died on the same day. Along the way several Russians who resembled Jews were beaten in the same way as Jews."[51]

This occurrence might have been explained by the remaining influence of Hitler's anti-Semitic propaganda, as Kiev had been occupied for more than two years. However, at approximately the same time, a similar letter was sent to the chairman of the Council of Nationalities of the Soviet Supreme of the USSR, N.M. Shvernik, from the town Rubtsovsk of the Altaí Region, which was situated thousands of kilometers from the front line. This letter described in detail a number of anti-Semitic excesses, including the one that took place on July 8, 1945 during a soccer game at the local stadium. It further mentioned the inexplicable inactivity of the town authorities, such as the prosecutor's office, the militia, and the local Party committee, which played a significant role in the provocation of the anti-Jewish disturbances.[52] This proves once again that the postwar upsurge of anti-Semitism in the USSR was not only a manifestation of the remaining vestiges of Goebbels's propaganda, but was also a natural result of the anti-Jewish policy that the Kremlin had begun to follow long before the war started. In this respect, it would be appropriate to give another example.

In July 1946 the head of the Stalin's personal office, A.N. Poskrebyshev, received a letter from a certain Ya.Ye. Braul, a professor of pathological anatomy and chairman of a Simferopol Medical Institute department in the Crimea. He wrote:

> . . . Upon my arrival to Simferopol after my release from the Red Army, I heard from many friends that in the Crimea Jews are not accepted to jobs, and that those who are already working are being fired by any means. I have a vacancy in my department. I have chosen for this position a knowledgeable and capable pathological anatomist . . . Kharkhurim Ilya Grigoryevich . . . . When I appealed to the director of the Medical Institute . . . and asked him to approve Kharkhurim for the position of an assistant, he replied . . . "What are you doing to me! I have already been 'burnt' by the Regional [Party] Committee because I have too many Jews working here!"

Later Braul decided to ask for advice from the head of the Department of

---

51. RTsKhIDNI, f. 17, op. 125, d. 310, l. 49–52 obverse.
52. RTsKhIDNI, f. 17, op. 125, d. 310, l. 47–48.

Marxism-Leninism, I.K. Dekhtyaryov, who declared to the professor that "he himself heard from Regional [Party] Committee functionaries that the Crimea has to be Russian and that no Jews should be accepted for work . . . . "[53] After having given an account of all these facts of anti-Semitism, Braul naïvely hoped that his letter would force the CC ACP(b) to call to order the Party leadership of the region, who at their own peril had gone too far in their protection of anti-Semites. How could he know that those he blamed were simply carrying out the instructions of the Moscow authorities?

Nevertheless, when Poskrebyshev sent this letter to Zhdanov, he in turn transmitted it to the secretary of the Crimean Regional Committee, N.V. Solovyev, who immediately accused Braul of slandering the regional Party organization and of propagandizing Jewish nationalism in the guise of fighting against anti-Semitism. Braul apparently realized how dangerous his own delusions were. In fact, things took a turn for the worse. In his reply to Zhdanov, Solovyev presented Braul's complaint as not just a calumny of a single offended Jew, but as the action of a broad nationalistic organization. He deliberately reminded the Party bosses at Old Square (who had not yet come to their senses after the JAC leaders dared to attempt establishing Jewish autonomy in the Crimea) that even before the war there had supposedly been a pro-American Zionist society, and that in November 1944 a religious meeting had been summoned in Simferopol, in which Braul had participated as well.[54]

Since this study touches upon a very important attribute of Jewry, namely Judaism, it should be pointed out that at this time, in the autumn of 1946, the freedom that had been allowed to the synagogues during the war was gradually being abolished. Before this time, and just by inertia, the second (and quite impressive) postwar memorial service for the six million Jews who had been annihilated by Nazis took place in the Moscow synagogue. Soon afterwards the Council of Religious Cult Affairs at the Council of Ministers of the USSR sent reports to the CC ACP(b) that sharply criticized, alongside other confessions, the situation in the Judaic communities. The reports claimed that the tragic losses sustained by the Jewish people during the war had led to a considerable growth of nationalistic moods as well as to the appearance of some sort of "Soviet Zionism." Its adherents did not want to see "the manner and styles in which the so-called

53. There is other evidence of the postwar wave of anti-Semitism in the Crimea. A certain Gordina, who in 1946 moved from the Crimea to Birobidzhan, where she worked as a City Committee lecturer, wrote in her autobiography: "The situation in the Crimea is such that it is impossible to work. Anti-Semitism is everywhere and nobody is fighting against it." That was why she moved to the Jewish Autonomous Region. Besides, she wanted to dedicate herself to transforming the Jewish people into a nation; for it was only through being a nation, she believed, that the Jews could avoid all the terrors they had had to survive during World War II. RTsKhIDNI, f. 17, op. 118, d. 39, l. 107.

54. RTsKhIDNI, f. 17, op. 125, d. 405, l. 21–26.

'Jewish problem' in the USSR had been resolved long ago," and declared the synagogue to be "the only place of national concentration and the only hearth of national culture." Based on this report, the authorities carried out a secret "crusade" against Jewish synagogues on Soviet territory (which, as of January 1, 1947, numbered 162). The first task was strongly to restrict Judaism, which traditionally constituted the basis of Jewish life, to the constrictive limits of cult rites. Specifically, the Council of Religious Cults and its local representatives were instructed to establish strict control over every Jewish community and all the rabbinate; to restrict considerably the so-called "zdoke" (charity based on nationality); to spread the fight against customs that "stir up nationalistic feeling," such as the baking of matzo, the ritual slaughter of cattle and fowls, the consuming of kosher meat, and the sale of places in the synagogue; to liquidate the so-called "Chevra Kadesha" (Jewish funeral fraternities), and so on.[55]

The materials on the investigation of the JAC noted that in summer of 1946 Molotov's wife, Zhemchuzhina, had met with Mikhoels at her office, and that Mikhoels had declared that the JAC continually received letters from different areas of the USSR, and that all of these letters concerned Jews being oppressed by the local authorities. He then asked to which of the Kremlin leaders he should personally address this matter—perhaps to Zhdanov or to Malenkov? Zhemchuzhina replied, "Zhdanov and Malenkov will not help you. All the power in this country is in Stalin's hands alone and nobody can influence him. I do not advise you to write to Stalin. He has a negative attitude toward Jews and so will not support us."

Despite the raging postwar anti-Semitism, the project of autonomy in the Crimea kept the Jews excited. On July 17, 1946, in the Moscow Polytechnic Museum, V. Lutskiĭ, an authority on the Near East, presented a lecture entitled "The Palestinian Problem." He was asked, "What is the attitude of the official bodies of the USSR toward the national problem of the Jewish people, in terms of territorial, national, and political consolidation similar to those of the other peoples of the USSR?" He was also asked, "Why is it impossible to arrange an autonomous Jewish formation in the USSR to counterbalance Palestine? . . . Don't we have enough land? There is, for example, the Crimean peninsula, which two years ago was completely free of the Germans of the former republic of Volga."[56]

The Jews had faith in the possibility of achieving equal rights with other peoples of the USSR, and of founding their own political system on their own territory. They did not abandon this faith until they witnessed the greatest event of modern Jewish history—the formation of the state of Israel in 1948. Once the

55. RTsKhIDNI, f. 17, op. 125, d. 405, l. 98–103; op. 117, d. 946, l. 144.

56. RTsKhIDNI, f. 17, op. 128, d. 1057, l. 118.

light of this Zionist dream beamed down upon the imagination of all Jews, the Crimean mirage slowly began to grow dim. It was definitively dissolved when Lozovskiĭ, Fefer, and its other creators vanished into Lubyanka's bowels.

The minutes of Fefer's interrogation present an absolute ending of the Crimean "project." Most likely, under pressure from his investigator, Fefer declared that the events in Palestine in 1948 had drawn importance to the issue of creating the Jewish Republic of Crimea. The appearance of an independent Israel, situated in immediate proximity to the peninsula, gave hopes to the creation of an "all-Jewish front." The writer Samuil Gordon was sent to the Crimea to prepare a series of essays about local Jewish collective farms. Upon his return, he informed the JAC leaders that, although the assimilation of the Jewish population had gone too far, the Crimean project was still feasible. Fefer also "confessed" that the JAC leaders planned to send their delegation to Israel to meet on "neutral grounds" with Ben Zion Goldberg and James Rosenberg in hopes of reviving the idea of Jewish autonomy in the Crimea. "However," as Fefer summed up, "the closing down of the JAC and the arrest of its members upset our plans . . . ."[57]

The Noose Tightens

Despite Stalin's enormous machinery of suppression that customarily disregarded everyone's rights, a small group, boldly upholding its small nation's rights, formed an invisible opposition in 1944 and continued for almost five years. Not even a dictator as powerful as Stalin could immediately and overtly rebuff his Jewish subjects' national movement. He had to bide his time for a number of reasons. For instance, the Jews, having suffered the most from Hitler's atrocities, had earned the deep-felt sympathy of the entire world; and Stalin had no choice but to take the sympathies of his Second World War allies into account. Also, international Jewry had expressed strong solidarity with Soviet Jewry. Additionally, Stalin had played the Jewish card in his Near Eastern policy, and this delayed the tragic outcome. Further, the Soviet Jews had heroically fought against the fascists; so it would be difficult to amass wide-scale social support of an anti-Jewish political campaign without adequate propagandistic preparation. And there were quite a number of Jews in the Communist Party despite the hecatombs of the war. As of January 1, 1946 there were 202 878 Jews in the Party out of a total of 5 513 649. (Comparatively, on January 1, 1941 the corresponding numbers were 176 884 and 3 872 465.)[58] It was much easier now for Stalin to brand the Ukrainian and Baltic nationalists as bourgeois nationalists, traitors, and enemies,

---

57. Document from the archives of the former KGB. *Translator's note:* Fefer's actual words for "upset our plans" would literally translate "scrambled our cards" or "scrambled our deck."

58. RTsKhIDNI, f. 17, op. 117, d. 611, l. 40.

and to accuse them of having collaborated with Germans during the war.

For these and other reasons,[59] the Stalinist regime refrained from an immediate overt attack on the Jewish national movement—a movement that had emerged in the course of the war initially as an elite movement, but was now steadily and speedily expanding. Stalin's government was thereby induced to choose a more subtle policy to slowly but surely strangle it.

Stalin was waiting for an opportunity to tighten the noose; but before he could do so he had to establish total control over the activities of the JAC and other Jewish institutions. To this effect, a wide network of intelligence service agencies infiltrated these institutions, and Soviet Jewry was isolated from the external world with increasing speed. Maximal efforts were made to assimilate the Jews; Jewish activities were hampered and hindered; Jews were intimidated and cowed; and most of the brightest and influential Jewish leaders were eliminated. Dogmatic propaganda, under the slogan of "Communist internationalism and Soviet patriotism," was stepped up. And lastly, Jews were discriminated against by means of various bureaucratic contrivances, Party apparatus intrigues, and so forth.

The Party apparatus and the MGB actively and methodically began this anti-Jewish policy immediately following the war. The first blow was dealt at the Sovinformburo and at its head, S.A. Lozovskií. Later, when testifying at trial, Fefer said that Lozovskií "had been the moving spirit behind the formation of the Jewish Antifascist Committee . . . he had been well informed of all its activity and was, in fact, its leader."[60] Among themselves the Jews admiringly referred to him as "Gabbi" (the foreman of a Jewish community). Stalin wanted the JAC to lose its authorized protector—the protector who had old connections with the Kremlin's elite circles—and to establish strict Party apparatus control over the JAC.[61]

---

59. For example, there was the Marxist-Leninist dogmatic idea of "proletarian internationalism" and "proletarian solidarity," which theoretically opposed any kind of national discrimination.

60. Document from the archives of the former KGB.

61. Perhaps it was the remaining influence of the Nazis' anti-Jewish propaganda that provoked this control. During the war the CC had received quite a few anti-Semitic publications edited by Goebbels's department. Typical examples of this kind of product are the separate issues of Russian-language fascist newspapers kept in the CC archives. The June 30, 1944 issue of one of these newspapers, pretentiously called *The Voice of Truth* (*Golos pravdy*), published a vile poem, whose title, "In the Style of A.A. Blok," referred to one of the greatest Russian poets of the early twentieth century:

> In the Informburo, bent over their pens,
> the Zhids make a din like carrion-crows;
> and replete with old superstitions
> are their tireless lies.
> And every night at a fixed time

A CC commission headed by G.F. Aleksandrov was sent to the Sovinformburo to find materials that would compromise its chief. The commission completed its inspection at the beginning of September 1945, and the CC Orgburo discussed the results. Aleksandrov maintained that since the war was over there was no further need for press coverage of operations, and therefore proposed that Sovinformburo activities cease as of October 1, 1945. He signed a summary document on the JAC situation:

> . . . Thus, for instance, in July 1945 in the trade union movement section [of Sovinformburo] . . . 170 out of 225 articles and pieces of information were written by insufficiently-qualified and little-known authors, such as I.S. Vatenberg, I.A. Arbat, S.I. Blyum, L.Z. Berkhina, Ts.Z. Vaínshteín, M.L. Berlyand, I.M. Vikker, M.I. Nekrich, N.L. Rudnik, A.A. Severin, L.F. Sosonkin, B.A. Khalip, A.F. Khavin, S.S. Khesin, etc. . . . Many authors, apparently because of the unquestionably poor quality of their articles, are ashamed to put their names to them. So, for instance, Broun signs his articles with the names of Stambulov and Melnikov; Grinberg writes them under the pen name of Gridnev, and Shneerson under that of Mikhaílov.[62]

Reading this artful conclusion, one can't but feel amazed at Aleksandrov's perfidious resourcefulness; for he was well aware that the real reason Jewish journalists used Russian pen names was that Stalin had instructed them to do so. As a matter of fact, D. Ortenberg (Vadimov), the former editor of *The Red Star* newspaper, maintained that Stalin had issued this directive as far back as the middle of the 1930s.[63]

Stalin did not support Aleksandrov's idea about immediately closing the Sovinformburo, but chose instead the tactic of gradually ousting Jews from it. Until Stalin's death the Sovinformburo was constantly bothered by innumerable inspection commissions sent by the CC, the Ministry of State Control, and so forth. What were these tireless inspectors interested in? On Stalin's personal orders, the CC ACP(b) commission in the summer of 1946 inspected the Sovinformburo's work[64] and drew up, in outline form, "reference no. 8," in

---

(or am I just dreaming it?),
grabbed by Lozovskií's hand,
The enemy croaks, driven into a corner . . . .

RTsKhIDNI, f. 17, op. 125, d. 338, l. 51 obverse.

62. RTsKhIDNI, f. 17, op. 125, d. 383, l. 45.

63. D. Ortenberg, *Sorok tretií: rasskaz khronika* [*Forty-Third: A Chronicle*] (Moscow, 1991), p. 399.

64. The second postwar inspection ensued mainly because Lozovskií had prepared and sent to the CC a resolution concerning the reorganization of the Sovinformburo into a Press and Information Ministry, with the implication that he was to become the minister. Stalin had rejected this proposal and

which the following shortcomings in personnel were noted:

> . . . a) the apparatus is cluttered up; b) employees selected according to personal and blood ties; c) unacceptable concentration of Jews.[65]

The members of the commission immediately sent Stalin a report with detailed tables on the Sovinformburo's national composition, reflecting this Jewish "concentration."[66] The verdict of the "directive body" was not long in coming. On July 24 Stalin signed a Politburo resolution dismissing Lozovskií from the post of deputy minister of foreign affairs; and, as Lozovskií formally remained the head of Sovinformburo, to appoint B.N. Ponomaryov (the former assistant to Comintern leader G. Dimitrov) as his senior deputy and S.I. Sokolov as his personnel deputy, though in actuality they would be inspectors and controllers.[67]

With the active participation of these two assistants, the CC ACP(b) issued its October 9, 1946 resolution, "On the Activity of the Soviet Informburo," which decreed that Lozovskií's department be given the status of an institution "attached to the USSR Council of Ministers." This resolution also stated that "the political direction and control over the work of the Sovinformburo were effected by the CC ACP(b)." Further, the resolution introduced obligatory Glavlit[68] censorship of all materials that the Sovinformburo and the JAC sent abroad. Additionally, under the pretext of staff reduction, the resolution envisaged a purge of Sovinformburo personnel, with the primary effect of dismissing the maximum possible number of Jews.[69]

Lozovskií, still head of the Sovinformburo, tried his best to oppose this Jewish persecution. Moreover, as B.N. Ponomaryov stated in a report to the CC, Lozovskií, despite this resolution, appointed to managing posts "a certain Sorkin, a certain Yevnovich, and a certain Dolitskií, who on political considerations were not deserving of appointment to the nomenclatura staff approved by the Central Committee; they were not even deserving of being kept as ordinary editors. . . . "[70]

---

undertook new steps to discredit Lozovskií.

65. RTsKhIDNI, f. 17, op. 125, d. 383, l. 150.

66. RTsKhIDNI, f. 17, op. 125, d. 383, l. 133.

67. RTsKhIDNI, f. 17, op. 117, d. 621, l. 20.

68. Glavlit was a directorate headed during the postwar period by the so-called "representative of the USSR Council of Ministers on Protection of the Military and State Secrets in Press." Glavlit openly and officially censored all published materials.

69. RTsKhIDNI, f. 17, op. 117, d. 621, l. 112–118. After this resolution had been approved, photo correspondents Khalip, Trakhman, and Gaft; Radio Department head S.V. Mikhelson, and others were dismissed from the Sovinformburo.

70. RTsKhIDNI, f. 17, op. 127, d. 1651, l. 2.

Meanwhile Lozovskiĭ's assistants aggravated the conflict between themselves and their supposed head by executing control over his activity. Then on June 19, 1947 the CC sent a new commission to the Sovinformburo; and, just as it had been preplanned, on June 25 Lozovskiĭ was replaced by P.N. Ponomaryov.[71] All Lozovskiĭ's supporters were dismissed. In a few months two JAC presidium members (M.I. Gubelman, leader of the trade unions of the state commerce workers and brother of the Party historian Ye. Yaroslavskiĭ; and Z. Brikker, leader of the cinema and radio workers) lost their jobs.

Now removed from political activity, Lozovskiĭ for some time was chairman of the Department of the History of International Relations and Foreign Policy at the CC ACP(b) High Party School, and until his arrest in January 1949 he was editor-in-chief of a diplomatic encyclopedia, which was then being prepared for publication.

Having dealt with Lozovskiĭ, the Party machinery took one more step toward putting an end to his offspring, the Jewish Antifascist Committee. The first real threat of its closure appeared in the summer and autumn of 1946, when in the course of inspecting the Sovinformburo, a commission (consisting of five people and headed by the state security colonel Tyurin) came to the JAC, which, of course, was subject to the Sovinformburo.[72] This was preceded, as Fefer later testified, by his and Mikhoels's summons to the CC, namely to A.S. Panyushkin (the deputy chief of the Department of Foreign Policy, and subsequently the Soviet ambassador to the USA),[73] who announced straightaway that "there is an opinion that the JAC should be closed down." Mikhoels considered this premature, "for fascism still exists and should be fought."[74]

A few days later several trucks appeared at the JAC headquarters on Kropotkinskaya Street. All the JAC files were loaded onto these trucks and taken to Lubyanka for inspection. At the end of September the commission presented to M. Suslov, head of the CC Foreign Policy Department, a "Report on the Activities of the Jewish Antifascist Committee," which contended that the JAC, instead of serving as a mouthpiece for Soviet propaganda abroad, had in fact become a "commissariat of Jewish affairs." To prove this point, the commission

---

71. RTsKhIDNI, f. 17, op. 116, d. 412, l. 3; op. 125, d. 509, l. 274.

72. At about the same time G.M. Popov, secretary of the CC of the Moscow Regional and Moscow City Committees of the ACP(b), granted Fefer, Kvitko, and Markish a reception. On behalf of the JAC, these three proposed the creation of a Jewish club and a Jewish printing house in Moscow. Ben Zion Goldberg promised to send the equipment for the printing house from America. But this proposal was rejected. In the summer of 1947 Mikhoels was forced to refuse a famous New York entrepreneur's invitation for his theater to tour the USA.

73. On August 1, 1946, a decision was made to transfer the JAC to the authority of the CC ACP(b) Department of Foreign Policy. This was done by August 25, 1946.

74. The Records of the Judicial Investigation of the JAC Case, vol. 1, p. 251.

quoted I. Erenburg: " . . . just for the sake of antifascist propaganda among Jews abroad there was no need to establish the JAC; for Jews least of all need antifascist propaganda. The JAC should see its main task in fighting anti-Semitism in our country."[75]

The commission further stressed that the JAC had "the intention of raising, before the government of the USSR, even the questions of territory" (meaning, obviously, new territories rather than Birobidzhan), and that it also had the intention of "organizing the study of Jewish history, for which purpose a commission consisting of eleven people was formed in February 1946."[76]

In addition, the JAC had constantly worked on behalf of poor Jews, soliciting for economic aid, interceding for them in settling residential and other problems, and finding jobs for them. The commission also blamed the JAC for having abandoned the "active militant ideological fight against Western, and especially against Zionist, propaganda," and for having become an "ideological captive" of Jewish nationalism and Zionism.

The investigating commission found it especially disquieting that international Jewish organizations had now and then applied to the JAC, and that the JAC attempted to render them assistance in solving humanitarian problems. Thus, in support of applications from international Jewish organizations, the JAC in the summer of 1946 even went so far as to appeal to the USSR Ministry of Internal Affairs for the release from Soviet camps of Hungarian and Italian POWs of Jewish origin.[77] At about the same time as the JAC made this appeal, Mikhoels and Fefer, at the request of American Jewish organizations, telegraphed a protest to the Polish government about anti-Semitic disturbances in Cracow and other Polish cities. The "Report" also noted that the JAC had acted as an intermediary in establishing relations between the Jewish-Ukrainian community in New York and the Ukraine's republican government bodies.[78]

One item made the investigating commission especially apprehensive. The JAC had sent to the foreign Jewish press many articles sympathetic toward "the Zionist idea of the creation of a Jewish state in Palestine" and "the idea of a mass emigration of Jews to Palestine. . . . The JAC paid excessively more attention to the work on Palestine, having sent there, in the period from June 1, 1945 through June 27, 1946, over 900 articles and other materials, or one-and-a-half times more than to England."

The conclusion the "Report" was virtually disastrous:

---

75. RTsKhIDNI, f. 17, op. 128, d. 868, l. 85–95.

76. RTsKhIDNI, f. 17, op. 128, d. 1057, l. 27.

77. These prisoners of war were employed at the eastern front in various auxiliary building detachments.

78. RTsKhIDNI, f. 17, op. 128, d. 1057, l. 87–88.

> The JAC employees . . . had not only joined the aggregate orchestra of the world's Zionists, but also found themselves siding with the policy of the American Baruchs,[79] who strive for implanting in Palestine a mass intelligence service of American imperialism by means of a mass migration of Jews.[80]

The inspectors also accused the JAC newspaper *Einikeit* (*Unity*) of "bourgeois nationalism." They even saw some hidden sedition in the Yiddish name of that publication: "For what unity of the Jews is the paper fighting?"[81]

The final conclusion, which was most likely formulated even before the inspection began, was that:

> . . . the JAC should be disbanded and its functions of propaganda abroad entrusted to the Sovinformburo. The JAC's publication, *Einikeit*, is not justifying its purpose, and should be closed down. The question of the expediency of the existence of a Jewish newspaper for the Jewish population is to be passed for consideration to the Department of the Press of the Directorate of Propaganda.[82]

The Party was working harmoniously and in full accord with the repressive structures of the all-embracing nomenclatura machinery after the war. On October 12, 1946 the MGB sent the CC ACP(b) and the Council of Ministers a report "On the Nationalistic Tendencies of Some Employees of the Jewish Antifascist Committee."[83] Together with the previous report, this served as a basis for a memorandum drawn up by M. Suslov and sent on October 19 to the CC secretaries A. Zhdanov, A. Kuznetsov, N. Patolichev, and G. Popov. (Suslov, later to be called "the gray cardinal," was apparently already preparing for himself the role of chief Party ideologist.) In this memorandum Suslov repeated the suggestion that the JAC be disbanded, and accompanied this with a fair portion of Marxist-Leninist dogmas on the benefit of assimilation:[84]

---

79. Bernard Baruch (1870–1965) was a prominent Jewish-American banker and one-time unofficial advisor to President Roosevelt. In March 1946 he was appointed US representative at the UN Commission on Atomic Energy. He retired in early 1947, and from 1953 acted as personal advisor to President D. Eisenhower.

80. RTsKhIDNI, f. 17, op. 128, d. 1057, l. 116–117.

81. RTsKhIDNI, f. 17, op. 128, d. 1057, l. 95.

82. RTsKhIDNI, f. 17, op. 128, d. 1057, l. 98.

83. *Izvestiya TsK KPSS*, 1989, no. 12, p. 36.

84. As the "struggle against assimilation" was going to officially figure in the JAC trial as the main point of the accusation, we can see that Stalin's apparatus considered the policy of assimilation one of practical, not merely theoretical, importance. And yet Stalin had earlier claimed that the "policy of assimilation is undoubtedly excluded from that arsenal of Marxism-Leninism, because of its anti-populist,

> As is known, Lenin and Stalin thought that one could not speak of the Jews, territorially scattered all over the world, economically disunited, and speaking different languages, as of one nation; that the entire course of history bore witness to the process of the Jews' merging with the surrounding populations; and that this inevitable process was a reliable and progressive way of solving the Jewish problem.[85]

After the expert examination in the CC secretariat on November 26, 1946, the memorandum was sent directly to Stalin.[86] However, there, at the very summit of power, this seemingly predetermined matter of closing down the JAC unexpectedly jammed. Stalin apparently did not want to rush things. It was not without reason that N. Bukharin called Stalin "a genius doser," for he knew the proper dose of action for each period of time.[87] Maybe the time was not ripe for a decisive action against the JAC, or maybe Stalin thought that the "Moor had not yet completed his task." In addition, international political consequences of liquidating the JAC were taken into account, and could not be ignored. Stalin could not fail to see that in the growing rivalry between the USSR and the USA for the British legacy in the Near East, the Jewish card would be of decisive importance. He had claimed as far back as June 1928 that "the main contradiction within the capitalist camp turned out to be the one between the American and the British capitalisms."[88]

The fate of the Jewish Antifascist Committee lay in the oscillating balance of high politics. Thus, in December 1946 the CC offered Fefer and Mikhoels an opportunity to draw up a draft on the closing of the JAC to be sent to foreign Jewish organizations, but the Ministry of State Security confiscated it once again and seized the JAC archives.[89] On January 7, 1947 G. Aleksandrov and M. Suslov submitted to Molotov and to CC secretary A. Kuznetsov a memorandum suggesting "the discontinuation of the activities of the Soviet Scientists' Antifascist Committee and the Jewish Antifascist Committee . . . in view of their having fully accomplished their tasks."[90] However, on February 2 the JAC's archives were

---

counterrevolutionary, and pernicious nature." Stalin, *Sochineniya* [*Works*], (Moscow, 1949), vol. 11, p. 347.

85. RTsKhIDNI, f. 17, op. 128, d. 868, l. 122.

86. *Izvestiya TsK KPSS*, ibid., p. 37.

87. Stephen F. Cohen, *Bukharin: politicheskaya biographiya–1888—1938* [*Bukharin: A Political Biography—1888–1938*] (Moscow, 1992), p. 412.

88. I.V. Stalin, *Sochineniya* [*Works*] (Moscow, 1949), vol. 11, p. 198.

89. The Records of the Judicial Investigation of the JAC Case, vol. 1, p. 254.

90. RTsKhIDNI, f. 17, op. 128, d. 1057, l. 2. Several documents testify that the authorities' intention to close down the JAC was serious indeed. One document, prepared by Aleksandrov and signed by Mikhoels, is a draft of a resolution on the necessity of the JAC's self-dissolution. Another document is the "Plan of measures concerning the intended cessation of activities by the JAC in the USSR," which

returned, and on the next day Fefer had a telephone conversation with Suslov, who told him that the JAC was to work as before and that no immediate changes were expected. Furthermore, three months later, at a meeting at the CC, the head of the section of public organizations of the Department of Foreign Policy, G.V. Shumeĭko, commended the JAC's propagandistic activity.[91]

There was one more piece of evidence regarding the vacillating attitude of top Party officials toward the JAC; this was a memorandum, then considered important, that M. Shcherbakov (the head of the CC Personnel Department) sent to CC secretary Kuznetsov. Entitled "On Nationalistic and Religious and Mystical Tendencies in Soviet Jewish Literature,"[92] this memo consisted of sharp criticisms of the wartime and postwar writings of such well-known Jewish literary men as P. Markish, I. Fefer, D. Bergelson, E. Fininberg, D. Gofshteĭn, and so forth, who were active JAC members. The report censured Markish, for instance, for saying, at a conference in late 1945 on Polish Jews in the USSR, that "the Jewish people cannot be divided into Polish Jewry, Soviet Jewry, American Jewry. One cannot divide a heart into parts without breaking it."[93] This supplied grounds for the conclusion that the main objective of the plot consisted in the propagation by Jewish literature of "the idea of the unification of Jewry in one state."[94] This memo maintained that Itsik Fefer's poems "Shadows of the Warsaw Ghetto,"[95] "The Turkish Scarf,"[96] and "I—a Jew"[97]; D. Gofshteĭn's "Bible"[98]; M. Talalayevskiĭ's "Envy"[99]; and D. Bergelson's play, *Prince Reubeni*,[100] also carried this idea of Jewish state unification. The memo especially emphasized that an American magazine called *Yiddish Culture* had printed *Prince Reubeni* in 1945. The memo went on sternly to denounce those writers—Perets Markish,

Mikhoels sent to the CC. This plan stipulated that a session of the JAC presidium be called on November 27 to declare the closing of the JAC. All the JAC's files were to be transmitted to the so-called "ISPA" (Idishe Sovyetishe Press-Agentur / Soviet-Yiddish Press Agency), nominally created within the Sovinformburo, which would continue distributing propaganda materials to the foreign Jewish press. The JAC's library, archives, and property were to be handed over to the editorial staff of *Einikeit*, which was reorganized into an "independent publication, i.e. a newspaper of the Jewish workers of the USSR." RTsKhIDNI, f. 17, op. 117, d. 938, l. 135, 143–146.

91. The Records of the Judicial Investigation of the JAC Case, vol. 1, p. 255.

92. These repetitious titles for Party bureaucratic works testifies to not only the intellectual poverty of their authors, but also to the existence, within Stalin's policies, of a singularly monolithic character.

93. RTsKhIDNI, f. 17, op. 125, d. 459, l. 24.

94. RTsKhIDNI, f. 17, op. 125, d. 459, l. 25.

95. "Teni varshavskogo getto."

96. "Turetskiĭ sharf."

97. "Ya—yevreĭ."

98. "Bibliya."

99. "Zavist'."

100. *Prints Reubeni.*

Der Nister, S. Gordon, and M. Lifshits—who had fallen under the influence of religious mystics. This memo cited some lines from D. Gofshteín's poem, "The Day,"[101] as an example of obsequiousness before foreign Jewry, which was also censured:

> I'm telling you, my heart simply melted with joy,
> when in Mr. Smith's report[102] on atomic energy
> and detonation experiments in the USA,
> I saw Albert Einstein's name in the topmost place.[103]

This Party document blamed not only writers and poets; it called to task literary critics; the Jewish section of the Soviet Writers' Union; and, first and foremost, the editorial board of *Einikeit*, which published many articles that "appeared to be groundlessly overemphasizing the role of Jews."[104] The memo recommended that the CC ACP(b) secretariat consider all these transgressions at its meeting.[105]

The situation then suddenly changed, and the matter did not reach the CC secretariat. On the contrary, in April 1947, as a counter-maneuver, Aleksandrov wrote a note to Zhdanov, in which he asserted, among other things, that "during the Great Patriotic War and the postwar period, the majority of works by Soviet Jewish writers were imbued with the ideas of Soviet patriotism and were full of optimism."[106] Just as the inveterate prosecutor of Christians, Saul, suddenly became the Christian apostle Paul, it would seem that Aleksandrov had undergone an inconceivable metamorphosis and had become enamored of the Jews. However, there was quite another reason for his transition. Apparently Aleksandrov, a Party official who had just been severely criticized, sensed the change in political weather.[107] Besides, he had to defend Agitprop's interests,

---

101. "Dyen'."

102. G.D. Smith, *Atomnaya energiya dlya voyennyh tselei* [*Atomic Energy for Military Aims*] (Moscow, 1946).

103. RTsKhIDNI, f. 17, op. 125, d. 459, l. 27.

104. RTsKhIDNI, f. 17, op. 125, d. 459, l. 29.

105. RTsKhIDNI, f. 17, op. 125, d. 459, l. 31.

106. RTsKhIDNI, f. 17, op. 125, d. 459, l. 32.

107. In 1947 Zhdanov organized a discussion about Aleksandrov's book, *History of Western European Philosophy* (*Istoriya zapadno-evropeiskoi filosofii*), at the Institute of Philosophy of the USSR Academy of Sciences. Aleksandrov had been awarded the Stalin Prize and been conferred an academician in 1946 for his book, *History of Western European Philosophy* (*Istoriya zapadno-evropeiskoi filosofii*). But Stalin did not long support Aleksandrov, for he did not like it when one of his circle stood out against the overall gray background. On June 24, at this philosophical discussion (which was unprecedented in scale), Zhdanov sharply criticized Aleksandrov for his apolitical views, his "objectivity" (i.e., his lack of class consciousness), and for his fawning attitude toward bourgeois philosophy. RTsKhIDNI, f. 17, op. 125, d.

which had been entrusted to him and which were now being intruded upon by a rival structure, the CC Personnel Directorate, whose criticisms of Jewish writers could only be perceived as a veiled attack upon the patron of those Jewish writers, namely Agitprop.

In actuality, Aleksandrov's negative attitude toward the Jews had not changed. Let us consider his stance toward the events related to the banning of the famous book on the holocaust, *The Black Book.* Preparations had begun in 1943, and the book was to be an international project with the participation of such intellectuals as Albert Einstein and Lion Feuchtwanger. In November 1946, long after the manuscript had been completed, its Russian editors, Erenburg, V. Grossman, Mikhoels, and Fefer (who all supported the book on behalf of the JAC), appealed to Zhdanov for assistance in publishing it.[108] On February 3, 1947 Aleksandrov signed a memo accusing the JAC and the Sovinformburo of having secretly sent the manuscript abroad; further, he suggested that its publication be forbidden in the USSR.[109]

477, l. 4–142; d. 492, l. 2–6.

108. RTsKhIDNI, f. 17, op. 125, d. 438, l. 124–125 obverse.

109. RTsKhIDNI, f. 17, op. 125, d. 438, l. 216–218. Albert Einstein and Ben Zion Goldberg had both conceived of the idea of writing the *Black Book* (*Chyornaya kniga*) at the same time. Early in 1943 Goldberg officially sought the JAC's cooperation in this matter.

Later, Fefer testified that in June 1943, during one of his and Mikhoels's meetings with Goldberg in the USA, Goldberg had once again asked them to participate in the collection and publication of documents on fascist atrocities toward the Jewish people, for an international publishing project. Fefer and Mikhoels immediately telegrammed Lozovskiĭ about this proposal. Lozovskiĭ, using his connections in the Ministry of Foreign Affairs and in the CC, was able promptly to obtain the official sanction of the Soviet leadership to carry out negotiations on this issue.

Upon Fefer's and Mikhoels's arrival in Moscow, the editorial board (which included Mikhoels, Epshteĭn, Fefer, Bergelson, Markish, Kvitko, Galkin, and Shimeliovich) commenced its activities. In conjunction with this project, a literary commission was created in spring of 1944 with Erenburg as its head. Its members included the writers V. Grossman, V. Lidin (Gomberg), and others. Their activity consisted of editing the materials received by the JAC on the Nazi annihilation of the Jews. In October 1944 the leaders of the JAC (Epshteĭn and Fefer) sent to the USA the first and rather raw version of the *Black Book* (consisting of 525 documents) at the request of A.A. Gromyko, the Soviet ambassador. A conflict then occurred among its editors and contributors when Erenburg protested that he had not been consulted about the literary commission's materials being sent to America. To ease tensions, Lozovskiĭ in February 1945 formed a "conciliatory" commission with S.L. Bregman as chairman. After having studied what the JAC and the literary commission had prepared, Erenburg's "easy-reading" version was approved with the materials collected by the JAC serving as its documentary basis.

In April 1945 *Pravda* published an article castigating Erenburg's anti-German extremism. So Erenburg passed the reigns of control over the *Black Book* editorial staff to V.S. Grossman. Then, that autumn, Grossman presented the completed manuscript to Lozovskiĭ. Later, after having been approved by the Glavlit censorship, the manuscript was sent to Der Emes publishing house. In early 1946 the JAC sent a few copies of the manuscript to Romania, Palestine, the USA, and other countries.

However, that same autumn the political temperature began to drop. The JAC was no longer

The story of the *Black Book* did not end there. The final outcome, the result of Kremlin intrigue, was very sad. The Politburo voted to dismiss G. Malenkov as CC secretary on May 4, 1946.[110] Zhdanov, now in Stalin's good graces, now

---

subject to Lozovskií, but was now under the authority of the CC. So M.A. Morozov, head of the Department of Publishing Houses of Agitprop, demanded from L.I. Strongin, the director of Der Emes, that the JAC leaders obtain permission to publish the *Black Book* directly from Zhdanov: "Because even if the book is already published, it cannot be released without being approved by the CC's secretary of ideology." As a result, Mikhoels, Fefer, Grossman and Erenburg wrote a letter on November 28, 1946 to Zhdanov, who sent it to Aleksandrov.

110. The Politburo decree states: "1. Establish that Comrade Malenkov, as chief of the aviation industry and of quality control of aircraft as well as chief of the air forces, is morally accountable for the scandalous neglect that was discovered in the work of these institutions (production and quality of aircraft); that he, having the knowledge of this negligence, did not inform the CC of the ACP(b) about it." This decree was approved when the "aircraft case" was in full swing.

The principal victims of the "aircraft case" were A.I. Shakhurin (the minister of the aircraft industry as well as a CC ACP(b) member) and A.A. Novikov (the commander of the Red Army Air Forces and chief marshal of aviation). The "aircraft case" was a touchstone for V.S. Abakumov, the head of the chief directorate of Smersh (short for *Smert' shpionam*, or Death to Spies), the counterintelligence service. Stalin was using Abakumov as part of his plan directed against the Malenkov-Beria grouping within the government, which, having subjected to its influence the major force of the country, namely the military-industrial complex, had gained enormous power during the war. Stalin always considered all the smallest details of his plans, which usually consisted of first gaining his future victim's favor, thus putting the victim off guard, and then striking the victim with an unexpected and crushing blow.

Soon after the war ended, Stalin, with the help of his long time protégé and advisor on aircraft affairs, A.S. Yakovlev (chief builder and deputy commissar of the aircraft industry), arranged for a group of chief builders to sign a letter principally blaming Shakhurin for allowing Soviet aviation to fall behind world standards. In November 1945, while this letter was being examined and studied (as bureaucratic procedure required), Stalin was on holiday in Sochi. Since Shakhurin also happened to be there at the time, Stalin invited him to M.I. Kalinin's seventieth birthday party at Kalinin's dacha near the Malyí Akhun mountain. According to what Shakhurin later said (in particular, to S.M. Sandler, the deputy minister of the aircraft industry), Stalin was very friendly and cordial to him that day. Later, when Shakhurin was to return to Moscow, Stalin asked A.N. Poskrebyshev (the head of the Special Section of the CC, i.e., Stalin's personal office) to see him off at the train station.

Upon his arrival in Moscow, Shakhurin learned that the Committee of Party Control of the CC ACP(b) was studying his case, and that he was accused of "unworthy conduct," in particular of obtaining eight cars and many other things from Germany for his personal use. As a result, his Party standing was affected, and on January 7, 1946 he was removed as commissar. Driven out of his senses and into despair, Shakhurin appealed to Malenkov for help. Malenkov was head of the Personnel Directorate of the CC and therefore responsible for the aircraft industry. He was confident that he had won Stalin's favor (indeed, on March 18, 1946 Stalin had made Malenkov and Beria members of the Politburo), and promised to help Shakhurin. So on March 29 Shakhurin was appointed deputy chairman of the Council of Ministers of the RSFSR, and the hard times now seemed to be in the past. It was at this moment that Stalin struck his blow. On April 7 Abakumov signed Shakhurin's arrest warrant. On that same day the heads of the Aircraft Department of the Personnel Directorate of the CC (A.V. Budnikov and G.M. Grigoryan), as well as the heads of the Military Air Forces (A.K. Repin, N.S. Shimanov, and N.P. Seleznev) were arrested. Then on April 23 A.A. Novikov was taken into custody. The Military Board

began to get rid of the protégés of the disgraced Party hierarchy. On September 17, 1947 came G. Aleksandrov's turn. This unsuccessful ideological Party leader was dismissed and appointed director of the Institute of Philosophy at the Academy of Sciences. The efficient, ascetic, and unpretentious M. Suslov was appointed to the now vacant post of head of the Agitprop Directorate.[111] All this was accomplished in the best tradition of the Stalinist bureaucratic Party school. Political life in Russia, as Winston Churchill once noted, was like a struggle of

---

of the Supreme Court (headed by V.V. Ulrikh) passed sentence on May 10–11, 1946: "The defendants deliberately and with prior collusion among themselves . . . armed the air forces with a large number of defective airplanes and engines, which resulted in a great number of accidents and catastrophes in the combat units of the air forces and in the deaths of pilots. . . . "

Shakhurin was sentenced to seven years of camp. The rest received sentences in decreasing order (Stalin's black humor is in evidence here): Repin, six years; Novikov, five years; Shimanov, four years; Seleznev, three years; and finally Malenkov's subjects Budnikov and Grigoryan each received two years—probably because they acted as a "pair." However, some of these sentences were later increased considerably.

For his work, Abakumov was made minister of state security. The previous minister of state security, V.N. Merkulov, who was Beria's protégé, was appointed head of the Chief Directorate of Soviet Property Abroad at the Council of Ministers of the USSR.

Stalin treated Malenkov relatively mildly, merely holding him under house arrest for some time. In August Malenkov was appointed deputy prime minister of the Council of Ministers of the USSR, and entrusted with agriculture. At almost the same time, Stalin had him head the construction of the strategic bomber TU-4. This atom-bomb carrier was an almost exact copy of the American "super-fortress," the B-29, three of which had been seized in 1944 after landing on the Soviet Pacific coast. Document from the archives of the former KGB; interview with S.M. Sandler.

111. RTsKhIDNI, f. 17, op. 121, d. 616, l. 6–86. Suslov was known for consenting to do whatever he was told; indeed, this was another reason for his appointment. As head of the Department on CC External Policy, he implicitly obeyed Zhdanov's will. On May 24, 1947 he was elected secretary of the CC and entrusted to introduce proper order to Agitprop. To trample Aleksandrov once and for all, and to remove Aleksandrov's allies from the Agitprop apparatus, Suslov (together with Zhdanov's group, which he had temporarily joined) in late September and early October 1947 organized sessions of a "court of honor" in the CC. Suslov chaired that court; and its presidium consisted of Stalin, Zhdanov, Poskrebyshev, G.M. Popov, D.T. Shepilov, M.F. Shkiryatov, and others. The court examined the actions of Aleksandrov's former subjects, namely Agitprop members B.L. Suchkov and K.S. Kuzakov, and former head of the Press Department of the CC Personnel Directorate M.I. Shcherbakov. In particular, the court accused Aleksandrov of having employed Suchkov in 1943. Suchkov, director of the State Publishing House of Foreign Literature, had been arrested in 1947 for giving the Americans secret information concerning the Soviet development of an atomic bomb as well as for information on postwar hunger in Moldavia. In addition, in 1946 he had attempted to obtain a retrial for his former Moscow Institute of Foreign Languages classmate Lev Kopelev, who had been sentenced to ten years of camp for "counterrevolutionary activities." (Kopelev, a future dissident, emigrated to West Germany in 1980.)

In one of his reports at the session of the "court of honor," A.A. Kuznetsov stigmatized Aleksandrov as a protector of politically dubious personnel. This "Zhdanovite," who replaced Malenkov as head of the CC Personnel Directorate, ended his statement with the following appeal: "Vigilance has to be the necessary quality of the Soviet people. It has to be, if you like, the national feature of the character of a Soviet Russian person."

bulldogs under the table: one did not see anything except the corpses when they were periodically taken away.

The corpse in this case was only political, not physical. The "internationalist" Zhdanovite Suslov had replaced the "chauvinist" Aleksandrov,[112] and this renewed the hopes of Mikhoels and other JAC leaders and urged them to action. On September 18, the day after Aleksandrov was dismissed, Mikhoels, this time acting personally on his own behalf and not officially on behalf of the JAC, again applied to Zhdanov to save the *Black Book*. Insisting that this topical and important work be published, he bluffed that he had enlisted the support of the Agitprop Directorate of the CC.[113] This white lie proved useless before the monolithic Stalinist apparatus. On October 7 M.A. Morozov, head of Agitprop's Publishing Houses Department, drew up and sent to Zhdanov "reference no. 76467," which stated that "the *Black Book* has been thoroughly examined by the Propaganda Directorate. The book contains serious political errors. Its publication in 1947 has not been sanctioned by the Propaganda Directorate. Hence the *Black Book* cannot be published."[114]

A few years passed before the authorities again discussed the matter of publishing the *Black Book*. But when they did, it was to accuse the JAC leaders of "bourgeois Jewish nationalism." (Those were the exact words that the expert investigation of February 26, 1952 used to characterize the *Black Book*.)[115]

A political chill had begun the previous year, 1946, as evidenced by the notorious CC resolution "On *The Star* and *Leningrad* Magazines," which marked the emergence of the dark phenomenon known as "Zhdanovism"[116] As the victorious year of 1945 receded further into the past, so did the people's hopes—built up through sufferings and unprecedented sacrifices—for a freer and more decent life. The chilly wind of the Cold War could now be felt in the political

---

112. These characterizations of the nomenclatura elite are, of course, clearly conditional, especially in respect to the high Party ideologists of this time. These political chameleons changed their roles from "chauvinists" to "internationalists" depending on the state of affairs. The "internationalist" Zhdanov who moved to Moscow in 1944 quickly noticed Stalin's chauvinistic moods and so became a great-power ideologist. Kuznetsov, Rodionov, and others who were helped by Zhdanov to receive high appointments in the Moscow Party and state apparatus also quickly changed their stripes. Even before the "great purge" of 1949 Zhdanov, Kuznetsov, and Suslov removed Jews from the CC ACP(b) apparatus, just as L.M. Kaganovich did in 1947 for the Ukrainian CC CP(b) apparatus.

113. RTsKhIDNI, f. 17, op. 125, d. 438, l. 219–220.

114. RTsKhIDNI, f. 17, op. 125, d. 438, l. 221.

115. The Records of the Preliminary Investigation of the JAC Case, vol. 25, p. 11.

116. L. Beladi, T. Kraus, *Stalin* (Moscow, 1989), pp. 291–292. No one has yet studied in sufficient depth the origins and essence of "Zhdanovism." I agree with those historians who believe that Zhdanov was playing a part directed by Stalin. For instance, just glancing over the record of the reports read at the August 14, 1946 meetings of the Orgburo of the CC ACP(b) reveals that Stalin was directing the spreading campaign. So when we talk about "Zhdanovism," we do so in a rather conditional manner.

atmosphere of the entire planet. The Cold War brought about the Truman Doctrine, the Bolshevization of Eastern Europe, and the creation of Cominform (the postwar successor to Comintern). The Iron Curtain that Stalin had pulled down over the border of his empire was becoming more hermetic and less permeable. February 15, 1947 saw a decree issued "On the Prohibition of Marriages Between Soviet Citizens and Foreigners." Some months later, on June 9 the Presidium of the USSR Soviet Supreme issued its decree "On the Responsibilities for the Divulging of State Secrets and the Loss of Documents Containing State Secrets," which aggravated the country's hysteria about spies. On July 16, the Politburo banned the publication of the *Journal of Physics* (whose editor-in-chief was academician P.L. Kapitsa) and of some other English-language periodicals. The stated reason was that such publications made it considerably easier for foreign intelligence services to spy on the achievements of Soviet science."[117]

The growing isolation from the external world was accompanied by the fanning of chauvinistic attitudes. On March 28, 1947 the Council of Ministers and the CC ACP(b) approved a resolution on creating "courts of honor" within the ministries and the central state committees. These courts were supposed to save a "triumphant people" from "bourgeois ideology; to carry out an irreconcilable struggle against the fawning before Western culture; to liquidate the underestimation of the importance of Russian science and culture in the development of world civilization."

The tightening of the ideological screws followed the totalitarian scheme tested by the Nazis in the early 1930s: first suppress nonconformity and the most obstinate intellectuals; then fan anti-Jewish hysteria. At the first stage the regime victimized mainly those who hindered the casting of the Iron Curtain.

On June 5, 1947, in the overcrowded club hall of the Council of Ministers, there took place the first session of the Ministry of Health Care's "court of honor." This session examined the case of the learned physicians N.G. Klyueva and her Jewish husband, G.I. Roskin, who had submitted their manuscript on KR, a "secret" anticancer medicine, for publication in the USA.[118] Present at the trial were well-known academicians, some of whom, with much gusto, stigmatized

117. RTsKhIDNI, f. 17, op. 117, d. 868, l. 5.

118. RTsKhIDNI, f. 17, op. 121, d. 258, l. 3–4. See also Ya. Rapoport, *Delo "KR"* (*The "KR" Case*); and V. Brodskií, B. Kalininikova, "Otkrytiye sostoyalos'," ("The Inauguration Took Place"), *Nauka i zhizn'* (*Science and Life*), 1988, no. 1.

The academician V.V. Parin, secretary of the USSR Academy of Medical Sciences, suffered the most. He had handed Klyueva's and Roskin's manuscript, *Methods of Cancer Biotherapy* (*Metody rakovoí bioterapii*), to some Americans when he was on business in the USA, and was thus sentenced to 25 years of camp for espionage. In a similar incident, the minister of health care, G.A. Miterev, lost his position and was appointed director of the Erisman Nursing Institute.

these "traitors of their homeland," not realizing that tomorrow they themselves could be branded as "cosmopolitans" or, worse yet, as "murderers in white coats." The academician B.I. Zbarskiĭ was especially diligent in condemning Klyueva and Roskin. At the end of his diatribe he exclaimed pathetically: "Clean yourselves of the disgrace and shame that you have inflicted upon yourselves by your unworthy deeds—you have never been patriots."[119] Another academician, Strashun,[120] who was partly responsible for this farce, furnished historical substantiation:

> The times when the "window to Europe" brought a fresh wind to our country have passed. Since October 1917 the fresh wind has been blowing not from the West to the East, but from the East to the West. The "New World" has stopped being the new world; it is our country that is now giving light to the whole world.[121]

Among the few at that trial who succeeded in maintaining their common sense was Lina Shtern, the first female academician in the USSR. She had moved to the Soviet Union from Switzerland in 1925 and later founded and headed the Institute of Physiology. In 1943 she sent Stalin a letter protesting the ousting of Jews from scientific and state institutions.[122] Her scientific reputation grew even more after the war, for she had discovered that the antibiotic streptomycin could

---

119. RTsKhIDNI, f. 17, op. 127, d. 1670, l. 105. Zbarskiĭ had participated in the embalming of Lenin's body. He was later to be arrested.

120. I.D. Strashun worked at the Institute of the Organization of Public Health and History of Medicine, a part of the USSR Academy of Medical Sciences.

121. RTsKhIDNI, f. 17, op. 127, d. 1670, l. 106.

122. In the summer of 1952, speaking as a defendant at the JAC trial, Shtern recalled that in 1943 P.G. Sergiev, the director of the Tropical Institute, talked to her at the request of G.A. Miterev, the minister of health care. Sergiev demanded that Shtern, as the editor-in-chief of the *Bulletin of Experimental Biology and Medicine* journal (*Byulleten' eksperimental'noĭ biologii i meditsin*), dismiss two Jewish employees from the editorial board. Sergiev referred to a CC resolution on the reduction, by up to 90 percent, of Jews in the governing body of medical workers. "You see," he explained, "Hitler circulates leaflets [saying] that there are Jews everywhere in the USSR, and this is humiliating for Russian culture." That same evening, Shtern told Ye.M. Yaroslavskiĭ about this strange conversation. Believing that no such directive existed, he recommended that she write Stalin, which she did. She was soon afterwards summoned to the CC. At Stalin's request, Malenkov met with her and invited N.N. Shatalin along. Stern harshly declared to these high-ranking Party functionaries that the persecution of Jews in recent times was being "carried out by an enemy, and that possibly even within the CC there were people who were giving such directives." Obviously not expecting such a categorical statement, a stunned Malenkov was only able to say that those "were intrigues of all manner of spy-saboteurs" who were sent by the Nazis to the Soviet rear. According to Shtern, Malenkov then "cursed Sergiev, and said that it was necessary to reestablish the editorial board as it was before."

Disapproving of Miterev's crude methods in the anti-Semitic purge, methods that had caused the apparatus an undesirable scandal, the CC soon reprimanded him. (The Records of the Judicial Investigation of the JAC Case, vol. 7a, pp. 14–16).

treat tuberculosis. This preparation was made in the US and categorized by the US Congress as a strategic material. Shtern's brother, a rich businessman named Bruno Stern who lived in the US, somehow obtained this preparation and was illegally sending it to his sister in the Soviet Union. Line Shtern, who was famous for her independent beliefs, said in the lobby that "this trial is a terrible thing . . . ."[123]

On June 17, 1947 the CC ACP(b) sent a "secret" letter, "On the Case of Professors Klyueva and Roskin," to the Party organizations of all institutions, plants, factories, collective farms, educational institutions, and so forth. Thus began a noisy propagandistic campaign against the "anti-patriots' fawning" before the West. Anti-Semitism played a substantial role in this campaign; however, the regime at first refrained from severe methods in regard to the intelligentsia, including the Jewish intelligentsia. Very few intellectuals were arrested.

The Jewish Antifascist Committee was subjected only to "sparing therapy." From June to July 1947 the CC drew up several memoranda and draft resolutions making the continued existence of the JAC contingent upon strict adherence to the principle that "the JAC's tasks do not include work among the Jewish population of the Soviet Union." The JAC's duty was "to broaden the decisive struggle against the attempts of international reactionaries and their Zionist agents to use the Jewish movement abroad for anti-Soviet and antidemocratic purposes."[124] The Party insisted that the JAC, in addition to activating anti-Zionist and anti-American propaganda, render other equally important services to the regime. One of the draft resolutions tactfully stated: "The committee has not used its relations with foreign Jewish scientists and public and political figures for the purpose of obtaining information useful to the Soviet state."[125] For some reason this resolution was never signed. The Party, which planned to subject the JAC leaders to a radical purge, confined itself to reprimanding them verbally.[126] In the meantime the Party showed them mercy. It was to some extent due to

---

123. RTsKhIDNI, f. 17, op. 127, d. 1670, l. 35, 39; Document from the archives of the former KGB. The reigning atmosphere in this "court of honor" was eloquently characterized by a remark from Klyueva. Driven to hysterics by accusations of "having sold the motherland to foreigners," she stated that "if the Americans were to treat their patients with medicine prepared in accordance with the technology passed to the USA, but from which something had been deliberately omitted, their patients would go into shock or die."

During the investigation Lina Shtern declared on March 18, 1949: "After Roskin's and Klyueva's 'courts of honor,' I cut all my relations with foreigners. But independently of this, I am guilty of having been sincere with foreigners during the time that I had broad contacts with them, and of having freely told them about the achievements of Soviet science, without taking into account that by so doing I had caused harm to the Soviet Union."

124. RTsKhIDNI, f. 17, op. 128, d. 1058, l. 134.

125. Ibid.

126. RTsKhIDNI, f. 17, op. 128, d. 1058, l. 135.

Mikhoels's great authority at home and abroad that the rate of repressions was considerably slowed.

"The Hand of Washington"

Immediately after the war the government severely restricted the JAC's international contacts and denied every attempt by committee members to meet the leaders of international Jewry abroad. However, the government did permit, for propagandistic purposes, pro-Soviet Jews to visit the Soviet Union from time to time.

The American journalist Ben Zion Goldberg arrived in Moscow at the end of 1945. The JAC had not invited him; rather, he came for journalistic purposes and for other business related to the Soviet publication of a book by his father-in-law, Sholem Aleichem (Solomon Rabinovich).[127] However, because Goldberg was first and foremost interested in the life of the Soviet Jews, Mikhoels and Fefer were required to take care of him. These two JAC leaders accompanied Goldberg on his visit to Kalinin, the chairman of the Supreme Soviet of the USSR, who repeated his promise to grant to the Jewish Autonomous Region in Birobidzhan the status of republic. He had first made this promise in the early 1930s, but had never fulfilled it. Though Goldberg urgently requested permission to visit Birobidzhan, he was not allowed to do so, for, he was told, it was in a region that was off-limits to foreigners. Instead, he was allowed to visit Stalingrad, as well as the Ukraine, Belorussia, Latvia, and Lithuania—regions that were traditionally beloved of the Jews.

Soviet intelligence focused its attention on Goldberg from the first day of his visit to his last. Fefer, who organized numerous meetings, discussions, and banquets for Goldberg in Moscow,[128] and who escorted him on his trips throughout the country, was, as mentioned above, an informant. On the basis of Fefer's reports, the MGB later informed Stalin:

> While in the Soviet Union Goldberg maintained contact with Mikhoels, Fefer, the executive secretary of the Jewish newspaper *Einikeit* Galkin, the writer Markish, and others. The leaders of the Jewish Antifascist Committee gave Goldberg an opportunity to meet with Jewish nationalists and clergy in Moscow, Leningrad, Riga,

127. During his visit, Goldberg, as heir to the copyrights of Sholem Aleichem, received from the Soviet government sixty thousand dollars.

128. Among the archival materials on the investigation of the JAC is a thick folder with documents "concerning the Moscow visit of the American spy Goldberg (aka Benjamin Waife)." These documents contain information about his visits to the Moscow Jewish community, the Jewish Theater, the Palace of Culture of the Stalin Automobile Plant, and so forth.

> Vilnius, Minsk, and Kiev. According to data presented by the agents, it is known that Goldberg visited the US Embassy in Moscow and informed Fefer of the nature of his meetings with the American ambassadors. In particular, Goldberg met with Ambassador Smith, [and] with [American] agents Davis and Thompson, who asked him about the intelligence data collected during his travel throughout the Soviet Union.[129]

However, someone at Lubyanka seemed to doubt that Fefer alone would be enough. Then a certain Mariya Vasilyevna Gordienko appeared on the scene. She was not very young, but she was rather self-assured, and she was to play the role of agent provocateur.

Some years later, at the court hearings of the Military Board of the Supreme Court, Fefer spoke of this Soviet Mata Hari:[130]

> Goldberg and I flew from Lvov to Mukachev, and as we were walking out of the airplane, we saw her standing there, in the airfield. I asked: "What are you doing here?" She answered: " . . . You are doing your business, and I am doing mine." She hinted that she was carrying out business of great importance, but I got the impression that she was an adventuress. I have not always been as old as I am now, and I am an expert in women. I know Goldberg to be a man with a delicate taste, but that woman's appearance was repulsive, and he would not be interested in intimate relations with her. I remember that once when I went to see Goldberg he told me that Gordienko had told him she was connected with military intelligence. I went to see the chief of the secret department of the Antifascist Committee right away . . . and told him about my conversation with Goldberg, that this woman had told the American that she was an officer [agent] of military intelligence, and I asked him to inform the security services of this fact.[131]

The chairman of the court replied to Fefer that Gordienko had been arrested and had given evidence of Goldberg's espionage activity, saying that she had supposedly been assigned various intelligence-seeking missions and that she had had intimate relations with him. Fefer understood that Goldberg's transformation from a "friend of the USSR" into an American spy, a spy with whom he had had long and rather close contact, made his position hopeless. So he defended himself

---

129. Document from the archives of the former KGB.

130. It turned out that Fefer had earlier made Gordienko's acquaintance when he had worked in Kiev in the 1930s.

131. The Records of the Judicial Investigation of the JAC Case, vol. 1, pp. 67, 68.

as best he could from the juridical machinery that was about to crush him. He repeated his arguments again and again:

> I have read her testimony, but I have my doubts about it, as there was so much falsehood in that woman that [I] should doubt everything [she testified]. Goldberg was frightened himself when he told me that the woman was involved in military intelligence . . . . That woman was very bad looking, even repulsive, and she could not attract him at all. A man of such taste as his could find a much better woman. He knew the feelings of many Jewish families and moved in a wide social circle, and that woman could not satisfy [his taste].[132]

Markish, the poet, spoke at the trial after Fefer. He even more vigorously opposed the accusation that he had cooperated with the "spy," whom he had happened to meet three times in Moscow:

> *Chairman:* You said that Goldberg turned out to be not only an editor, but also an experienced American spy, and that Fefer and Epshteín mentioned his name worshipfully.
>
> *Markish:* It was unknown to me that he was a spy. A year and a half have elapsed since that scoundrel brought dishonor to our country; yet, strange though it may seem, even the MGB did not know that [he was a spy]. A year and a half later Simonov and Galaktionov visited the USA, met him [Goldberg], and were interviewed by him.[133]
>
> Where did my personal relations with him begin? I had no contacts with the [Jewish Antifascist] Committee [people during Goldberg's stay in the USSR]. The girl that rang me up said that Sholem Aleichem's son-in-law, the chairman of the American Committee of Antifascist Scientists, had arrived and we ask you to come too. I went. Such a person arrived, such a dear person. There was no meeting of the [JAC] presidium [at that time]. I was there only for half an hour. There was a photographer who took a photograph of me right next to him [Goldberg].
>
> *Chairman:* Had you ever met him anywhere any time before?
>
> *Markish:* No, I hadn't. A week later I got a call from the Union of Soviet Writers and was asked to come to the banquet organized in Goldberg's honor. I don't think that Fadeyev would do this for any personal reasons. Therefore, at first the low-ranking people were deceived and then the higher ones were deceived too. The Union of Soviet Writers was deceived. Goldberg is a very clever, cunning

132. The Records of the Judicial Investigation of the JAC Case, vol. 1, p. 68

133. The writers K. Simonov and I. Erenburg, along with *Pravda* correspondent M. Galaktionov, had visited the USA in May 1947.

person . . . . He began his speech at the banquet . . . : "Comrades, let me propose my first toast to the best writer in the Soviet Union, who has written such an immortal creation as the Constitution of the Soviet Union!" Everybody was delighted. At the end of the banquet . . . he approached me and said, "I am very much interested in your play.[134] Come over some time." I dropped by his room at the National Hotel at about one in the afternoon. By that time my Russian book, which I have already mentioned, had been published. I was in a cheerful mood. It must be said that the best American poets are compelled to go from door to door to sell their books themselves. I don't have to do the same in the Soviet Union . . . .

Chairman: Did you have a tête-à-tête?

Markish: Yes I did. When we began to talk of the play, he praised me, and then asked, "Tell me what life is like in Russia, in the Soviet Union in general, for Jewish writers. [You] know, when Leínik[135] got ill recently and was to be sent to the hospital, some of his friends went from door to door to collect money for his admission to the hospital."

I took out my book, published by the State Publishing House, and showed it to him. He looked at the book and said, "Tell me, please, have you been given any money for it? Because over in America no one gives a damn about men of letters." I answered, "Yes, I have received 120 000 rubles for this book, and if you add to that the royalties from the various magazines that have published it, it comes to 30 to 40 thousand more." This almost drove him mad. He was shocked by my information. Prior to the present unhappy occasion that has brought me to this bench, I considered myself to be one of the Soviet Union's luckiest writers. . . .

Then Goldberg skipped over to the matter of the situation of the Jews. He asked, "Why did the Birobidzhan undertaking fail?" I answered, "Is there any Jew so silly as to exchange Moscow for Birobidzhan?" Further I said that when a book by Sholem Aleichem is published in Russian in hundreds of thousands of copies, it is able to feed the people;[136] but when it is published in Yiddish, it does not find such an audience, as our Jews are accustomed to Russian culture. They long for great culture and have no nationalist enthusiasm. They do not speak Yiddish, [so] what are they going to do in Birobidzhan[?] In ten years not even their children will speak Yiddish there. . . .

Chairman: Was Nusinov[137] present during your meeting?

---

134. *The Insurrection in the Ghetto* (*Vosstaniye v getto*).

135. This is how it is spelled in the transcript. The person actually mentioned was H. Leivick (pseudonym for Leivick Halpern, 1888–1962), a Jewish-American writer originally from Russia.

136. *Translator's note:* In other words, authors can live on the royalties.

137. Isaak Markovich Nusinov was a literary scholar and professor of the Moscow Lenin Institute of

Markish: It [the meeting with Nusinov] took place afterwards . . . . Goldberg had soon left; I was not interested in where he had gone. Three months later he arrived here again. One day in the afternoon he called on me at my flat, and while we were talking he said that he had visited either Denmark or Norway. Then we talked about life [and] sat down at the table to have dinner. During the conversation he would repeatedly say the words "OK!" and "All right!" Once my son[138] said some words to him in English. Goldberg was very much surprised and said, "My! Do you speak English?" My son answered, "Yes." "Where are you going to study?" My son answered that he was going to enter the Department of Romance Languages of the Philological Faculty of the [Moscow] University. He asked, "What for?" And my son answered, "We must know our enemies." . . .

Chairman: According to your story, Goldberg glorified Soviet power, didn't he? But during the investigation you gave evidence that during your conversation with Goldberg he " . . . paid great attention to the fate of the Jews, who were too much separated by war, . . . and stressed that the Soviet Jews were too isolated, that they were 'under seven seals' and were isolated from the rest of the Jewish world . . . that the Soviet Jews were in the process of assimilation and were breaking from the 'Israeli tree.' Therefore, he supported more frequent meetings of the Soviet Jews with the Jews from the USA and Europe, and to get acquainted with the national [roots] of the Jews . . . ."

Markish: That conversation took place during our first meeting, but that was not the way he said it. When we talked about the great success of the Jews in the Soviet Union, he said that it should be shown to the whole world, and let the Jews not be ashamed of showing their achievements . . . .

Chairman: And how do you explain this statement of Goldberg's: "Send Mikhoels and Fefer abroad once more and we shall turn the whole world around?"

Markish: Yes, at one of the banquets he said something like that: "Let me take Mikhoels and Fefer to America and we shall turn the world around." That is, they had been in America once and had performed miracles there; and if they were to be sent there again, they would perform even more miracles than before."[139]

Education. His 1941 book, *Pushkin and World Literature* (*Pushkin i mirovaya literatura*) examined the creative work of the Russian poet within the context of European civilization. In 1947 the literary bosses N.A. Tikhonov and A.A. Fadeyev criticized this book and called Nusinov "a passportless hobo in humanity," i.e., a "cosmopolitan."

138. Simon (Shimon) Markish.

139. The Records of the Judicial Investigation of the JAC Case, vol. 1, pp. 186–193.

While in Moscow, Goldberg gathered materials for his book, *Britain Against Peace*, and asked for Lozovskiĭ's help. Lozovskiĭ accordingly contacted the Specialized Institution Number 205 (attached to the CC), which supplied a review of British foreign policy. Goldberg received propagandistic information concerning the economies of the various regions of the Soviet Union, achievements in the sphere of national policy and culture, and in particular the development of Jewish literature, Jewish theater, and so forth. The JAC agreed regularly to send such information to the USA to be published mainly in Goldberg's pro-Soviet publications, such as *Der Tog*[140] and *Einikeit (N.Y.)* Of course, Lozovskiĭ and the other JAC leaders had no idea that all this innocent literature would be declared either secret or nationalistic, or that it would come to be seen as evidence of criminal espionage.

It should be noted that the MGB was diligently preparing its own version of this affair, intending to expose the JAC's espionage activities with American intelligence services. The main point of the accusation, "nationalistic activity," could include anything (Yiddish literature and drama, social journalism, any public activity of the JAC, or even the careless statements of its members), as the matter dealt with interpretation. But to prove cooperation with Western special services more accurate and detailed facts were needed. However, since there were no such facts, the facts had to be invented through falsification, which was a speciality of Stalin's bodies.[141]

To strengthen its case, the MGB capitalized, in addition to Goldberg, on one other foreigner who had cooperated with the JAC: Paul (Peisakh) Novick, the editor of *Morning Freiheit*, an American Communist newspaper. Novick had visited the Soviet Union from September 1946 through January 1947—much later than Goldberg—and the state intelligence services were not at all worried that Novick had been a member of the American Communist Party since 1921 and was, like Goldberg, considered by the FBI to be a "Moscow agent." (Incidentally the FBI and the Immigration Service had even wanted to deprive Goldberg of his American citizenship.)[142] Also like Goldberg, Novick, on his return to the United States, continued to write pro-Soviet articles and books at his own risk. But the most unbelievable aspect of this story was that the "investigation had at its disposal documents testifying that Goldberg was a foreign agent of the MGB of the USSR abroad."[143] These exact words were later used by the general prosecutor of the USSR, R.A. Rudenko, in his report to the CPSU CC on the

---

140. *Der Tog—New York Yiddish Daily.*

141. *Translator's note:* "Bodies" usually refers to the various secret intelligence services; though it can also mean the political or state "organs."

142. S. Redlich, *Propaganda and Nationalism in Wartime Russia: The Jewish Antifascist Committee in the USSR, 1941–1948* (Boulder, Colorado, 1982), p. 154.

143. RTsKhIDNI, f. 589, op. 3, d. 15624, l. 367.

results of the 1955 rehabilitation of those subjected to repression in connection with JAC case. This is yet another proof that the cynicism of Abakumov's department was boundless.

With the simplest falsifications, the MGB leaders could convert their foreign agents into their antipodes, and use them as puppets in cases fabricated to give short shrift to politically disagreeable persons and organizations. There was no hint of human decency in these diabolical manipulations, nor was there any hint of professional ethics. A very similar method was applied to Fefer, who was used to incriminate the rest of the JAC members, and was then tossed off like an old overcoat and sent to death together with the others.

The Personal Enemy of Stalin

Coincidentally—or most likely intentionally—it happened that, before getting down to the business of vanquishing the JAC, the special services launched an operation to expose a mythical American-Zionist plot allegedly directed personally against the "leader of peoples" and his family. The main purpose of this political provocation was to liquidate the leader of Soviet Jewry, Mikhoels. To attain this goal, Stalin did not spare even his relatives, who were suspected of having connections with Jewish bourgeois nationalists. At Stalin's order the MGB fabricated a special case whose central figure was a little-known senior scientist of the Institute of Economics of the USSR Academy of Science, I.I. Goldshteín. He was not chosen randomly. Although he had never been a member of the JAC, he had long been well acquainted with Z.G. Grinberg, a senior scientist at the Institute of World Literature at the USSR Academy of Science who happened to be Mikhoels's closest aide in the JAC on matters concerning the Jewish scientific intelligentsia.

Goldshteín and Grinberg had been members of the Bund even before the revolution, but had gotten to know each other only at the end of 1941 in evacuation in Tashkent. At that time Grinberg was already often speaking about Mikhoels in his conversations with his new friend. Mikhoels and his theater were then in the Uzbekistan capital, and so Goldshteín had no opportunity to meet with him personally.

Goldshteín's and Mikhoels's first encounter took place in 1945 at the Jewish Theater in Moscow, when Goldshteín and his wife were invited there for a soirée dedicated to the thirtieth anniversary of the death of Isaac Leib Peretz, a Jewish writer who had lived in Poland and who was Goldshteín's uncle. After delivering his speech, Mikhoels went up to Goldshteín and his wife and told him to come to the theater more often. After this brief encounter they did not meet again until the autumn of 1946, when Grinberg brought Goldshteín to the JAC's office at

Kropotkinskaya 10, where a long and serious conversation took place. Later, during the investigation, Goldshteĭn said that the main reason for—and principle topic of—that conversation was his acquaintance with Stalin's relatives, about which he informed Grinberg. Yevgeniya Aleksandrovna Alliluyeva, whom Goldshteĭn had known since 1929 when they had worked together at the Soviet Commercial Office in Berlin, was the central subject of the conversation. Beginning in 1943 he had from time to time visited her at her apartment, a large gray building called the House of Government on the Moscow river embankment.[144] Ye.A. Alliluyeva's first husband was Stalin's brother-in-law, P.S. Alliluyev, who had died unexpectedly in 1938 of a heart attack. (This occurred after he returned from his holidays and learned that many of his colleagues at the Armored Directorate of the Red Army had been arrested as enemies of the people.) P.S. Alliluyev's sister, Anna S. Alliluyeva, also had to overcome personal tragedy. Her husband, S.F. Redens, who had headed the Moscow Directorate of the NKVD, was transferred to Kazakhstan, later recalled to Moscow, taken into custody on November 21, 1938, and shot as a state criminal on January 21, 1941. Then in 1943 her son was imprisoned. Stalin no longer kept in touch with his late wife's relatives. Those of them who survived fell into disgrace; they were deprived of their Kremlin passes and were forbidden from using the governmental dachas. The perceptive functionaries could sense who was out of the leader's favor, and so even reduced the Alliluyevs' living space.

Not long after her husband's death, Ye.A. Alliluyeva married N.V. Molochnikov, a senior builder at the State Institute of Plant Projects of the Ministry of Ferrous Metallurgy, whom she had known since 1930. As it turned out, Yevgeniya Aleksandrovna's new husband had long been informing the "organs" about the life of the beleaguered Alliluyev "clan."

Ye.A. Alliluyeva's personal life, which had seemingly improved, was again disturbed; she and all her relatives realized that, deprived of all former privileges, they were to vegetate as outcasts. After years of bearing a grudge against Stalin, they now began to pour forth all manner of gossip and lamentations about the misfortunes he had willed upon them. They began openly to discuss the circumstances regarding Nadezhda Alliluyeva's death[145] and other taboo family secrets. Stalin was regularly informed about all of this. His discontent with the Alliluyev family grew considerably after the 1946 publication of A.S. Alliluyeva's *Memoirs*.[146] Stalin grew even more furious when, to advertise her book, the

---

144. *Translator's note:* The House of Government was also known as the House at the Embankment. It was situated near the Kremlin, and many high-ranking Party functionaries lived there.

145. Nadezhda Alliluyeva (1901–1932) was Stalin's second and last wife. Stalin was apparently responsible for her murder.

146. *Vospominaniya.*

author traveled across the country and, with an openness that was intolerable at that time, recounted to the working masses her version of the history of the Party and of the state leader's family. Accompanying Alliluyeva on her trips was the journalist R.M. Azarkh, whom she had known since 1920 when they had worked together in Ukraine. Azarkh was later arrested and accused of persuading Alliluyeva to send Mikhoels a copy of *Memoirs*, along with her father's book, *The Path That Was Taken.*[147]

The storm unexpectedly broke on May 14, 1947 when *Pravda* published an article by P.N. Fedoseyev eloquently entitled "Irresponsible Inventions." Fedoseyev criticized A.S. Alliluyeva for contrasting her "inventions," which "distort historical reality," with Stalin's *Brief Course on the History of the ACP(b).*[148] Nobody in the Kremlin circles ever doubted that Fedoseyev had written his article at Stalin's personal order. Notorious for his instability, Alliluyeva's brother Fyodor exclaimed in a fit of temper: "It's a crusade against the Alliluyevs launched with Stalin's consent."[149]

This and other upheavals in Stalin's relationship with late wife's family were one of the topics that Mikhoels and Goldshteín discussed during their encounter. The JAC leader was primarily interested in what Ye.A. Alliluyeva had told Goldshteín about Svetlana Stalina and her husband Grigorií Morozov. The dictator's daughter and the Jewish youth (who was later to become a famous legal expert) had studied at the same school and were married in the spring of 1944. At that time Morozov was already a student at the Moscow Institute of Foreign Relations (attached to the Ministry of Foreign Affairs). Stalin did not approve of this marriage but did not stand in its way. Hiding his hostility toward his son-in-law, he never met with him, and moved the couple from the Kremlin to the House at the Embankment. Once, long before the end of the war, Stalin let his feelings out, maliciously saying to his daughter, "He is far too thrifty, your young man. . . . Look, it's scary at the front; people are shooting there—and he found himself a soft site at the rear."[150]

At the investigation Goldshteín testified that Mikhoels had hoped, in that time of growing postwar anti-Semitism in the USSR, that Morozov would be able somehow to influence his all-powerful relative and thus soften the anti-Jewish policy. For this reason, Mikhoels had asked Goldshteín if he could be introduced to Grigorií Morozov and Svetlana. This happened in December 1946, during one of the family meetings at Ye.A. Alliluyeva's.

---

147. *Proídennyí put'.*

148. *Istoriya vsesoyuznoí kommunisticheskoí partii (bol'shevikov). Kratkií kurs* (Moscow, 1941).

149. Document from the archives of the former KGB.

150. S.I. Alliluyeva, *Dvadtsat' pisem k drugu* [*Twenty Letters to a Friend*] (Moscow: Izvestiya, 1990), p. 143.

However, Mikhoels soon afterwards had to abandon his illusions. In May 1947 the young couple had a disagreement and separated. Their divorce was apparently due not only to "personal reasons," as Svetlana later wrote.[151] It was most likely brought about by Stalin's intervention, for he had long seen his family's relations with Jewry as a burden. There is nothing strange about his cutting them off. The power and cruelty of his predecessors Ivan the Terrible and Peter the Great impressed him, and like them he was ready to sacrifice anything without hesitation, including his family and close friends, for the sake of his unshakable power.

It was also the compromising material that Stalin regularly received on his son-in-law's friends and relatives that made him put a stop the relationship between his daughter and her husband.[152] The report from the special services contained a good deal of information on G.I. Morozov's father, I.G. Morozov, who had been born in Mogilev to a rich Jewish family. And I.G. Morozov's father, G.V. Moroz, had lived in a place called Mstislavichi where he had his own farm with a hospital at which he offered medical care to the local landowners.

I.G. Morozov had been involved in commerce, and in 1922 opened his own pharmacy in Moscow, but was given a one-year prison sentence in 1924 for bribing a functionary. After his release, Morozov quit private business (private business was quite dangerous at that time) and became a state functionary. At the time that his son married Stalin's daughter he was working as a modest bookkeeper at one of the state enterprises in Moscow. However, as of that moment the life of this insignificant Soviet functionary miraculously changed. He became a guest at the Barvikha governmental sanatorium. Introducing himself as an old Bolshevik and professor, he entered the circle of the influential Soviet elite, having become acquainted with P.S. Zhemchuzhina; R.S. Zemlyachka; and the

---

151. Ibid, p. 144.

152. He and Svetlana were been living in the House of Government on the Bersenyevskaya embankment; and the MGB leaders, whose agents vigilantly spied on their every move, had long been "studying" their frequent guest, Anna A. Leíkind. The State Security Office's examination established that Leíkind (who from 1945 through 1947 given Morozov English lessons) had left Russia as a child before the revolution together with her parents and had lived in the USA until her return in 1934. Until 1922 she had worked at the World Jewish Congress in New York, and later at the Jewish Telegraphic Agency. She had more than once met with Zionist-Revisionist leader V.I. Zhabotinskií, a native of Odessa now living in France who from time to time visited America to propagate Zionism, and who had cooperated with many Russian periodicals. Anna Leíkind had been the stenographer at his appearances and, with time, gained his friendship and trust.

State Security was interested not only in Leíkind's past. Those in Lubyanka were informed that she had spent New Year's Eve 1947 at the Vatenbergs (who were JAC members) in the company of P. Novick, an American journalist who was interested in her student Morozov and his wife Svetlana. Stalin was, of course, informed about this, and must have regarded this information as further proof of what so frightened him, namely, the "underhanded plotting of Zionists."

director of the Institute of Physiology of the USSR Academy of Science, academician L.S. Shtern, among others. In 1945 Shtern employed him as her deputy in the Administrative and Household Equipment Section. Having found himself in a promising situation, I.G. Morozov was careless enough not to understand that his persona had become an object of increased attention on the part of the MGB. In conversations with his relatives and acquaintances he boasted about his new contacts within the Party structure without thinking about the possible consequences of his negligence; he would not forget to mention that he was on good terms with Stalin, who invited him to Kremlin receptions. In early 1948 Morozov paid for his carelessness as well as for his dangerous lies. He was taken to Lubyanka and charged with "the perpetration of anti-Soviet activity and the dissemination of slanderous lies against the head of the Soviet state."[153]

Stalin no longer trusted his relatives; and starting in mid-December 1947, and based on analogous accusations, the relatives of Stalin's late wife were arrested. On December 10 Ye.A. Alliluyeva became the first victim. She was accused of "having organized, over a long period of time, several anti-Soviet meetings at her apartment, during which she disseminated foul slander regarding the head of the Soviet government." At about the same time her husband, N.V. Molochnikov, was arrested; and on January 6, 1948 her daughter, Malyí Theater actress K.P. Alliluyeva (Politkovskaya), was summoned. Anna S. Alliluyeva, who was a member of the Union of Soviet Writers, was taken into custody on January 29, 1948. Among other things, it was claimed that "after the arrest of her husband S.F. Redens in 1938 she hid her anger against the leader of the Party and the Soviet government, and up to the day of her arrest carried out anti-Soviet agitation."[154] It was for the same reason that Anna's friends L.A. Shatunovskaya (a theater expert), and Lev Tumerman (Shatunovskaya's husband, a professor of physics), were arrested. Those who lived in the same building with Stalin's relatives (E.S. Gorelik, the wife of deputy minister of the military forces at the rear A.V. Khrulyov; and radar expert Major General G.A. Uger and his Russian wife) were arrested as well.

During her interrogation, on December 16, 1947, Ye.A. Alliluyeva said to the investigator that her old friend, I.I. Goldshtein, once while visiting her, had asked about Stalin, his daughter Svetlana, and her relations with Grigorií Morozov. This was enough for Goldshtein to be taken to Lubyanka within three days. His arrest was carried out at Abakumov's personal order and without procurator's sanction. From the beginning Stalin gave the MGB leaders instructions regarding the course the investigation was to take. In July 1953 the arrested former deputy head of the MGB's Department to Investigate Cases of Special Importance,

153. Document from the archives of the former KGB.

154. Document from the archives of the former KGB.

V.I. Komarov, testified that in late 1947 and early 1948 Abakumov had called his office at the Lefortovo prison and said that "those in this instance [i.e., Stalin] consider that Goldshteín expressed interest in the personal life of the head of the Soviet government not at his own initiative, but because he was backed by foreign intelligence . . . ."[155] The investigation did not possess any information confirming this story, but was required to resort to blackmail and to fabricating facts. Therefore Goldshteín's wife, M.A. Krzhevskaya, was also arrested.

Colonel G.A. Sorokin was interrogating prisoners at the Sukhanovo prison near Moscow when M.T. Likhachyov, the deputy head of the Department to Investigate Cases of Special Importance, entrusted him with the investigation of Goldshteín's case and recalled him to Lubyanka to "untangle Goldshteín's espionage connections and reveal his [true] face as a spy."[156] What happened later becomes clear from Sorokin's written statement, dated January 3, 1954, to the commission for investigating the activity of former MGB leaders:

> . . . I had never received any materials that pointed to Goldshteín's being a spy, or any case against him; and, as I learned later, there were none in the MGB's possession . . . . Sometime later Komarov showed up at Goldshteín's interrogation session and said that Abakumov had ordered the application of physical methods to Goldshteín. . . . Komarov carried out [this directive] that very same evening, with my participation. On the next day, with Komarov away, Goldshteín testified to me that Grinberg had told him that the JAC presidium had been taken over by inveterate bourgeois nationalists who, distorting the national policy of the Party and of the Soviet government, perform functions outside the committee's scope and carry out nationalistic activity. In addition, Goldshteín testified that Mikhoels carried out espionage activities, and revealed a great interest in the personal life of the head of the Soviet government in the Kremlin. According to Goldshteín, Mikhoels had given this information to the American Jews . . . .[157]

The last sentence above demonstrates the enormous task that Stalin put to the MGB. It was one thing was to discuss the head of the Soviet government among family and friends; it was quite another to collect information about this person in order to transmit it to enemy intelligence services. To prove that this indeed was the crime, the investigators had to make use of "physical methods." What that meant in practice, Goldshteín himself later described. On October 2,

---

155. Document from the archives of the former KGB.

156. RTsKhIDNI, f. 589, op. 3, d. 15624, l. 343.

157. RTsKhIDNI, f. 589, op. 3, d. 15624, l. 344–346.

1953, while at the Vladimirskaya prison, he wrote to Malenkov:

> On December 19, 1947 I was arrested in Moscow by the MGB and taken to Lubyanka, and later to the investigation prison at Lefortovo. Here, and without being informed of the reasons for my arrest, I was asked to confess and tell of my allegedly hostile activity against the motherland . . . . They started to beat me with a rubber baton on the soft parts of my body and on my bare heels. They beat me until I could not stand nor sit . . . . After a while I was asked to sign a confession (allegedly dictated by me), in which I confessed my guilt. I . . . declined to sign this confession. Then the investigator, Sorokin, and one other colonel . . . started to beat me with such force that my face was swollen for several weeks, and I could hardly hear for several months, especially with my left ear . . . . This was followed by a new interrogation and new beatings. In total, I was beaten eight times, [and was] asked only for more and more new confessions. Exhausted by these day-and-night interrogations, terrorized by tortures, swearing, and threats, I fell into a deep despair and total moral miasma, and started to incriminate myself and others in very serious crimes."[158]

Abakumov visited the Lefortovo Prison to witness personally the "confession" forced out of Goldshteín. He lost no time in putting to Goldshteín, who could hardly move his mouth, detailed questions, pointedly asking him, "So, you say that Mikhoels is a swine?" "Yes, he is," Goldshteín replied. Abakumov followed with a similar question about Fefer, to which Goldshteín gave a negative response.[159] Satisfied with what he heard, Abakumov ordered the preparation of the minutes of the interrogation, which would include Goldshteín's confession. This was the first record made after Goldshteín's arrest.

This document was soon prepared, and it was edited by Colonel Ya.M. Broverman, who worked at Abakumov's secretariat and specialized in this kind of "intellectual" work. This document was later sent to Stalin. In the last version of the minutes, dated January 9, 1948, Goldshteín's testimony was formulated as follows,

> Mikhoels gave me the task of getting to know Grigorií Morozov. "You have to notice all the smallest details of the relationship between Svetlana and Grigorií and take these details into account. On the basis of your information we will be able to come up with a good plan of action and inform our American friends, who are interested in

---

158. RTsKhIDNI, f. 589, op. 3, d. 15624, l. 342.

159. The Records of the Judicial Investigation of the JAC Case, vol. 1, pp. 57–58.

this matter."[160]

On the basis of the evidence allegedly given by Goldshteín, Z.G. Grinberg was arrested as far back as December 28, 1947 without procurator's sanction. Grinberg was allegedly the link between Goldshteín and Mikhoels, and the MGB was endeavoring to coerce him into slandering the JAC leaders. Colonel M.T. Likhachyov conducted Grinberg's case. Years later, on May 26, 1953, Likhachyov was arrested as accessory to Abakumov and stated:

> During the interrogations Grinberg for a long period of time would not confess, and there was nothing on which to establish his guilt except for Goldshteín's testimonies . . . but later he began to testify, giving many details of the activity carried out by the JAC, which managed to get the Jewish population to group around it, and aroused nationalistic feelings and thus became the center for the Jewish nationalists. He named Lozovskií, Mikhoels, Fefer, and others as being the main ringleaders of Jewish nationalistic activity. He also said that this subversive activity is directed by the Americans . . . . "[161]

Likhachyov obtained this testimony by threatening the prisoners and by cynically lying to them. Grinberg wrote to him on April 19, 1949,

> Four months ago you officially informed me that my case was closed and that I would soon be released. Unfortunately, this didn't happen. I've been under arrest for sixteen months, and I'm getting weaker and weaker.[162]

On December 22, 1949, before his promised release, Grinberg died of a heart attack in the internal prison of the MGB.

Goldshteín was forced to slander not only Grinberg but also R.S. Levina, who had long worked with him at the Institute of World Economics and Politics and who was a close friend. During the war, while in evacuation in Tashkent, Levina had sheltered Goldshteín in her kitchen. Later they coauthored some monographs on "German Imperialism." And now, because Levina had been deputy director of the Institute of World Economics and Politics through 1945, Goldshteín was forced to make it appear as though she had been the leader of the group of Jewish nationalists that allegedly existed there. This old and gravely ill woman was arrested on January 10, 1948. The investigators dug up everything they could

---

160. Document from the archives of the former KGB.

161. RTsKhIDNI, f. 589, op. 3, d. 15624, l. 341–342.

162. RTsKhIDNI, f. 589, op. 3, d. 15624, l. 321–322.

about her past, and documented that her father, Saul Levin, had emigrated to the USA in 1911 and had worked in Louisville, Kentucky as an agent of a leather firm; and that as a girl she had lived in Penza (central Russia) from 1917 through 1918, where she had been a member of the "Union of Jewish Youth." But these were not the most important facts. During her first interrogation, Levina was shocked to hear from the investigator that, beginning in 1946, she had grouped around herself, at her institute, Jewish nationalists, and that she had induced them to carry out anti-Soviet activities. At the same time, she had supposedly been receiving instructions from Mikhoels's on how to participate in "active work for the good of the Jewish nation." In addition, Levina was accused of having asked Goldshteín, whom she knew was acquainted with Stalin's relatives, to use their good offices in getting her book nominated for the Stalin Prize, and also to get her son Mikhail (who had been arrested in 1944) released from prison. Levina thoroughly denied these accusations. Then, to break the spirit of this stubborn "nationalist," Abakumov called for a confrontation between her and Goldshteín, who was to be "worked on" in advance. However, in March 1948, when Goldshteín was escorted to the confrontation room and saw Levina, he could not overcome his remorse and declined to play the part he had rehearsed. The irritated investigator stopped the interrogation and the accused were escorted back to their cells. Goldshteín was then beaten over the next two days. The next confrontation followed the scenario that the investigators had planned.[163]

Despite the psychological shock of being "exposed" by her colleague, Levina nevertheless continued to insist that she was innocent. But the investigators still had in their stock such drastic remedies as deprivation of sleep and lengthy "standing" interrogations that ended usually when Levina fainted, fell down, and was then cruelly beaten. These remedies were employed to make Levina compliant. Colonels Sorokin and Likhachyov tortured their victim in a barbaric manner. Having flown into rage, they broke the old lady's front teeth. They hit her all over her body with a rubber baton—on her buttocks, legs, back and genitals. After this refined operation, Levina confessed. On May 29, 1948, by a resolution of the Special Meeting of the MGB, she was sentenced to 10 years of camp.[164]

As the main suspect in the case, Goldshteín was interrogated for the next year and a half, and his testimony was used against the imprisoned leaders of the JAC. On October 29, 1949 the Special Meeting brought this investigation to the foreground, classified Goldshteín as "an especially dangerous spy," and sentenced him to the MGB prison for 25 years. On November 10 he was sent to the

---

163. Document from the archives of the former KGB.

164. Ibid. On March 6, 1954 the USSR Supreme Court release Levina, who was then ill and almost insane.

Verkhneuralsk Central near Magnitogorsk. He was later transferred to the Vladimirskaya Prison, where he died on October 30, 1953.[165]

Having thus acquired "evidence" on the existence of an American-Zionist plot, the MGB fixed Mikhoels's fate. Tormented by his paranoia, Stalin could not feel safe while Mikhoels, the ringleader of the plotters, who had with their help lured into his traps the frivolous Alliluyevs, was still alive. The dictator could relax only after having dealt with Mikhoels, who had become his personal enemy, and who sought (as the dictator believed) to be the king off stage as well as on.

The MGB's political investigation acquired a clearly anti-Semitic nature with the "Mikhoels-Alliluyevs case." M.D. Ryumin, the former head of the Department to Investigate Cases of Special Importance to the MGB, was arrested after Stalin's death and in June 1953 frankly admitted:

> From late 1947 the tendency to consider persons of Jewish nationality as enemies of the Soviet state (which emanated from Abakumov and was later carried out by Leonov, Likhachyov, and Komarov) became clearly noticeable in the work of the Department to Investigate Cases of Special Importance. This directive led to the unreasonable arrest of persons of Jewish nationality accused of anti-Soviet nationalist activity and of American espionage.[166]

Obviously, such "innovative" work by the MGB was a result of the growing Judeophobia that had first been fanned by Stalin himself.

The Teacher Departs

Lidiya Shatunovskaya wrote that Stalin had planned the "Mikhoels-Alliluyeva case" to be a "most important anti-Jewish political action."[167] An open trial was supposedly prepared as the signal for the "final solution to the Jewish problem" in the Stalinist manner, i.e., all Soviet Jews were to migrate to the Far East region of the Soviet Union to live in the Birobidzhan taiga's severe conditions. Rumor had it that barracks were being built and that cattle cars were ready for the deportation.[168]

Such a claim is not original; rather it is traditional in the popular literature of this Jewish exile and is common in scientific and historical works.[169] It can be

---

165. Document from the archives of the former KGB.

166. V.P. Naumov, "Ministr skazal: 'Pobit' yego'" ("The Minister Said: 'Beat Him Up'"), *Moskovskiye novosti* (*Moscow News*), 1994, no. 2.

167. Lidiya Shatunovskaya, *Zhizn' v Kremle* [*Life in the Kremlin*] (New York, 1982), p. 309.

168. Ibid., pp. 335–336.

169. See for example Benjamin Pinkus, *The Jews of the Soviet Union* (Cambridge, 1988), p. 180.

said that this claim is a result of, and bears the stamp of, the postwar mentality of the European Jews, who had experienced the greatest tragedy in their history, and who lived in anticipation of a new national catastrophe. Those fears, so characteristic of a totalitarian society, resulted from the impossibility of obtaining objective information, independent of the information supplied by the state. The postwar Soviet-Jewish mentality was based on all manner of rumors, myths, illusions, utopian hopes, and disturbed expectations that corresponded to the irrational, closed, and basically secret political system.[170]

I think the supposition, made by Shatunovskaya and others, that a massive anti-Jewish policy was being prepared from the beginning of 1948 is to a considerable degree the result of such aberrations. Even a general knowledge of the Soviet and world political situations at that time, as well as a general knowledge of Stalin's psychology, allows us to conclude that Stalin could not dare begin a public anti-Semitic trial. First, to do so would bring about diplomatic complications, for in 1947 and 1948 the Soviet Union had actively supported the project of forming of an independent Jewish state in the Near Eastern part of the USSR. Second, it is hard to imagine that Stalin would dare give publicity to the circumstances of his personal life, and, in particular, to his conflict with his late wife's relatives. Third, Stalin would have found an open trial over Mikhoels unacceptable not, as Mikhoels's daughters put it, because he was afraid of losing his psychological duel with him (far stronger political enemies had been broken and forced to say whatever was needed), but rather because the dictator preferred to deal with disagreeable persons secretly. The domestic and international reaction to such a scandalous trial (using, as it would, false evidence) could easily go wrong. Why would Stalin risk this? Rather than deal with a martyr suffering for his

---

170. In the wave of sensationalistic exposés of Stalinist evils, some seemingly factual recent publications actually mythologize history. Thus Memorial, a center of scientific and cultural research, published in 1991 (through A. Vaísberg) "M.A. Suslov's Reception by the Jewish Antifascist Committee." This was an extract from the recollections of Ye.I. Dolitskií, a former Sovinformburo employee and GULAG prisoner. This work states that in mid-November 1948 some JAC members were invited to the Central Committee, where Suslov suggested that the migration of all Soviet Jews to the Birobidzhan Region be discussed. Lozovskií and Markish took the stage after Suslov, and refused to take part in such a discussion, as they suspected a secret threat to Jewish national interests was afoot. The next day all the JAC members who had taken part in that meeting were arrested. According to this document, Suslov was simply following directives from Stalin, who was thus making preparations for the mass deportation and genocide of the Jews.

This legend is pure fiction, replete with mistakes and illogical statements. It is nothing more than an odd mixture of the faint echoes of sometimes real but usually imaginary events that took place probably from 1944 through 1946, when questions about Jewish state organization and the JAC's postwar fate were being discussed. Ye.I. Dolitskií, "Yevreískií antifashistskií komitet u M.A. Suslova" ("M.A. Suslov's Reception by the Jewish Antifascist Committee"), in A. Vaísberg, ed., *Zven'ya: Istoricheskii al'manakh* (*Links: A Historical Miscellany*), Part 1 (Moscow: Progress/Phoenix/Atheneum, 1991), pp. 535–554.

people, it would be simpler and much safer to declare that an enemy had been the victim of a tragic accident. Such cynical logic, it seems to me, had from the end of 1947 determined Mikhoels's tragic end. His assassination has become a question of when and how. Soon after Stalin's death, the imprisoned former minister of state security, Viktor Abakumov, stated:

> As far as I can remember, in 1948 the head of the Soviet government, I.V. Stalin, gave me instructions to carry out an urgent task for the officers of the MGB of the USSR—to organize Mikhoels's liquidation. He entrusted this matter to special persons. Then it was learned that Mikhoels had arrived in Minsk with his friend, whose last name I do not recall.[171] When Stalin was informed about this he immediately gave orders to carry out the liquidation right in Minsk . . . .[172]

The operation was planned and carried out by the deputy minister of state security, S.I. Ogoltsov, and the minister of state security of Belorussia, L.F. Tsanava. With the help of an agent, they were

> . . . to invite Mikhoels to visit some acquaintances in the evening, to provide him with a car at the hotel . . . to bring him to the vicinity of Tsanava's dacha, and to kill him there; then to take the corpse out to a deserted street, place it across the road leading to the hotel, and then to have a truck run over it . . . . [173]

This was all to occur on the evening of January 12, 1948.

The Stalin Prize Committee sent Golubov-Potapov (who, it was later learned, was an MGB secret agent)[174] and Mikhoels to Minsk, where the two spent the day with actors and employees of theaters in Minsk. At six o'clock in the evening they had dinner and went to their hotel, telling their Minsk colleagues that they would be busy for the remainder of the evening, as they intended to visit an acquaintance of Golubov-Potapov's, an engineer named Sergeyev (or Sergeí). At about eight o'clock they left the hotel and declined the offer of the use of a car. The next morning their corpses were found on one of the deserted streets of

---

171. Mikhoels, together with drama study specialist V.I. Golubov-Potapov, left for Minsk on January 7, 1948.

172. *Argumenty i fakty* (*Arguments and Facts*), 1992, no. 19.

173. Ibid.

174. In order to maintain complete secrecy, Golubov-Potapov was also doomed to death. The executors of Stalin's will were later awarded with Orders. Stalin in particular appreciated minister of state security L.F. Tsanava's role in the murder, and on August 12, 1950 he signed a Politburo resolution to award Tsanava with the Order of Lenin. This honor was in connection with his fiftieth birthday and for his "services rendered to the state." RTsKhIDNI, f. 17, op. 119, d. 1, l. 35.

that town.

At first everything looked like a tragic accident. Therefore, in order to make this case seem criminal, the investigation was entrusted to the militia. A group of officers of the Central Directorate of the Ministry of Internal Affairs was sent to Minsk and, a month after the actor's death, presented a confidential report on their results to Colonel General I.A. Serov, the deputy minister of internal affairs. This investigation was doomed to failure from the beginning. The militia's report stated:

> Both corpses were pressed into the snow, as it had been snowing from the evening of January 12 and a severe wind had been blowing. All the clothes of the dead, [their] money, documents, and wristwatches (Mikhoels had a gold watch) remained safe. Mikhoels's watch was missing only its glass; however, his watch, as well as Golubov-Potapov's, were in motion at the moment of the corpses' examination.
>
> According to the forensic investigation of the corpses carried out on January 13 by Prilutskiĭ, the chief forensic expert of the Ministry of Health Care of the BSSR [Belorussian Soviet Socialist Republic], and by the expert physicians Naumovich and Karelina, it was established that the deaths of Mikhoels and Golubov-Potapov had followed as a result of being run over by a heavy truck. The deceased turned out to have all their ribs broken and their lung tissue ruptured; Mikhoels had a fracture of the vertebrae, while Golubov-Potapov that of the hip. All injuries occurred while they were still alive.
>
> Judging by the beginning of the development of putrefaction, their deaths occurred 15–16 hours before the investigation of the corpses had begun, i.e., approximately at 8 in the evening on January 12, soon after they had left the hotel.
>
> The state of the food in their stomachs confirmed that the food had been ingested approximately two hours before the death, and the composition of the food corresponded to what they had been served in the restaurant. Nothing indicated that Mikhoels and Golubov-Potapov had died owing to some causes other than that of being accidentally run over.
>
> As a result of the investigation . . . the story about Mikhoels and Golubov-Potapov going to the engineer Sergeyev's, Golubov-Potapov's acquaintance, before they were struck by a heavy truck, was disconfirmed.
>
> All the information collected leads [us] to conclude that Mikhoels and Golubov-Potapov, for some reason or other, intended to visit another person and thoroughly disguised their plans, giving their acquaintances the fictitious name of Sergeyev, an engineer.
>
> In connection with this, an additional plan of measures was later

> developed and approved by the minister of state security of the BSSR, Lieutenant General Tsanava, and the minister of internal affairs of the BSSR, Belchenko. Since Mikhoels's and Golubov-Potapov's acquaintances belonged mainly to the artistic community, it was expedient for the MGB staff to design further investigations; hence, *the information that was collected, along with the [further] measures concerning those persons, was entrusted to the Second Directorate of the MGB of the USSR, and all the remaining examinations of their contacts were carried out by the Second Directorate.* [Emphasis added.]
>
> Measures to identify the vehicle and the driver who committed the crime were taken by the operational staff of the militia and the traffic police of the Gosavto Inspektsiya [State Motor Vehicle Inspection]. All trucks that were not in their garages on the night of January 12 were checked . . . and thoroughly examined; then the same operation was carried out with the rest of the trucks. Nothing dealing with the case was discovered. Apparently, there were no traces on the truck that ran over [Mikhoels and Golubov-Potapov] . . . .
>
> It is necessary to note that it is very difficult to discover the name of the driver, who has vanished. The Minsk truck fleet consists of more than four thousand vehicles. Besides, a considerable number of trucks arrives in Minsk daily from other regions, as well as from military subdivisions located in the Minsk Region . . . .
>
> Thus, despite the measures taken, it was impossible to discover the name of the driver who ran over Mikhoels and Golubov-Potapov . . . .[175]

Different results could hardly be expected, since the investigation was carried out under the control of the very persons who had planned the crime. Everything was arranged so perfectly that even the most honest professionals from the militia could not get at the root of the crime. Neither could anyone else, as the MGB nipped in the bud any attempts to lift the veil of mystery that surrounded Mikhoels's death. In connection with this, it is necessary to mention Lev Sheínin, the author of the popular detective stories, *Notes of an Investigator.*[176] Sheínin worked as the chief assistant to the prosecutor general and the attorney general, and was chief of the Department of the Office of Investigation. He had known Mikhoels well, and had often called him and dropped by the theater. Sometimes Mikhoels had asked him for help in examining the fate of some arrested Jew. According to the testimony of V.L. Zuskin, the Jewish Theater art director who was subsequently arrested, Sheínin more than once discussed with Mikhoels a play and screenplay he had written entitled *Mendel Beílis,* based on archival documents,

175. GARF, f. 9401, op. 1, d. 2894, l. 329–332.

176. *Zapiski sledovatelya.*

about the exposure of the so-called ritual murder of the boy Andreí Yushchinskií that took place in Kiev in 1911. The film director Eízenshteín (Eisenstein) became interested in the screenplay and supposedly offered the role of Beílis to Zuskin. However, in early 1941 Agitprop canceled this project. Sheínin's attempt in 1946 to arrange for Mikhoels's attendance at the Nuremberg trials also failed.

After Mikhoels's death, stubborn rumors began to circulate in the Jewish community that Sheínin had supposedly undertaken at his own risk an investigation of the Minsk tragedy; that, together with a group of investigators, he had flown to the spot where the artist and his friend were killed, interrogated witnesses, and so forth. As with other cases, the desired facts displaced the real facts. As Shimeliovich testified during the investigation, this was because many Jews insisted at Mikhoels's funeral that the investigation of his death be passed on to "their own" attorney. When taken to Lubyanka, Sheínin thoroughly denied that he had participated in the examination of Mikhoels's case, saying that he had been in Kazakhstan in January 1948, when Mikhoels had died. But all this happened afterwards; and at first the rumor about the noble investigator seeking the truth about the death of his great fellow tribesman pleased the self-esteem of the senior assistant of the attorney general. Then these rumors reached, through the all-knowing "bodies," the ears of the dictator, and Sheínin had to pay dearly for his popularity.

In December 1949 A.S. Bakakin, the deputy chief of the CC Administrative Department, sent several memos to G.M. Malenkov, suggesting that the latter discharge Sheínin from the staff of the USSR Public Prosecutor's Office. Since no fault could be found, Sheínin was charged with general shortcomings (such as groundless actions brought against somebody, unlawful arrests, bribery, the abuse of power on the side of investigators, and so forth). Personal accusations were even more significant. As the head of the Department of Investigation of the Office of Public Prosecution of the USSR from 1936, Sheínin "overlooked shortcomings," "grew accustomed to them," "tried to color the truth and describe the situation in the Office of Public Prosecutor of the USSR in the best light," "likes sensationalism," and so forth. The list of charges concluded with a rather vague statement: "Sheínin was unscrupulous in his numerous personal acquaintances."[177] On December 26, 1949 Stalin signed a Politburo resolution "to release Comrade Sheínin L.R. from his duties as chief of the Prosecutor's Department of Investigation of the USSR Office of Public Prosecutor in connection with his transfer to another job."[178] Everything indicated that the anti-Jewish purge in the police juridical system had come to a decisive stage; for now it was not only Jews who were its victims, but also those who sympathized

177. RTsKhIDNI, f. 17, op. 118, d. 639, l. 12–15, 17–18.

178. RTsKhIDNI, f. 17, op. 118, d. 639, l. 10.

with them.[179]

At first the CC wanted to give Sheínin the directorship of the All-Union Scientific Research Institute of Criminalistics at the USSR Office of Public Prosecution, but Stalin did not approve of this. Unemployed, Sheínin earned his living by writing. In 1950 he even received the Stalin Prize for his screenplay, *The Meeting on the River Elba*,[180] which he co-authored with the Brothers Tur. It seemed that this disfavored investigator had fallen into luck. But that was a mere illusion. For in that very same year the USW leaders accused Sheínin of suggesting cosmopolitan and nationalistic ideas in his works. But for some reason, the MGB was not yet interested in the newly-fledged literary man. Abakumov was later on pay for this lapse.

However, let us return to the events that followed the Mikhoels's tragic death. The Soviet Jews were mourning, for they had lost their teacher, their rabbi, their national support, their hope, their leader, their patron. Though the majority of Soviet Jews had been assimilated and were divorced from their native language and culture, many saw his death as a national tragedy. In those days of grief—grief not only for the Soviet Jews but for all those who admired Mikhoels's talent—*Pravda* published a wordy, hypocritical obituary notice, calling Mikhoels "an active builder of Soviet artistic culture," and "a great public figure who devoted his life to the service of the Soviet people."[181] At the civil funeral rites on January 16, the writer Aleksandr Fadeyev[182] called him "a particularly wholehearted, optimistic person with a crystal-clear soul."[183]

It seemed that the all-powerful MGB had gotten its way: the personal enemy of the "leader of all the peoples" had been destroyed, and, more importantly,

---

179. At the end of 1949 N.V. Zaítsev, a military prosecutor who was also attached to the Department of Investigation of the Prosecutor's Office of the USSR, was removed from his post and dismissed from the Party. This relatively young prosecutor had imprudently fallen in love with a person under his investigation, a certain R., a Jew, the daughter of the famous movie director Yu.Ya.R., who had more than once been awarded the Stalin Prize. Even after R. was sent to one of the strictly regimented camps situated in the suburbs of Moscow, Zaítsev found opportunities to see her. With the help of hush money, and under the pretext of the necessity of conducting "educational work," Zaítsev obtained from the camp administration permission to stay with R. in private. Often their dates lasted until three o'clock in the morning. At each of these visits Zaítsev gave R. flowers, sweets, books, various gifts, and once he even gave her his photograph. This romantic story (which so resembled the one in Liliana Cavani's famous film about the romance between an SS guard and one of his prisoners in a concentration camp) had a rather sad ending. Someone squealed on Zaítsev, who was put to shame and dismissed from his work and from the Party. R. was transferred to an even more remote camp.

180. *Vstrecha na El'be.*

181. *Pravda*, January 15, 1948.

182. Fadeyev was at that time general secretary of the USW as well as chairman of the Stalin Prize Committee in art and culture.

183. *Pravda*, January 17, 1948.

without a hint of the real cause.[184] However, not everybody believed the official version—at least not those who had worked closely with him in the JAC and at the Jewish Theater. In the grim atmosphere of frequent shadowings and even more frequent arrests, their intuition could not deceive them: Mikhoels's death was an intentional act thoroughly planned by the authorities.[185]

While Mikhoels's disfigured body was still lying in its coffin in the hall of the Jewish Theater, Perets Markish wrote a poem dedicated "To Mikhoels—the Inextinguishable Torch,"[186] which read in part:

> The broken face with numerous scars
> was hidden under biting snow and greedy darkness,
> but his eyes flowed as two streams of tears,
> and in his broken chest the stubborn cry is gurgling:
>
> O Eternity! I am murdered, lifeless.
> I approach your desecrated threshold;
> I, like my people, retain the evil traces
> in order that you, looking at our wounds, should recognize us . . . .
>
> The stream of people flows—no end of your friends
> who are mourning for you at funeral repast;
> six million victims, innocent and tortured,
> are rising from the ditches and stinking holes in honor of you.

Some years later, fighting for his life in court, Markish was forced to admit that he had written that poem in an affected state, and had authored but 12 of the 93 lines; the remainder having been written by others. At the same time he insisted that the poem had never been published. Fefer immediately refuted this, saying that *Einikeit* had published it. When Markish was asked why he believed that Mikhoels had been killed, he replied:

---

184. RTsKhIDNI, f. 17, op. 128, d. 1152, l. 198. Had the MGB not removed all traces of government complicity in Mikhoels's death, Stalin would have suffered international complications. Considering the reaction to Mikhoels's death in the USA, Australia, France, Argentina, Yugoslavia, and other countries that held mass meetings in his honor, it is not difficult to imagine what the scope of those complications would have been. For instance, on February 14 the American Committee of Jewish Writers, Artists, and Scientists organized a rally in Manhattan Center in honor of this great Jewish actor, which was attended by over 2 000 people.

185. Fefer later told the investigator that, soon after Mikhoels's death, he had had a meeting in Minsk with the Jewish literary man Isaak Platner (arrested in 1949), who straightaway declared that none of the Jews in the Belorussian capital believed that the artist's death was accidental, but rather saw it as a planned murder intended to "cut the head of the Jewish community."

186. "Mikhoelsu—neugasimyĭ svetil'nik."

> There was a troubling situation the first day after his death, and somebody from the Art Affairs Committee said that Mikhoels had been killed. One can be killed in an accident. For two days I had been obsessed by the thought that he had fallen victim. Then there was talk that he was drunk. For the first few days after his death there was no certainty about the causes of his death. It should be said that he had an acquaintance, commander-in-chief of the Belorussian military region Trofimenko (their wives were friends), and even that family did not know the details of his death. The situation, when even his relatives and close friends did not know the cause of his death made me feel uncertain. That's what I was thinking; perhaps I was wrong. And therefore the poem was written under the influence of those emotions . . . . The essence of the situation made me do that. . . . When rumors about his death emerged, it was known that some fascists sent by the Mikolajczyk[187] people had appeared in Belorussia, and it was quite possible that he was killed by one of these.[188]

Jewish circles closely connected with the Kremlin leadership also greeted the story of Mikhoels's accidental death with skepticism. Polina Zhemchuzhina, the wife of foreign affairs minister Vyacheslav Molotov, had spent six hours at Mikhoels's funeral and declared to Fefer and Zuskin[189] that Mikhoels had been murdered. This became known in late 1948 during the course of the investigation of the JAC case. Fefer's and Zuskin's "confessions" could have been made under pressure from the security organs, which collected compromising information on Zhemchuzhina, whom Mikhoels, according to the testimony of Fefer and others, had compared to the Biblical heroine Esther and called "a true Jewish daughter."[190] The investigators arranged for Zuskin and Zhemchuzhina to have a

187. Stanislaw Mikolajczyk was the Polish prime minister of emigrant government in London in 1943 through 1944. In 1945 he became a member of the Provisional Government of People's Poland; and in 1947 he again emigrated.

188. Document from the archives of the former KGB; The Records of the Judicial Investigation of the JAC Case, vol. 1, pp. 178–179.

189. After Mikhoels's death Veniamin Lvovich Zuskin became art director of the Moscow State Jewish Theater. It should be pointed out that on November 24, 1946, the day of the twenty-fifth anniversary of Zuskin's work as a director, Mikhoels, as if he had had a premonition of his death, presented Zuskin with a wallet, and enclosed with it a letter that read, "Whether you want it or not, one way or the other; but in case I die, you are obliged to take my position in the theater. Get seriously prepared for it." And when Zuskin visited Mikhoels in his study after the rehearsal (about two or three days before Mikhoels's ill-fated trip to Minsk), Mikhoels made him sit at his desk and said significantly, "Here, you will be sitting in this chair soon, very soon . . . . " The Records of the Preliminary Investigation of the JAC Case, vol. 23, pp. 118–119.

190. Rumor had it that Zhemchuzhina had played a major role in organizing the twentieth anniversary celebration of the Jewish Theater in 1939, and of arranging for Mikhoels to be conferred with

face-to-face confrontation on December 26, 1948:

> *Question to Zuskin:* Was Zhemchuzhina present at Mikhoels's funeral?
>
> *Zuskin:* Yes, she was. It happened the following way. On the evening of January 15, 1948 I was standing near the coffin and taking the wreaths from all the [Party and State] organizations, and when I saw Polina Semyonovna I greeted her and expressed my condolences at Mikhoels's death. During our conversation Polina Semyonovna asked me what I thought about it—was it an accident or a murder? I answered, referring to the official information we had received: Mikhoels was killed as a result of a car accident; he was found at seven o'clock in the morning in the street not far from the hotel. But Polina Semyonovna disagreed and said that the matter was not as simple as they wanted to paint it; it was murder.[191]

However, not many people doubted the official version. It was mainly those closely connected with the top officials and who had access to additional information who expressed skepticism. The majority of Jews believed what was written in the newspapers. As even Ilya Erenburg was later compelled to admit: "The [official] version seemed to be the convincing version in the spring of 1948."[192]

At that time Stalin thoroughly concealed his hatred toward the actor who had been killed at his order. The State Jewish Theater was now named after Mikhoels, and performances in his memory were arranged and broadly advertised, and were attended by the elite of Jewish and Russian culture. The JAC presidium decided at their meeting of April 27 that Boris Shimeliovich, who had been a close friend of Mikhoels, should propose to the Moscow City Council that the name of Malaya Bronnaya Street be changed to Mikhoels Street.[193]

The Party's upper echelons were now discussing the question of Mikhoels's successor at the JAC; yet at the same time CC ACP(b) officials were also discussing the radical purge of the JAC's staff. To be more exact, in March and April 1948 these officials suggested, in a memo to CC secretaries A.A. Kuznetsov and M.A. Suslov, that for the sake of:

---

the title of "People's Artist of the USSR" and awarded with an Order.

191. RTsKhIDNI, f. 589, op. 3, d. 6188, l. 10, 11.

192. I.G. Erenburg, *Lyudi, gody, zhizn'* [*People, Years, Life*], in *Sobr. soch.* [*Complete Works*] (Moscow, 1967), vol. 9, p. 566. The truth is that this statement could be a result of Erenburg's usual slyness. If we can trust the testimony Shimeliovich gave during the investigation, Erenburg supposedly "declared during Mikhoels's funeral": "A few days ago Mikhoels died at the very place where tens of thousands of Jews have already been annihilated," thus implying that Mikhoels's death was not accidental.

193. RTsKhIDNI, f. 17, op. 128, d. 444, l. 170.

> . . . normalizing the situation in the Jewish Antifascist Committee and transforming it into an efficient body for uniting democratic Jewish forces abroad . . . [that] I. Fefer, A. Frumkin, S. Galkin, L. Shtern, S. Bregman, D. Bergelson, G. Zhits, I. Yuzefovich, L. Kvitko, and others should be dismissed as committee presidium members. . . . While Ya. Kreízer, M. Gubelman, B. Shimeliovich, V. Zuskin, P. Markish, L. Gonor, and G. Kheífets should be left there.

In addition, the CC officials recommended the poet S. Marshak, the architect B. Iofan, the general D. Dragunskií, the composers M. Blanter and I. Dunayevskií, the violinist D. Oístrakh, the writer B. Gorbatov, the ballet dancer M. Plisetskaya, and others be elected to the committee's presidium. The biochemist B. Zbarskií, the general Ya. Kreízer, S. Marshak, and B. Iofan were proposed as candidates for JAC chairman.[194]

However, the Ministry of State Security had quite different plans. Minister V. Abakumov and his assistants relished Stalin's praise of Mikhoels's elimination and were encouraged by it (as well as by the Orders, promotions, prizes, and so forth). Thus they began to fabricate a large-scale case about an American-Zionist espionage center in the USSR, which had supposedly been formed under the umbrella of the JAC. It was with this idea in mind that the story of the "conspiracy" between the Alliluyevas and Mikhoels was first concocted (in connection with the disappearance of the main "espionage link," the dead Mikhoels) and then later closed.

On May 29, 1948 Stalin's Themis, the MGB, sentenced Yevgeniya Alliluyeva to ten years' imprisonment for anti-Soviet agitation. On that same day her daughter, Kira Pavlovna, was sentenced to five years' exile to the Ivanovo Region for "supplying information about the personal life of [Stalin's] family to those who worked at the American Embassy."[195] Anna Alliluyeva was sentenced to five years' imprisonment "for the distribution of slanderous fabrications about the head of the Soviet government"; and when her term approached its end, the special tribunal, on December 27, 1952, doubled it.[196] L. Shatunovskaya and her husband, L. Tumerman, who were involved in the same case, were sentenced to 25 years' imprisonment.[197] Then, on October 29, 1949

---

194. RTsKhIDNI, f. 17, op. 127, d. 1714, l. 3.

195. The person referred to here was a certain Zaítsev, who had worked at the US Embassy in Moscow and was declared a spy.

196. It apparently turned out that during the investigation one of Anna Alliluyeva's arrested relatives declared that "A.S. Alliluyeva claimed that Stalin became more and more unbearable with age, and subjected to repressions persons who were disagreeable to him, and that Russia had never before seen such a dictator."

197. A. Vaksberg, "Stalin protiv yevreyev" ("Stalin Against the Jews"), *Detektiv i politika* (*Detective Stories and Politics*), 1992, no. 3, p. 189.

the Special Meeting sentenced I. Goldshteín to this same term.[198] Other persons arrested in connection with this case were sentenced to various terms in concentration camps.

Another step the MGB took in this direction was to search for new compromising information to discredit the JAC, ban its activity, and obtain Stalin's sanction to arrest its leaders. Thus at the beginning of 1948 three Sovinformburo employees were arrested: Press Department head Yefim Ilyich Dolitskií,[199] the editor-translator Yakov Guralskií,[200] and Grigorií Sorkin. These people had been hired by Lozovskií[201] and were considered his confederates. With Mikhoels dead, the MGB became particularly interested in S. Lozovskií. This is not remarkable. Similarly, on March 1, 1948, during Zakhar Grinberg's interrogation, M.T. Likhachyov asked mostly about the "JAC's criminal activity" in general; then, on April 19, the investigator's questions dealt almost exclusively with Lozovskií's "nationalistic tendencies." The MGB used every method it could. Thus, G.Z. Sorkin, who until his arrest[202] had been in charge of the Photo Information Department of the Sovinformburo, was beaten and brutally tortured with a rubber baton in the Lefortovo prison for almost an entire month (January 24 to February 22, 1948). His torturers demanded that he "confess" to the espionage activity of Lozovskií and other JAC leaders, who had supposedly "sold themselves to the Americans and the Zionists." After the investigators had forced from Sorkin all the information they wanted, the court sentenced him to 25 years of camp.[203]

---

198. Golshteín's sentence was delayed because he was being used in the JAC case.

199. After his arrest in March 1948, Dolitskií (1901–1984) was forced to testify to the espionage activities of Lozovskií, Markish, and other JAC leaders. He was sentenced to ten years' imprisonment, seven of which he spent in Dubrovlag (Mordovia).

200. Yakov (Abram) Yakovlevich Guralskií (Kheífets), together with his wife, Ester Dreksler, came to the USSR in 1934 from the USA, worked in Comintern as secretary to G.Ye. Zinovyev, and was a state security service agent. He was arrested on December 25, 1947, and on November 17, 1950 the Special Meeting sentenced him to ten years of camp. Since he had been involved with falsifying materials sent to the MGB, he also claimed, without adducing any proof, that foreign intelligence service agents were active within the Party and state apparatus. Thus, on June 23, 1955 the Supreme Court of the USSR denied him rehabilitation because he had provided incorrect information to the State Security service. *Ogonek* (*A Small light*), 1988, no. 20, p. 26.

201. In 1949 other Sovinformburo employees who worked with Lozovskií were arrested, among them S.S. Khesin, M.M. Borodin (Gruzenberg), former British citizen George Hanna, and others. According to a resolution of the Special Meeting of September 14, 1949, Hanna was sentenced to 25 years of camp for espionage activities.

202. Among other things, he was incriminated with the transmission of "secret" photo materials on the technology of the anticancer medicine 'KR,' on the construction of the dam at Lake Sevan in Armenia, and on the Caucasus Metallurgical Plant, to the American journalist Robert Magidov, who was accused of espionage and later expelled from the country.

203. A. Vaksberg, "Stalin protiv yevreyev" ("Stalin Against the Jews"), *Detektiv i politika* (*Detective*

The MGB waged its secret war against the JAC (which the state security bodies defined as the organizational center of bourgeois Jewish nationalists in the USSR) not only in Moscow, but also in other regions where the Jewish population lived more or less in communities. The MGB headquarters directed and coordinated this repression on a country-wide scale. On March 26, 1948 minister of state security V. Abakumov submitted a report to the USSR Council of Ministers (Stalin and Molotov) and to the CC ACP(b) (Zhdanov and Kuznetsov), in which he detailed the first stage of actions, which were aimed at laying the groundwork for the preliminary imputation against the JAC. The following extracts from this top secret document testify to the seriousness of these accusations.

> The USSR Ministry of State Security, as a result of the measures carried out by the Cheka[204] officers, has established that the Jewish Antifascist Committee members, being active nationalists and oriented toward the Americans, actually carry out anti-Soviet nationalistic activity. The pro-American influence upon JAC activity became especially evident after the leaders of the committee, Mikhoels and Fefer, visited the United States of America, where they made contact with influential Jewish public figures, some of whom are linked with the American intelligence service. S.M. Mikhoels, the former chairman of the committee's presidium, who was known long before the war as an active nationalist, was some kind of banner of the nationalistically-minded Jewish circles . . . . Mikhoels and his supporters, as it has been discovered by information agents and during the investigation of the case of the Jewish nationalists, used the Jewish Antifascist Committee as an umbrella for carrying out anti-Soviet activity. . . . According to the agents' data, Jewish Antifascist Committee members Fefer, Kvitko, Bergelson, Markish, and others are linked with the Jewish nationalists of the Ukraine and Belorussia. Visiting these regions, [they] have contacts with them, inform them about the situation in the committee, and direct their anti-Soviet activity. The MGB of the Ukrainian SSR in Kiev is developing a plan for[205] the Jewish nationalistic group headed by the writer D.N. Gofshtein, a member of the Jewish Antifascist Committee presidium. This group unites

Stories and Politics), 1992, no. 3, p. 176.

204. Cheka, or Ch.K., was an abbreviation for the Extraordinary Meeting, which from 1918 through 1922 functioned as the political police. Employees of the state security have ever since traditionally called themselves "Chekists."

205. *Translator's note:* The Russian word we here render as "Developing a plan for" is almost untranslatable. The verb *razrabatyvat'* (or the noun *razrabotka*) essentially means collecting all information on a suspect (group, organization, or person), and planning tactics to incriminate and then punish that suspect.

> writers, journalists, and artists of the Jewish intelligentsia and is carrying out hostile activity among them for "the national unity of the Jews and the creation of an independent Jewish state 'of a bourgeois kind'." . . . The members of the nationalistic group maintain relations with the Jewish communities in Kiev, Chernovtsy, and Lvov. An analogous nationalistic group, headed by a fellow of the Academy of Sciences of the Ukrainian SSR, E.G. Spivak (Ph.D. in philology), has been discovered by the MGB of the Ukrainian SSR in Kiev among scientists. In Belarus the Jewish nationalistic group headed by I.M. Platner, a member of the Union of Soviet Writers of Belarus, has been unmasked by security services, who are working out the tactics of their investigation [*razrabotka*]. Until 1930 Platner lived in America, where he was a member of the nationalistic organization, "Poalei Zion," and participated in the International Congress of Zionists. The agents discovered that the participants of the nationalistic Jewish groups in the Ukraine and Belarus make contact, via the Jewish Antifascist Committee, with Jewish nationalistic functionaries who used to come to the Soviet Union from abroad . . . ."[206]

The report was of an informational character and did not contain any concrete proposals regarding the JAC. Rules characteristic of Soviet bureaucracy made it clear that taking the initiative for a proposal was punishable; so the MGB considered it reasonable to wait for instructions from above, and had no doubts that the orders would be adequate to the "exposures" described in the report. However, those "above" did not rush to get their orders out—and there were reasons for this.

The Peak of the Illusions

The spring of 1948 saw the formation of the state of Israel in the Middle East, and the rivalry between the USSR and the USA intensified in that part of the world. At such a decisive moment Stalin, who hoped for a socialist Israel to be the Soviet vanguard in the Mediterranean area, could not begin an overt anti-Jewish campaign in his country. Nothing could prevent Soviet propaganda and diplomacy from presenting the USSR as the best friend of the Jews in Palestine. The leader of the Soviet delegation at the United Nations General Assembly, Andreí Gromyko,[207] declared at the Political Committee of the General Assembly

---

206. Document from the archives of the former KGB.

207. According to Russian writer and historian Zinovií Sheínis, Gromyko's speeches on the Palestinian question had been written by the Ministry of Foreign Affairs counselor Boris Shteín. *Arkhivy raskryvayut taíny . . . Mezhdunarodnye voprosy: sobytiya i lyudi* [*The Archives Reveal the Mysteries . . . International Issues: Events and People*] (Moscow, 1991), p. 308.

on April 20: "The heavy sacrifices of the Jewish people during the tyranny of Hitlerites in Europe emphasize the necessity of, and justify the demands of, the Jews to create their own independent state in Palestine."[208] When on May 14 the world learned about the birth of the state of Israel, the Soviet Union was almost the first country to recognize it officially. After thus giving its moral support, the USSR began to supply military aid (directly and through Czechoslovakia) to the young state that had started a war with its neighboring Arab countries.[209] On July 12 the Israeli newspaper *Kol-ha'Am*[210] reported that "the armament supplies that arrived in our country in the first weeks of the existence of the state of Israel have given our state a chance to resist." Even writer/journalist Arthur Koestler, who in 1940 had published his well-known anti-Soviet novel, *Darkness at Noon*, was forced to admit that "those ships aroused a feeling of gratitude among the Jews toward the Soviet Union, while Bevin's[211] policy has undermined the faith in Western democracies."[212]

However, Stalin soon had to conclude that by supporting Israel the USSR stimulated the already intensive growth of national consciousness among Soviet Jews, who now suddenly felt they were an integral part of international Jewry. The Jewish Antifascist Committee telegrammed greetings to the provisional president of Israel, Chaim Weizmann. The Ministry of Foreign Affairs and the CC had thoroughly agreed upon the text before it was sent. Meanwhile hundreds of Jews, by phone or in person, demanded of the JAC that more drastic measures be taken for actual, rather than formal, solidarity with Israel. It seemed that all Jews, regardless of age, profession, or social status, felt responsible for the distant little state that had become a symbol of national revival. Even the Soviet Jews who had seemed irrevocably assimilated were now under the spell of the Middle Eastern miracle. Yekaterina Davidovna (Golda Gorbman) was a fanatic Bolshevik and internationalist and wife of Marshal Kliment Voroshilov, and in her youth she had been excommunicated as an unbeliever; but now she struck her relatives dumb by saying, "Now at last we have our motherland, too."[213]

In connection with the creation of Israel, the Moscow Choral Synagogue[214] organized in June 1948 a ceremonial divine service, attended by 10 000 people

---

208. *Pravda*, April 23, 1948.

209. It is interesting to note that in autumn of 1948 the UN Security Council's Permanent Representative of the Ukraine, D.Z. Manuilskií, suggested, in order to cool tensions, that the Palestinian Arab refugees (over 500 000 people) be moved to Soviet Central Asia where an Arab Union Republic or Autonomous Region could be created.

210. *All People*.

211. Ernest Bevin was the British foreign secretary from 1945 to 1951.

212. RTsKhIDNI, f. 17, op. 128, d. 446, l. 20.

213. L.N. Vasilyeva, *Kremlevskiye zheny* [*The Kremlin Wives*] (Moscow, 1992), p. 236.

214. *Editor's note:* Also known as the Great Synagogue.

who filled the building and flowed out into the streets. Inside the synagogue were posters, some of which read: "The Jewish people are alive," and "On May 14, 1948 was proclaimed the state of Israel." Identical services took place in Tashkent, Chernovtsy, and other towns.[215]

Workers, students, intelligentsia, servicemen, and even prisoners addressed the JAC. Some of them offered to take collections for the purchase of arms for the Israeli army. For example, I.B. Klionskiĭ, a Leningrad Kirov Institute of Advanced Medical Studies employee, suggested in a letter to the *Pravda* editorial staff that one thousand rubles be sent to the "voluntary fund to arm the struggling Palestinian army" and, in particular, for the construction of the "Iosif Vissarionovich Stalin" air squadron. Others wanted to go to Palestine[216] to fight as volunteers. And there were other suggestions, such as that made by those citizens of the town of Zhmerinka (Vinnitsa Region) who asked the authorities permission for their entire community of over 500 people to emigrate to Israel.[217] There were also suggestions that a Jewish Committee to Aid the Israeli Independence Fighters be created in place of the JAC.[218]

Here is a letter typical of the many sent to the JAC:

> To the Jewish Antifascist Committee:
>
> Last week I sent you an application asking to help me get an exit visa to fight as a volunteer in the army of the state of Israel, which is fighting for its independence. I have not received an answer. Now, with a struggle to the death; when the war is becoming all the more difficult; when the blood of our brothers and sisters is being shed; when the Arab fascist gangs, with the support of Anglo-American imperialism, are trying to strangle and drown the heroic Jewish people in blood; we, the Soviet Jews, cannot be silent and sit waiting. We must render active help for the devoted heroes to achieve victory, and we must actively participate, fighting shoulder-to-shoulder with our brothers. This is our sacred duty. One cannot be idle when the sacred war breaks out; one must fight.

---

215. RTsKhIDNI, f. 17, op. 118, d. 351, l. 148.

216. For example, D.A. Dragunskiĭ (colonel of the Tank Troops and twice a hero of the Soviet Union) and the Jewish activist I.G. Rogachevskiĭ proposed to the JAC that a special Jewish division be formed and sent to Palestine. Rogachevskiĭ was later arrested and incriminated with pro-Israeli propaganda and with having frequently written letters to Stalin, particularly in 1946, regarding the creation of a Jewish republic in the Crimea and the opening of Jewish schools.

217. There were persistent rumors among the Jews that, immediately upon the Soviet recognition of Israel, every Soviet Jew would automatically be given the right of repatriation. In this regard they alluded to Lenin, who let the Finns and Poles go to their native lands once they had become independent after the great October Revolution.

218. RTsKhIDNI, f. 17, op. 128, d. 445, l. 64; GARF, f. 8114, op. 1, d. 8, l. 58.

Therefore I ask you once more to help me, or advise me where to go in regard to this matter.

Yu.B. Shmerler. Novosibirsk,
Demyan Bednyí Street, 15a.[219]

This and other similar letters went unanswered. Letters such as this, along with conversations in person or on the telephone, were thoroughly recorded and passed to the authorities together with the names, addresses, and telephone numbers of their authors. What happened later is not difficult to imagine—at best, such people were fired.

However, the mass repressions occurred later. Meanwhile the Jews' euphoria at getting their own state continued. On September 3, 1948 Golda Meir (whose name at that time was Myerson) arrived in Moscow as an envoy extraordinary and minister plenipotentiary of the state of Israel.[220] On the first Saturday of her stay in Moscow she attended to the synagogue, where she often later appeared. Especially impressive was her attendance at synagogue on the Jewish new year, Rosh Hashanah. This event unexpectedly turned into an inspiring manifestation of Jewish national unity. Some 15 or 20 thousand people, most of whom could not fit inside the synagogue, participated in this service, which in reality became a celebration of the foundation of the Jewish state. Meir's next visit to the synagogue was on October 4, Yom Kippur, the Day of Atonement. On that day Rabbi Sh. Shlifer read the prayer, "Next Time in Jerusalem," with such emotion that he elicited a thunderous burst of excitement from the crowd.

Of course, Stalin would not tolerate such things, especially now that the illusions of transforming Israel into a Middle Eastern Soviet satellite had been shattered. The ever increasing military, political, and economic activity from the USA left no room for Stalin to realize his imperial plans. Washington officials were in no hurry to recognize Israel *de jure*; nonetheless they sent a contingent of several thousand servicemen under the guise of UN observers. As well-known American politician Henry Morgenthau[221] declared: "I want the entire world to

---

219. GARF, f. 8114, op. 1, d. 20, l. 60.

220. Meir had been born in 1898 and emigrated to America with her parents when she was eight. It is interesting to note that in summer of 1948, upon learning of Israel's decision to send Meir to Moscow, the MGB ordered Ukrainian state security agents to establish, in accordance with the synagogue records and other archival documents, all the facts related to Meir's family. Once Meir arrived in Moscow, the authorities, who considered her an agent of world Zionism, monitored her every step. The MGB believed that Meir supposedly had a "personal assignment from the Mapai party (an Israeli Labor Party) to establish contacts with Soviet Jews in order to get them actively involved in all-Zionist activities."

221. Henry Morgenthau Younger (1891–1967) was secretary of the treasury under President Franklin D. Roosevelt (1934–1945), and was later elected director of Joint. From 1951 through 1954 he was president of the board of directors of an American corporation on the financing and development

understand that if peace is achieved in Israel, I believe that Israel will be the only state in the Mediterranean basin that we can rely upon as a bastion against Communism."[222] Further, the Palestine Economic Corporation, founded and controlled by the American Zionists, was used as a shock brigade.[223]

There were many indications of America's victory over the Soviet Union in regard to influence on Israel. One quite significant event occurred on August 21, 1948 at the Habimah Theater in Tel Aviv: as a prelude to the opera *Thaïs*, the orchestra played only the Israeli and US anthems, ignoring the Soviet anthem. The Soviet ambassadors in the audience then left as a sign of protest.[224]

On August 2 Ben Zion Goldberg wrote to Fefer from New York:

> The prestige of the Soviet Union among the Zionist public (and, at present, all Jews almost everywhere constitute the Zionist public) has greatly increased. This prestige is so high that the Zionist leaders are even afraid to admit this, fearing that the left movement could increase. They justify themselves by saying that this should not be admitted lest America be displeased. They cannot set America against them for two reasons—first because America controls the majority in the UN, and second because America could impose sanctions against the collection of money for Israel. And the state of Israel without American dollars is not a state, and the country is not a country. The state of Israel will depend upon the bread of American Jewry for quite a long time—twenty years if not more.[225]

This letter well reflected public opinion in Israel at the time. There was one more event of great significance: Golda Meir, who was inclined toward the USA, became the first Israeli envoy to the USSR. This could not possibly have pleased the Soviet authorities, who demonstrated their discontent on September 16 by ordering the Ukrainian MGB in Kiev to arrest the Jewish poet David Gofshteĭn, who had not long before wired Meir about the urgent necessity of reviving the Hebrew language.[226] Other JAC leaders were left alone for some time yet.

---

of Israel.

222. RTsKhIDNI, f. 17, op. 128, d. 446, l. 270.

223. On September 19, 1948 the American Bund weekly, *Forward* (*Forverts*), published M. Rudenskiĭ's article, "American Corporation Invested Substantial Fixed Capital into the Economy of Israel."

224. RTsKhIDNI, f. 17, op. 128, d. 446, l. 201.

225. GARF, f. 8114, op. 1, d. 910, l. 175–176.

226. It should be noted that Gofshteĭn, a strong supporter of the rebirth of Hebrew, as far back as 1930 had signed a letter to the Soviet government on the necessity of studying this language in institutions of higher education. It was for this reason that he was dismissed from the Association of Proletarian Writers.

The King is Dead! Long Live the King?

The JAC's political importance for the regime was declining, and it became evident both to moderates in the CC and to the Jewish intelligentsia that it was only by convincing Stalin that the Soviet Jews supported the policy of unforced, gradual assimilation that he could be kept from taking the radical anti-Jewish measures urged by the MGB.[227] Considering the wave of repressions that was then beginning, this was a reasonable alternative to the fatal romanticism of the growing Jewish self-identity that so provoked anti-Semitic reactions. To realize this alternative, finding a national leader was of decisive importance. The writer and publicist, Ilya Erenburg,[228] who was respected at home and among

227. To demonstrate to the authorities the Soviet Jewry's political loyalty, *Einikeit*, on September 7, 1948, published an article by Lev Goldberg criticizing Zionism .

228. Stalin and his ideological apparatus made a considerable effort to put Erenburg's journalistic talents to their service. During the war his emotional and witty anti-German appearances, articles, and leaflets had enjoyed great popularity. Because of this he was even forgiven for his overt criticism of the anti-Semitic mood in the country—a mood that had been fanned not simply with the connivance of, but even with the participation of, the Party propaganda leaders. Indeed, the resultant frictions between Erenburg on the one hand and A.S. Shcherbakov and G.F. Aleksandrov on the other resulted in Stalin's ordering Aleksandrov to give a lesson in obedience to the obstinate literary man. So on April 14, 1945 *Pravda* ran Aleksandrov's article, "Comrade Erenburg Oversimplifies" ("Tovarishch Erenburg unroshchayeb"), in which, by criticizing Erenburg's propaganda of groundless hatred toward the Germans, Aleksandrov gave vent to his own Judeophobia and Germanophilia. Thus was the head of Agitprop able simultaneously to carry out Stalin's order to initiate a change in the psychological orientation of the troops entering Germany. Soon afterwards, on April 20, the General Headquarters issued a decree insisting that the Red Army "change the attitude toward the German prisoners of war, as well as toward the civil population, and improve their treatment." Upon being given this threatening warning, Erenburg realized exactly what was wanted of him. In the summer of 1945 he severed relations with the JAC and refused to finish editing the *Black Book*. So in 1948, the year of the JAC's defeat, he was awarded the Stalin Prize. During the Cold War Erenburg became the herald of anti-Americanism. Now when he criticized anti-Semites, he criticized only American anti-Semites. (See, for example, his article "Supermen of America" ["'Sverkhzeloveku' Ameriki"] in *Bolshevik*, no. 30, November 1949.) The following facts testify to Erenburg's contradictory nature. At an official reception in Moscow in November 1948, Erenburg found himself standing next to Golda Meir and deliberately declared aloud that he "hated those Jews of Russian origin who only speak English." These words shocked the head of the Israeli mission. It is said that at this reception he also criticized the film director Mark Donskoí, who mentioned the possibility of limiting the number of the Soviet Jews emigrating to Israel. He then loudly warned the representative of the Israeli embassy, M. Namir, that any pretensions in this respect would encounter "a strong resistance." At the same time, Erenburg sent, on November 21, 1948, a letter to *Pravda*'s editor-in-chief, P.N. Pospelov, asking him to publish material on an anti-Semitic action of V.S. Vasilevskií, the head of the *Literary Gazette*'s Department of Communist Education. When Vasilevskií had gotten drunk in a restaurant, he called a customer he disliked a "Zhid mug." This incident ended in court, which symbolically sentenced Vasilevskií to a one-year suspended sentence and ordered the material that Erenburg wished to publish to be sent to the archives. RTsKhIDNI, f. 629, op. 1, d. 110, l. 12-13.

On June 30, 1950 Stalin signed a Politburo resolution appointing Erenburg deputy chairman of the

intellectuals abroad, was best suited for that role. So popular was he that Soviet Jews distributed among themselves naïve and clumsy poems of Jewish consciousness that were ascribed to Erenburg and Margarita Aliger, but which were most likely of popular origin.[229]

Margarita Aliger set the tone for the national fate:

Warming my hands in an alien dwelling,
I will not dare to ask:
Who are we? We are the Jews.
How did you dare forget this?! . . .

I ask Marx and Einstein,
who are full of great wisdom;
have they perhaps learned this secret
of nations before the eternity of wars?

Have we not given everything we had—
all our riches—without unnecessary words?
What have they done wrong,
Erenburg, Bagritskií, and Sverdlov? . . .

Answer, please, in the name of honor
of the tribe that has been damned from ancient times—
boys missing,
youths who were killed in battles.

Eternal smell of humiliation,
lamentation of mothers and wives,
in the camps of death and annihilation
our people have been shot and burnt.

Children crushed with tanks;
the label "Jud" and the nickname "Zhid";
there are almost none of us left in this world;
nothing can bring us back to life . . . .

Soviet Peace Committee; and soon afterwards Erenburg was elected vice president of the World Peace Council. Erenburg so assumed the role of Stalin's special messenger of propaganda that even during and after the "thaw," which he had so tactfully anticipated, he could not abandon his piety toward Stalin. For example, he noted in his memoirs *People, Years, Life* (*Lyudi, gody, zhizn*) that "Stalin's nature, his favorite methods of struggle, resembled that of the brilliant politicians of the Italian Renaissance."

229. Yelena Sotnik, a Ukrainian student from the town of Stalino (Donetsk), found such poems at the house of a Jewish friend and sent them to Erenburg. Sotnik was later accused of bourgeois nationalism.

Erenburg responded to Aliger with another poem:

I do not know how to answer your question;
I should say: It was fated that we suffer;
our fault is that we are Jews;
our fault is that we are clever.

Our fault is that our children
are striving for knowledge and living wisdom,
and that we are scattered throughout all the world,
and that we have no single motherland.

Hundreds of thousands of lives have we sacrificed;
worthy of legends, we also traversed our path
so that we could hear: "Who? The Jews?
They were fighting in the rear for Tashkent."

So that, after the torments and tortures of Auschwitz,
those whom death by mere chance forgot,
those who have lost all their near and dear ones,
could hear: "Zhid, you were not beaten hard enough!" . . .

They wished to kill us in a filthy ghetto,
to burn us in the furnaces and to drown us in blood.
But I believe that, in spite of all that,
we shall live, Comrade Aliger.

We shall live, and we shall be able
to make our talents sparkle and to prove
that our people, that poor Jews,
have every right to live and flourish.

And hundreds of thousands of modern Maccabees
will be resurrected as a lesson for the future.
And I am proud, proud, not sorry,
that I am a Jew, Comrade Aliger.[230]

These were not merely poems. These works reflected the agonizing attempts to answer the questions that the war and Stalin's anti-Semitism had raised; they reflected the Soviet Jews' struggle for national survival; they reflected the struggle to obtain a new national perspective that was obviously not within the

230. RTsKhIDNI, f. 17, op. 132, d. 12, l. 116–123.

framework of Soviet patriotism (i.e., of forced assimilation), but was based rather on a national-historical renaissance. The Jewish youth were the most active participants in this process. Few people know of the informal group that was established in September 1945 at the Moscow State University, which consisted primarily of Jewish senior students: M.A. Akivis, V.A. Edelshteín, A.Kh. Lifshits, N.Ya. Gindina, L.V. Goldshteín, O.K. Budnevich, and others.[231] Edelshteín was a senior math student who had joined the Party while in the army. From 1941 to 1945 he was recognized as the group's leader, and suggested that the group be named "Confidential Commonwealth."[232] He wrote the group's statutes and its hymn (also called *Confidential Commonwealth*), and proposed the motto and distinctive membership logo. Meetings were usually held at a member's apartment, and in November 1948 Erenburg's poem was read and discussed at one of these meetings. When the MSU administration discovered the group in the summer of 1949, its members were dismissed from the Party and from Komsomol, and were later expelled from the university.[233] Their fate is unknown, and needs to be researched.

It was at this decisive moment for the movement toward Jewish self-identity that Stalin quite possibly took a fancy to the idea of placing at the head of the Soviet Jewry Erenburg, who would be a guiding star leading the Jews toward assimilation. In Stalin's view Erenburg must have been far better than Mikhoels, the impulsive and uncontrollable "bourgeois nationalist" whose charisma survived even after his death.

It was at this time that *Pravda* published Erenburg's article, "In Regard to a Letter"[234] which caused a sensation. This article answered a letter by a certain (fictitious) Aleksandr R., a Jewish student from Munich who had complained to Erenburg of West German anti-Semitism and who had stated that emigration to

---

231. The documents of the investigation of the JAC case contain information about another group of Jewish students at the Moscow State University. This group was headed by Leopold Vydrin, the son of F.I. Vydrin, who was known in Moscow Jewish circles as an expert in Hebrew and Jewish history. During the war, Leopold, who was at the front, was taken prisoner by the Germans and miraculously survived. In 1945 the British and American troops freed him from a concentration camp. Though he wanted to go to Palestine, he could not leave his elderly parents and so returned to the USSR. After entering the Moscow State University, he and Z.G. Grinberg strove to have the Department of Eastern Languages begin a program in Hebrew. In the spring of 1948 Vydrin, as head of the delegation of Jewish youth, visited Erenburg at his apartment and asked him to appeal to the Soviet Jews, through the press, in the struggle for Israel's independence. Realizing what this could cost him, Erenburg rejected the proposal. Vydrin was later arrested, along with others who had closely cooperated with him, such as Ts.Ya. Plotkin (a *Moscow News* employee), M.D. Baazov (an employee of the technical school of the Ministry of the Food Industry, and whose rabbi father was personally acquainted with Chaim Weizmann).

232. "Tesnoe sodruzhestvo." This may also be translated "Intimate Commonwealth."

233. RTsKhIDNI, f. 17, op. 118, d. 828, l. 27–33.

234. "Po povodu odnogo pis'ma," *Pravda*, September 21, 1948.

Israel would be the universal means of settling the Jewish problem.[235] This was just a simple bit of journalistic mystification that provided Erenburg with an opportunity to fulfill the enormous task given to him by the Stalinist propaganda machine: by using his erudition and his brilliant polemicist potential, he was to dethrone Zionism in the eyes of the Soviet Jews—not only as an idea about the international brotherhood of all Jews, but also as the idea behind the creation of Israel. The main thrust of the article was that Jewish solidarity was based not on some vague national bond that exists only in Zionist fantasies, but rather that it was based on the vital necessity of protecting Jews from a common enemy: anti-Semitism. As Erenburg remarked:

> The obscurantists say that there is a certain mystical connection among Jews throughout the world. However, a Jew in Tunisia has little in common with a Jew in Chicago, who speaks American and thinks American too. If there is actually any tie that binds them, it is not of a mystical nature; the tie is engendered by anti-Semitism. If one day a madman appeared and declared that all red-haired and snub-nosed persons should be persecuted and victimized, we would witness the natural solidarity of all the red-haired and the snub-nosed. The unprecedented atrocities of the German fascists—who first proclaimed and then in many countries afterwards carried out racial propaganda and the general extermination of the Jewish population—at first with abusive actions and then with the furnaces of Majdanek—all this gave rise to the sentiment of deep connection among the Jews of different countries. This is the solidarity of an abused and indignant people.[236]

Erenburg used all these arguments, which were generally correct, to lay the foundation for his cunning and false main conclusion; namely, that in the USSR there was not and could not be any anti-Semitism, since the Lenin-Stalin national policy had worked as an antidote to it. Hence, he argued, the Soviet Jews had

---

235. In reality this letter was a fiction. As Perets Markish testified in court: "In 1948 we, the writers, were summoned to Fadeyev. Bergelson, Fefer, Galkin and I were present.... This occurred after Erenburg's article, "In Regard to a Letter," was published in *Pravda*. Who cares how this letter was created? Then Fefer suddenly addressed Fadeyev and said, "Do you know, Aleksandr Aleksandrovich, how this letter appeared? When I was in the CC, the secretary [Suslov] told me that Erenburg had not received any letter; that this was a political maneuver." Records of the Court, vol. 1, p. 187.

Fefer testified during this investigation that S. Rabinovich, the deputy editor-in-chief of *Einikeit*, had told him that he had learned from Erenburg himself about the CC's proposal to write an article attacking the "active behavior" of the Jews in connection with Golda Meir's arrival in Moscow. Erenburg told Fefer that he had agreed to this on the condition that the article also attack anti-Semitism, a subject about which he had been prohibited from writing in the central press. Erenburg also said that he had not received any letters, and that he himself was Aleksandr R.

236. *Pravda*, September 21, 1948.

nothing to fear regarding the accursed "Jewish question," and they therefore should "look not to the Middle East, but to the future."[237]

The enthusiasm of this article, which Erenburg wrote perhaps with good intentions in an effort to avoid a Jewish-versus-Bolshevik extremism, did not extinguish any passions. The Jews did not see in this article a call for prudence; rather they saw the emergence of collaboration with the assimilationist ideology of the regime. Critical letters poured into the *Pravda* office, and into the *Einikeit* office, which had reprinted Erenburg's article. Asked one *Einikeit* reader:

> Who gave Erenburg the right to speak on behalf of the Soviet Jews? It is known that Erenburg has never been interested in the public life of the Jews. I wonder whether he has seen any Jews at all? Erenburg . . . is one of those 'Paris' Soviet patriots who would have forgotten that his mother was called Hanna[238] if Hitler had not kicked him out of [Paris]. . . . Erenburg probably has as much in common with the Jews as the red-haired have in common with the red-haired, or the snub-nosed with the snub-nosed, when they are being persecuted. . . . Erenburg compares Israel with a steamship occupied with Jews who have escaped from Majdanek. If a Frenchman spoke this way about France the French people would tear him to pieces. Unfortunately, the Jews cannot allow themselves to do the same; they only feel malice and hatred toward him. Let Erenburg know that he will be damned by the people and that he will never whitewash himself.[239]

Another reader also declared in plain words:

> According to Erenburg . . . the Jews must be assimilated. . . . If Mikhoels could read the article by Erenburg in *Einikeit* he would shudder in his grave from grief and sorrow . . . . The Jewish people do not wish to listen to Erenburg's advice.[240]

Einikeit also received poems addressed to Erenburg:

---

237. Ibid.

238. Until 1940 Erenburg had been the Paris correspondent for *Izvestiya*. In August 1941 he declared at a Jewish antifascist meeting (broadcast by radio) that he was a Russian writer. The Nazis then reminded him that his mother's name was Hanna and that he himself was a proud Jew. (*Pravda*, August 25, 1941.)

239. GARF, f. 8114, op. 1, d. 20, l. 39–40.

240. GARF, f. 8114, op. 1, d. 20, l. 38.

What are your thoughts? What are we to believe?
Your *Pravda* essay or your answer to Aliger?
When are you telling lies, Jewish Quisling?
When are you writing the truth—then or today?

O writer, "Conscience of the World," come to your senses!
Are you a Jew? Are you in your right mind?
And how dare your worshipful lyre
play so false a sound! And on such strings!

The Jews are hundreds of times stronger than you, writer.
It was only you who dared write such nonsense;
only you, who have spent your life in foreign lands,
could manage to break the links with your people.

What are you looking for? Esteem? Or money? Glory?
Have you not got enough despicable goods?
Perhaps it is the devil's work, no more,
and you decided that you were Bar-Kokhba[241] himself?

A simple soul! Can you be a hero?
An eternal slave and snake cannot be a leader.
You, a writer without a homeland, an outcast,
will not lead the Jewish people against the foe. . . .[242]

It was a complete fiasco. Stalin now saw how ineffective assimilationist therapy was. He had long had on reserve the surgical cure for national problems, a cure that had been devised by Abakumov's department. Without even a second thought, Stalin now put it into practice.

Doomed to Death

November 20, 1948 saw the appearance of "Item #81: 'On the Jewish Antifascist Committee'." This was under the top secret Party seal "Special File"[243] in the Record of the Proceedings #66 of the CC ACP(b) Politburo session. This document stated that "The following resolution of the Bureau of the Council of Ministers of the USSR should be approved." It continued:

---

241. Bar-Kokhba was the leader of the anti-Roman uprising in 132–135 AD.

242. GARF, f. 8114, op. 1, d. 20, l. 53–54.

243. "Special File" ("Osobaya papka") was the highest degree of secrecy in Stalin's Party and state machinery.

> The Bureau of the Council of Ministers of the USSR charges the USSR Ministry of State Security with the immediate dismissal of the Jewish Antifascist Committee, as the facts show that this Committee is the center of anti-Soviet propaganda that regularly delivers anti-Soviet information to organs of foreign intelligence services.
>
> In accordance with the above, the publishing organs of this Committee should be closed and their files should be confiscated. In the meantime nobody should be arrested.[244]

This resolution was approved on that same day and sent to Malenkov and Abakumov for execution. The next morning, even though it was a Sunday, a group of officers from the MGB arrived at Kropotkinskaya 10 and searched the headquarters of the now abolished JAC. All the documents were confiscated and taken to Lubyanka. *Einikeit*'s last issue was dated November 20; and on November 25 the Politburo signed a resolution announcing the closing of Der Emes, a publisher of Yiddish literature. To avoid charges of anti-Semitism or persecution of national culture, the resolution offered a neutral explanation: "the circle of readers of Yiddish is extremely insignificant," and "most of the books released by the publishing house Der Emes do not find distribution."[245]

Mikhoels's former office in the Jewish Theater, which after his death had been converted into a memorial museum, was also searched. At the same time inquests were made of JAC members and of others who had connections with the JAC. However, as the Politburo's November 20 resolution stated, nobody was arrested—yet. Stalin evidently thought that the MGB should first present more serious evidence of the JAC's "criminal activity."

This did not suit the MGB, for such evidence could only be fabricated if JAC members would slander themselves; and unless they were arrested and threatened with physical torture, they would not likely do so. However, Abakumov soon sent Stalin the interrogation record of Z. Grinberg and I. Goldshteín, who had been arrested and from whom the necessary facts had been "squeezed." Thence followed the order to arrest the two key JAC figures, Fefer[246] and Zuskin, Mikhoels's successors in the JAC and at the Jewish Theater. The choice of Abakumov, the secret policy chief, was not accidental, for the MGB was required to fabricate evidence that the JAC had performed espionage activity for the USA and had distributed nationalistic propaganda within the Soviet Union and abroad. The MGB hoped to use Fefer firstly to obtain the necessary testimony about the JAC in general; secondly to obtain information about his journey to America and

---

244. *Izvestiya TsK KPSS*, 1989, no. 12, p. 37.

245. RTsKhIDNI, f. 17, op. 118, d. 231, l. 82.

246. As far back as 1948 Fefer apparently sensed the impending danger and, at a presidium meeting on October 21, tried in vain to get dismissed as executive secretary.

his subsequent contacts abroad, which they could then interpret as collaboration with Western intelligence services; and finally to get a confession from him about the "nationalistic activity" of *Einikeit* and of the Jewish section of the Union of Soviet Writers (Fefer had played a leading role in both institutions).

The MGB interrogators planned to get from Zuskin new compromising materials on his deceased friend Mikhoels, whom they wished to paint as the organizer of the Zionist underground in the USSR. Further, they planned to have Zuskin "help" present the Jewish Theater as the major center of Jewish nationalistic propaganda.

There was one more circumstance that led to the primary importance of arresting these two leaders: the MGB considered them the most vulnerable to psychological pressure. Zuskin and Fefer had already been morally broken at the preliminary investigations, and it would not be difficult to make them admit both to their own guilt and to the accusations made against the JAC in general. The MGB was certain of this, for Zuskin had developed a serious form of nervous exhaustion, and Fefer, as an MGB secret agent, thought it was his duty to collaborate with the investigators.

Thus on December 24, 1948 Fefer and Zuskin were sent to Lubyanka. Zuskin was actually arrested in the hospital while asleep. (His sleep was induced for his nervous condition.) The MGB immediately began intensive interrogations in order to fabricate new accusations and to obtain formal grounds for arresting other JAC members. The MGB did not have much trouble with Fefer. As he later explained at the trial, "The night of my arrest Abakumov told me that if I did not give confessional evidence, they would beat me. So I was scared, and as a result I gave false evidence at the preliminary investigation."[247]

Then came Shimeliovich's and Yuzefovich's turn. Shimeliovich had served a long term as the head of Botkin, Moscow's largest hospital, and of all the JAC members, it was he who had the closest and friendliest relations with Mikhoels, and it was he who heartily supported Mikhoels's attempt to convert the JAC into an organization representing the interests of Soviet Jewry. Shimeliovich was himself an active and energetic specialist and organizer. For example, for his effective assistance to the starving people in Russia in 1923 he had been awarded in 1923 with an official letter of recognition from the USSR Central Executive Committee. Upon arriving in Lubyanka, this proud and courageous man refused to give the necessary evidence for the investigation. He was thus transferred to the Lefortovo prison, where he was subjected to refined tortures. On May 15, 1949 he declared in a written statement to the MGB leadership:

---

247. RTsKhIDNI, f. 589, op. 3, d. 15624, l. 341.

> Four months have passed since the day of my arrest. During this time I repeatedly declared: I am not a traitor or criminal. My interrogation record, drawn up by the investigator, has been signed by me in a languorous state of mind, and vague consciousness. Such a state was a direct result of the methodical battery of sneer and insult that went on around the clock daily for one month.[248]

In spite of all their efforts, the executioners could not break Shimeliovich. When, at closed legal proceedings, the chairman of the court asked if he would admit his guilt, Shimeliovich answered, "I have never admitted [it] and never shall."[249] And in his final statement at the trial, instead of appealing for leniency, he declared:

> I ask the court to appeal to the corresponding institutions with the request to forbid corporal punishments in the prison .... to disabuse some MGB employees of the idea that the Investigation Department is the 'holy of holies' ... On the basis of what I said at the trial, I would ask that some MGB employees, including Abakumov, be made fully responsible."[250]

Yuzefovich, whom the investigators expected to slander Lozovskií (whom he had known since 1917 when they worked in the trade unions), stood firm and thus failed to avoid the torture chamber. What he suffered there was made clear from his statement of June 6, 1952, at the hearings of the Military Collegium of the Supreme Court of the USSR:

> At the very beginning of the inquest I gave true evidence and declared to the investigators that I didn't believe I had committed a criminal offense.... After this, I was called by Abakumov, the Minister of State Security, who said that if I didn't give confessional testimony he would transfer me to the Lefortovo prison, where I would be beaten. And prior to this, I had already been "crushed." I refused Abakumov's [advice] and was transferred to the Lefortovo prison, where I was beaten with a rubber baton and trampled upon when I fell down. In connection with this, I decided to sign any evidence and to just wait

248. RTsKhIDNI, f. 589, op. 3, d. 15624, l. 340.

249. Document from the archives of the former KGB; The Records of the Judicial Investigation of the JAC Case, vol. 1, p. 15.

250. Ibid. Shimeliovich was interrogated by M.D. Ryumin, who was notorious for his cruelty, and who, in particular, forced him to "confess" that his article on the Botkin Hospital, "The Letter Overseas" ("Pis'mo za okean"), which was sent to the American press in 1948, was of an "espionage" nature. The Records of the Judicial Investigation of the JAC Case, vol. 7a, pp. 141–142.

for the day of the trial.[251]

Thus Yuzefovich, though tempered by the tsarist penitentiary system (having been imprisoned in the Warsaw citadel, Lomzhinskaya, and other prisons), could not withstand the brutal tortures of the Soviet jailers and gave the required testimonies, including testimony against Lozovskií.[252] All evidence obtained in this manner was immediately sent to Stalin and to the CC, where, under Malenkov's and Shkiryatov's supervision, the court examination on "a personal case" against CC ACP(b) member Lozovskií was already in full swing.

The Party apparatus and the political police machinery coordinated themselves and worked synchronously. The MGB had arrested Shimeliovich and Yuzefovich on January 13, 1949. It was on this same day that Lozovskií was called to the Central Committee, where Malenkov and Shkiryatov interrogated him for several hours to obtain testimony about criminal acts. Malenkov and Shkiryatov then proposed a Politburo resolution, which stated in particular that:

> . . . the Central Committee of the All-Union Communist Party (b) member, Lozovskií, having long been leader of the Sovinformburo, devoted himself to the questions of the Jewish Antifascist Committee's activity. Yet he did not help expose the anti-Soviet activity of this committee. And that is not all, for by his politically harmful behavior he even contributed to helping the leading workers of the Jewish Antifascist Committee conduct nationalistic and espionage work hostile to the Party and Government."[253]

This project was accepted on January 18, and Lozovskií, "because of his politically unreliable connections and for behavior unworthy of a member of the All-Union Communist Party (Bolshevik) Central Committee, was withdrawn from the Central Committee of the All-Union Communist Party (Bolshevik) and expelled from the Party."[254] Two days later Lozovskií was summoned to the CC, where Shkiryatov read him this resolution. The next day Lozovskií sent a letter to Stalin: "For the last time, I beg you to listen to me, and take into consideration that I have never betrayed either the Party or the CC." But his plea for mercy was never heard. Civil punishment followed Party punishment. On January 26

---

251. RTsKhIDNI, f. 589, op. 3, d. 15624, l. 340.

252. Yuzefovich's interrogation was extensive. He "confessed" that Lozovskií had actively participated in the composition of the Crimean brief and had, after the war, met with Ben Zion Goldberg, an "American spy," and delivered "secret documents" to him. On January 26 Abakumov sent this interrogation record to the Kremlin, and on that same day Stalin issued an order for Lozovskií's arrest.

253. RTsKhIDNI, f. 589, op. 3, d. 15624, l. 308.

254. *Izvestiya TsK KPSS*, 1989, no. 12, p. 37.

Lozovskií was arrested and taken into custody.

From January 24 to 28, 1949 other representatives of the Jewish intelligentsia were placed behind bars; namely, the writers Leíba Kvitko, Perets Markish, and David Bergelson; academician and biochemist Lina Shtern; editors Emiliya Teumin and Ilya Vatenberg; and Vatenberg's wife, the translator Chaíka Vatenberg-Ostrovskaya. They were all later to be convicted in the JAC case.

Repressions then fell as if from the horn of plenty upon the most eminent representatives of the Jewish community and of Jewish culture. These repressions could be considered simply as manifestations of the personal pathologies of the Stalinist leadership. However, this is not exactly the case. Though Stalin and many of those in his inner circle were infected with a bacillus of anti-Semitism, this defect played only an auxiliary role. The main reason for the persecutions was the tyrant's pathological fear of losing power, whether it be by the opposition, by a palace revolution, or by the notorious Zionist plot. It is possible that Stalin knew the writing of Jacob de Haas (secretary to Theodor Herzl, one of the initiators of Zionism), concerning the secret mission of the Zionist organization:

> The real organization does not flaunt its actual abilities with or without cause. In need, however, one cannot lose sight of this form of demonstration. The great force of the American Zionist organization consists of its innumerable contacts and bonds, of its thorough knowledge about those who were in charge of the human resources that served as the base of these contacts. Did not the Englishmen need to obtain a reliable informant in Odessa; did they not need to have a warrant agent in Kharbin? And when President Wilson requested in a short period of time generalized information in a thousand words, which would set forth in detail what forces stand for Kerenskií rising to power in Russia . . . the New York [Zionist] Center provided these services, pretending nothing, but achieving much respect and favor of the public figures who signed the great deeds. Thousands of Zionists have been working everywhere, faithfully serving from their deeply echeloned positions . . . . "[255]

There is no doubt that some in Stalin's circle could derive a benefit by playing, at times, on his terror of the omnipresent secret agents of world Zionism. The MGB leaders were the primary culprits, for their prestige directly depended on the number of spies they caught and plots they uncovered. To all appearances, the all-powerful "organs" had once again detonated the repressions in a regime that had reached critical mass.

If only for the sake of objectivity, I should mention that some researchers

---

255. *Menorah Journal* (USA), February 1928.

ascribe the anti-Jewish campaign initiative to Malenkov, who ranked among the out-and-out anti-Semites. Such a statement is supported by numerous facts, as we have seen above. Nonetheless, strange as it may seem, the circumstances of Lozovskií's tragic fate actually cast doubt upon Malenkov's anti-Semitism and upon his interest in defeating the JAC. At the CC Malenkov had worked with his relative and good friend Mikhail Abramovich Shamberg. As far back as March 1936 Malenkov arranged to have the 34-year-old Shamberg transferred from the Odessa Regional Party Committee to Moscow. Then in 1942 Shamberg, an intelligent and thorough Party functionary, was given a crucial appointment as head of the Central Committee's Organization-Instruction Department. By 1946 Malenkov's star had faded a little (having been dismissed as CC secretary), but Shamberg managed to remain in the Party's central apparatus, although he had been demoted to inspector. Shamberg was not vain; so in mid-1948, when Malenkov was reinstated as CC secretary, Shamberg remained satisfied with his modest position, especially now that his son had married Malenkov's daughter and now that Malenkov was back in Stalin's good graces.

Soon, however, the Jews came upon hard times. Stalin's daughter, Svetlana Alliluyeva, remembers when, in late 1948, her father said in a fit of anger: "... you don't understand! The whole senior generation is infected with Zionism, and they teach the youth .... The Zionists tossed you up to your first husband."[256]

Stalin demanded that Malenkov have his daughter Volya divorce her husband. But the major ordeal was yet to come. It is important to realize, however, that what had happened to Lozovskií could also have happened to Shamberg. B.N. Chernousov, the head of the Department of the Party Trade Union and Komsomol Organs of the CC ACP(b), clearly stated the dramatic nature of the situation:

> I think it necessary to inform you of the following. This morning S.A. Lozovskií said to me that, by a decision of the Central Committee ACP(b), he was dismissed from the Central Committee ACP(b) and expelled from the Party because of his connection with the leaders of the Jewish nationalistic espionage center within the former Jewish Antifascist Committee.
>
> Since 1924 I have been married to Lozovskií's daughter, V.S. Dridzo (a member of the CPSU(b) since 1920, she works in the Historical Library). My sister, S.A. Shamberg, is his wife ([she has been] a member of the CPSU(b) since 1919, [and] she is an employee

256. *Translator's note:* In other words, the Zionists arranged things in such a way that Svetlana would meet Grigorií Morozov. Svetlana I. Alliluyeva, *Dvadtsat' pisem k drugu* [*Twenty Letters to a Friend*] (Moscow: Izvestiya, 1990), p. 149.

of MOGES).[257]

I shall say the following about my relations with Lozovskiĭ. I have never had any official connections with him. Therefore, the facts that have now been revealed were not known to me. When, some time ago, I learned about the closing of the Jewish Antifascist Committee, it did not occur to me that this could be connected with Lozovskiĭ's former work in the Sovinformburo.

I of course visited him at his apartment. During our meetings we had the usual common conversations on political or literary topics that were well known from the press. There was no talk about business. In particular, not even once was there talk about any question connected with the activity of the Jewish Antifascist Committee. . . .

Considering that I am related to a person who has been expelled from the Party, I suppose that it will be difficult for me to continue working in the apparatus of the ACP(b) Central Committee. I ask you to resolve the question about my further work.

January 21, 1949[258]

Malenkov did not abandon his former Jewish relation to misfortune. Instead, he transferred Shamberg to the remotest depths of the province and gave him the post of deputy head of the Executive Committee of the Kostroma Regional Council, where Shamberg remained until Stalin's death.

On the day of Lozovskiĭ's arrest, one other "fallen angel" was also taken prisoner. Polina Semyonovna Zhemchuzhina, the former wife of Politburo member and minister of foreign affairs Vyacheslav Molotov, had only one hour earlier been ejected from the high Party elite. Polina Zhemchuzhina (whose real name was Perl Karpovskaya) was an remarkable person. She was born in 1897 in the Yekaterinoslavskaya province; at twenty-one she joined the Bolshevik Party. After the civil war of 1918–1919 she went to Moscow, where she began her impetuous ascent into society, and where she met Molotov, whom she married in 1921. Through her marriage she was introduced into a privileged circle of the high Soviet hierarchy and became best friends with Stalin's wife, Nadezhda Alliluyeva, who happened to live in the adjacent flat in the Kremlin. After Alliluyeva's tragic death in late 1932 Zhemchuzhina became the first among the Kremlin wives. In addition to being the wife of a high-ranking elite, she also tried her hand at a career. She managed the perfumery Trust Zhirkost (abbreviated TeZhe); in November 1937 she became the deputy people's commissar of the Food Industry; in 1938 she headed this commissariat; and in January 1939 she

257. MOGES = the Moscow Thermoelectric Power Station / Moskovskaya Gosudarstvennaya Elektrostanusiya.

258. RTsKhIDNI, f. 17, op. 118, d. 296, l. 63–64.

was appointed people's commissar of the fishing industry. Later that year, at the Eighteenth Party Congress, she was elected as a candidate member of the ACP(b) Central Committee. But later her fate was not so favorable.

Only several months had passed since the Eighteenth Party Congress when the NKVD found within Zhemchuzhina's commissariat a great number of "vandals" and "saboteurs." Worse, the NKVD found an entire network of German agents nested there. The Zhemchuzhina question was submitted to the Politburo, and the accusations were serious and fraught with the most dramatic consequences. Stalin proposed that she be removed from the body of candidate members of the ACP(b) Central Committee. The blow was softened at the discussion of this proposal, when Molotov abstained from voting. Nonetheless, Stalin's proposal predictably prevailed.[259] However, without the usual unanimous vote, Stalin was compelled to agree upon the relatively liberal variant of the resolution on Zhemchuzhina approved by the Politburo on October 24, 1939. In particular, this resolution proposed:

> 1. To consider the evidence of some of those who have been arrested regarding Comrade Zhemchuzhina's involvement in saboteur and espionage work, as well as their statements about the lack of objectivity of the conduct of the investigation, to be slanderous.
>
> 2. To admit that Comrade Zhemchuzhina exhibited hastiness in regard to her connections, due to which many hostile espionage elements were found in Comrade Zhemchuzhina's circle, and that this unwittingly made their espionage activity easier.
>
> 3. To dismiss Comrade Zhemchuzhina from the post of people's commissar of the fishing industry, and entrust the secretaries of the Central Committee Comrades Andreyev, Malenkov, and Zhdanov with seeking employment for Zhemchuzhina.[260]

They soon found work for her: by decree of the Orgburo on November 20, 1939 Polina Zhemchuzhina was appointed head of the Chief Administration of the Textile-Haberdashery Industry of the People's Commissariat of Light Industry of the RSFSR.[261] This time Stalin had to back down. However, he could not forget or leave unpunished even the least important circumstances that went against his will. His revenge wait ten years—on May 10, 1948 Zhemchuzhina was dismissed "due to poor health."

---

259. In February 1941 the Party Forum approved this proposal supposedly because Zhemchuzhina had not been able to cope with her duties. See *Rezolyutsii XVIII Vsesoyuznoi konferentsii VKP(b)* [*Resolutions of the XVIII All-Union Conference of the ACP(b)*] (Moscow, 1941), p. 21.

260. RTsKhIDNI, f. 17, op. 3, d. 1015, l. 30–31.

261. RTsKhIDNI, f. 17, op. 116, d. 22, l. 71.

Fig. 1. S. Mikhoels and I. Fefer at Sholem Aleichem's tombstone in Brooklyn Cemetery (N.Y.) during their 1943 visit to the United States. From left to right: B.Z. Goldberg, S. Mikhoels, I. Fefer, Mrs. Goldberg (Sholem Aleichem's daughter), and the Goldberg's son Mitchell (courtesy of GARF).

Fig. 2. *(Top)* Reception of Professor Mikhoels and Colonel Fefer by Mayor Kelly of Chicago in his office, 1943 (courtesy of GARF).

Fig. 3. *(Bottom)* B.Z. Goldberg during his 1946 visit to the Soviet Union as guest of the Jewish Antifascist Committee (JAC). From left to right: L. Kvitko, V. Zuskin, B.Z. Goldberg, L. Shtern, General Aaron Kats, I. Fefer (courtesy of GARF).

Fig. 4. *(Top)* Paul Novick during his 1946 visit to the Soviet Union, at the JAC. From left to right: P. Novick, Dr. B. Shimeliovich (standing), pilot Paulina Gelman, poet Shmuel Khaíkin, Ukrainian poet Maksim Rylskií, I. Fefer, S. Mikhoels (courtesy of GARF)
Fig. 5. *(Bottom)* Ilya Erenburg and Albert Einstein, 1946.

Fig. 6. Solomon Mikhoels, 1948.

Fig. 7. Perets Markish.

Fig. 8. *(Left)* Aleksandr Bakhmutskiĭ, leader of the Party organization of Birobidzhan.

Fig. 9. *(Right)* Poet David Gofshteĭn (Hofstein).

Fig. 10. *(Right)* Writer Shmuel (Samuil) Persov.

Fig. 11. *(Bottom)* Svetlana Stalina and her husband Grigorií Morozov, October 1945.

Fig. 12. *(Below)* Paulina Zhemchuzhina, her husband Vyacheslav Molotov, and their daughter Svetlana at a country cottage.

Fig. 13. The funeral of S. Mikhoels, January 1948. From left to right: theater producer Yu. Zavadskií, V. Zuskin, theater producer A. Tairov, I. Fefer, and writer I. Altman.

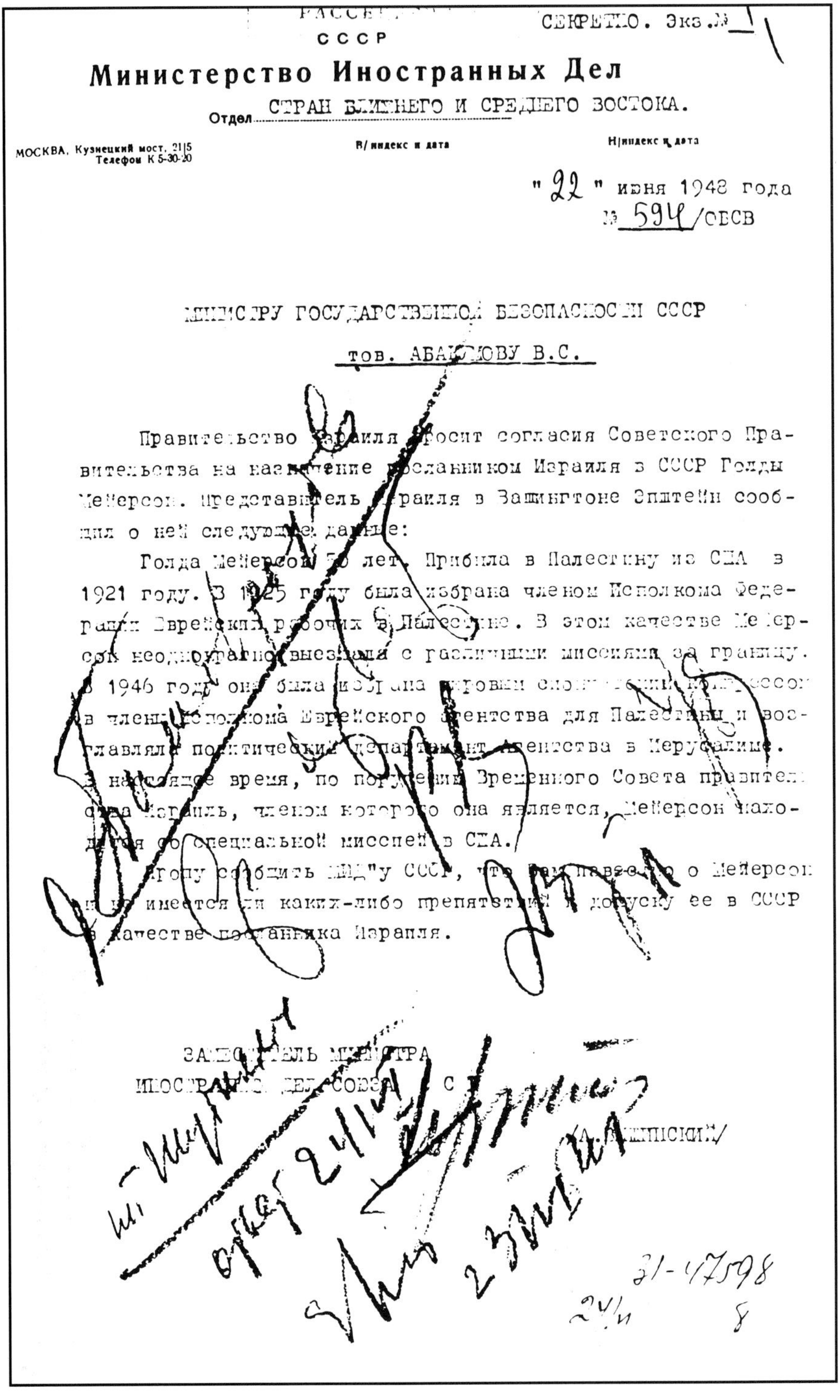

СЕКРЕТНО. Экз.№ 1

СССР

Министерство Иностранных Дел

Отдел СТРАН БЛИЖНЕГО И СРЕДНЕГО ВОСТОКА.

МОСКВА, Кузнецкий мост, 21/5
Телефон К 5-30-20

В/ индекс и дата

Н/индекс и дата

"22" июня 1948 года
№ 594/ОБСВ

МИНИСТРУ ГОСУДАРСТВЕННОЙ БЕЗОПАСНОСТИ СССР

тов. АБАКУМОВУ В.С.

Правительство Израиля просит согласия Советского Правительства на назначение посланником Израиля в СССР Голды Мейерсон. Представитель Израиля в Вашингтоне Эпштейн сообщил о ней следующие данные:

Голда Мейерсон 50 лет. Прибыла в Палестину из США в 1921 году. В 1925 году была избрана членом Исполкома Федерации Еврейских рабочих в Палестине. В этом качестве Мейерсон неоднократно выезжала с различными миссиями за границу. В 1946 году она была избрана мировым сионистским конгрессом в члены Исполкома Еврейского агентства для Палестины и возглавляла политический департамент Агентства в Иерусалиме. В настоящее время, по поручению Временного Совета правительства Израиль, членом которого она является, Мейерсон находится со специальной миссией в США.

Прошу сообщить МИД'у СССР, что Вам известно о Мейерсон и не имеется ли каких-либо препятствий к допуску ее в СССР в качестве посланника Израиля.

ЗАМЕСТИТЕЛЬ МИНИСТРА
ИНОСТРАННЫХ ДЕЛ СОЮЗА ССР
/А.ВЫШИНСКИЙ/

Fig. 14. A letter from the Soviet Ministry of Foreign Affairs to the Ministry of State Security about a secret inquiry of Golda Meir (Myerson), June 1948.

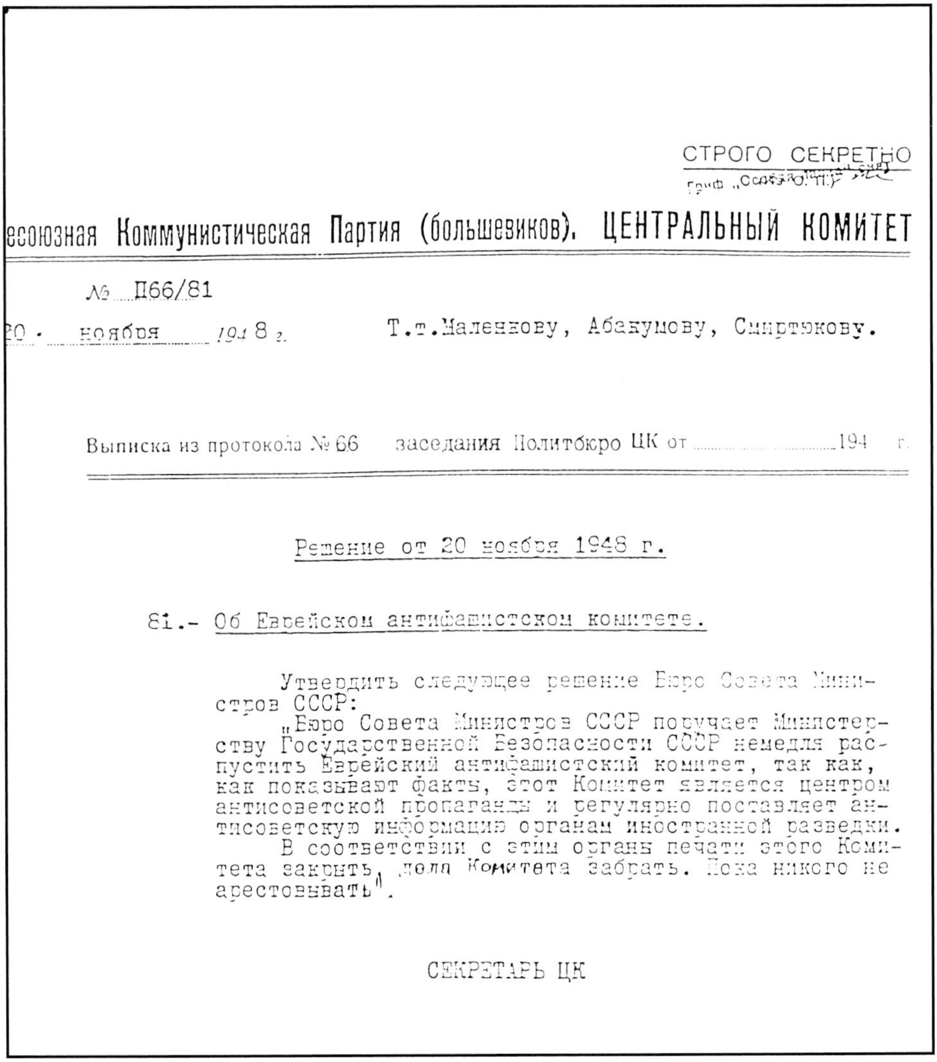

СТРОГО СЕКРЕТНО

Гриф „[illegible] О. П."

есоюзная Коммунистическая Партия (большевиков). ЦЕНТРАЛЬНЫЙ КОМИТЕТ

№ П66/81

20 · ноября 1948 г.

Т.т. Маленкову, Абакумову, Смиртюкову.

Выписка из протокола № 66 заседания Политбюро ЦК от .... 194 г.

Решение от 20 ноября 1948 г.

81.- Об Еврейском антифашистском комитете.

Утвердить следующее решение Бюро Совета Министров СССР:

„Бюро Совета Министров СССР поручает Министерству Государственной Безопасности СССР немедля распустить Еврейский антифашистский комитет, так как, как показывают факты, этот Комитет является центром антисоветской пропаганды и регулярно поставляет антисоветскую информацию органам иностранной разведки.

В соответствии с этим органы печати этого Комитета закрыть, дела Комитета забрать. Пока никого не арестовывать".

СЕКРЕТАРЬ ЦК

Fig. 15. Document concerning a secret decision of the Politburo of the CC ACP(b) to close the JAC, November 1948.

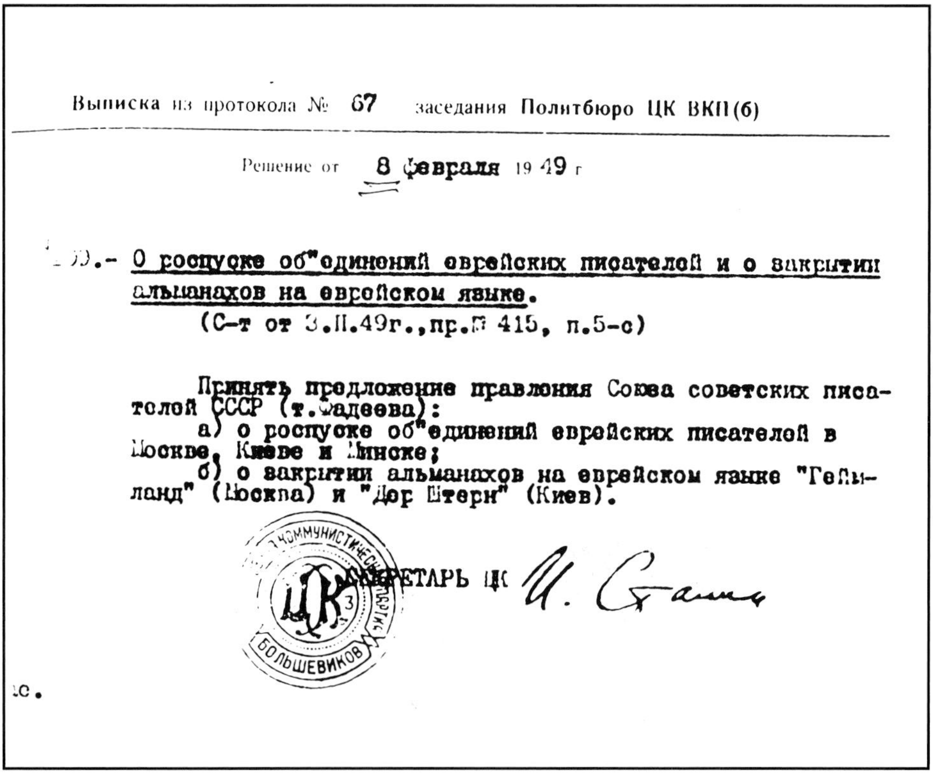

Выписка из протокола № 67 заседания Политбюро ЦК ВКП(б)

Решение от 8 февраля 1949 г

[illegible].- **О роспуске об"единений еврейских писателей и о закрытии альманахов на еврейском языке.**

(С-т от 3.II.49г., пр.№ 415, п.5-с)

Принять предложение правления Союза советских писателей СССР (т.Фадеева):

а) о роспуске об"единений еврейских писателей в Москве, Киеве и Минске;

б) о закрытии альманахов на еврейском языке "Геймланд" (Москва) и "Дер Штерн" (Киев).

КОММУНИСТИЧЕСКОЙ ПАРТИИ БОЛЬШЕВИКОВ ЦК

СЕКРЕТАРЬ ЦК И. Сталин

ic.

Fig. 16. Document indicating the Politburo's decision to close and disband organizations of Jewish writers and to suppress Yiddish publications.

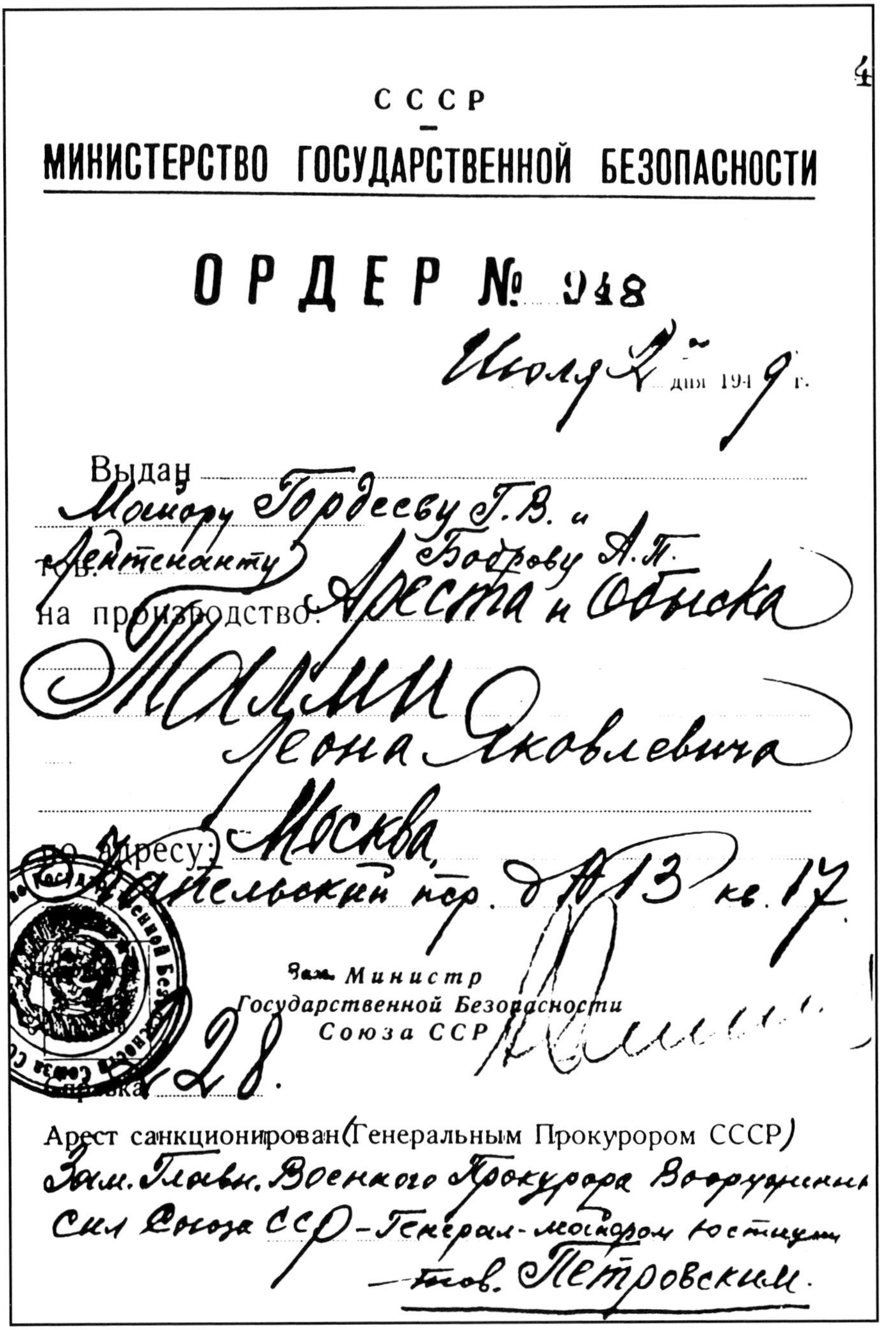

4

С С С Р

МИНИСТЕРСТВО ГОСУДАРСТВЕННОЙ БЕЗОПАСНОСТИ

ОРДЕР № 948

Июля 2 дня 1949 г.

Выдан Майору Гордееву Г.В. и

тов. Лейтенанту Боброву А.П.

на производство Ареста и Обыска

Талми

Леона Яковлевича

по адресу: Москва,

Капельский пер. д. 13 кв. 17.

Зам. Министр
Государственной Безопасности
Союза ССР

Справка 28.

Арест санкционирован (Генеральным Прокурором СССР) Зам. Главн. Военного Прокурора Вооруженных Сил Союза ССР – Генерал-майором юстиции тов. Петровским.

Fig. 17. A warrant to arrest L. Talmi.

Fig. 18. S. Lozovkskií (prison photo).

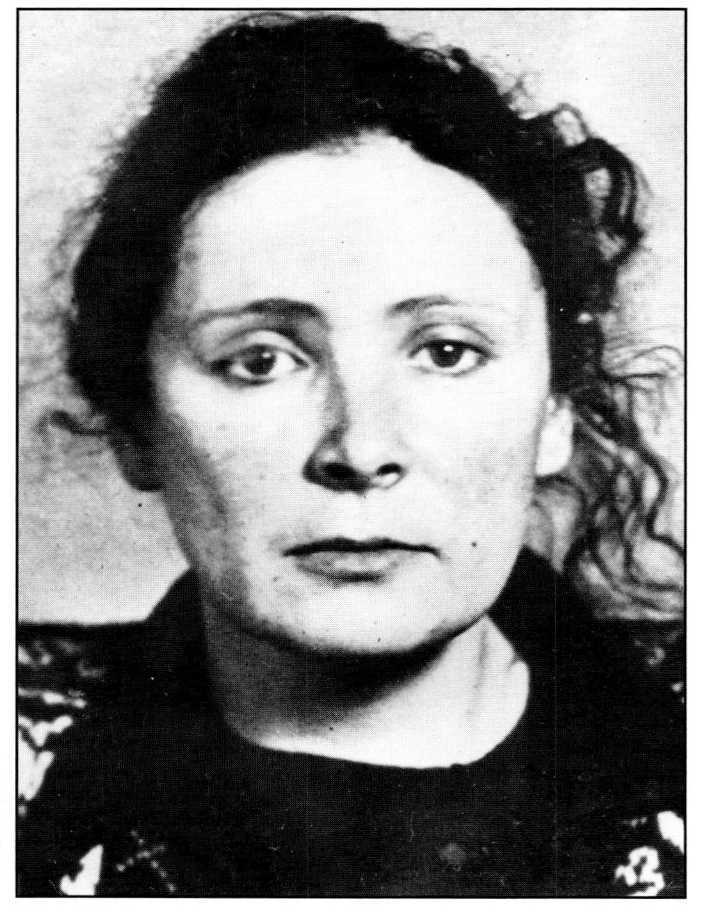

Fig. 19. E. Teumin (prison photo).

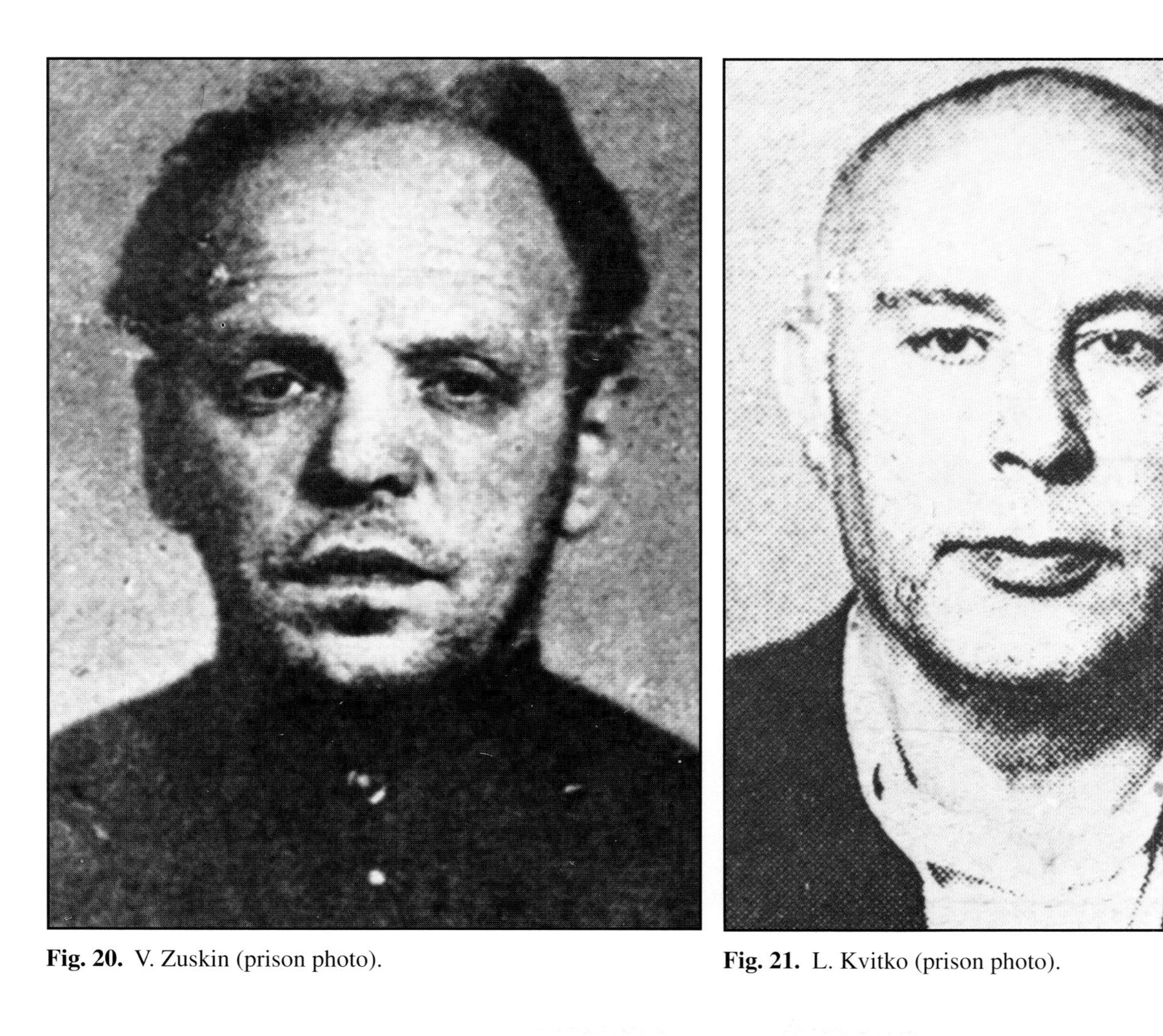

Fig. 20. V. Zuskin (prison photo).

Fig. 21. L. Kvitko (prison photo).

Fig. 22. D. Bergelson (prison photo).

Fig. 23. L. Talmi (prison photo).

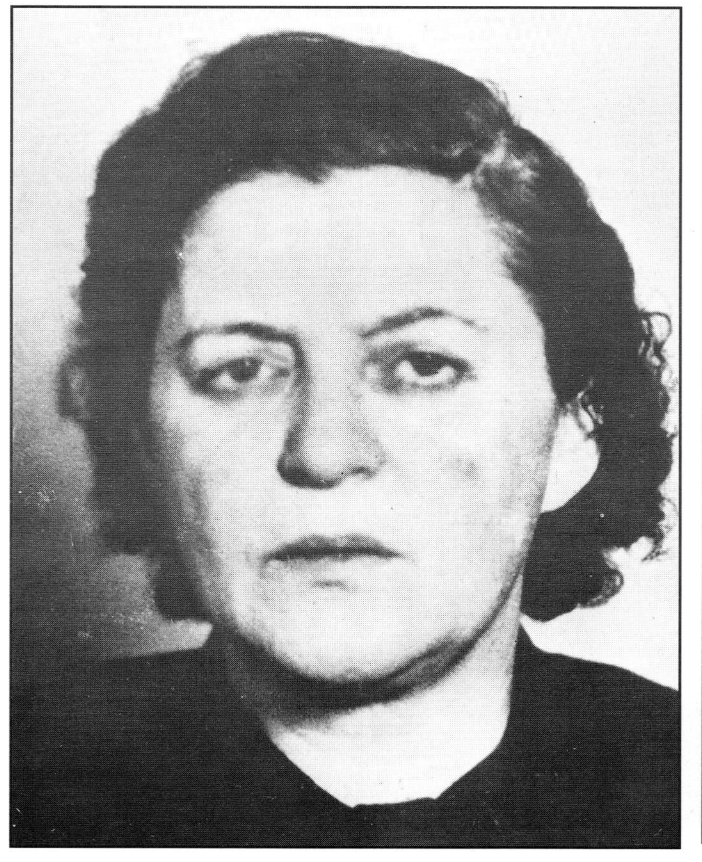

Fig. 24. Ch. Vatenberg-Ostrovskaya (prison photo).

Fig. 25. I. Vatenberg (prison photo).

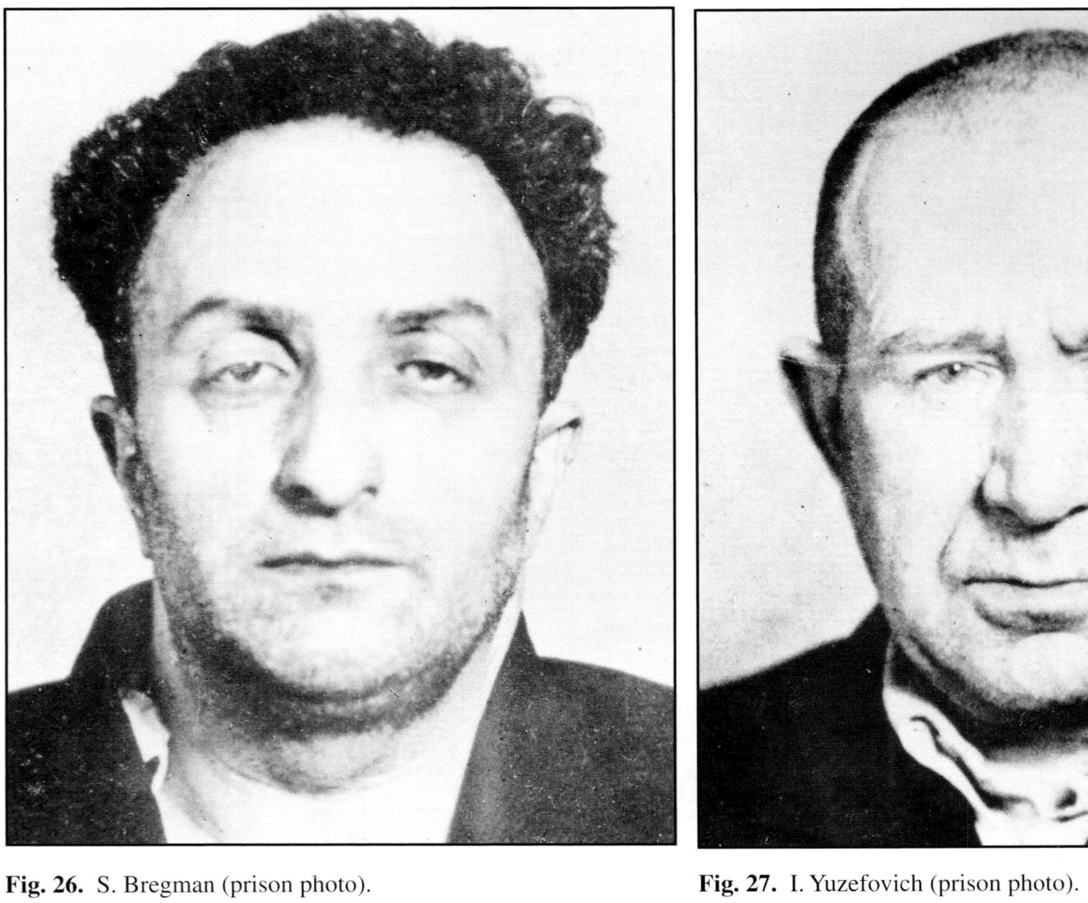

Fig. 26. S. Bregman (prison photo).

Fig. 27. I. Yuzefovich (prison photo).

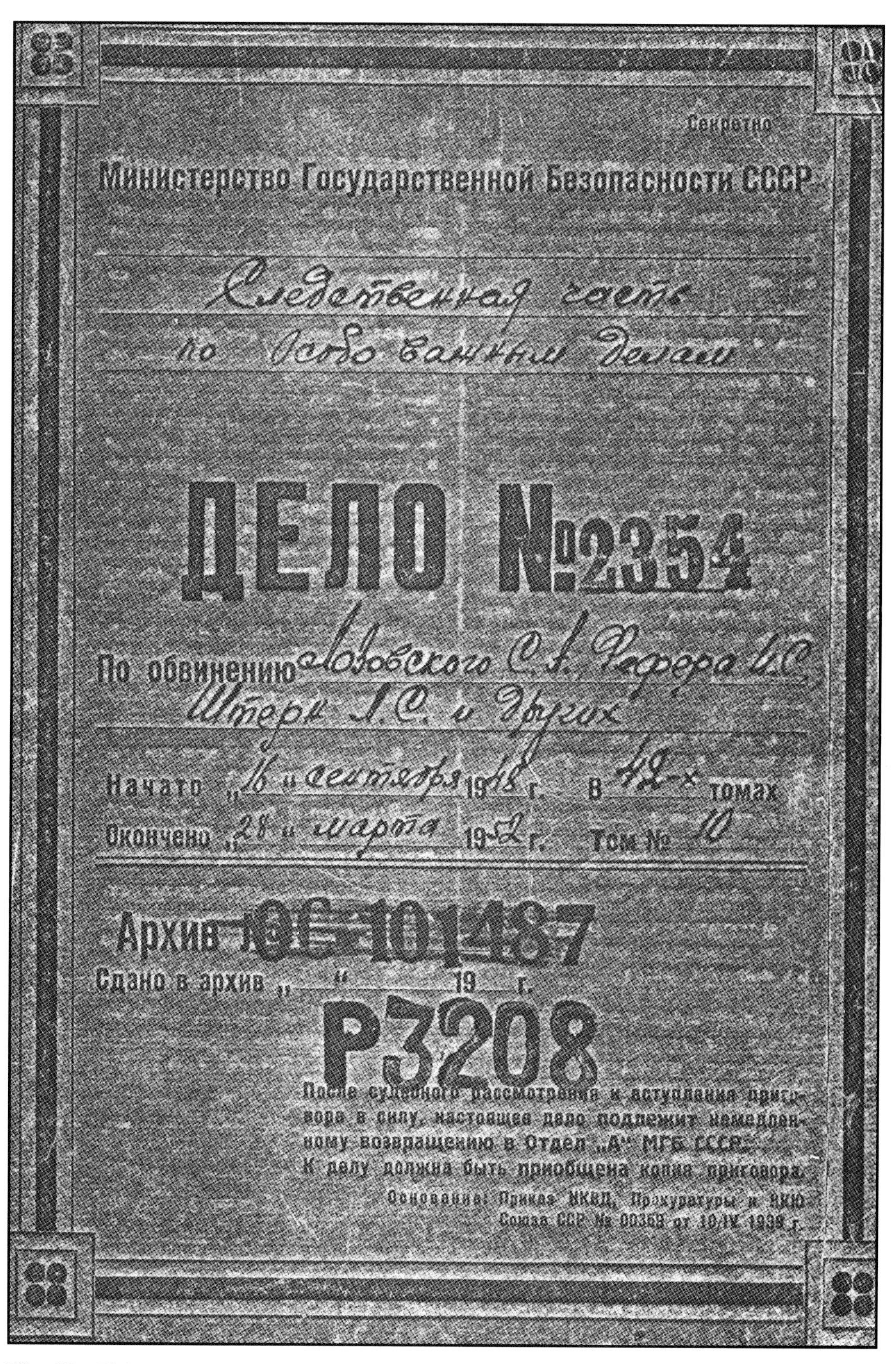

Секретно

Министерство Государственной Безопасности СССР

Следственная часть
по особо важным делам

ДЕЛО №2354

По обвинению Лозовского С.А., Фефера И.С.,
Штерн Л.С. и других

Начато „16“ сентября 1948 г. в 42-х томах
Окончено „28“ марта 1952 г. Том № 10

Архив № ОС 101487

Сдано в архив „ “ 19 г.

Р3208

После судебного рассмотрения и вступления приговора в силу, настоящее дело подлежит немедленному возвращению в Отдел „А“ МГБ СССР.
К делу должна быть приобщена копия приговора.

Основание: Приказ НКВД, Прокуратуры и НКЮ
Союза ССР № 00359 от 10/IV 1939 г.

Fig. 28. Title page of the file on the JAC case, with records of the preliminary investigation, in the Ministry of State Security.

ХРАНИТЬ ВЕЧНО　　　　СОВЕРШЕННО СЕКРЕТНО

Военная коллегия
Верховного Суда Союза ССР

По картотеке № 0065/52
По архивной описи №

СУДЕБНОЕ
ПРОИЗВОДСТВО ПО ДЕЛУ

Фефера И.С. и друг.
по ст. ст. 58-1 „а", 58-10 ч. II и 58-11
Уголовного Кодекса РСФСР
(Всего 15 человек)

том №1　Р3208

Начато „8" апреля 1952 года
Окончено „25" ноября 1952 года
На 272 листах

Fig. 29. Title page of the file on the JAC case, with records of the judicial investigation.

оп-0065/52

Совершенно секретно
экз.№ 1

ПРОТОКОЛ

ЗАКРЫТОГО СУДЕБНОГО ЗАСЕДАНИЯ ВОЕННОЙ КОЛЛЕГИИ ВЕРХОВНОГО СУДА СССР

/ стенограмма /

8 мая -18 июля 1952 года гор. Москва

в составе:

Председательствующего-генерал-лейтенанта юстиции ЧЕПЦОВА,
Членов: генерал-майора юстиции ДМИТРИЕВА и
генерал-майора юстиции ЗАРЯНОВА

при секретаре-старшем лейтенанте АФАНАСЬЕВЕ М.,

без участия представителей государственного обвинения и защиты.

12 час.00 мин.8 мая 1952г.

ПРЕД-ЩИЙ: - Заседание Военной Коллегии Верховного Суда СССР об"являю открытым. Будет слушаться дело по обвинению ЛОЗОВСКОГО, ФЕФЕРА, БРЕГМАНА и других в измене Родине.

Секретарь доложил, что обвиняемые: ЛОЗОВСКИЙ С.А., ФЕФЕР И.С., БРЕГМАН С.Л., ЮЗЕФОВИЧ И.С., ШИМЕЛИОВИЧ Б.А., КВИТКО Л.М., МАРКИШ П.Д., БЕРГЕЛЬСОН Д.Р., ГОФШТЕЙН Д.Н., ЗУСКИН В.Л., ШТЕРН Л.С., ТАЛЬМИ Л.Я., ВАТЕНБЕРГ И.С., ТЕУМИН Э.И. и ВАТЕНБЕРГ-ОСТРОВСКАЯ Ч.С. в судебное заседание доставлены под конвоем.

Председательствующий удостоверяется в самоличности подсудимых, которые о себе показали:

Fig. 30. First page of the record of the JAC trial.

Совершенно секретно
Экз.№ 8

ПРИГОВОР

ИМЕНЕМ СОЮЗА СОВЕТСКИХ СОЦИАЛИСТИЧЕСКИХ РЕСПУБЛИК

ВОЕННАЯ КОЛЛЕГИЯ ВЕРХОВНОГО СУДА СОЮЗА ССР

в составе:

Председательствующего - генерал-лейтенанта юстиции ЧЕПЦОВА

Членов: генерал-майора юстиции ДМИТРИЕВА и генерал-майора юстиции ЗАРЯНОВА

при секретаре - старшем лейтенанте АФАНАСЬЕВЕ М.

в закрытом судебном заседании, в гор. Москве

II-18 июля 1952 года, рассмотрела дело по обвинению:

I. ЛОЗОВСКОГО Соломона Абрамовича, 1878 года рождения, уроженца села Даниловка, Запорожского района, Днепропетровской области еврея, гражданина СССР, женатого, с незаконченным высшим образованием, исключенного в 1949 году из ВКП/б/, быв. начальника Совинформбюро;

2. ФЕФЕРА Исаака Соломоновича, 1900 года рождения, уроженца мест.Шпола, Киевской области, еврея, гражданина СССР, женатого с незаконченным высшим образованием, члена ВКП/б/ с 1919 года еврейского поэта, быв.секретаря Еврейского Антифашистского комитета;

3. ЮЗЕФОВИЧА Иосифа Сигизмундовича, 1890 года рождения, уроженца гор.Варшавы, еврея, гражданина СССР, женатого, с высшим образованием, члена ВКП/б/ с 1917 года, быв. научного сотрудника Института Истории Академии Наук СССР;

4. ШИМЕЛИОВИЧА Бориса Абрамовича, 1892 года рождения, уроженца гор.Риги, еврея, гражданина СССР, женатого, с высшим образованием, члена ВКП/б/ с 1920 года, быв. главного врача Центральной клинической больницы им.Боткина;

5. КВИТКО Лейба Моисеевича, 1890 года рождения, уроженца села Голосково, Одесской области, еврея, гражданина СССР, женатого, с домашним образованием, члена ВКП/б/ с 1941 [illegible] поэта, члена Союза советских писателей СССР;

Fig. 31. First *(above)* and last *(next page)* pages of the sentence delivered in the JAC trial.

12.

√ ГОФШТЕЙНА - "Знак почета";

ТЕУМИН - "Знак почета" и

√ ШТЕРН - "Трудовое Красное Знамя" и "Красная Звезда".

Приговор окончательный и кассационному обжалованию не подлежит.

Подлинный за надлежащими подписями.

С подлинным верно: Судебный секретарь Военной Коллегии
Старший лейтенант

/АФАНАСЬЕВ/

Приговор исполнен. 12 августа 1952 года.

Figs. 32 *(above)* **and 33** *(next page).* Two cartoons from *Crocodile* magazine (March 1949), criticizing "cosmopolitans."

Рис. К. ЕЛИСЕЕВА

БЕСПАЧПОРТНЫЙ БРОДЯГА

«...Признаюсь, жалки и неприятны мне спокойные скептики, абстрактные человеки, беспачпортные бродяги в человечестве...»

КРОКОДИЛ

№ 8 МОСКВА 20 МАРТА 1949 ИЗДАНИЕ ГАЗЕТЫ «ПРАВДА» ГОД ИЗДАНИЯ XXVIII ЦЕНА НОМЕРА — 1 р. 20

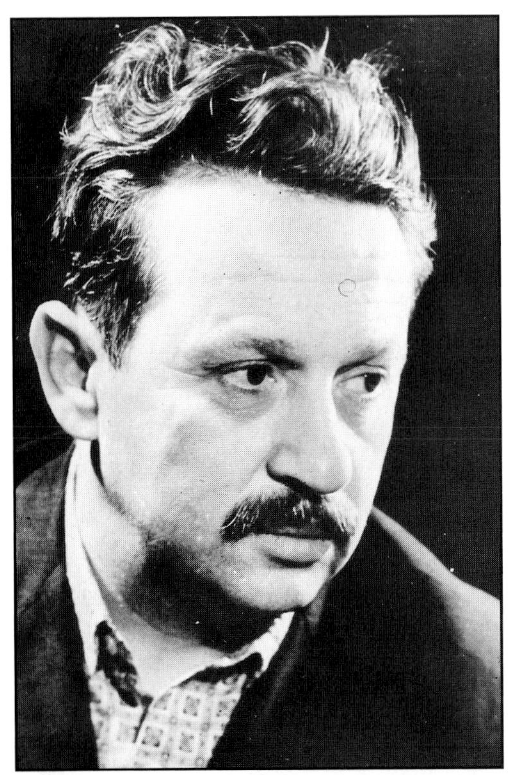

Fig. 34. *(Left)* An example of a "cosmopolitan"—theater critic A. Borshchagovskiĭ.

Fig. 35. *(Bottom)* Office workers from the Stalin Automobile Factory in Moscow. From the left, the first man sitting in the front row is A. Eidinov, and the fifth is A. Likhachyov, the director of the factory.

Совершенно секретно

Товарищу С Т А Л И Н У И.В.

При этом представляю Вам заявление заведующей кабинетом электрокардиографии кремлевской больницы – врача ТИМАШУК М.Ф. в отношении состояния здоровья товарища Жданова А.А..

Как видно из заявления ТИМАШУК, последняя настаивает на своем заключении, что у товарища Жданова инфаркт миокарда в области передней стенки левого желудочка и межжелудочковой перегородки, в то время как начальник Санупра Кремля ЕГОРОВ и академик ВИНОГРАДОВ предложили ей переделать заключение не указывая на инфаркт миокарда.

Приложение:– Заявление т.ТИМАШУК и электрокардиография товарища Жданова.

В. Абакумов

АБАКУМОВ.

30 августа 1948 года.

Fig. 36. A letter to Stalin from Abakumov with the report by Dr. L. Timashuk, 1948. At the foot of the page, in Stalin's hand, is written: "Send to the archives."

PARTITO COMUNISTA ITALIANO

IL SEGRETARIO GENERALE

Rome, le 15 février 1949

Cher Professeur Kogan,

je vous remercie des salutations que vous m'avez fait parvenir par le camarade Giuliano Pajetta.

Par la même occasion je tiens a vous remercier ,de même que votre frère, pour les soins attentifs prêtés à notre camarade.

Bien à vous

Palmiro Togliatti

Fig. 37. A letter to Professor B. Kogan from the leader of the Italian communists, P. Togliatti.

Fig. 38. Professor Ya. Etinger.

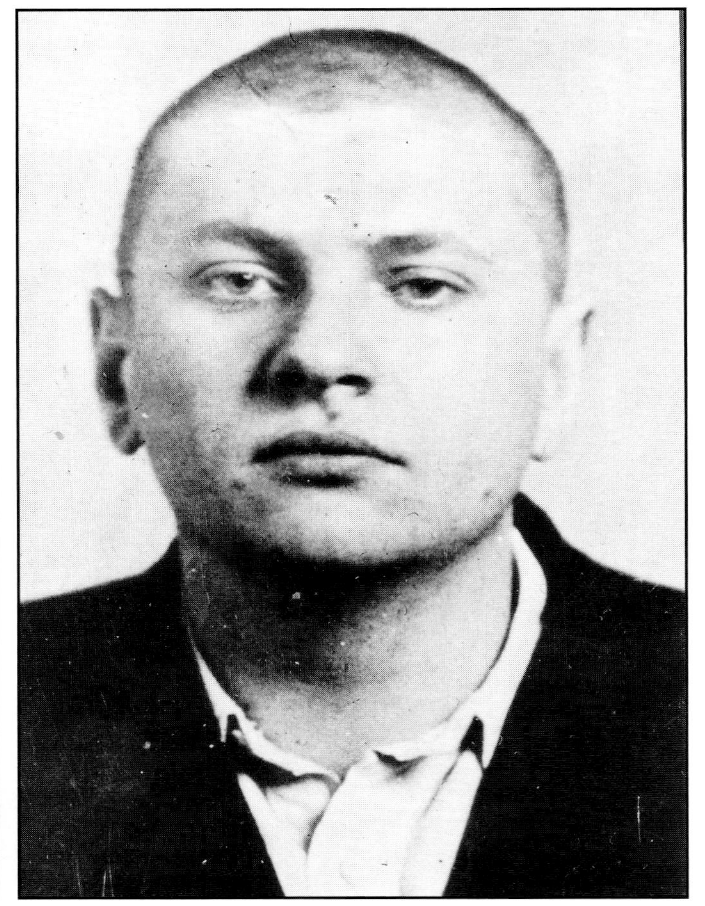

Fig. 39. Ya. Ya. Etinger, Professor Etinger's son (prison photo).

Fig. 41. Professor M. Vovsi

Fig. 40. Professor V. Vinogradov.

Fig. 42. Professor V. Zakusov.

Медкарточка № 4581.

Фамилия Коган

Имя, отчество Борис Борисович

Место работы Леч. Сан. Упр. Кремля

Должность врач терапевт.

Год рожд. 1896 п/ст. 1917.

« 22 » ноября 1937 г.

Ист. бол. № 22698

Нач. Лечсанупра
Кремля

Fig. 43. *(Top)* Medical card of Professor B. Kogan.
Fig. 44. *(Bottom)* Professor V. Nezlin *(left)* and Professor M. Kogan *(right)*.

Fig. 45. Chief of Kremlin hospital, Professor P. Yegorov

Fig. 46. Professor Ya. Tyomkin.

Fig. 47. Professor V. Vasilenko.

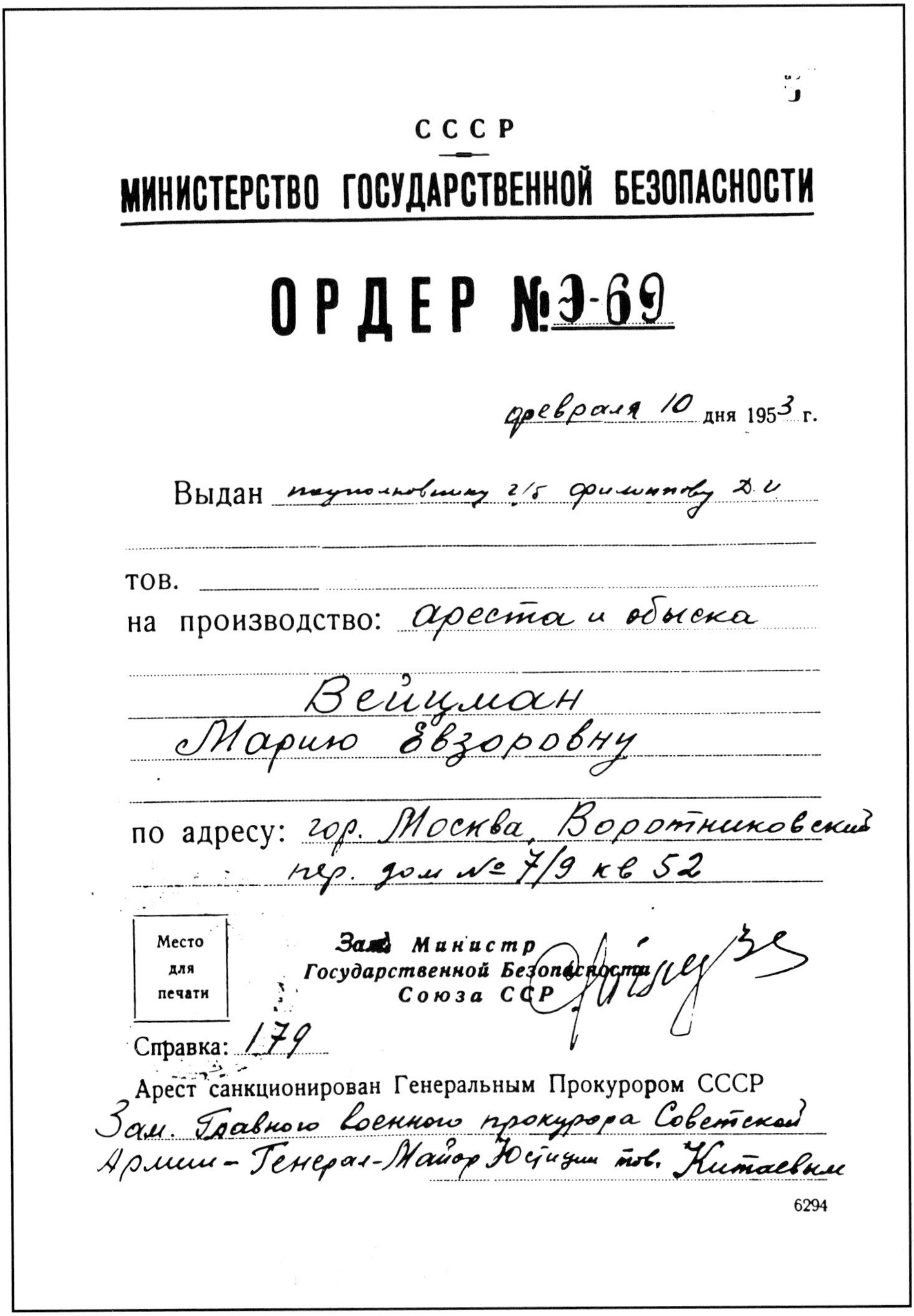

СССР

МИНИСТЕРСТВО ГОСУДАРСТВЕННОЙ БЕЗОПАСНОСТИ

ОРДЕР №Э-69

февраля 10 дня 1953 г.

Выдан уполномоченному г/б Филиппову Д. И.

тов.

на производство: ареста и обыска

Вейцман

Марию Евзоровну

по адресу: гор. Москва, Воротниковский пер. дом № 7/9 кв 52

Место для печати

Зам. Министр Государственной Безопасности Союза ССР

Справка: 179

Арест санкционирован Генеральным Прокурором СССР Зам. Главного военного прокурора Советской Армии - Генерал-Майор Юстиции тов. Китаевым

6294

Fig. 48. A warrant to arrest M. Veĭtsman (Weizmann)

Fig. 49. Professor B. Zbarskiĭ.

Fig. 50. Dr. S. Karpaí with her daughter, 1948.

ПРЕЗИДИУМ АКАДЕМИИ МЕДИЦИНСКИХ НАУК СОЮЗА ССР

ПОСТАНОВЛЕНИЕ

г. Москва — 14. января 1953 г.

6. Об исключении из списка действительных членов и членов-корреспондентов АМН СССР Виноградова В.И., Вовси М.С., Гринштейна А.М., Егорова П.И. как врагов народа.

Докладчик: Академик-секретарь АМН СССР
А.И. Н Е С Т Е Р О В

ПОСТАНОВИЛИ:

В соответствии с постановлением Общего собрания Академии медицинских наук СССР от 14 января 1953 г., принятого на основании ст.19 Устава АМН СССР, и с к л ю ч и т ь из списка действительных членов АМН СССР Вовси М.С., Виноградова В.И., Гринштейна А.М., из списка членов-корреспондентов АМН СССР Егорова П.И. как врагов народа.

П.п. Президент
Академии медицинских наук СССР
Академик (Н.Н.Аничков)

Академик-секретарь
Академии медицинских наук СССР (А.И.Нестеров)

верно: Воз

Fig. 51. A resolution of the Presidium of the Soviet Academy of Medical Sciences to exclude "killer-doctors" from membership.

Fig. 52. A cartoon from *Crocodile* magazine (January 1953) concerning the “doctors’ plot.”

N30

Пролетарии всех стран, соединяйтесь!

СЕКРЕТНО

Коммунистическая Партия Советского Союза. ЦЕНТРАЛЬНЫЙ КОМИТЕТ

Тов.Берия Л.П.

№ П3/I
3.1У.1953г.

Членам ЦК КПСС.
Первым секретарям ЦК Компартий союзных республик, крайкомов и обкомов КПСС.

ВЫПИСКА из протокола № 3 заседания ПРЕЗИДИУМА ЦК КПСС от 3 апреля 1953 года.

Доклад и предложения МВД СССР по "делу о врачах-вредителях".

(т.т.Берия,Ворошилов,Булганин,Первухин, Каганович,Сабуров,Микоян,Хрущев, Молотов,Маленков)

1. Принять предложение Министерства внутренних дел СССР:

а) о полной реабилитации и освобождении из-под стражи врачей и членов их семей, арестованных по так называемому "делу о врачах-вредителях", в количестве 37 человек;

б) о привлечении к уголовной ответственности работников б.МГБ СССР, особо изощрявшихся в фабрикации этого провокационного дела и в грубейших извращениях советских законов.

2. Утвердить прилагаемый текст сообщения для опубликования в центральной печати.

3. Предложить б.Министру государственной безопасности СССР т.Игнатьеву С.Д. представить в Президиум ЦК КПСС об"яснение о допущенных Министерством государственной безопасности грубейших извращениях советских законов и фальсификации следственных материалов.

4. Принять к сведению сообщение тов.Л.П.Берия о том, что Министерством внутренних дел СССР проводятся меры, исключающие возможность повторения впредь подобных извращений в работе органов МВД.

5. Отменить Указ Президиума Верховного Совета СССР от 20 января 1953 г. о награждении орденом Ленина врача Тимашук Л.Ф., как неправильный, в связи с выявившимися в настоящее время действительными обстоятельствами.

Fig. 53. A resolution of the presidium of the Central Committee of the CPSU, adopting the report of the Ministry of Internal Affairs on the “doctors’ plot.”

In the course of the investigation of the JAC case, which was to start a couple of months later, Abakumov (the minister of state security) sent to Stalin the minutes of Z.G. Grinberg's interrogation on December 17, the same day that they had been prepared. These minutes contained Grinberg's new "confession" concerning Zhemchuzhina's involvement in the nationalistic activities of Mikhoels, Lozovskií, and others.

Since Zhemchuzhina was a Party member and—most importantly—a Politburo member's wife, Stalin ordered M.F. Shkiryatov, the real head of the CPC at the CC ACP(b),[262] to get involved in the investigation conducted by Abakumov. Thus was created a Party-police mechanism. On December 26, 1948 Shkiryatov and Abakumov conducted a number of confrontations at Old Square between Zhemchuzhina on the one hand, and M.S. Slutskií (a member of the so-called "twenty," i.e., the board of the Moscow synagogue), Fefer, and Zuskin, and on the other. All three had been arrested by that time; they agreed to cooperate with the investigation and were instructed correspondingly before the confrontations.

On the evening of December 27 the minutes of the confrontations and a memo prepared by Shkiryatov and Abakumov were sent to Stalin. Zhemchuzhina was accused of "politically unworthy behavior," in particular, she was incriminated with the following transgressions:

> For a long period of time . . . [she] had contacts with persons who turned out to be enemies of the people, had a close relationship with them, supported their nationalistic actions, and was their advisor. . . . She conducted negotiations with them; she met Mikhoels on more than one occasion [and], using her position, helped transmit . . . politically harmful, slanderous statements to governmental bodies. She made arrangements for Mikhoels's speech on America at one of the clubs, thus promoting the popularization of the American Jewish anti-Soviet circles. Advertising her close contacts with Mikhoels, she attended his funeral, showed concern for his family; and, by talking about it to Zuskin, gave the nationalists a reason to disseminate provocative gossip about Mikhoels's violent death. Having ignored the rudimentary norms of behavior for a Party member, she attended a Jewish religious service in the synagogue on March 14, 1945,[263] and this discrediting incident became the priceless property of the Jewish religious circles . . . .[264]

---

262. A. Andreyev was only the nominal head of the CPC.

263. This was part of a worldwide religious memorial service for the six million Jews who had been killed by the Nazis during World War II.

264. RTsKhIDNI, f. 589, op. 3, d. 6188, l. 7–24.

On January 21, 1949, Zhemchuzhina was summoned to the CC and arrested. Once in Lubyanka, she was accused of even more crimes, such as her correspondence with her brother, Sam Karp, an American businessman who, at her request, met with Mikhoels in New York in 1943. At a Politburo session of December 30 Zhemchuzhina was dismissed from the Party. This time Molotov voted "yes." He later remembered when, "during the Politburo session, he [Stalin] read the material that the Chekists had collected for him on Polina Semyonovna, my knees trembled."[265] By this time Molotov and Zhemchuzhina had already divorced at Stalin's order and she had moved in with her brother and sister.[266] The dictator no longer trusted his old comrade-in-arms. As early as March 4, 1949 Molotov was dismissed as minister of foreign affairs and head of the Information Committee at the USSR Council of Ministers.[267]

In addition, Zhemchuzhina was accused of numerous faults and abuses in regard to her work, such as losing secret documents, illegally obtaining extra supply funds, making additions to documents, giving out undeserved bonuses, nepotism, favoritism, and so forth.

At the interrogations Zhemchuzhina, despite her weak health, maintained her composure with an enviable firmness and denied all accusations. To break her spirit and to amuse Stalin, Abakumov's people prepared a rather unpleasant surprise for her. As some of Zhemchuzhina's closest assistants at the Chief Administrative Board were arrested with her, the department heads decided to use them not only to expose her faults at work, but also to testify to their chief's intimate vices as well. A certain Ivan Alekseyevich Kh., a young family man, was quickly persuaded to "admit" that Zhemchuzhina had used her position to persuade him to live with her. This is what was required to destroy her composure. Insulted as a person and humiliated as a woman, she called her accuser a scoundrel. The investigation also tried to incriminate Zhemchuzhina with establishing contacts with the International Zionism. They remembered that in 1943 Zhemchuzhina, at Mikhoels's request, met with her brother, the businessman Sam Karp, in New York. The vigilant organs also noted that at a diplomatic reception in honor of Golda Meir, Zhemchuzhina had had a genteel conversation with the guest of honor. But apparently this was not enough to accuse Zhemchuzhina of actual espionage, though Meir had caused Stalin serious distress in this respect. Meir, who had proposed a forthcoming exodus to the

---

265. F.I. Chuyev, *Sto sorok besed s Molotovym* (Moscow, 1991), p. 473. Published in English as *Molotov Remembers: Inside Kremlin Politics. Conversations with Felix Chuev* (Chicago: I.R. Dee, 1993).

266. P.S. Zhemchuzhina's brother, V.I. Karpovskií, was also arrested.

267. This committee had been created in September 1947 to direct the united secret services of the USSR, namely the MGB's External Intelligence Service of the USSR, and the Chief Intelligence Directorate of the Armed Forces of the USSR. Its office was in the building next to the All-Union Agricultural Exhibition, where the Institute of Marxism-Leninism was later situated.

Promised Land, became a legend in the eyes of the Soviet Jews. Stalin could not help but be put on his guard. It was only on April 19, 1949, when Golda Meir left for Israel to accept her appointment as minister of labor, that the fears that tormented Stalin disappeared. Mordekhai Namir, the temporary charge d'affaires, had been appointed her successor in Moscow. Interestingly, Namir was of Russian origin and, before the revolution, had headed the right Zionist-Socialists in Odessa.

The investigation took Zhemchuzhina's recent social status into consideration, and sentenced her to a relatively mile punishment: a five-year exile in the Kustanaí region of Kazakhstan. Nonetheless, the burden of these undeserved offenses was so heavy that she became addicted to alcohol. Later, however, she regained control of herself and would not lower herself morally.

Dora Moiseyevna Khazan was also ostracized. She was the Soviet Union's grand dame number two, the wife of the deputy chairman of the Council of Ministers of the USSR and chairman of the Party Control Commission of the CC ACP(b), A.A. Andreyev. In 1938 she became deputy people's commissar of light industry, and later she moved on to become deputy people's commissar of the textile industry. In early 1949 she was demoted to being the director of the Central Scientific Research Institute of the Woolen Industry of the Ministry of Light Industry. Then on September 22 of that same year, Alekseí Kosygin, the minister of light industry, informed Georgií Malenkov that the Ministry's board considered the work of the Central Scientific Research Institute "absolutely unsatisfactory," and that the board had decided to dismiss Khazan.[268]

In the meantime, beginning in mid-January 1949, the large-scale attempt to root out the "Zionist plot" entered its final phase. Major General A.G. Leonov, the head of the Department to Investigate Cases of Special Importance to the MGB, was placed in charge of the investigation into the "criminal activity of the Jewish nationalists." Leonov, and his assistants, colonels M.T. Likhachyov and V.I. Komarov, contributed more than anyone to the creation of the "case of the Jewish Antifascist Committee." The investigators P.I. Grishayev, B.N. Kuzmin, N.M. Konyakhin, G.A. Sorokin, A.F. Rassypninskií, and others (35 in all) also directly participated in this case.

Komarov was especially thorough. We can judge his character from a letter that this crony of the dethroned Abakumov sent, after his arrest, to Stalin on February 18, 1953, when the anti-Semitic "doctor's plot" was in full swing.

> Dear Comrade Stalin,
>
> . . . Everyone in the Investigation Department knows how much I hated the enemies. I was merciless with them; as they say, I tore their

268. RTsKhIDNI, f. 17, op. 118, d. 562, l. 117–117 obverse, 125.

> souls apart forcing them to confess their hostile affairs and connections. . . . The arrested were literally shaking in front of me, they feared me as they would a fire . . . . The minister himself didn't scare them as did I during the interrogations. The arrested enemies knew very well my hatred toward them and felt it through their skin; they saw in me an investigator who carried out a cruel punitive policy in regard to them, and therefore, as other investigators told me, they tried by any means to avoid meeting with me or . . . being interrogated by me . . . . I was especially merciless with, and I hated the most, the Jewish nationalists, in whom I saw the most dangerous and malicious enemies . . . . In 1948 I was the first to discover, during the interrogation of the arrested, that the Jewish nationalists were interested in obtaining information about the leaders of our Party and government, and as a result of this we later learned about the existence of the Jewish Antifascist Committee . . . . Having learned of the crimes committed by the Jewish nationalists, I grew full of anger toward them, and I ask you to give me an opportunity to take vengeance upon the enemies, with all my hatred for their crimes, for the harm they have caused to our state . . . .[269]

Intensive interrogations of the accused and planned confrontations among them were conducted through early 1950. At Abakumov's order the accused were officially informed in March 1950 that the investigation of their case had ceased. The interest of the leaders of the Department to Investigate Cases of Special Importance in the arrested JAC leaders diminished considerably over the following months. At that time all the forces of the MGB's investigation apparatus were directed toward creating a new anti-Semitic hoax, namely, the "branch" case about the espionage activities of M.S. Aízenshtadt-Zheleznova, N.Ya. Levin, S.D. Persov, and others who worked at the JAC editorial board, and about their "criminal connection" with the leaders of the "Zionist" group unmasked at the Moscow Stalin Automobile Plant (we shall talk of this later). At the same time, Abakumov and his assistants were preparing the legal punishment for the arrested Party and government leaders who belonged to the so-called Leningrad group.

The MGB had no time for the JAC members, who were languishing in Lubyanka. Maybe the MGB people did not know what to do with them, for the "evidence" they had collected could not be considered serious even at that time. Only with regard to Fefer, whose case was still under investigation, could they bring more or less grounded accusations, although these were of doubtful value since Fefer secretly cooperated with the MGB. Therefore, the investigation of JAC case was put aside.

---

269. The records for the revision of the JAC case, vol. 1, p. 23.

This state of affairs continued through mid-1951, when there took place a drastic cleansing within the MGB. This long-brewing perturbation was caused by a letter that M.D. Ryumin (the lieutenant-colonel of the Department to Investigate Cases of Special Importance) sent to Stalin on June 2. Ryumin accused the MGB leaders, primarily minister Abakumov, of having deliberately concealed the terrorist plans by nationalists and enemy agents against the Soviet leadership.[270] Ryumin also accused the chief of the secret police of intentionally halting the investigation of an anti-Soviet youth organization "of a Trotskyite nature" called the Union of Struggle for the Revolutionary Cause (SDR). Created in August 1950, the SDR included freshmen and senior high school students, mainly children of repressed Jews. An 18-year-old history student, B.V. Slutskiĭ, headed the SDR, and he was supported by those who held the same views, among them V.L. Furman, Ye.Z. Gurevich, S.S. Pechuro, G.G. Mazur, I.I. Arginskaya, M.A. Ulanovskaya, F.M. Voin, I.L. Vannikov, N.Ye. Uflyand, and A.Ye. Reĭf. They were all arrested in January, February, and March 1951. It then became known that Gurevich, for instance, not satisfied with the publication of antigovernmental leaflets, more than once proposed an act of terrorism against Malenkov who, he thought, was responsible for all the troubles that had fallen upon the Jews. Ryumin noted that Abakumov tried to show that such activities of this criminal organization were an inoffensive and childish game of politics. For this purpose, Abakumov ordered that "generalized" minutes of the SDR "leader" Slutskiĭ be prepared and sent to the CC, and that Slutskiĭ's evidence concerning the planned acts of terrorism be withdrawn from the minutes. In early 1952 the Military Collegium sentenced Slutskiĭ, Furman, and Gurevich to death. Eleven of their friends were sentenced to 25 years of camp, and two to ten years of camp.

The Kremlin welcomed Ryumin's denunciation of Abakumov as if it were expected. While Ryumin's denunciation may or may not have appeared with Stalin's help, it certainly appeared with the participation of Beria and Malenkov, who had long dreamt of being done with their hated Abakumov.[271]

Beria and Malenkov joined a commission established by the Politburo and

---

270. It was in part Ryumin's phenomenal adventurism and excessive vanity and ambition that made him take this step. But another factor here was the MGB Personnel Directorate's hesitation about the information he had submitted on his relatives, for the investigation had discovered that he had concealed his "socially alien" ancestry when applying to the state security organs. The investigation learned that Ryumin's father had been a rich cattle trader before the revolution, and that his father-in-law had fought in Kolchak's army during the civil war. Worried that this investigation would result in a dismissal at best, Ryumin found a way out by slandering Abakumov.

271. As far back as December 31, 1950 Malenkov, to establish total control over Abakumov and his office, personally signed (which was possible in rare cases) a Politburo resolution to have V.Ye. Makarov, previously the head of the Administrative Department of the CC ACP(b), replace M.G. Svinelupov as vice minister of state security on personnel. This resolution also gave Makarov the "duties of control over the work of the Party organization of the MGB organs." RTsKhIDNI, f. 17, op. 119, d. 177, l. 10.

initiated an investigation into the activities of the MGB leaders. According to their report, on July 11 Stalin had signed a top secret letter of the CC ACP(b), "On a Bad Situation at the MGB of the USSR." The following day Abakumov was further accused of appropriating enemy property taken from Germany, of lacking personal modesty, of demoralization, and of other transgressions. He was arrested and sent to Matrosskaya Tishina, the Ministry of Internal Affair's solitary confinement prison. Almost all his deputies, and almost all the heads of the department of the MGB—and primarily the Department to Investigate Cases of Special Importance who had been in close contact with Abakumov—found themselves behind bars.

L.L. Shvartsman was taken into custody on July 13, 1951. This former investigator had made his career back in the 1930s by falsifying the case of M.Ye. Koltsov (a journalist), A.V. Kosarev (the head of Komsomol), and others who were subsequently shot. Finding himself in his former victims' place, he behaved strangely at the interrogations. He was clearly under psychological stress, and "confessed" that he had participated in the killing of S.M. Kirov, that he had had sexual contacts not only with his own son and daughter, but also with Abakumov and (at night when he broke into the British embassy) with British ambassador Archibald Clark Kerr. Shvartsman further confessed that, in 1945 and 1946, he had been a devout Jewish nationalist, and had later headed a group of legal-organ employees who shared his views. The former investigator went on to slander workers at the MGB Central Apparatus as Zionist-plotters; namely S.G. Pavlovskií, N.M. Borodin, and L.F. Raíkhman (the leaders of the Second Main Directorate);[272] N.I. Eítingon (the deputy head of the Special Bureau, who had been one of the organizers of L.D. Trotskií's murder in 1940); A.Ya. Sverdlov (recruited by the MGB in mid-1930s—in lieu of being incarcerated—when he was arrested in the case of the so-called Youth Counterrevolutionary Organization); M.I. Belkin (the deputy head of the First Directorate of the Foreign Intelligence Service who, in 1949, as head of the Directorate of Counterintelligence of the MGB Central Troops of the Red Army situated in Vienna, was one of the main initiators of the show trial of the Hungarian minister of foreign affairs, Laszlo Reich); Aron Palkin (the head of the "D" Department), and others. L.Ye. Itkin (the deputy head of the Investigation Department of the Directorate of Counter-Intelligence of the Moscow Military District) was also included in that group. A.P. Doron (the MGB public procurator) was also arrested for being a suspected member of this organization of Jewish nationalists.

On September 21, 1951 Shvartsman testified at the interrogation that he had had criminal contacts with L.R. Sheínin, the former officer of the Public Procurator's Office, and that he had supposedly long prevented his arrest as a

---

272. The Second Main Directorate was the domestic counterintelligence service.

member of this organization.[273] On October 20, Sheínin was taken into custody, and was released only in late 1953. Shvartsman, who was responsible for Sheínin's arrest, was sentenced by the Military Board of the Supreme Court and shot in early March 1955.

I.M. Broslavskií, Sheínin's former deputy at the Investigation Department of the Public Procurator's Office, along with his other colleagues, also suffered. In particular, in August 1951 M.Yu. Roginskií, the senior assistant of the procurator general (who had participated in 1946 in the Nuremberg trials as deputy senior procurator from the USSR), was dismissed from his post. In December the same happened to M.Z. Altshuller, the deputy head of the Department of Supervision on the Militia Organs. And in January 1952 M.Ya. Lvov, the procurator of the Department on Special Affairs, was dismissed as well. This list went on. It was also discovered that the nationalistic group inside the MGB, "fearing it would be unmasked by its allies in the JAC (Lozovskií, Fefer, and others), tried to conceal its activities." This discovery was made with the active participation of Ryumin, a skillful investigator of the rank of colonel, whom Stalin had appointed not only as head of the investigation of the "Zionist plot," but also as head of the Department to Investigate Cases of Special Importance. Ryumin was later promoted to the rank of general and appointed vice minister of state security.

He demonstrated his official enthusiasm, examining the protracted investigation of the JAC case, and gave it a new impetus. On the basis of his report, S.D. Ignatyev, the new minister of state security,[274] wrote on August 24

---

273. Shvartsman slandered himself with this statement. The tortured Shimeliovich, on March 11, 1949, had "confessed" that Sheínin was an active nationalist and Mikhoels's friend. But Shimeliovich had made this confession not to Shvartsman, but to Ryumin. To prove his accusation, Shimeliovich said that he had visited Sheínin in the summer of 1948 at his dacha in Serebryannyí Bor, and that he had allegedly heard Sheínin say that it would be good to move to Israel where one could live the rest of one's life quietly, without fear, without thinking about tomorrow. Sheínin also alluded to other items that proved the nationalistic nature of his beliefs, particularly the play he had coauthored with the Brothers Tur (a collective pen-name for L.D. Tubelskií and P.L. Ryzheí), *To Whom Time Is Subject* (*Komu podchinyaetsya vremya*), about an underground group, headed by a watchmaker named Rubinshteín, that operated in the Lithuanian ghetto during the war. The Vakhtangov Theater had staged this play to great success. When Sheínin was arrested, the investigation used this play, together with his other dramatic works—*Beílis's Case* (*Delo Beílisa*) and *A Confrontation* (*Ochnaya stavka*)—as "evidence" of his criminal activity. Sheínin was forced to admit that he headed a nationalistic group of Jewish playwrights that included K.Ya. Finn, A.A. Kron, Ts.Z. Solodar, and others.

274. Though Ignatyev was appointed to this post, he retained his position as head of the Department of the Party, Trade Union, and Komsomol Organs of the CC ACP(b), a post he had served since 1950. His right hand in cleansing the MGB's central apparatus and peripheral organs of "Abakumovites" was A.A. Yepishev. In September the latter was appointed vice minister on personnel of the MGB. This occurred only shortly after he had been moved from Odessa (where he had been first secretary of the Regional Committee) to Moscow to become inspector of the CC. As Khrushchev's man before the war, he was personnel secretary in Khrushchev's CC of the Ukrainian CP(b). However, there

to Malenkov and Beria, telling them that "there are almost no documents to substantiate the evidence given by the arrested about the espionage and nationalistic activity they carried out under the concealment of the JAC." However, the former leaders of the MGB did not give due importance to the examination of the evidence given by the arrested. As was claimed, this evidence contained quite a few facts regarding American espionage. Ignatyev assured the Kremlin bosses that the inactivity under his precursor was a thing of the past, and that the Jewish nationalists' espionage connections "will be fully investigated."[275]

On January 19, 1952 the investigation on the case of the former JAC leaders officially resumed. According to a preplanned scheme to unmask the related alleged espionage plot of the American-Zionist agents, preparations for a closed trial were initiated. Final interrogations were being conducted to determine the degree of secrecy and the ideological perspective of the official and literary materials that had been prepared and published by those who now found themselves imprisoned. These published materials were to be used as evidence of criminal activities. The first stage of this investigation (1949–1950) had followed conventional legal norms—at least formally and for show. But the current proceedings gravely violated even these norms.

On March 5 fifteen cases were brought forth, mainly because the biographies of those under investigation contained facts regarding affairs abroad. Such a selection was dictated by a scheme that the investigation had worked out regarding the Zionist plot in the USSR. The cases of Lozovskií, Fefer, Yuzefovich, Shimeliovich, Kvitko, Markish, Bergelson, Gofshteín, Zuskin, Leon Ya. Talmi,[276]

---

are different opinions regarding his relations with Khrushchev. See, for example, an article by American political scientist A. Sulla in the *Military-Historical Journal* (*Voyenno-istoricheskií zhurnal*), 1993, no. 3, pp. 62–70. Nevertheless, it was Khrushchev who in 1962 appointed Yepishev head of the General Political Directorate of the Army and Navy, a position he maintained up to the time of M.S. Gorbachev.

According to a CC resolution of August 23, 1951 Ignatyev, Yepishev, and others were appointed to leading positions at the MGB; namely, V.I. Alidin became secretary of the Kherson Regional Committee; V.A. Golik became secretary of the Vinnitsa Regional Committee; N.G. Yermolov became secretary of the Voroshilovgrad Regional Committee; N.K. Mazhar became secretary of the Tyumen Regional Committee; S.N. Lyalin became secretary of the Tula Regional Committee; N.R. Mironov became secretary of the Kirovograd Regional Committee; M.P. Svetlichnyí became secretary of the Kustanaí Regional Committee; A.I. Stepanets and A.N. Bezotvetnykh (a leaders of the CC apparatus) became secretaries of the Chelyabinsk Regional Committee. Some of them later climbed quite high up the official ladder, for example, N.R. Mironov, who became the head of the CC Administrative Department. RTsKhIDNI, f. 17, op. 119, d. 43, l. 219–220.

275. Document from the archives of the former KGB.

276. Talmi was a Sovinformburo employee and a journalist/translator who had lived for a good length of time in the USA, where he had been a member of the American Socialist Party. He was arrested on July 3, 1949, making him the last of the "Jewish nationalists" to be apprehended. Though he had not played an active role in the JAC, the Ministry of State Security needed to support its story of an American-Zionist plot.

I.S. Vatenberg, Ch.S. Vatenberg-Ostrovskaya, E.I. Teumin, Shtern, and S.L. Bregman were combined into a joint case, whose inquests, minutes, and other preliminary examination documents consisted of 42 volumes. Ryumin approved the accusations on March 31, 1952, and on April 3 Ignatyev forwarded this to Stalin, with copies to Malenkov and Beria.[277] On April 7 the summary investigation was transmitted to the MCSC.

The tribunal's work (which the official documents referred to as the closed meeting of the Military Board of the Supreme Court) began at 12 o'clock on May 8. The judges entered the Dzerzhinskiĭ club hall of the Ministry of State Security, and the accused were escorted in. The opening process took place in the presence of the investigators and other state security employees. A. Cheptsov, the lieutenant general of justice, took the chair. Dmitriev and I. Zaryanov, the major generals of justice, were assigned to be members of the Military Collegium, and M. Afanasyev, the senior lieutenant, was assigned secretary. The meetings were conducted without the participation of representatives for the prosecution, defense, or witnesses.

Only Fefer and Teumin admitted to the court's accusations; Lozovskiĭ, Markish, Shimeliovich, and Bregman categorically rejected the accusations; and the remainder of the defendants agreed only partially. From the start the court had to make every effort to conceal the groundlessness of the accusations, which were based only upon fabrications. For instance, during the preliminary investigation the court attempted to establish that Lozovskiĭ had delivered secret material on English foreign diplomacy from Institute No. 205[278] to Ben Zion Goldberg, the American journalist. In response, Lozovskiĭ reasonably requested that the court attach this material to the case file. Ryumin would not allow this, as the secrets were obviously forged. N.N. Pukhlov, the former director of Institute No. 205, when questioned in the course of the trial, declared that the material in question was merely a review based on data published in the foreign press, and was not secret.[279] Nevertheless, the court trusted completely the results of the so-called experts, who, following the investigators' dictates, concluded during the preliminary investigation that the materials prepared by the JAC were secret and nationalistic.

This trial was a fiction, a mere formal action directed by the Ministry of State

277. Ryumin prepared the accompanying letter, which stated: "Here is . . . a copy of the accusation in the case of the Jewish nationalists and American spies Lozovskiĭ, Fefer, and others. I inform you that the investigative case was forwarded to the MCSC with a proposal to sentence Lozovskiĭ, Fefer, and their allies, except for Shtern, to death. Shtern should be sent to the outlying areas of the country for 10 years." Thus was the fate of the arrested JAC leaders sealed before the actual sentence was passed.

278. *Translator's note:* Institute No. 205 was the Institute of Scientific Information attached to the Department of External Policy of the CC ACP(b).

279. RTsKhIDNI, f. 589, op. 3, d. 15624, l. 339.

Security on Stalin's orders. Aleksandr Cheptsov, the chairman of the Military Collegium, later claimed that Ignatyev and Ryumin had informed him, before the trial had begun, that the Politburo had approved a resolution to execute all the accused except for L.S. Shtern.[280] Cheptsov, though, had his doubts about what he had been told, and thought Ryumin was bluffing. Ryumin, after all, was an upstart who had obtained Stalin's special confidence and who had placed under his command Ignatyev, who had no experience in the affairs of the political police. Cheptsov was a professional who had successfully climbed the official ladder, starting as a senior clerical worker in 1926 and finally achieving, in 1948, the chairmanship of the Military Collegium of the Supreme Court. He could not but feel indignant at Ryumin's unceremonious attitude toward the trial. Moreover, the accused were subjected to psychological and physical treatment between their meetings with the investigators. And since the trial was held at Lubyanka, Ryumin installed listening devices in the judges' consultative room.[281]

To neutralize at least somewhat the total control of the Ministry of State Security, Cheptsov transferred some of the closed inquests of the accused, the witnesses, and the experts to the Military Collegium building. He was completely convinced that the JAC case had been fabricated by the inquest, and in July 1952 he interrupted the trial and submitted the case for a supplementary examination. This made a fight with the omnipotent Ryumin inevitable. To protect himself, Cheptsov addressed the leaders of the various power organizations; namely G.N. Safonov, the procurator general of the USSR; A.A. Volin, the chairman of the Supreme Court of the USSR; M.F. Shkiryatov, the chairman of the Party Control Commission; N.M. Shvernik, the chairman of the Presidium of the Supreme Soviet of the USSR; G.P. Gromov, the head of the Administrative Department of the CC ACP(b); and P.K. Ponomarenko, the secretary of the CC. All these officials sympathized with Cheptsov and unanimously agreed that this problem could be resolved only by Malenkov.

Cheptsov soon met with Malenkov; Ryumin and Ignatyev were also present. Malenkov listened to Cheptsov's arguments about the supplementary examination of the case, and to his complaints about Ryumin's unlawful actions. Ryumin responded adroitly and immediately, and Malenkov said to Cheptsov: "Well, do you want to bring us to these criminals' knees? The people have approved the sentence on this case. The Politburo of the Central Committee has investigated this case three times. Carry out the Politburo's resolution."[282] The circle was

280. *Izvestiya TsK KPSS*, 1989, no. 12, p. 38.

281. This and the following facts related to the JAC trial are given as they appear in a letter from Aleksandr A. Cheptsov, the chairman of the MCSC, to Marshal G.K. Zhukov, a member of the CC CPSU presidium. Excerpts are published in *Detektiv i politika* (*Detective Stories and Politics*), 1992, no. 3, pp. 196–201.

282. *Detektiv i politika* (*Detective Stories and Politics*), 1992, no. 3, p. 200.

closed; it was apparent that Malenkov's words clearly reflected Stalin's will.

It was some years later that Cheptsov sent G.K. Zhukov (the minister of defense) a verbose memo dated August 15, 1957 favorably recounting his actions during the JAC trial. This démarche of an experienced Soviet legal expert, who signed more than one death sentence in the cases of the Jewish nationalists, was not accidental. A CC session in late June 1957 sharply criticized G.M. Malenkov for his participation in "anti-Party groups," and removed him from the CC presidium. He was then exiled to eastern Kazakhstan to direct the work of the power stations. Cheptsov could not afford to lose his guard. The very same Zhukov, who then became a member of the CC presidium, during that session harshly accused Malenkov of being Stalin's close aide in organizing the postwar repressions in the country."[283]

Cheptsov saw the unexpected squabble in the corridors of power as a favorable opportunity to dissociate himself from the formerly omnipotent, but now toppled, grandee; and so he transferred his own guilt to Abakumov, blaming him for the former regime's crimes. So, taking this chance, Cheptsov now tried to convince Zhukov that during the investigation of the JAC case he had been guided exclusively by the desire to "establish objective truth," and that he had striven against Ryumin's "unlawful actions." Yet after Stalin's death, and in the course of the investigation of Ryumin's crimes, P.I. Grishayev, a former investigator in the JAC case, declared that, according to Ryumin:

> . . . during the investigation of JAC case, Comrade Cheptsov appealed to the "instance" when he spoke of the shortcomings and violations in the case; however . . . Comrade Cheptsov criticized the case for being of a doubtful nature, and for the arrested not being unmasked and the roots of their crimes not being discovered."[284]

Between July 11 and 18, 1952 the MCSC condemned Lozovskiĭ, Fefer, Yuzefovich, Shimeliovich, Kvitko, Markish, Bergelson, Gofshteĭn, Zuskin, Talmi, Vatenberg, Vatenberg-Ostrovskaya, and Teumin to death. Shtern was sentenced to three and one-half years in prison, followed by five years in the town of Dzhambul in Kazakhstan. S.L. Bregman, the former deputy minister of state control of the RSFSR and also involved in the JAC case, was then suffering from heart, kidney, and vascular diseases. Unable to withstand the ordeal, he fell

---

283. At the June 1957 session of the CC CPSU, Procurator General R.A. Rudenko asked Malenkov whether he had informed Stalin of Cheptsov's request for further inquiry into the JAC case. Malenkov replied, "I did not dare not tell Stalin all that he said." *Istoricheskiĭ arkhiv* (*Historical Archives*), 1991, no. 1, p. 59.

284. A.N. Yakovlev, ed., *Reabilitatsiya: Politicheskiye protsessy 30—50-kh godov* [*Rehabilitation: Political Processes of the 30s Through the 50s*] (Moscow, 1992), p. 326.

unconscious on June 16, 1952 and was hospitalized at the medical unit of the Butyrskaya prison. Accordingly, the Military Board ceased examining his case, and on July 9 separated his case from the others. Then on January 23, 1953 Bregman passed away in the prison hospital due to "heart failure."[285]

The sentences were, of course, entirely disproportionate to the "crimes." For example, the artist Zuskin pled guilty to the charge that "together with Mikhoels he directed plays in the theater in which the Jewish olden times, small town traditions and mode of life, and the tragic predestination of the Jews were portrayed, thus exciting the nationalistic moods of the Jewish spectators; [and that he] had sent a number of articles to America on the nationalistic nature of the state of the arts in the USSR."[286]

The poet Kvitko was shot on the grounds that "having returned to the USSR in 1925 from abroad, he joined the nationalistic Jewish literary group 'Fight,' headed by the Trotskyites in Kharkov. Being, from the beginning of its establishment, assistant to the executive secretary of the JAC, he entered the criminal plot with the committee leaders and helped them in collecting materials about the USSR economy to be sent to the USA."[287]

The accused all appealed for mercy to the Presidium of the Supreme Soviet of the USSR, categorically denying their faults. Their appeals were denied, and they were executed on August 12, 1952.

The JAC case was only the tip of the iceberg. The larger—and almost invisible—part of the repressions consisted of a great number of other cases, all fabricated by the Ministry of State Security in connection with the JAC's defeat. These related cases had 110 victims—ten were shot; 20 were sentenced to 25 years in reform camps, 3 were sentenced to 20 years in reform camps; 11 to 15 years of exile, 50 to 10 years, 2 to 8 years, 1 to 7 years, 2 to 5 years, and 1 to 10 years. As for the remaining 10 people, 5 died during the course of the examination, and the other 5 cases were closed shortly after their arrest.[288] Among those who suffered the accusations of espionage, Zionism, and nationalistic activity, the large majority were public figures of the Jewish national culture. It was from the end of 1948 through the beginning of 1949 that this culture was defeated.

---

285. RTsKhIDNI, f. 589, op. 3, d. 15624, l. 323–329.

286. RTsKhIDNI, f. 589, op. 3, d. 15624, l. 324.

287. RTsKhIDNI, f. 589, op. 3, d. 15624, l. 325.

288. *Izvestiya TsK KPSS*, 1989, no. 12, p. 40.

Three

Ethnocide

Having rated Zionism with American imperialism as the wickedest of postwar enemies, the Stalinist leadership declared war against it. The Soviet Jews became involuntary hostages and had to prove their loyalty to the regime. They wanted to dispel any suspicions that they might become a Zionist "fifth column" in the USSR. The only way out was radical assimilation—a forced, agonizing, and not at all bloodless process that eliminated all that made a Jew a Jew. National culture, traditions, originality, history, language were all cut off from the youth. Thus under the control of state security, Judaism did not present a serious threat to the regime. Stalin perceived the Jewish cultural and intellectual elite—who widely influenced the hearts and minds of their fellow tribesmen through theater, radio, museums, Yiddish publications, and so forth—as the primary potential conveyor of Zionist ideas. Accordingly, in early 1949 Stalin would not confine himself to the elimination of the JAC, but struck a blow to the hearth of Jewish culture.

Arrests of the Intellectuals

On February 8 he signed the Politburo resolution (prepared by Fadeyev) on closing the Jewish writers' unions in Moscow, Kiev, and Minsk, and on closing the Yiddish literary periodicals *Geimland* (Moscow) and *Der Stern* (Kiev)[1]. For the

---

1. It is extremely significant that it was Fadeyev himself who had initiated the creation of the Union of Jewish Writers in Moscow. The chairman of this union, L.M. Kvitko, testified to this at the closed proceedings of the JAC case in May 1952. Fadeyev had also proposed the publication of Yiddish literary anthologies in Moscow and Kiev. The CC secretariat approved his proposal on July 28, 1947. RTsKhIDNI, f. 17, op. 117, d. 877, l. 18–19.

sake of "orientation," the CC apparatus prepared for Stalin a certificate justifying these maneuvers. This certificate showed that 45 Jewish writers were members of the Moscow union, 6 were members of the Minsk union, and 26 were members of the Kievan union. It also showed that the principle of national uniformity that lay in the unions' organizational grounds was erroneous.[2] Further, the certificate stated that the unions had no perspective for a quantitative growth in personnel, and that there was little demand for Jewish writings. Finally, it condemned the anthology journals as especially nationalistic. "Incriminating" fragments from the writings in question, together with negative commentaries, were the basis of these rather categorical appraisals. For example, the certificate claimed that Der Nister's essay, "With the Immigrants to Birobidzhan,"[3] develops Zionist ideas with such statements as "Let the house of Israel again be built" and "How good it is that, in the USSR, there have already appeared brave little Davids who must actively arm themselves still more with the pride and self-respect of David, with his love to his people . . . so that no Goliaths may ever frighten them."[4] There was another argument, too: "publication of the anthologies *Geimland* and *Der Stern* is unprofitable."[5]

To carry out the formalities, Fadeyev coordinated his Kiev and *Der Stern* proposals with Ukrainian CC CP(b) secretary N.S. Khrushchev; and coordinated his Minsk proposal with Belorussian CP(b) secretary N.I. Gusarov. In actuality, this Politburo resolution was a mere formality; there was no need to close the Jewish literary unions or publications, as almost all the Jewish writers had been arrested.

In late January 1949, together with the JAC activists mentioned in the previous chapter, the literati Goldshteín, Markish, Kvitko, Bergelson, and Fefer, the writer Pinsokh M. Kaganovich (Der Nister), the poet Samuil Galkin, the critic and playwright Íekhezkiil Dobrushin, the writers Dmitrií Stonov and Noyakh Lurye, and others were taken to Lubyanka. Literati and journalists who had worked with the JAC and *Einikeit* in preparing articles, essays, reports, and other materials for further publication abroad also found themselves in Lubyanka. It was they who suffered most.

On April 4 Miriam S. Aízenshtadt was arrested. Aízenshtadt, who published her articles under the pen name "Zheleznova," was an extremely energetic and forceful journalist. Her husband, Leopold Aízenshtadt, was a lieutenant colonel and editor of a Ministry of Armed Forces illustrated publication, and Zheleznova

---

2. In other words, it was erroneous because Stalin's ideologists were opposed to the principle of isolation (including cultural isolation) of national minorities. This principle, they believed, was an obstacle to assimilation.

3. "S pereselentsami v Birobidzhan."

4. RTsKhIDNI, f. 17, op. 118, d. 305, l. 21–22.

5. RTsKhIDNI, f. 17, op. 118, d. 305, l. 22; Document from the archives of the former KGB.

used his connections to gain access to military headquarters, offices of the higher nomenclatura, and defense plants. In 1943 she wrote an essay about L.R. Gonor, the director of the Barricades Plant in Stalingrad. After the war she published essays about vocational schools and the Moscow Stalin Automobile Plant's Palace of Culture. At Mikhoels's request she contacted the leaders of the Military Department Award Board,[6] and, on the basis of the information she obtained from them, prepared 30 essays about 85 Jews who had been awarded as Heroes of the Soviet Union during the war. She sent these essays to Ben Zion Goldberg, the American journalist, in April 1946. That same year she wrote to Suslov about a collection of M.Ye. Saltykov-Shchedrin's works, protesting the inclusion of a satirical tale of a Jewish usurer, a tale she considered anti-Semitic. On November 22, 1950 a closed session of the MCSC,[7] headed by A.A. Cheptsov, sentenced her to death. In April 1954 this very same Cheptsov told the mother of Ye.S. Kazarinskaya (a journalist who had been shot) that her daughter had been sentenced to ten years of prison without the right of maintaining correspondence, and that she had died in the camp from pneumonia on October 10, 1951.[8]

That same day the MCSC also sentenced the writer Samuil D. Persov to death. Like Aĭzenshtadt-Zheleznova, he had cooperated, through the JAC, with the American Jewish press. The Americans were interested in learning about Stalin's daughter, Svetlana, and in 1943 they asked Persov to send them materials on such things as what she considered important in her life, her cultural tastes, her attitude toward the West, and how she spent her leisure time. During the war Persov traveled extensively throughout the country, visiting Belorussia, Lithuania, and the Ukraine, and collecting a wealth of material about Jewish heroes, from simple fighters in the partisan detachments to generals. He gathered information on Jews who had made great contributions to creating Soviet military equipment, such as S.A. Lavochkin, a rabbi's son and aircraft designer; and A.I. Bykhovskiĭ, director of the Artillery Plant in Motovilikha (Perm). He sent all this material to the USA.

After the war Persov actively participated in the preparation of a book called *The Partisan Flame*,[9] which was to be published by Der Emes. However, the editor-in-chief, M.S. Belenkiĭ, later recalled that in 1946 the CC had deemed this work harmful and nationalistic, and ordered all copies to be destroyed. Nonetheless Persov continued working. In 1946 and 1947 he prepared a series of

---

6. In particular she cooperated with Aron Tokar, the deputy head of the Department of the Directorate on Awards and Conferrals of Military Ranks of the Ministry of Armed Forces of the USSR, who was subsequently arrested and, on July 23, 1951, sentenced to 25 years of camp.

7. Military Collegium of the Supreme Court of the USSR.

8. Document from the archives of the former KGB.

9. *Partizanskaya slava.*

essays entitled "The Jews from the Stalin Plant in Moscow,"[10] some articles about V.E. Dymshits, manager of the Zaporozhstroí trust, and other articles on Dinamo, the Moscow Electrical Machinery Construction Plant.

Zheleznova, Persov, and the others had sent all this material and more to America. The investigation now concluded that this material had been coded espionage information related to the Soviet Union's industrial potential. Accordingly the Moscow Stalin Automobile Plant and the other institutions that Persov and his colleagues had described in the essays became the objects of operative "study" by the state security organs as potential centers of American-Zionist agents. (We shall learn more about this below.) Moreover, Persov, under torture, "mentioned" some names. For example, in describing his 1946 meeting with Ben Zion Goldberg, Persov claimed he had mentioned some influential Soviet Jews, among them the academic B.I. Zbarskií, who headed the Biochemistry Laboratory attached to Lenin's Mausoleum. Upon hearing this, the American visitor supposedly exclaimed, "So, Lenin's body is guarded by the Jews!" It is not surprising that Zbarskií was later arrested.[11]

The investigation materials contained extensive lists of Jewish literati, journalists, and those who had been so imprudent as to send articles, essays, or other writings to the JAC editorial board for further publication in the Jewish press abroad. Almost all of these people were sooner or later captured by the millstone of Stalin's punitive machine which cruelly and methodically ground out their fates. On January 25, 1950 the poet/playwright S.Z. Galkin was sentenced to ten years of camp. S.V. Gordon, a Jewish literary man, was sentenced to fifteen years on July 21, 1951. His term was longer probably because he had seen Kuíbyshev during the war and had later prepared, for the JAC, material on Aviation Plant No. 1 and State Bearing Plant No. 4. After the war Gordon continued actively cooperating with the JAC and *Einikeit*. On several occasions he had taken business trips to the Crimea and the Ukraine, and had visited Birobidzhan, which was closed to visitors.[12]

On February 25, 1952 the Jewish Ukrainian writer A.Ya. Kagan was sentenced to the so-called Abakumovian "quarter," i.e., to 25 years in reform camps. Such a long term was primarily for his "crimes" of publishing his article on "The Jews in Kiev"[13] in the West and for giving the JAC, in 1948, material on

10. "Yevreí zavoda imeni Stalina v Moskve." The plant director, A.F. Eídinov, had allowed Persov to visit, introduced him to the Jewish machine-operators, and described the technical characteristics of the new governmental car ZIS-110. Persov also met with B.Yu. Persin, director of the Food Department; and F.B. Belikhina, director of the plant's Palace of Culture. In 1950 all these people became the subjects of repression.

11. Document from the archives of the former KGB.

12. Document from the archives of the former KGB.

13. "Yevreí v Kieve."

Dashava-Kiev, a "strategic" gas pipeline.[14] Other Jewish literati and journalists were dealt with in a similar manner.

After Stalin's death, those who survived were released. In exchange for the health and joy that had been robbed of them, they were given rehabilitation certificates; but their health and their faith in justice were forever lost. Less fortunate were those who never lived to escape the tenacious arms of the GULAG. On October 31, 1950 Professor I.M. Nusinov died in the Lefortovo prison "from a tumor of the hard brain membrane." His crime was having sent, in 1947, 15 articles to the USA through the JAC. Then in December 1950 the Jewish literary patriarch, Der Nister, died from heart disease while in camp. His crime was that he, together with Ukrainian migrants, had in July 1947 gone to Birobidzhan and had written about this in an essay. It was this essay with which he was incriminated.[15]

A no less savage reprisal was prepared for the JAC staff and the *Einikeit* employees who had solicited, edited, and published the pieces and then, through the Sovinformburo, sent them abroad. According to the MGB, the JAC and *Einikeit*, having created a broad network of staff writers and freelance correspondents,[16] thus collected "espionage" information throughout the Soviet Union. Abakumov, with his assistants from the MGB's Department to Investigate Cases of Special Importance, threatened the Kremlin leadership with this large-scale activity of the "Zionist agents," and thus obtained permission to carry out the mass arrests of Jews. From 1949 through 1951 S.N. Khaĭkin and N.Ya. Levin (the JAC editors-in-chief), A.Yu. Gontar (the senior editor), G.M. Kheĭfets (the executive assistant of the JAC who regulated the sending of the articles abroad), M.M. Grubian (the JAC editor at the Belorussian news desk), S.O. Kotlyar (the director of the JAC editorial Board), and others were taken into custody. *Einikeit*'s editor-in-chief Gershon Zhits, his deputy Semyon Rabinovich, and other *Einikeit* employees suffered the same fate. Lev Strongin (the director of Der Emes), Moiseĭ Belenkiĭ (the editor-in-chief who in 1946 had also been the director of the Jewish School of Arts), and others were arrested. All endured the terrors of Stalin's prisons and camps. Kotlyar died in prison in 1951. Zhits died in the Butyrskaya

14. Ibid.

15. Ibid.

16. According to the investigation materials, the "spies," (in reality, the network of ordinary JAC correspondents) divided their tasks as follows: Persov and Zheleznova collected "intelligence" information on Moscow and the Moscow Region, A. Kagan on the Ukraine, I. Platner on Belorussia, G. Osherovich on Lithuania, Z. Kagan on Latvia, and I. Emiot on Birobidzhan. The list went on. In addition, the investigation had an extensive list of freelance correspondents for *Einikeit*, which included the employees of Dinamo, Red Proletarian (Krasnyĭ Proletariĭ), the Stalin Automobile Plant, and Metrostroĭ (all Moscow enterprises); some scientists, including the academics I.I. Mints, S.I. Volfkovich, A.N. Frumkin, B.I. Zbarskiĭ; and others.

prison hospital on October 8, 1954. The former editor-in-chief of the JAC, Naum Levin, was arrested on September 17, 1949, when he was an editor for a book publisher called Physical Training and Sports. On November 22, 1950 a closed session of the MCSC, headed by A.A. Cheptsov, sentenced him to death.[17]

Having interrogated dozens of suspects, the MGB obtained information not only on those who had had relatively stable and long-lasting relations with the JAC, but also about those who had only occasionally contacted the JAC. Thus Natan Zabara, a journalist who from 1945 through January 1947 had worked in Berlin as the Soviet correspondent for *Tägliche Rundschau* (a publication of the Soviet occupation administration), was taken into custody. On September 11, 1950 he testified, during the interrogation, that while in Berlin he had often met with Erich Nelgans, the head of Misrachi, the local Zionist organization. Nelgans had introduced Zabara to Eisenberg and Rock, American servicemen who represented Joint; and to Captain Shubov, the rabbi of the American garrison in Berlin.[18] The five of them together supposedly spread propaganda among Soviet Jews stationed in Berlin—civil as well as military—suggesting they move to Palestine. These new acquaintances provided Zabara with Zionist literature (i.e., such as the texts of Chaim Weizmann's public speeches); and in early 1947 Zabara illegally brought this the USSR and transmitted it to his good friends Fefer and Mikhoels at the JAC.

Meanwhile, like ripples in a pond, the persecutions drifted outwards from Moscow to other cities and regions. Jewish national and cultural institutions were abolished in Leningrad, the Baltics, Moldavia, the Ukraine, and the Far East Region; and all who had contacts with these organizations were arrested. Z.M. Akselrod, the executive secretary of the periodical anthology *Der Stern*; E.G. Spivak, the director of the office of Jewish culture at the Academy of Sciences of the Ukraine; the writer M. Talalayevskií, and others were arrested in Kiev. Spivak died in the MGB's internal prison on April 4, 1950.

Denied the influx of youth, the Judaic religion was thus doomed to extinction. Yet this religion had not represented a serious threat to the regime, for it was completely under the control of the state security organs, and this was why the majority of the Jewish community's leaders did not suffer at that time. The repressive regime preserved them for the sake of show. However, on August 18,

17. Document from the archives of the former KGB. This sentence took into account the accusation that in 1946, having established contacts with the American spy B.Z. Goldberg who visited the USSR, Levin had been given an espionage assignment. In that same year, Levin entrusted S.D. Persov with collecting materials on the Moscow Stalin Automobile Plant that were later sent to the USA. On January 26, 1956 the MCSC revoked the sentence of November 22, 1950 and, for lack of corpus delicti, halted the investigation of Levin's case.

18. In the archival documents, Erich Nelgans, Eisenberg, Rock, and Shubov are transliterated into Russian. The correct German and American spellings are uncertain.

1951 Ignatyev, the minister of state security, sent Malenkov a note accusing S.M. Shlifer (a member of the board of directors of the Moscow Synagogue) of having contacts with functionaries of the Israeli diplomatic mission in Moscow and with the leaders of the JAC, and therefore suggesting that he be arrested. Nonetheless, the CC would not sanction this arrest. The functionaries at Old Square were apparently counting on later using Shlifer to their advantage in propagandistic operations. Thus it was no accident that in January 1953 Shlifer made a statement practically supporting the accusations set forth against the "doctor-saboteurs."

Since Shlifer's arrest misfired, the MGB had to satisfy itself with jailing a number of "Jewish clerics" of a lower rank. Thus on November 19, 1950 one of the oldest members of the Moscow Jewish community, I.M. Averbukh, was taken to Lubyanka.[19] Other religious activists—Gurari, Dubinin, Zilberman, and

---

19. According to the resolution of the Special Meeting of May 12, 1951, I.M. Averbukh was for five years incarcerated in the special MGB prison and his property was confiscated. Averbukh was then already over 70 and had long led the life of an inconspicuous Soviet pensioner; so in order to justify its repressive action, the MGB remembered his postwar membership on the board of the Moscow synagogue. He was later accused of having been a leader of the "Zionist Underground Center of Jewish Clerics and Nationalists," an organization of the "Misrachi" party, created in 1902. According to the materials used in the investigation, this center was founded in 1922 when Dr. I.B. Rosen, the president of Agro-Joint (the American Agricultural Jewish Society), visited Moscow. Rosen began actively to finance the Jewish religious community in Moscow, some of whose leaders (mainly those of the orthodox Hasidic stance) were members of "Misrachi." Funds were sent through Merkoz (Center), Misrachi's administrative body, in order to maintain the peripheral Jewish communities in Kiev, Minsk, Rostov-na-Donu, Kharkov, Leningrad, as well as illegal heders and yeshivot. The leaders of the Moscow community—represented by Sh.Ya. Medalye [Medaliah] (the Hasidic senior rabbi of the synagogue), M.D. Braude (the director of the board of the Moscow community), E.Ya. Sheptovitskií (Braude's deputy), A.L. Fuks, and others—maintained steady contacts with Rabbi Shekhter in Kiev, the Hasidic Rabbi Leívika Shneerson in Dnepropetrovsk, Rabbi Bogatin in Saratov, and so forth. Medaliah and others were later accused also of having established contacts with the Jewish community in Riga (Rabbi Shneerson) and with the London Jewish Committee.

In late 1937 an NKVD secret informant tipped off Lubyanka that Medaliah and one of the leaders of the Moscow community, I.S. Uryson, had declared to their accomplices that "The Jewish religion in the USSR is constantly repressed, it's forced to go underground. Meanwhile it flourishes in the West. The Jewish people don't exist as a nation. Birobidzhan is a Soviet colony. The Jewish people have to unite . . . in order to escape from the attack of communism in the USSR." The mass arrests of "Zionist-religionists" now started. Braude, Medaliah, Rabinovich (Medaliah's son-in-law), Sheptovitskií, and others were taken into custody. Averbukh was able to avoid this fate perhaps because he had moved from Moscow and had vanished into the province for a while. However, 13 years later the inevitable happened: the punitive palm of the "organs" caught this old religious Jew and put him into the depths of the GULAG.

Many years passed, and though Averbukh had long since passed away, the accusations of political crimes brought against him ("participation in an anti-Soviet nationalistic organization, anti-Soviet propaganda") remained. It was only on May 5, 1993 that the Judicial Collegium of the Supreme Court of

Tverskoí—also found themselves in Lubyanka.

The Museum of Local Lore, History, and Economy of the Jewish Autonomous Region in Birobidzhan was closed. So was the Jewish Museum in Vilnius, the Historical-Ethnographic Museum of Georgian Jewry in Tbilisi. Aron (Aharon) Krikheli, the director of that museum, was arrested as well. Then Moscow International Radio's Yiddish broadcasts were terminated in mid-February 1949.[20]

The Closing of the Theaters

The Jewish theaters were in their last months. The strangulation of these theaters paralleled the apparatus games. The process began with two decrees (March 4, 1948 and February 6, 1949) of the Council of Ministers of the USSR "On the Reduction of State Subsidies for Theaters" and "On Measures to Improve Their Financial Activity." These decrees at first significantly reduced financial aid to many theaters, including Jewish theaters, and then entirely eliminated it. It would seem that, devoid of subsidy, all the theaters would face identical disasters. However, this was not to be. The state continued to fund theaters—including national theaters—except for the Jewish ones. On July 6, 1949 the Cultural Bureau of the Council of Ministers increased subsidies to Yakut theaters by 1 800 000 rubles, to Tuva theaters by 500 000 rubles, and to the Altaí Mountain theaters by 450 000 rubles.[21]

References to their unprofitability served to camouflage the true reason for the cessation of funds to Jewish theaters. Stalin saw the Jewish theaters as hotbeds of Zionism, and from the end of 1948 the Stalinist leadership planned to liquidate them. It is indeed true that the younger generation of Jews did not, for the most part, speak Yiddish, and had drifted far from their national culture. Accordingly the attendance at the Jewish theaters did indeed steadily decline over the years. Yet even some of the assimilated Jewish intelligentsia tried to promote season tickets for the Moscow Jewish Theater. Golda Meir had been solemnly received at the Moscow Jewish Theater (which was displaying the Israeli flag) on September 16, 1948. She knew of the theater's disastrous financial state and bought several such season tickets to be passed on to Jews who needed them.

Nonetheless, as is well known, in a totalitarian state politics and ideology always predominate over economics, and the case of the Jewish theaters was no exception. On February 8, 1949 N.I. Gusarov, secretary of the CP(b) CC of Belorussia, wrote to Malenkov for permission to close down BELGOSET,

---

the Russian Federation disaffirmed the resolution of the Special Meeting of May 12, 1951.

20. B. Pinkus, *The Jews of the Soviet Union* (Cambridge, 1988), pp. 203–205.

21. RTsKhIDNI, f. 17, op. 132, d. 240, l. 89.

emphasizing political reasons:

> The Jewish Dramatic Theater of the BSSR has consistently presented an ideologically incorrect political repertoire, idealizing, in its plays, the patriarchal lifestyle of the petit bourgeois layers of the prerevolutionary Jewish population, and praising life in the capitalist countries. For a long time the leading playwright of this theater was I. Fefer, who has now been exposed as a Jewish nationalist. In a number of his productions (for example, in Galkin's play, *The Musician*)[22] he portrayed America as the "Promised Land," the only place where Jewish talents can flourish and find fulfillment. The theater produced *Wandering Stars*[23] by Sholem Aleichem (directed by I. Dobrushin), but misinterpreted the meaning of Sholem Aleichem's work and propagandized a pro-American attitude, and thus the theater serves the purpose of inculcating in the consciousness of the Jewish population the idea that the Jewish theater is not a typical cultural establishment, but the center of the special "Jewish deed."
>
> The propaganda of this special "Jewish deed" assumes a character in contraposition to the socialist interests of the working people of all other nationalities of the USSR. Nationalistic moods have long been spread among the theater's workers [to the effect] that Russians and Belorussians had not defended the Jews from the Germans and had helped the Germans destroy them, and were therefore guilty of the deaths of thousands of Jews. Such slanderous inventions became more intense, especially after the leader of the Jewish nationalists, Mikhoels, visited Minsk.
>
> The Jewish Theater serves an insignificant portion of the Minsk population, and it is unprofitable. The theater does not have its own premises; therefore it continues to rehearse twice a week at the Belorussian Yanka Kupala State Dramatic Theater, which is the leading theater in the republic and serves the majority of the Minsk population . . . . "[24]

Though the Party leaders in Moscow had apparently planned to issue an order to close the theater, they were in no hurry to implement that plan. More exactly, they made a show of not participating in closing Jewish cultural establishments. Like Cæsar's wife, the CC CPSU(b) had to remain above reproach—and God forbid that someone would have reason to accuse its members of anti-Semitism. The task of bringing about the "soft" suffocation (i.e.,

22. *Muzykant.*
23. *Bluzhdayushchiye zvyozdy. Editor's note:* The English version was published as *Wandering Star.*
24. RTsKhIDNI, f. 17, op. 132, d. 239, l. 4–5.

repression without obvious brute force) of Jewish culture fell onto the shoulders of Dmitriĭ Trofimovich Shepilov.

Shepilov, born in 1905, had come to the apparatus in 1935. He served in the Political Department of the Soviet Army from 1941–1946, and from 1946–1947 he served as editor for *Pravda*'s Propaganda Department and as first deputy chairman of the Directorate of Propaganda and Agitation. When this directorate was reorganized in the summer of 1948 and became the Department of Propaganda and Agitation of the Central Committee, Shepilov was appointed its chief. Since he had graduated from the Moscow State University and had had a long record of service in the apparatus, Shepilov's reputation, in contrast to Aleksandrov's, was not tainted with chauvinism. He was known as a sensible person and the liberal high-ranking Party official in intellectual circles.

Malenkov ordered an investigation the Belorussian State Jewish Theater (BELGOSET), and Shepilov prepared a CPSU(b) CC secretariat resolution stating that the responsibility for closing the theater lay with the Belorussian government itself. And that is exactly what happened. The press of the Belorussian republic launched a polemical campaign to discredit the theater and to accuse its director, Viktor Golovchiner, of producing nationalistic and cosmopolitan plays. In March 1949 the Belorussian Council of Ministers approved the decree to dissolve the Belorussian State Jewish Theater.[25]

Nonetheless, every cloud has a silver lining. The tendency of the CPSU(b) CC apparatus employees to use strangers' hands to pull chestnuts out of the fire actually helped the Moscow State Jewish Theater (GOSET) stay afloat for almost one year after the ethnocide began in late 1948. This theater's situation was tense.[26] On February 23, 1949 the CAA sent a letter to the council's chairman, Kliment Voroshilov, and to CC secretary Georgiĭ Malenkov, stating that "the Moscow Jewish Theater causes the state great losses and cannot work in the future in self-sufficient conditions," and that the council should close it on March 1.[27] The CAA supported its position by attaching several documents of facts and figures. One of these documents detailed the theater's financial state and pointed out that the average attendance was at best 45.5 percent of capacity in 1948, and that by January and February it had dropped to between 20 and 25 percent of capacity. Predictably, the certificate omitted the main reason for this drop; namely, the fear of being accused of bourgeois nationalism and ending up in Lubyanka. Instead, it mentioned only the declining interest, for "the children and

25. RTsKhIDNI, f. 17, op. 132, d. 239, l. 6.

26. There is an interesting story here. *Izvestiya* had stopped advertising the plays at the BELGOSET (which had by now been renamed the Mikhoels Belorussian State Jewish Theater) in mid-January 1949. Then in late April the paper began to run the ads again, but only under the name of the Jewish Theater.

27. RTsKhIDNI, f. 17, op. 132, d. 239, l. 8, 18.

youth, almost without exception, do not attend Jewish plays."[28]

After the war Stalin's bureaucracy acted more cautiously and cynically. It significantly sharpened its tools of repression, adding to the obviously political methods of struggle of the 1930s (such as political processes headed by the opposition) economic levers that, though seemingly far from political, were just as efficient. So if in 1948 the Jewish Theater received a subsidy of 578 000, in 1949 it lost the subsidy completely.[29]

But the tried-and-true weapons from the police and ideological arsenals had not become rusty for lack of use. The MGB studied the dossiers of State Jewish Theater employees and actors and prepared a list, with particular attention paid to the biographical data of those with relatives abroad.[30] And the CAA officials drew up a memo with extremely negative reviews of the plays being staged.[31] The Department of Propaganda and Agitation of the CC requested this material, and upon receiving it sent a memo to Stalin and Malenkov:

> . . . Lately the theater has fallen into a complete ideological and artistic decay. The theater's repertoire is extremely unsatisfactory in regard to its ideological-artistic quality and is limited by the narrow frames of the national subjects. The theater has not staged the works of the classic Russian playwrights or the plays of modern Soviet authors. Its repertoire is littered with the ideologically defective plays of the dramatist-nationalists. (The theater has produced plays by the repressed authors Fefer, Markish, [and] Dobrushin.) .
>
> . . . The theater personnel is littered with people who are not good artists and are not worthy of political confidence. After S. Mikhoels's death, V. Zuskin—now repressed—was appointed artistic leader of the theater. Neither the producer nor the actors who are cast are great masters. Out of 55 artists there are only 4 Communists and 6 Komsomol members. Many artists are immigrants from abroad and through their relatives have connections abroad.
>
> . . . The Department of Propaganda and Agitation considers it expedient to accept the suggestion of the Committee of Art Affairs at the Council of Ministers of the USSR (Comrade Lebedev) regarding the liquidation of the Moscow State Jewish Theater. We ask that the decree of the CC of the CPSU(b) on this question be approved.[32]

The decree was not approved. The CC followed the new procedures and

28. RTsKhIDNI, f. 17, op. 132, d. 239, l. 10.
29. RTsKhIDNI, f. 17, op. 132, d. 239, l. 10.
30. RTsKhIDNI, f. 17, op. 132, d. 239, l. 11–15.
31. RTsKhIDNI, f. 17, op. 132, d. 239, l. 16–17.
32. RTsKhIDNI, f. 17, op. 132, d. 239, l. 20–23.

stayed in the background, entrusting the decision on the theater's future to the CAA. On November 14, 1949 the CAA chairman, P. Lebedev, told M. Suslov that he had issued a decree to liquidate the GOSET as of December 1, "due to lack of profit."[33] Earlier, in February 1949, the Mikhoels Jewish School of Art in Moscow had been closed,[34] and then in September the same fate befell the Sholem Aleichem Theater in the Ukrainian town of Chernovtsy.[35]

In 1950 the curtain closed for its last time at the famous Moscow Chamber Theater, which had for 35 years been headed by its founder, A.Ya. Tairov (Kornblit), who had been a close friend of Mikhoels and shared his views. Tairov died that same year, unable to tolerate the continual chauvinistic persecutions that had begun in 1936 after the performance of the farcical opera *The Bogatyrs*,[36] in which the official critics saw "aesthetic-formalistic eccentricity."

The L.M. Kaganovich State Jewish Theater in Birobidzhan, directed by Ye.L. Gelfand, could not avoid sharing the same fate. The decree of the Council of Ministers of the RSFSR of October 22, 1949[37] ordered its closing, in accordance with Stalin's all-embracing plan to liquidate the rudiments of Jewish autonomy in this region. One reason for Stalin's plan was that, after the war, the strategic role of the Soviet Far East in the global opposition between the USSR and the USA became more acute—and Stalin could not allow the eastern borders to be weakened by Zionism.

The End of Red Zion

The migration of Jews to the area near the Tikhonkaya train station, where Birobidzhan was later created, was proposed by a March 28, 1928 resolution approved by CPC. A few years passed, and on May 4, 1934 Politburo decided to transform the Birobidzhan national district into the Jewish Autonomous Region within the Far East (later the Khabarovsk) Krai (territory). The Bolsheviks made no effort to conceal that the establishment of Jewish autonomy in Soviet Siberia was a Communist response to Theodor Herzl's bourgeois project of reviving the Jewish state in Palestine. The Soviet Jewish Autonomous Region was to symbolize the incarnation of the idea of the proletarian Zion.

In its first years the Jewish Autonomous Region experienced rapid economic growth. Residents of the European parts of the USSR were moving there. The highest rates of exploration of the virgin Birobidzhanian lands occurred from 1935

33. RTsKhIDNI, f. 17, op. 132, d. 239, l. 24–25.

34. RTsKhIDNI, f. 17, op. 132, d. 239, l. 1–3.

35. B. Pinkus, *The Jews of the Soviet Union* (Cambridge, 1988), p. 203.

36. *Translator's note:* The Bogatyrs were heroes of Russian folklore.

37. RTsKhIDNI, f. 17, op. 132, d. 240, l. 162.

through 1938, when almost 20 000 people migrated to the region. In 1930 its population was 32 000 people; in 1939 it was 109 000, including 17 700 Jews.[38] However the organized migration to the Jewish Autonomous Region later almost ceased (firstly because of the Soviet-Japanese armed conflict in Far East, and secondly because the USSR joined World War II).

After the war the Jewish leaders endeavored to restore and revitalize the Jewish Autonomous Region, which had begun to decay, and so appealed for help to Moscow. On December 4, 1945, the first secretary of the regional Party committee of Jewish Autonomous Region, A.N. Bakhmutskií, and the chairman of the regional executive committee, M.N. Zilbershteín, sent a letter to Stalin requesting social and economic support of the region, and also proposing that the region be transformed into an independent autonomous republic, subject directly to Moscow. They gave the following reasons for this project, "now that the Soviet state has saved millions of Jews from physical extermination by Nazis, there is a clear necessity for the further development of Jewish statehood in the USSR."[39] This proposal of the Jewish Autonomous Region leadership to the center[40] was accepted only partially.

Material and technical help to the region was rendered promptly and on a large scale. On January 26, 1946 there appeared a special resolution of the CPC of RSFSR "On Measures for the Strengthening and Further Development of the Economy of the Jewish Autonomous Region." This resolution stated that plans were underway to send to Birobidzhan 50 teachers and 20 doctors, with "first choice given to those of Jewish nationality." Even Aleksandrov's propagandistic office prepared a quite extensive CC secretariat resolution of April 4, 1946 "On Measures for Helping the Regional Committee of the ACP(b) of Jewish Autonomous Region in Organizing Mass Political, Cultural, and Educational Work Among the Population." They allowed the *Birobidzhaner Stern* newspaper to publish three times a week rather than once; the *Birobidzhan Star*[41] newspaper expanded to four columns and grew to a circulation of 10 000 copies; a regional publishing house was created; and sanction was given to publish a quarterly literary and social-political miscellany in Yiddish.[42]

Nonetheless, the proposal to transform the Jewish Autonomous Region into a republic was immediately and decisively rejected as "unwarranted." It seemed that the question was now settled. But the anti-Semitic atmosphere was growing throughout the country. After February 1948, when a commission from the CC

38. RTsKhIDNI, f. 17, op. 117, d. 600, l. 45.

39. RTsKhIDNI, f. 17, op. 117, d. 600, l. 47.

40. *Translator's note:* The center = Moscow.

41. *Birobidzhanskaya zvezda.*

42. RTsKhIDNI, f. 17, op. 117, d. 597, l. 44–45.

Directorate on Personnel, headed by D.S. Polyanskií (a Politburo member from 1960 until 1976), visited the Soviet Far East, Stalin's bureaucracy considerably increased its project of finding faults with this region's leadership. Upon his return to Moscow, Polyanskií informed A.A. Kuznetsov, secretary of the CC ACP(b), not so much about real mistakes as about imaginary errors, miscalculations, and abuses of the secretary of the Jewish Autonomous Region's Regional Party Committee, A.N. Bakhmutskií. He went on to do the same for other leaders of the Jewish Autonomous Region, naming abuses in regard to all fields—ideological matters, personnel matters, economic matters, and so forth.

The ninth wave of criticism came in May 1949, when A. Gusev, the secretary of the Khabarovsk Krai Party Committee, along with Ye. Karasev, the head of the Department of the Party Organs of the Khabarovsk Krai Party Committee, sent the report of all these faults to Suslov and Ponomarenko, the CC secretaries.[43] As always, the MGB made a special effort, in particular through general S.A. Goglidze, who in March 1948 was appointed Far East representative of the MGB. And in early June 1949 Abakumov, at Shkiryatov's request, sent the CC compromising material on Bakhmutskií.[44]

Feeling the dark clouds gathering above them, the Birobidzhan leaders hurriedly sent penitential letters to Moscow, assuring the Party leaders of their devotion and ability to improve. These multipage letters of conviction and self-reproach allow us, to some extent, to reconstruct the situation. First, Bakhmutskií was accused of being swept away by the idea of Jewish statehood. In particular, he had referred to a promise Kalinin had made in 1931 at the Congress of OZET (the Company for Settling Jewish Toilers in Agriculture),[45] namely, to create a Jewish republic once the Jewish population had reached 20 or 30 000. In 1945 Kalinin sent Stalin a note requesting that the autonomous region be converted into an autonomous republic.[46]

Secondly, Bakhmutskií and other Jewish Autonomous Region leaders were accused of harebrained nationalistic plans, such as making the creation of a State Jewish University in Birobidzhan a top priority, of making the region's polytechnical education Jewish, and of changing the regional newspaper,

---

43. RTsKhIDNI, op. 118, d. 428, l. 40–53; f. 589, op. 3, d. 6592, l. 59.

44. See for example RTsKhIDNI, f. 17, op. 127, d. 1702, l. 187–192, 203–204, 194–196; op. 118, d. 39, l. 105–110.

45. The CPC of the USSR founded OZET by a resolution dated December 22, 1924. The first head of the Public Committee was Yu. Larin (M.A. Lurye). It was dismissed on May 11, 1938 by a decision of the Politburo of the CPSU(b).

46. Attached to the note were projects of the resolution of the CPC of the USSR and of the CC ACP(b). The note was never answered. But Bakhmutskií did not submit; he publicly defended his project, particularly in February 1946 when he visited the JAC, and in March 1947 when he met with the Jewish community in Moscow at the editorial offices of *Einikeit*. RTsKhIDNI, op. 118, d. 428, l. 59.

Birobidzhaner Stern, into an All-Union newspaper.

Thirdly, the Khabarovsk Territory Committee and, through it, the state security organs and Moscow, became aware of the existence of a "nationalistic organization" in Birobidzhan that "entrenched itself" in the editorial offices of the *Birobidzhaner Stern*, the *Birobidzhan* (a literary anthology journal), the Regional Radio Committee, the museum, and some other "ideological" institutions as well. This organization supposedly included the poetess Lyubov (Leva) Vasserman, who had returned from Palestine; Boris I. (Buzi) Miller, the editor of *Birobidzhaner Stern*;[47] the writer Grigoriǐ Rabinkov; the poet Izrail Goldvasser (Emiot); the actor Feǐvel Aronis; the Ukrainian literatus Iosif Kerler; the painter Tsimerinov (who claimed that the territory chosen for the Jewish Autonomous Region and the investigation of its natural resources was mainly to the credit of the Americans), the medical doctor Mitsengendler (a former member of Kharbin's Zionist organization), the translator Ber Slutskiǐ, Semyon Sinyavskiǐ (who escorted the trains of European migrants), the employees of the regional museum, the "former Bund member" Faktor, G. Grinberg, and others. Z.S. Brokhin (the secretary of ideology of the Regional Committee of the Jewish Autonomous Region), S.N. Kushnir (the secretary of propaganda of the Birobidzhan City Committee), Oksegorn (the chairman of the Regional Radio Committee), Druyan (the head of the City Planning Committee), Rabkin (the regional prosecutor), Gekhman (the chairman of the Regional Court), and others were also supposedly involved in this "nationalistic organization."[48]

This nationalism was supposedly manifested in Birobidzhan in the summer of 1947 when Bakhmutskiǐ ordered that certain children's homes be used exclusively for Jewish children. Children of other nationalities were transferred to other children's homes. Bakhmutskiǐ and M.Ye. Levitin, the Regional Executive Committee chairman,[49] were also accused of having been "oriented mainly toward Jewish personnel." This was proved by some appropriate figures: Jews constituted 54 percent of the nomenclatura Party and Komsomol workers of the region, and constituted 56 percent of the regional Soviet workers. However, the leading staff

---

47. The fate of Miller (1913–1988) was typical of those residents of Birobidzhan accused of nationalism. Arrested on May 31, 1950, the Special Tribunal sentenced him to 10 years of camp for conducting "subversive activity against the national policy of the ACP(b) and the Soviet government, with the aim of isolating the Jewish Autonomous Region from the other regions of the USSR; and, by propagating the nationalistic views in his works, of undermining the unity and the friendship of the peoples of the USSR." (See *Birobidzhanskaya zvezda* [*Birobidzhanian Star*], April 20, 1993.) Emiot, Slutskiǐ, Rabinkov, Vasserman, and others were arrested as well.

48. RTsKhIDNI, op. 127, d. 1702, l. 189–191.

49. Before his appointment to this post in 1947, Levitin had worked as regional prosecutor of Birobidzhan.

of the ideological establishments was 80 to 90 percent Jewish.[50]

Bakhmutskii's contacts with the JAC were seriously criticized. So in one of his notes to the CC he explained himself:

> I had long known of the anti-Birobidzhanian trends in the attitudes of many Antifascist Committee workers, and their activity provoked my great displeasure. I did not have personal connections with any of the former members of the Antifascist Committee. As far back as 1943 I received a telegram that I, along with my predecessor, was elected a member of the Jewish Antifascist Committee. As a member of this committee, I had to be present only twice. . . . I did not afterwards attend and I took no part in its activities. Rumors had reached me; and further, during my visits to the committee I myself paid particular attention to the unhealthy atmosphere in the committee. It was only this that induced me, in November 1948, to inform on the unhealthy situation in this committee.
>
> At a reception for Comrade Chernousov, the head of the Department of the Party, Trade Union, and Komsomol organs of the CPSU(b) Central Committee, I offered him my remarks on the work of this committee:
>
> (a) that the situation is stagnant in the committee, and all sorts of discontented elements gather, grumble, and gossip there.
> (b) that the leading committee workers, Fefer and Zhits, are in a rebellious mood; that they are trying to transform the committee into a special center for decision-making on Jewish questions, and so on.
> (c) that, in connection with the creation of the state of Israel, Zionist, unpatriotic, and anti-Soviet moods predominate in the committee; that they gather letters from former frontline Soviet Jewish soldiers aimed at creating a special legion for the protection of Israel; that they entertain the idea of collecting donations to acquire weapons for them, etc.
> (d) Comrade Chernousov was informed by me about a number of facts concerning Israeli ambassador Meierson's [sic] provocative activity in Moscow.
>
> I repeat once again, I have never had any personal connections with the criminals, villains, [and] enemies of the people of the former Antifascist Committee.[51]

---

50. RTsKhIDNI, f. 17, op. 118, d. 428, l. 46.
51. RTsKhIDNI, f. 17, op. 118, d. 428, l. 65–66.

Most of all, Moscow was displeased by the Jewish Autonomous Region's cooperation with various American Jewish public organizations, such as Ambidzhan.[52] Totalitarian thinking called forth an acute fit of xenophobia. Bakhmutskiĭ vainly tried to justify himself. He explained that back in the 1930s American, Canadian, Mexican, Cuban, and other foreign Jewish organizations had helped the Jewish Autonomous Region by providing it with machinery, equipment, materials, clothes, foods, and so on; and that all this was done with the permission of the authorities. He was accused of offering for publication in *Pravda*, on May 30, 1944, a telegram addressed to Stalin, which indicated that the workers of the Jewish Autonomous Region had gathered a relief fund of 1 662 000 rubles for children who had suffered from the German occupation. This telegram further requested permission for the Regional Executive Committee to organize two children's homes for Jewish orphans, which would house 2 000 to 2 500 people) and to use the relief fund for this purpose. Although no Jewish orphans from the Soviet Union's western regions had been sent to Birobidzhan, this initiative served as propaganda to further American assistance to the JAC after the war. Indeed, from 1945 through 1948 the region received various commodities and gifts worth over 6 million rubles.[53]

The Jewish Autonomous Region's governing body was accused of attempting to delude the Soviet government by claiming that Ambidzhan was a progressive Jewish charitable organization; and by further claiming that if the Jewish Autonomous Region were to refuse its help, hundreds of millions of dollars would instead be sent to Israel and other places.

On these grounds, it was concluded that "Comrades Bakhmutskiĭ and Levitin did not lead an appropriate struggle against the spreading of pro-American and nationalistic attitudes, and that they were subservient to the US." The compromising materials were more than enough for the Politburo to pass a resolution on June 25, 1949 "On the Mistakes of the Secretary of the Regional Party Committee of the Jewish Autonomous Region of Khabarovsk Krai,

---

52. Ambidzhan was the American-Birobidzhan Committee. On April 15, 1948 Stalin signed a Politburo resolution voting down the Jewish Autonomous Region's proposal to invite Ambidzhan's vice president, Yakov P. Budish, to the USSR. Mikhoels and Fefer had met Budish in New York in summer of 1943, when he represented the interests of those American Jews who, unlike Joint leader Rosenberg, favored the development of Jewish autonomy in Birobidzhan rather than the Crimea. Budish supposedly declared, "We are interested not only in the Jewish Autonomous Region, but in the whole [Soviet] Far East." RTsKhIDNI, f. 17, op. 118, d. 26, 168; Document from the archives of the former KGB.

53. RTsKhIDNI, f. 17, op. 118, d. 428, l. 48, 52–53. Enclosed in one parcel from America was a note: "Friends: All these things were collected and piled in Ronya Levy's house. My husband has devoted his life and health to the assistance of his fellowmen in Russia.... All these things are sent to you in commemoration of the late Mr. Max Levy.... " Also, five electric generators were labeled: "Gift from Joseph and David Morgenstern. Cleveland, Ohio." There are other examples of such notes and inscriptions.

Comrade Bakhmutskií A.N., and the of Chairman of the Committee, Comrade Levitin M.Ye.":

> . . . Comrades Bakhmutskií and Levitin have committed serious political errors in ideological work and in building the economy. . . . Comrades Bakhmutskií and Levitin not only failed to give a correct political evaluation of the regional organizations' long-standing connections with the American-Birobidzhan Committee in the USA, but also accepted crumbs from this committee, thus widening the connections by which they contributed to the spreading of pro-American and bourgeois-nationalistic attitudes among some portions of the region's population.
>
> Comrades Bakhmutskií and Levitin also failed to give a correct political evaluation of the Jewish Autonomous Region's citizens' numerous private connections with America as a channel for perpetrating hostile propaganda, and to the parcels obtained by the citizens being a matter that depreciates the dignity of Soviet citizens.
>
> In his writings and oratory Comrade Bakhmutskií made political errors, claiming that the Jewish region is being and will be built only by Jewish hands . . . .

This list of transgressions was followed by resolutions, among them:

> 1. Relieve Comrade Bakhmutskií A.N. of his post as first secretary of the Regional Committee of the CPSU(b) of the Jewish Autonomous Region, and [relieve] Levitin of his post as chairman of the Regional Executive Committee. Rebuke Comrades Bakhmutskií A.N. and Levitin M.Ye. with a reprimand for their improper behavior in relations with the American-Birobidzhan Committee in the USA. . . .
>
> Secretary of the Central Committee I. Stalin[54]

Aleksandr Naumovich Bakhmutskií, the son of a pharmacist in Belgorod, was a hard-core Communist who had worked at the Hammer and Sickle metallurgical plant in Moscow in the 1920s and was a Party employee at the Dinamo plant in the 1930s. This Politburo resolution was a cruel blow to him. In the hopes of being forgiven, he wrote a confessional letter to Malenkov,[55] but all was in vain. On February 18 the Jewish Autonomous Region's CPSU(b) Regional Committee accused Bakhmutskií of bourgeois nationalism and expelled him from the Party.[56]

---

54. RTsKhIDNI, f. 17, op. 118, d. 428, l. 31–32.
55. RTsKhIDNI, f. 17, op. 132, d. 102, l. 9–14.
56. A resolution of the CPSU(b) CC Politburo on October 4, 1949 removed Bakhmutskií from the

After Bakhmutskiĭ and Levitin[57] were dismissed, dozens of functionaries who had worked with them were also released from their posts. One such functionary was Ya.I. Yarmitskiĭ, the deputy chairman of the Regional Executive Committee who had helped form a Jewish religious community in Birobidzhan by opening a synagogue[58] and by supporting the separation of the town's cemetery into Russian and Jewish sections. Also dismissed were M.Z. Spivakovskiĭ, the head of the MGB's Regional Directorate; Branzburg, editor of the *Birobidzhaner Stern* newspaper; Naum M. Fridman; and others as well.

Pavel Vasilyevich Simonov was appointed the new secretary of the Regional Party Committee. This was not a chance appointment. Simonov was a Russian who had previously worked as an instructor at the Department of the CPSU(b) CC. His duty in Birobidzhan was now to cleanse the personnel of those "infected with Jewish bourgeois nationalism." In early August 1949 the Seventh Regional Party Conference of the Jewish Autonomous Region, under Simonov's leadership, elected 42 Russians and 16 Jews to the new body of the CPSU(b) Regional Committee.[59]

At the suggestion of the new regional Party leadership, of the Politburo of the ACP(b) adopted a resolution on January 30, 1950 to the effect that "the further acceptance by the Jewish Autonomous Region of any gifts from 'Ambidzhan'" would be considered inadvisable. With the Politburo's blessing, the new leadership immediately sent a telegram to New York on behalf of the Regional Council of the Jewish Autonomous Region, which read:

> We thank Ambidzhan for the gifts. At the same time, expressing the wish of the Jewish Autonomous Region, we consider it necessary to inform you that there is no need to send any more gifts in the future.[60]

However, Simonov later disappointed his bosses in Moscow, in particular because of his persistently asking that the CC reopen the Birobidzhan Jewish Theater.[61] The Politburo passed a resolution on August 21, 1952 to remove Simonov. In his place, the Politburo appointed A.P. Shitikov, who had been in the apparatus of the Khabarovsk Krai Party Committee.[62]

---

body of the Supreme Soviet of the USSR. RTsKhIDNI, f. 17, op. 118, d. 544, l. 25.

57. Levitin was later arrested.

58. The synagogue opened in 1947. At the Jewish New Year that year (September 24) about 400 or 450 people were present. RTsKhIDNI, f. 17, op. 118, d. 39, l. 110.

59. RTsKhIDNI, f. 17, op. 118, d. 494, l. 151–158.

60. RTsKhIDNI, f. 17, op. 118, d. 715, l. 158–159.

61. RTsKhIDNI, f. 17, op. 132, d. 240, l. 161.

62. RTsKhIDNI, f. 17, op. 119, d. 1053, l. 108.

Accused of treason and anti-Soviet propaganda, Bakhmutskiĭ was arrested on January 28, 1951 and tried by the Supreme Court on February 20–23, 1952. He was sentenced to death, but at the last moment his sentence was reduced to 25 years' imprisonment. (He was released on January 23, 1956, shortly before the Twentieth Party Congress, and the following month his Party membership was reinstated.)[63]

At this same session, the MCSC, headed by Major General A.G. Suslin, sentenced to varying prison terms such Jewish Autonomous Region leaders as M.N. Zilbershteĭn, who until 1947 had been chairman of the Regional Executive Committee; M.Ye. Levitin; Z.S. Brokhin, the secretary of the Regional Executive Committee; A.M. Rutenberg, the editor of the *Birobidzhan* literary anthology; Kh.I. Maltinskiĭ, the editor of the *Birobidzhaner Stern*; N.M. Fridman, the executive editor of the *Birobidzhan Star* newspaper; and M.M. Fradkin.[64] On December 28, 1955 their sentence was also revoked, and all of them were released.

This massive repressiion almost totally deprived the Jewish population of the region of its administrative and intellectual elite, and now the prospect of turning Birobidzhan into a flourishing Soviet Jewish Republic was gone forever. Ilya Erenburg's gloomy prophecy that the Jewish Autonomous Region would become a large Jewish ghetto within the Soviet Union did not come true. But the writer B.I. Miller's assessment was much closer to the truth: "The Jewish Autonomous Region did not fulfill our hopes; it became instead a factory for Jewish assimilation."[65]

---

63. RTsKhIDNI, f. 589, op. 3 d. 6592, l. 154–169.
64. RTsKhIDNI, f. 589, op. 3, d. 6592, l. 175.
65. Document from the archives of the former KGB.

Four

Attacking the "Cosmopolitans"

On January 28, 1949 *Pravda* ran an editorial called "On an Unpatriotic Group of Theater Critics." Inexpressive as the title was, the piece was destined to become a notable milestone in the genesis of postwar Stalinism. With this editorial, *Pravda*, the main Party and state publication, subjected to scathing criticism a few critics known only to a small number of professionals in Moscow's theatrical circles. But now these critics—Abram Gurvich, Iosif Yuzovskiǐ, Aleksandr Borshchagovskiǐ, Yakov Varshavskiǐ, Leonid Malyugin, Grigoriǐ Boyadzhiev, and Yefim Kholodov—were suddenly infamous throughout the country; they were symbols of the insidious forces destroying the solid base of Soviet patriotism.[1] *Pravda* accused these seven people of "having lost a sense of responsibility toward the people, of having become bearers of a stateless cosmopolitanism detestable and hostile to Soviet man."[2]

The inquisitorial spirit, propagandistic scope, and enthusiasm of this editorial all suggested that Stalin's invisible presence lay behind it. There was nothing mystical about this intuition. According to Konstantin Simonov, a popular writer who was in the dictator's good graces and privy to some of the Kremlin's political secrets, the editorial was written at Stalin's direct initiative.

---

1. On the following day *Literary Gazette* (*Literaturnaya gazeta*) added one more name to this unpatriotic group: Iogann Altman. Then on January 31 the newspaper *Culture and Life* (*Kul'tura i zhizn*) cleared things up by supplying Kholodov's real name, Meyerovich, in brackets after his pen name.

2. Alexander Werth, an English journalist who during the war had been a correspondent in Moscow, wrote in the *Manchester Guardian* (April 25, 1949): "In Russia cosmopolitanism has now become a philosophical concept and has been given a place of honour in the vocabulary of Soviet polemical writing, along with formalism, bourgeois nationalism, anti-patriotism, anti-Sovietism, comparativism, Hegel-mongering, and toadying to the West."

Though it looks as though the largest caliber of the ideological artillery was fired at a trifling target, this was not at all the case. That this editorial was not at all fortuitous was confirmed by subsequent developments. As a matter of fact, this editorial served as a signal for starting a large-scale purge of the entire state and Party machinery, beginning with the Politburo and ending with the remote provincial offices. The culmination of this purge was the notorious "doctor's plot."

This new purge had a distinctive feature: it was accompanied by an intense popular eruption of anti-Semitism, which had been building since the war. It is noteworthy that reprisals against "stateless cosmopolitans," first in the sphere of theater criticism and then in other spheres of cultural and public life, came at the height of the struggle against so-called Jewish bourgeois nationalists, during which a number of Jewish writers and poets were arrested and prosecuted. Was this just a coincidence? Hardly. Rather, these events constituted two sides of the same coin. Or maybe we can more accurately say they constituted "two sides of the same Moon": on the face was the tumultuous propaganda campaign and the scourging of unpatriotic intellectuals who had lost touch with the native soil; but on the "invisible" side, screened from the public, was the MGB's highly secret repressive actions, aimed at annihilating Jewish culture and annihilating its propagators as well. When properly coordinated, propaganda and police attacks are a powerful deterrent, and this was especially true for assimilated Jewry who held important positions in the artistic and intellectual spheres in the country.

However, anti-Semitism, both latent and patent, could not have been a self-sufficient cause; rather, it was an indicator that the totalitarian regime was strengthening itself. In the late 1940s the Soviet empire endured another attack of Stalinist paranoia, caused by external (Cold War) and internal (power struggle) factors. The Kremlin ruler was seeing the American-Zionist threat everywhere.

In the final analysis, it was this idée fixe that provoked the unprecedented struggle against "cosmopolitans and unpatriotic intellectuals." And this all began with one seemingly ordinary intrigue, one intrigue among many that was carefully thought out and later enacted in art organizations and in the corridors of power.

THE NOMENCLATURA'S OPPOSITION

After the war some Moscow critics formed an association attached to the All-Russia Theater Society. Among the members of this association were some that *Pravda* later branded as "anti-patriotic" cosmopolitans. Grigorií Boyadzhiev, a learned art critic, was elected chairman of this group in 1947, succeeding Iosif Yuzovskií, a specialist in Western theater and in Maksim Gorkií's dramaturgy. This association resembled somewhat a Western guild of professional critics, and it had influential patrons. Theater critics were members of the Union of Soviet Writers (USW); and among the

USW's leadership were such patrons as Aleksandr Kron (Kreín), head of the dramaturgy commission; and most importantly Konstantin M. Simonov, the young but already well-known writer who served as the USW's deputy general secretary. Another patron was Dmitrií Shepilov, from the ACP(b) CC's Agitprop Department. Some other Agitprop employees were also patrons, such as B.S. Ryurikov (the Art Section chief) and his subordinates V.N. Prokofyev and D.S. Pisarevskií, who were art critics more than they were Party functionaries.[3] Stalin sympathized with Shepilov and hoped he would fill the intellectual gap left by G.F. Aleksandrov's fall.

Such a distinguished patronage filled the ambitious critics with illusions of extensive opportunities and of their having the right to give bold appraisals and judgments. Prestigious journals and newspapers[4] would often publish their articles. Further, these critics had long-standing connections with the editorial boards of these journals and newspapers, and some were even on the staffs. The "anti-patriotic" critics' articles were especially often published by newspapers such as *Culture and Life*[5] (whose chief editor was Shepilov), *Izvestiya*, *Soviet Art*,[6] and in such magazines as *New World*,[7] and *Theater*.[8]

The association of theater critics enjoyed some organizational and creative autonomy and was, to a certain extent, opposed to Aleksandr Fadeyev, the leader of the Union of Soviet Writers. They redoubled their opposition to Fadeyev because, among other things, a fairly energetic group of demagogues held key positions in the USW by making use of Fadeyev's "human weaknesses," namely, ambition and alcohol. This demagogic group included playwrights Anatolií Surov[9] and Boris Romashov, and the writer Arkadií Perventsev among others; and it was led by the USW's board secretary Anatolií Sofronov, the author of a number of plainly mediocre comedies. The members of this group declared themselves to be the true bearers of the methods of socialist realism in literature.

The conflict between the two art groups (which was complicated by the favoritism, nepotism, and clan interests characteristic of any totalitarian state) was aggravated ever more until, at last, there arose a situation in which a decisive fight was unavoidable. Moreover, the Propaganda and Agitation Department decided to

---

3. Prokofyev was an art critic and a specialist in the works of K. Stanislavskií.

4. For instance, A.M. Borshchagovskií published in *Izvestiya* (February 24, 1948) a favorable review of American playwright Arthur Miller's *All My Sons*, which was produced at the Vakhtangov Theater.

5. *Kul'tura i zhizn'.*

6. *Sovyetskoye iskusstvo.*

7. *Novyí mir.*

8. *Teatr.*

9. Surov was a two-time winner of the Stalin Prize and author of the play *Decent People* (*Poryadochnye lyudi*). In 1952 he was denounced as a plagiarist and expelled from the Union of Soviet Writers.

avail itself of the opportunity, with the aid of theater critics, seriously to criticize Fadeyev for his shortcomings in the sphere of dramaturgy and, if possible, even to remove him as USW general secretary. Fadeyev had always annoyed the apparatus ideologists by his overtly arrogant attitude toward them, which was based on his special relations with Stalin. To have the tolerant and predictable Konstantin Simonov (who was, by the way, also one of Stalin's favorites) in place of the "recalcitrant" Fadeyev would have suited the Propaganda and Agitation Department—and it would have suited the theater critics even more.

The attack upon Fadeyev began in the spirit of traditional Party bureaucracy tactics: the Propaganda and Agitation Department checked up on the implementation of the CPSU(b) CC's resolution of August 26, 1946 "On the Repertoire of Drama Theaters and on Measures for Its Improvement." Agitprop invited the cooperation of theater critics for collecting materials and preparing a report to the CC secretariat. With Shepilov's sanction, a consultative meeting took place at the Arts Section of the Propaganda and Agitation Department on November 27, 1948. Participating in this meeting were theater critics and journalists V.F. Zalesskií, Ya.L. Varshavskií, G.N. Boyadzhiev, I.L. Altman, I.I. Yuzovskií, A.P. Matskin, A.M. Borshchagovskií, L.A. Malyugin; *Theater* magazine editor G.S. Kalashnikov; playwright A.A. Kron, and others. Their assignment was to submit in a week's time their suggestions along with materials concerning the repertoire of theaters and theater critique.[10] A few more of these consultative meetings took place in the first half of December and, as a result, Ryurikov, Prokofyev, and Pisarevskií, (the Agitprop employees who had conducted the meetings) placed on Shepilov's table a draft of a report that subjected to sharp criticism the playwrights Sofronov, Virta, Romashov, and Surov for such plays as *Moscow Character,*[11] *Daily Bread,*[12] *Great Power,*[13] and *Free Passage.*[14] The report also criticized the Moscow Academic Art Theater and the Malyí Theater for staging some of these plays. However, circumstances suddenly changed, and the report was put aside.

The more impatient theater critics were inspired by the Propaganda Department's support and were confident of winning. Accordingly they began openly and quite sharply to criticize the USW leadership—primarily Fadeyev—for serious shortcomings in the sphere of dramaturgy. At the end of November there was an art conference in Moscow, held under the auspices of the All-Russia Theater Society of the Arts Committee and the USW's Dramaturgy Commission,

---

10. RTsKhIDNI, f. 17, op. 132, d. 229, l. 9.

11. *Moskovskií kharakter.*

12. *Khleb nash nasushchnyí.*

13. *Velikaya sila.*

14. *Zelenaya ulitsa.*

devoted to the plays presented through the thirty-first anniversary of the Great October Revolution. A. Borshchagovskiĭ was the main speaker, and he maintained that Soviet drama of recent years was, with rare exceptions, ideologically and artistically helpless, and that the theaters were passing through another crisis. He denounced Sofronov, Surov, and other playwrights patronized by Fadeyev, and found support for his denunciation from L.A. Malyugin and from the producers F. Kaverin, A. Popov, and I. Bersenev.[15] But the matter went further than mere rhetoric. Ryurikov and Prokofyev, who were both Agitprop employees, visited M. Kedrov, the director of the Moscow Academic Art Theater, and demanded that he cease performances of A. Surov's play *Free Passage* since, in their opinion, it needed revision.[16]

The Agitprop leaders, in a note to G. Malenkov, attacked Fadeyev once again on December 14, 1948. Fadeyev maintained authority over the Soviet Writer publishing house, which published a series called "The Library of the Collected Works of Soviet Literature," which included Ilya Ilf's and Yevgeniĭ Petrov's books *The Twelve Chairs*[17] and *The Golden Calf*.[18] These two works had been declared "slanderous," and were condemned for discrediting Soviet life and the state apparatus from a position of "bourgeois-intelligentsia haughtiness" and "vulgar scoffing." Shepilov and his subordinates even prepared a draft for a CC ACP(b) resolution to "point out to the secretariat of the Union of Soviet Writers of the USSR [Comrade Fadeyev]'s unsatisfactory control over the publishing activity of the Union of Soviet Writers."

This draft was never approved. Fadeyev countered the new attack without great losses. On January 26, 1949 he proposed to Malenkov that G.A. Yartsev, the director of the Soviet Writer publishing house, be dismissed, "to introduce order."[19] Fadeyev at the same time attempted to vindicate himself fully in the eyes of the Party bosses, and so disclosed that approximately 30 books recognized as "ideologically defective" had been excluded from the 1949 publishing schedule. These books included an anthology of S. Yesenin's poems and Yu. Olesha's story, "The Three Fat Men" ("Tri tolstyaka")[20]

In order to parry the attacks, Fadeyev started to concentrate his forces for a retaliatory blow. He enlisted the support of P.I. Lebedev, the chairman of the

---

15. *Literary Gazette* published a short report on this conference on December 4, 1948, which gave an obvious preference to the critics as against their opponents, the playwrights.

16. RTsKhIDNI, f. 17, op. 132, d. 337, l. 9–10.

17. *Dvenadtsat' stul'yev.*

18. *Zolotoĭ telyonok.*

19. In fact, it was not until October 28, 1949 that Yartsev was dismissed by a resolution of the CC secretariat. Apparently, the secretariat remembered him only after "relations were cleared up" among the nomenclatura factions.

20. RTsKhIDNI, f. 17, op. 118, d. 557, l. 143–158.

CAA; G.M. Popov, secretary of the ACP(b) CC's Moscow Committee and of the Moscow City Committee (who also patronized Sofronov); P. Pospelov, the editor of *Pravda*; and Malenkov, the CC secretary who had long been dreaming of laying his hands on the Party's Propaganda Department, formerly the domain of his late rival, Zhdanov.[21] It is important to realize that Malenkov would never dared to have taken this step on his own, and it became obvious whose position Stalin, the higher arbiter, would take in this conflict. However, to prepare for this, Fadeyev's champions arranged for a certain Anna Begicheva to send a letter to the "highest name."

The choice of Begicheva for this task was not at all accidental. She was a journalist on the *Izvestiya* newspaper staff, an educated woman of simple origin, born into a peasant family. She had formerly been a collector of Ukrainian folk songs, and was now being "badgered" and "slighted" by aesthete cosmopolitan critics for her adherence to the people's communist art.[22] Her denunciatory message of December 8, 1948 began with a hysterical and almost panicky appeal:

> Comrade Stalin!
>
> There are enemies actively operating in the art circles. I am answering for these words with my own life.[23]

Begicheva went on to expose these "enemies" with unflinching resolve:

> A group of leading theater critics, . . . masked cosmopolitans, formalists, occupying key positions in criticism . . . is deliberately disorienting theaters and influencing the opinions of none-too-clever chief editors of even such newspapers as *Soviet Art* and *Izvestiya*. Their leaders are Yuzovskií, Matskin, Gurvich, Altman, Boyadzhiev, Varshavskií, Borshchagovskií, Gozenpund, Malyugin. These critics, by pushing mediocre plays, are opening up the theaters to such libelers and slanderers of our present-day reality as Mass, Chervinskií, the Brothers Tur, Prut, Finn, Laskin, etc.
>
> Cosmopolitans have everywhere entrenched themselves in the art circles. They head the literary departments of theaters; they teach in institutions of higher education; they lead such critical associations as those of the Theater Society and the Writers Union; they have penetrated *Pravda* . . . *Culture and Life* . . . *Izvestiya* . . . .
>
> Theirs is a firmly united group. With their skepticism, disbelief,

21. Incidentally, it was Zhdanov who appointed Shepilov head of the Propaganda Department; and it was Zhdanov's assistant, A.N. Kuznetsov, who subsequently became Shepilov's assistant.

22. A similar scenario would be employed in January 1953, when physician Lidiya Timashuk, another patriotic woman of "simple" origin, addressed Stalin to expose the subversive doctors' plot.

23. RTsKhIDNI, f. 17, op. 132, d. 337, l. 75.

> [and] disdainful attitude toward anything new, they are depraving the theatrical youth and none-too-clever people by inculcating in them aesthete tastes, which are, incidentally, conducive also to the commonplace foreign films flooding our screens (obsequiousness before the West, a negative attitude to the new things sprouting in our life).
>
> . . . It is very difficult to fight them. They are respected and everywhere fill key posts. Their numerous adherents and puppets ostracize those people who deign to oppose them, creating around them an atmosphere of contempt, and presenting their opposition, which is based on principle, as a squabble.
>
> A deliberate conspiracy of silence is organized around Soviet Communistic plays.[24] These art connoisseurs did not recommend that such plays as *Great Power, Daily Bread, The Offense,*[25] and *Moscow Character* be reviewed, and the newspapers obediently followed their "expert advice."
>
> . . . All these cosmopolitans pursue their own interests and care not in the least for Soviet "peasant" art (Yuzovskii's view of L. Leonov's works). They have no national pride, ideals, or principles; they are guided exclusively by considerations of their own careers and the propagation of the European-American views that negate the very existence of Soviet art. These "subtle connoisseurs" are hindering and impeding terribly the development of art.

The entire letter continued in this same grandiloquent style:

> Comrade Stalin! I no longer have any personal ends to pursue. I am fifty. My life has already been lived through. Not even my robust health can any longer bear the strain of the lifelong struggle I have carried on against enemies in art circles. Personally I have not attained anything; for, though everywhere valued as a talented worker, I was invariably dismissed because of my unbending nature.
>
> My effort is like digging a well with a needle, but I am all the more happy when suddenly life-giving water starts spurting out of it, if your [i.e., Stalin's] penetrating gaze happens to be turned to that side.
>
> I consider the plays *Great Power* by Romashov, *The Offense* by Surov, *Moscow Character* by Sofronov, and *Lenushka*[26] by Leonov to

24. Those who approved of the achievements, including the literary achievements, of the West were not the only ones subjected to criticism. Those who did not join the conformist chorus of praise for the latest "masterpiece" of socialist realism were also criticized. The criticism was based on Stalin's directive that "the method of keeping silent as a special form of ignoring was, as a matter of fact, a type of criticism—stupid and laughable, but a type of criticism."

25. *Obida.*

26. *Lenushka = Helen.*

> be achievements in Soviet dramaturgy, milestones in the development of Soviet people's art. I've been openly fighting for them, knowing that behind me stands the man whose sublimely pure Leninist teaching I confess with all my heart and conscience. It is this that gave me the conviction of my rightness and the strength to go on fighting. I am glad I was not wrong.[27]

TRIAL OF STRENGTH

Meanwhile the day of the opening of the USW's twelfth plenum (December 18) was drawing nearer.[28] Fadeyev, his champions, and his patrons were preparing themselves with special care for this event, secretly perfecting the plan for their decisive battle with the "cosmopolitan critics." Agitprop insisted on putting the session off and disapproved of the report written by the USW leadership. The session opened despite this; and, despite Agitprop's further disapproval, Sofronov was the main speaker. Sofronov was self-assured, and even somewhat defiant, confident of support from above. Nonetheless, he limited himself to some general remarks and personal attacks on the theater critics who censured his plays.

Fadeyev later took the floor. He spoke more resolutely, accusing theater critics of ideological sabotage, which consisted of "trying, first of all, to knock down those Soviet playwrights who reflected new features in Soviet life."[29] These speeches set the tone for a discussion that concluded by adopting a resolution censuring a group of theater critics[30] for discrediting Soviet Communist dramaturgy.

Indignant at the manifest disobedience, Agitprop's leaders were unable to assess the situation soberly during the few days that followed. Neither could they understand the strange behavior of Fadeyev and his adherents. Shepilov forbade *Literary Gazette* from printing the plenum's resolution. The newspaper *Soviet Art* already had its article (containing Sofronov's report and Fadeyev's speech) typeset and ready; but at the last moment this was put aside and only a short review was published in its place. The editorial board applied to the Propaganda Department for instructions on how to cover the results of the twelfth plenum, but received

---

27. RTsKhIDNI, f. 17, op. 132, d. 337, l. 75–80. The provocative nature of this letter is especially evident once we learn that as far back as February 1948 Begicheva had sent a letter to the MGB denouncing the "unpatriotic" activity of such "aesthetizing" critics as Altman, Varshavskiĭ, and Yuzovskiĭ. No punitive action was taken at that time, but the authorities did make note of these future "cosmopolitans."

28. A Politburo resolution of November 16, 1948, signed by Stalin, stated that this plenum was to have been held on December 15. The three-day delay testifies again to the increasing intrigues within the highest Party circles.

29. A.M. Borshchagovskiĭ, *Zapiski balovnya sud'by* [*Notes of a Favorite of Fortune*] (Moscow: Sovyetskiĭ pisatel, 1991), p. 54.

30. On January 28, 1949 *Pravda* branded seven theater critics as "anti-patriotic."

only an evasive answer: the Union of Soviet Writers was an art organization; reporting on its resolutions was not obligatory for *Soviet Art*, which should have its own policy.[31]

On December 22 *Literary Gazette* gave an exposition of Fadeyev's speech; and on the next day *Pravda* published Sofronov's article, "For the Further Development of Soviet Dramaturgy," in which he asserted that "formalists and stateless cosmopolitans were still pursuing activities in theatrical critique." It was only after these two articles were published that Shepilov and his assistants understood the true essence of the situation. They started calling the critics, asking them to write letters to Stalin explaining that Fadeyev and his adherents were deceiving the Party. But the critics were so dispirited and afraid that they point-blank refused. Only Borshchagovskií reluctantly agreed to attempt some retaliatory measures, though he would not venture to write to Stalin. He wrote instead to Shepilov. Konstantin Simonov helped edit this letter in hopes of repairing some of the damage. (According to some reports, Simonov had offered Borshchagovskií membership in the *New World* editorial board back in the summer of 1946.)[32] All was in vain, for Simonov, Shepilov and his assistants, and the critics who were siding with them all sustained defeat. And the events that soon followed convinced them of it.

Stalin meanwhile saw that he had to act decisively—and this reveals his involvement in these matters. He signed a Politburo resolution "On the Suspension of the English Version of the *Moscow News* newspaper"[33] on January 20, 1949. This document marked the coming of the storm. The nomenclatura jingoists perceived *Moscow News* as being somehow tainted by Western liberalism and as being a breeding ground for cosmopolitan ideas. Hence this newspaper had long had one foot in the grave.[34] As far back as January 5,

31. RTsKhIDNI, f. 17, op. 132, d. 237, l. 27–28.

32. RTsKhIDNI, f. 17, op. 132, d. 237, l. 13.

33. RTsKhIDNI, f. 17, op. 118, d. 290, l. 22.

34. At the end of 1948 M.M. Borodin (Gruzenberg), the editor of *Moscow News*, had a chance meeting with I.S. Yuzefovich on the street. As if sensing his forthcoming arrest, he declared, "We, Iosif Sigizmundovich, are no longer part of the family . . . . " And this was exactly what happened. On March 21, 1949 Borodin was arrested because he had been in China from 1923 through 1927 as the Soviet advisor to Kuomintang. He was accused of having betrayed the interests of the Chinese revolution. But this was only a part of Borodin's imaginary "crimes," which he firmly denied in his statement written in prison on March 24, 1950, " . . . I was incriminated with crimes that I have never committed, such as: hostile activity, including espionage in favor of the USA and Britain. After my sincere assertion that these accusations were entirely groundless, I was taken to Lubyanka and mentally and physically tortured there, subject to foul language, beaten with a stick on different parts of my body . . . despite my age (I was then 65) and diseases. I was convinced that I would not be able to overcome this torture and that my death was inevitable, and I started to give absurd testimonies without realizing it . . . . " The old man's health was declining noticeably, and he died shortly thereafter, before the investigation reached its end. Document

1948, Shepilov insistently recommended that Zhdanov take measures to close the newspaper, particularly on the grounds that "the editorial staff in terms of nationalities could be characterized by the following data: Russians–1, Armenians–1, Jews–23, others–3."[35] On July 12 Zhdanov agreed to take this measure and signed a draft of a corresponding Politburo resolution. Afterwards he fell ill and went to the Valdaí sanatorium, and thus was this issue withdrawn from the agenda.

THE REORGANIZATION OF AGITPROP

And thus, half a year later, Stalin buried yet another publication based only on the fictitious reason that it supposedly "was poorly managed and did not have a wide circulation." It is possible that Shepilov, when once again presenting this old project at the Politburo session, wanted to demonstrate his loyalty to Stalin and to beg Stalin's forgiveness for his indiscreet flirting with theater critics. This Agitprop head, who had risen headlong to the ideological Olympus of the Party, had everything to lose and someone to be afraid of. Not long before signing of the *Moscow News* resolution, Shepilov saw Stalin and cautiously mentioned the theater critics' complaints of persecution by the leaders of the USW. Stalin replied sharply and with irritation, "It is a typically anti-patriotic attack against the CC member Comrade Fadeyev."[36] It so happened that on the previous day Stalin had received G.M. Popov (the secretary of the CC's Moscow Regional Committee and of the ACP(b)'s Moscow City Committee), who had a reputation for being crude and extremely chauvinistic. In reporting on the state of affairs in the capital, Popov incidentally mentioned to Stalin that Fadeyev had been tormented by cosmopolitan critics, who in turn were supported by Agitprop; but that Fadeyev, on account of his modesty, would not apply to Stalin for help.[37]

Stalin's harsh reply had a sobering effect upon Shepilov, but the belated enlightenment engendered panic. And though Shepilov and his allies preferred to attack as a united front, they all escaped separately on their own—and some of them at any cost. So on January 23, 1949 Shepilov and his assistant A.N. Kuznetsov sent a memo to Malenkov in which they not only dissociated themselves from their protégés, but also brought serious accusations against them. And among their accusations, they hinted at an item that was then important—the national origins of the majority of the critics:[38]

---

from the archives of the former KGB.

35. RTsKhIDNI, f. 17, op. 118, d. 35, l. 39–46.

36. Borshchagovskií, *Zapiski balovnya sud'by*, p. 54.

37. Ibid., pp. 68–69.

38. Many Jewish intellectuals had been arrested that month.

In a number of documents and directives the ACP(b) Central Committee has stressed the presence of serious shortcomings in the sphere of literary critique. The facts show that the state of affairs in theater criticism is especially disquieting. The activity of an unpatriotic bourgeois-aesthete group, which has formed here, is seriously injurious to the cause of the development of Soviet theater and dramaturgy. This group, which includes critics Yu. (and I.I.) Yuzovskií, A. Gurvich, L. Malyugin, I. Altman, A. Borshchagovskií, G. Boyadzhiev, etc., has secured a monopolistic position and is setting the fashion in a number of publications and in such organizations as the All-Russia Theater Society and the Union of Soviet Writers Dramaturgy Commission.

The critics who form the group have consistently discredited the best works of Soviet dramaturgy, the best performances of Soviet theaters devoted to the most important subjects of the present.

. . . The trends of the group are set mainly by A. Gurvich and Yu. Yuzovskií. Two years ago A. Gurvich was denounced by the newspaper *Culture and Life*, and since then has not written anything on questions of Soviet dramaturgy.[39] Yuzovskií writes only articles on Shakespeare and Gorkií, showing a lordly disdain toward Soviet theater and dramaturgy. Nevertheless these critics retain influence on other members of the group.

. . . This group of critics has succeeded in getting access to the pages of leading newspapers. Thus A. Borshchagovskií and L. Malyugin had a few articles printed in *Pravda*; Yu. Yuzovskií—as well as G. Boyadzhiev, and A. Borshchagovskií—in *Culture and Life*; A. Matskin, L. Malyugin, A. Borshchagovskií in *Izvestiya*; etc.

. . . In September 1948 the Propaganda and Agitation Department reported to the ACP(b) Central Committee on the situation in the All-Russia Theater Society; it was decided to replace the leadership of the society. A rotten, stagnant atmosphere had arisen in this society, conducive to the appearance of antisocial bourgeois-aesthete mental attitudes. Instead of fighting the manifestations of formalism and the lack of ideals in theatrical art, the society's leaders adopted a conciliatory attitude toward these alien influences.

. . . In December 1948 there was a re-election in the Theater Society's Critique Section. The re-election meeting was held under the predominant influence of this group, which was elected almost in its entirety to the new bureau of the section. . . . Among nine elected critics, only one was a Russian. It is worth noting that the national composition of the ARTS[40] Critique Section is utterly unsatisfactory: only 15 percent of its members are Russians.

39. After one such "denunciation" Gurvich suffered a heart attack.

40. The All-Union Theater Association.

> The ACP(b) Central Committee's Propaganda and Agitation Department instructed the Arts Committee at the RSFSR Council of Ministers and the new leadership of the All-Union Theater Association to annul the results of these re-elections and recommended that they concentrate on working on the theater critics in the Union of Soviet Writers.
>
> . . . The aesthete critics have entrenched themselves in the *Soviet Art* newspaper and *Theater* magazine. V. Vdovichenko, *Soviet Art*'s editor, along with Malyugin, who sat on the editorial board and dealt with issues of dramaturgy and theater, gave ample opportunity for such critics as Boyadzhiev, Borshchagovskií, Matskin, etc., to publish their articles in the paper's pages. Further, two staff members, Varshavskií and K. Rudnitskií, wrote for the paper under three or four pseudonyms, thereby depriving young authors of the opportunity to have their articles published.[41]

Enclosed with the memo was the draft of the Agitprop resolution that had not been approved.[42]

On January 24, 1949 Malenkov chaired a CC Orgburo session, at which, with Stalin's blessing, a decision was made to begin a large-scale propagandistic campaign against the so-called anti-patriotic stateless cosmopolitan forces in the ideological sphere. The attack on theater critics served as a signal to begin a complete purge of all political, administrative, and social structures from the Politburo to the managerial staffs of factories. This jingoistic ballyhoo in the mass media served as a kind of cover for the Party police actions undertaken at that time, namely, the so-called "Leningrad case"[43] and the JAC case.

---

41. RTsKhIDNI, f. 17, op. 137, d. 237, l. 50–53.

42. RTsKhIDNI, f. 17, op. 137, d. 237, l. 55–56.

43. The "Leningrad case" came at the beginning of the purge. Stalin saw this purge as a guarantee of preserving his absolute rule, and so it continued, with varying intensity, throughout the Soviet Union until his death. To purge the highest echelons of power, Stalin used his favorite method of playing one group of high nomenclatura officials against another in order to remove, by other people's hands, those whom he thought dangerous for himself or no longer needed. Thus for the "Leningrad case" in late 1948 Stalin let Malenkov, Beria, and Shkiryatov deal with the late A. Zhdanov's protégés, their old rivals in the struggle for power.

When Zhdanov was CC secretary and Number Two in the Kremlin (his favorite phrase then was "Comrade Stalin and I have decided . . . ") he transferred many officials from the provinces, mainly Leningrad, to the central Party and government bodies. Thus N.A. Voznesenskií, A.A. Kuznetsov, and M.I. Rodionov found themselves in Moscow. Voznesenskií was a Politburo member and the deputy chairman of the USSR Council of Ministers. In early 1949 he also occupied the post of chairman of the USSR State Planning Committee. Kuznetsov was the CPSU(b) CC secretary, and Rodionov was chairman of the RSFSR Council of Ministers.

Malenkov, Beria, and Shkiryatov made use of various far-fetched accusations against Voznesenskií, Kuznetsov, and Rodionov, such as their illegal arrangement in Leningrad of an All-Union wholesale fair,

DECLARATION OF WAR AGAINST THE "COSMOPOLITANS"

At its session, the Orgburo considered a draft for a *Pravda* editorial, written under the direct guidance of Pyotr Pospelov,[44] *Pravda*'s chief editor. The title of the draft was "The Epigoni of Bourgeois Aestheticism: On an Unpatriotic Group of Theater Critics."[45] However, after the reorganized Agitprop revised it and after Stalin edited it, the title was shortened to simply: "On an Unpatriotic Group of Theater Critics."

Another item on the Orgburo session's agenda was the question of theater critics and their supporters among the CC staff. As to the former all was clear: they were liable to immediate dismissal, and the CPSU(b) members among them were liable to expulsion from the Party. As to the latter, Shepilov was faced with a dilemma: either he could take responsibility himself for conniving with the frondeur critics and resign, or he could find scapegoats among his subordinates and mobilize his renovated Agitprop staff for a decisive struggle against cosmopolitanism. He chose the latter. Between late January and late March 1949 a number of people were dismissed from Agitprop "for patronizing the anti-patriotic group of theater critics." Among them were I.V. Sergievskií, a consultant;[46] B.S. Ryurikov, head of the Arts Section;[47] and his assistant, V.N. Prokofyev.[48]

---

their falsification of the voting results at the Leningrad Party conference in late December 1948, their falsification of state accounting documents, their loss of secret documents, and so forth. Malenkov, Beria, and Shkiryatov went on to accuse those who were somehow connected with Zhdanov of anti-Party activity and of various other offenses. (Among the accused were P.S. Popkov, Ya.F. Kapustin, P.G. Lazutin, G.F. Badayev, I.S. Kharitonov, P.I. Levin, and N.V. Solovyev.) All the accused were dismissed from their posts. They were later arrested, and in the autumn of 1950 they were executed by firing squad.

In March 1949, in connection with the "Leningrad case" and the JAC case, Stalin dismissed V. Molotov as minister of foreign affairs, and he dismissed N. Bulganin as minister of the armed forces. Also, since A. Mikoyan's son, Sergo, was married to Kuznetsov's daughter, Alla, Stalin dismissed him as minister of foreign trade.

The MGB and Stalin concentrated their attention on the "Leningrad case" as it directly involved Party and state leaders. On the other hand, they temporarily pushed the JAC case to the background, and "remembered" it only after Zhdanov's group had been dealt with once and for all.

44. According to Borshchagovskií, the authors of this article were A. Fadeyev and D. Zaslavskií, a *Pravda* editorial staffer who was rather skilled at eradicating ideological heresies. Borshchagovskií, *Izvestiya*, February 24, 1948, p. 74.

45. RTsKhIDNI, f. 17, op. 118, d. 315, l. 98.

46. RTsKhIDNI, f. 17, op. 118, d. 325, l. 231–232.

47. RTsKhIDNI, f. 17, op. 118, d. 325, l. 231–232. Ryurikov was sent to the disposal of the Gorkií Regional Party Committee. In March 1950 he was sent back to Moscow and appointed deputy to K.M. Simonov, who was then appointed editor-in-chief of the *Literary Gazette*.

48. RTsKhIDNI, f. 17, op. 116, d. 412, l. 12; d. 343, l. 45–46. Prokofyev was sent to the disposal of the Sverdlovsk Regional Party Committee.

But this happened later. At the time in question Shepilov published an eloquently-titled article, "Hostile Positions (On the Underhanded Plotting of an Unpatriotic Group of Theater Critics)," in *Culture and Life*.[49] This article, alongside *Pravda*'s editorial of January 28, played a part in the Party's directive in starting a new witch-hunt, this time with "unpatriotic critics" serving as the witches.

"Working on" the Union of Soviet Writers

Different critics differently bore the trials they had to undergo at the dictator's will. At the Orgburo session Malenkov cried out about the young critic Aleksandr Borshchagovskiĭ: "Not to be allowed anywhere near the sacred pursuit of the Soviet press!"[50] Borshchagovskiĭ then took the advice of his patron Simonov and stopped attending meetings, kept away from other critics, and hid himself from the public eye for a while.[51] On January 31, 1949, by decision of the CC secretariat, he was removed from the *New World* magazine editorial board and dismissed from the Central Red Army Theater, where he had headed the literature department.[52]

Leonid Malyugin suffered a similar fate. By the same January 31, 1949 CC secretariat decision, he was dismissed as editorial board member of *Soviet Art* on February 16.[53] But it was Iogann Altman who suffered the most of all. He was a Party member of long standing, having joined the Bolshevik Party in 1920 after a brief membership with the party of the left Socialist-Revolutionaries. He was fanatically devoted to the idea of socialism, and among his colleagues and friends he was respectfully referred to as "our ardent Iogann." In June 1947 G.F. Aleksandrov dismissed him from the editorial staff of *Flag*[54] magazine. Altman was for some reason not mentioned in the *Pravda* editorial of January 28;[55] but the next day the *Literary Gazette* put this right. Obeying Anatoliĭ Sofronov's diktat, the editorial staff branded Altman as an inveterate cosmopolitan. Soon afterwards Altman was accused of having connections with "Zionist plotters" and was thrown out of the Party. Since Altman would not confess, Fadeyev began in the autumn of 1949 to exert pressure to have him

---

49. *Kul'tura i zhizn'*, January 31, 1949.

50. Borshchagovskiĭ, *Izvestiya*, February 24, 1948, p. 69. *Translator's note:* A more exact translation would be "Not to be allowed within gunshot range of the sacred pursuit of the Soviet press!"

51. In 1953 he re-emerged from the literary "underground" by writing a historical patriotic novel, *The Russian Flag* (*Russkiĭ flag*).

52. RTsKhIDNI, f. 17, op. 116, d. 412, l. 13.

53. RTsKhIDNI, f. 17, op. 118, d. 310, l. 62–64.

54. *Znamya*.

55. Apparently Fadeyev was for some time unsure if it was worthwhile to victimize Altman, who was an old friend since the days of the Russian Association of Proletarian Writers.

expelled from the Union of Soviet Writers. He sent a denunciatory memo to Stalin, Malenkov, Suslov, Popov, and Shkiryatov on September 22, in which he wrote:

> It is expedient additionally to verify the facts about Altman's close communication with bourgeois Jewish nationalists at the Jewish Theater and at the Moscow section of Jewish Writers, for Altman's close connection with them is widely known in literary circles. Comrade Korneíchuk A.Ye.[56] informed me of Altman's privately making use of his connections in the circles of eminent men of literature and art to distribute season tickets for the Jewish Theater,[57] i.e., of his actively supporting this artificial method of rendering assistance to the theater by means of "private charity," instead of trying to improve its repertoire and standard of performance.[58]

One year later Fadeyev achieved his goal: Altman was expelled from the Union of Soviet Writers on September 9, 1950. With his support and professional protection gone, the refractory critic was arrested and taken to Lubyanka on March 5, 1953 for "subversive activity in the area of theatrical arts." On May 29 he was released. Yet the burden of offenses and trials he had borne did not allow him long to enjoy his freedom—he died shortly thereafter from heart failure. Altman was the only Moscow theater critic to have been expelled from the Union of Soviet Writers and arrested.

Certain questions now arise: Why was it mainly those who represented Jewish national literature, art, and public organizations who were subjected to mass arrests, exiles, and execution? Why, on the other hand, was the persecution of "stateless cosmopolitans" confined to administrative measures (dismissals from work, from the Party, and so on)? And why did these "stateless cosmopolitans" not always end up in the MGB's torture-chambers? Why was the attitude toward the Jews different? The answer is apparently that Stalinism classified the Jews as bourgeois nationalists, potential agents of the West who led separatist and other subversive activities against the Soviet state. They were almost automatically included in the category of political criminals and sometimes even traitors of the motherland, and hence were subject to severe punishments—including physical extermination. "Traitors to the motherland" were not involved so much in politics

---

56. A.Ye. Korneíchuk was the author of a play called *In the Ukraine Steppes* (*V stepyakh ukrainy*) which was criticized by "cosmopolitans."

57. In 1947 Altman had been appointed head of the Literature Department of the Jewish Theater at Fadeyev's request. When the theater lost subscribers in the spring of 1948, it issued season tickets, just as other theaters did. The distribution of season tickets was not then regarded as wrong or criminal.

58. RTsKhIDNI, f. 17, op. 132, d. 229, l. 34.

as in ideology; they did not encroach upon the political basis of the Soviet state. They were accused of advocating "national nihilism" primarily toward the Russian people. Further, their "servility" before the West aided imperialism, and it especially aided American propaganda in its long-term aim of imposing Anglo-Saxon culture upon the entire world (this was later called American Cultural Imperialism). To put it simply, they were accused of carrying out a global Americanization of humanity.

Other "cosmopolitans" were seen as transmitters of American influence in the Soviet state. So, to neutralize them the Stalinist government merely kicked them out of the ideological sphere, dismissed them from work and so on, unless, of course, the MGB accused them of anything serious. The Stalinist regime's attitude toward so-called Jewish bourgeois nationalists and "stateless cosmopolitans" reflected its phenomenal hypocrisy and perfidy. The regime exterminated Jewish bourgeois nationalists for their devotion to a national religious idea, to their traditions, to their native culture, to their language, and so forth. And yet the regime persecuted the "stateless cosmopolitans," who for the most part were assimilated Jews, for just the opposite reason; namely, for striving to deny their national identity, and for attempting to dissolve into "the united humanity of the people of the world." The Stalinist regime classified this attitude as the advocacy of cosmopolitanism.

Hard times then fell upon the writer Boris Gorbatov, who suffered the heat of anti-Semitism in the Union of Soviet Writers. His wife Tatyana Okunevskaya, a popular actress, was accused of espionage and of having had an intimate affair with the Yugoslavian ambassador. The MGB then arrested her. In relation to this, Boris Gorbatov was forced to withdraw his candidature from the USW Party Bureau. Nikolaí Gribachov then became Party leader of the USW. (Gribachov was a poet who wrote "Collective Farm Bolshevik"[59] and was Anatolií Sofronov's protégé.) Gorbatov actually remained secretary of the Party group of the USW board. He then left Moscow for almost half a year because he did not want to participate in the hearings of the "personal cases" of "anti-patriots" and returned to Moscow only when the unmasking campaign was ended. He was more than once accused of having "never on any occasion defined his attitude toward the struggle against the cosmopolitan critics, which allowed them to consider him their man."[60]

Other critics suffered differently. For example, in order to save his Party membership and job, Yakov Varshavskií, a critic on the *Soviet Art* staff, became a "literary Negro slave" of Anatolií Surov, an editorial board member and Stalin Prize-winner. For Surov, Varshavskií wrote everything from personal letters

---

59. "Kolkhoz 'Bol'shevik'."

60. RTsKhIDNI, f. 17, op. 118, d. 714, l. 136.

to plays.

In early February 1949 Varshavskiĭ informed Surov of his, so to say, understanding of the situation regarding theater critics. "Does the group of unpatriotic critics exist as a unit, as a united front?" he rhetorically asked. He went on to answer his own question:

> The group exists as a united front, attached to the All-Russia Theater Society in the form of an association of theater critics. The Theater Society financially supported Yuzovskiĭ and Gurvich, who were idle for years on end, having been deprived of the opportunity to express their views in the press. For a long time the association's chairman was Yuzovskiĭ, then Boyadzhiev . . . . As the association's leader, G. Boyadzhiev confidentially suggested that critics regularly gather on the first of every month at the Aragvi restaurant for a "heart-to-heart talk." The purpose of such gatherings of only elderly, eminent, carefully chosen critics was no doubt to forge a caste of theater critics, screened from public observation, and to consolidate critics averse to the "prevailing" views. It was to be a kind of rebellion, opposing the "official" viewpoint on theater life. I was present at the first such gathering, presided by I. Altman.[61]

This denunciation soon fell into the hands of Dmitriĭ Shepilov, who passed it on to Malenkov with a note:

> I also present for your consideration Ya. Varshavskiĭ's letter to Surov, in which there is, in particular, information that the unpatriotic group of critics tried to organize itself (and maybe did so) on an ideological platform deeply hostile to our Soviet system . . . . I have informed Comrade Abakumov of the particular gatherings of the unpatriotic group at the Aragvi.[62]

By using such arguments, it was very easy to rebuff "unpatriotic" critics as plotters, and this is what happened at a closed Party meeting of the Union of Soviet Writers on February 9 and 10. Anatoliĭ Sofronov delivered the main speech and set the tone for the openly anti-Semitic course of the discussion. It is noteworthy that Sofronov, Surov, and their adherents deliberately and intensively capitalized on the nationality of the majority of critics who had been branded as cosmopolitans. This was not accidental, and the critics could not but guess that. This played a significant role in Stalin's sanctioning a campaign against "stateless

---

61. RTsKhIDNI, f. 17, op. 132, d. 229, l. 13.
62. RTsKhIDNI, f. 17, op. 132, d. 229, l. 8.

cosmopolitan" critics. At this meeting (which took place at the Iskusstvo [Art] publishing house), Surov stressed:

> One should look to bourgeois nationalism for the roots of cosmopolitanism. It is through the soil of bourgeois nationalism that sustenance was given to such double-dealers and traitors as Yuzovskií, Gurvich, and the like. Such despicable monsters must be removed from our ranks.[63]

THE CAMPAIGN GROWS

The "fifth item" became the key point in the further development of the campaign. The USW meeting denounced not only theater critics, but also a number of literary critics of Jewish nationality, among them L.M. Subotskií, F.M. Levin, D.S. Danin, B.V. Yakovlev (Kholtsman), A.M. Leítes, and A.I. Erlikh.[64]

In February 1949 the CC ACP(b) received a letter from a group of employees of the Leningrad Institute of Literature (Pushkin House) of the Academy of Sciences. This letter alleged that for twelve years there had been a secret anti-patriotic group of literary men and philologists within this scientific institute who had now been exposed. The letter claimed that this group had seized up to 80 percent of the seats in the Scientific Council. Such world famous scientists as B.M. Eíkhenbaum, V.M. Zhirmunskií, M.K. Azadovskií, G.A. Byalyí, and G.A. Gukovskií[65] were among those alleged to be active members. The letter accused them all of formalism, of propagandizing the comparativist theories of A.N. Veselovskií,[66] and of concealing their real nationalities by writing "Russian" in response to questionnaires.

The letter went on to denounce P.I. Lebedev-Polyanskií and L.A. Plotkin. Lebedev-Polyanskií was an academician who directed the Leningrad Institute of Literature from 1937 to 1948, and Plotkin was his successor after his death. The Pushkin House employees maintained that both were patrons of "cosmopolitan formalists." Lebedev-Polyanskií "was blinded by the flattery and groveling," while

---

63. *Vechernyaya Moskva* (*Moscow Evening*), February 19, 1949.

64. *Pravda*, February 11, 1949.

65. Gukovskií (1902–1950) was soon kicked out of the Pushkin House and the Leningrad University and was then arrested. He was rehabilitated after his death.

66. Veselovskií (1838–1906) was a Russian literary man and an academician of the Petersburg Academy of Sciences (1880). He was also a representative of the comparative historical literary science, having studied Russian literature in the context of Slavic, Byzantine, and Western European literature as well as from the context of world folklore. A discussion on Veselovskií's activities, which took place as per a CC ACP(b) resolution in 1948, branded him the father of "comparativism," which was now seen as a formalistic-cosmopolitan trend in Soviet literary science.

Plotkin ran the whole show at the institute, creating all the favorable conditions for the activities of the group that "was welded together by long-lasting relationships of families and friends, mutual protection, homogeneous (Jewish) national composition, and anti-patriotic (anti-Russian) tendencies." The letter incriminated the "cosmopolitans" with a long list of actions, the most "monstrous" of which was that they had succeeded in changing the name of the Institute of Russian Literature to the Institute of Literature. Actually, a resolution of the General Meeting of the Academy of Sciences of the USSR had decreed this name change in 1935, when a Western European literature section was opened within the institute. The letter writers ignored this bit of information.[67]

The Pushkin House employees moaned about Jewish domination, and their cries were heard. By order of the CC, the Academy of Sciences soon restored the original name to the institute. This was done discreetly, and the initiators of the intrigue possibly did not even notice it, for they were too busy struggling against "Jewish nationalism." In actuality, they were pursuing a major goal; namely, they were hoping for higher salaries and for appointments to administrative positions that were becoming vacant as a result of the widespread personnel purge.

Sometime later something very similar occurred in Moscow, at the Gorkií Institute of World Literature at the Academy of Sciences of the USSR. A.M. Yegolin,[68] formerly deputy to G.F. Aleksandrov in Agitprop, was appointed director of the Gorkií Institute in January 1948. In the spring of 1949 he took measures to bring its scientific staff "into a healthy state." He dismissed V.Ya. Kirpotin, T.L. Motylyova,[69] B.V. Yakovlev (Kholtsman), I.I. Yuzovskií, and other scientists of Jewish nationality who were branded as cosmopolitans.[70] Professor B.A. Byalik, who was left in the Institute, was forced to incriminate himself. In particular, he had to confess that his article "Gorkií and Mayakovskií," in which he claimed that Mayakovskií's poetry had been nurtured by the works of the Jewish poet Kh.N. Byalik, was "faulty."

The anti-Semitic hysteria grew day after day, gathering momentum and involving new names, regions, and spheres of activity. On February 10 the president of the USSR Academy of Arts, A.M. Gerasimov, denounced in *Pravda* the art critics A.M. Efros, A.G. Romm, O.M. Beskin, I.L. Matsa, D.Ye. Arkin,

---

67. RTsKhIDNI, f. 17, op. 118, d. 408, l. 1–4.

68. Yegolin had replaced V.F. Shishmaryov as director of the Gorkií Institute. Shishmaryov had been a student of the academician A.N. Veselovskií, and Fadeyev accused him of "comparativism" and servility before the West for having the institute publish the first volume of the "ideologically defective" *History of American Literature* (*Istoriya amerikanskoí literatury*). A.I. Startsev, one of the authors of this book, was later arrested.

69. On March 19, 1949 the CC secretariat, at Sofronov's suggestion, dismissed Tamara Lazarevna Motylyova from the editorial staff of *Soviet Literature*. RTsKhIDNI, f. 17, op. 118, d. 335, l. 226–230.

70. RTsKhIDNI, f. 17, op. 118, d. 784, l. 15–20.

and others. On February 11 *Culture and Life* printed an article by A.G. Dementyev, B.F. Chirskov, and M.A. Shuvalova on the process of the "denunciation of cosmopolitans" in Leningrad. (Dementyev was executive secretary of the USW's Leningrad section, and Chirskov was a playwright.) The three authors adduced numerous facts about the "unpatriotic activity" of Leningrad critics S.D. Dreíden, I.I. Shneíderman, I.B. Berezark, S.L. Tsimbal, and drama studies specialist M.O. Yankovskií. They accused these five people of towing the Yuzovskií/Gurvich line in their articles and speeches. Then on February 20 *Culture and Life* printed a piece by Tikhon N. Khrennikov (the chairman of organization committee of the Union of Soviet Composers),[71] who attacked the musicologists D.V. Zhitomirskií, L.A. Mazel, S.I. Shlifshteín, A.S. Ogolevets, I.F. Belza, M.S. Pekelis, and a professor at the Leningrad Conservatory, S.L. Ginzburg.

This bacchanalia of censuring raged everywhere. Grigorií Brovman, a critic and head of the Art Department at the Gorkií Institute of Literature in Moscow, had invited three of his confederates to lecture at that institute; namely, the critics Fyodor Levin, Lev Subotskií, and the poet Pavel Antokolskií. But because these three had all undergone ideological trials and had been ostracized, Brovman was accused of unpatriotic activity. Three students who were close to them (G. Pozhenyan, K. Levin, and Goldshteín) also suffered. Even earlier, on August 14, 1948, by a resolution of the Special Meeting, N.M. Korzhavin (Mandel), a third-year university student who was later to become a famous poet, was sent out of Moscow for "disseminating rumors of anti-Soviet nature."[72]

This was a logical ending of the old conflict that had begun for

---

71. Khrennikov had headed the Union of Soviet Composers for 43 years. He later acknowledged that to a large extent he had been forced to write the article for *Culture and Life*. Despite his objections, Agitprop—and primarily Suslov and Shepilov—had insistently "recommended" that he purge the Union of Jewish musicians. They referred to the outpouring of anonymous letters threatening to deal with Khrennikov for the protection that he supposedly gave to Jews. (It seems that these letters were written at somebody's order.) Countering this ordeal was beyond the capability of this young head of an artistic organization. Finding himself between the hammer of Agitprop and the sledge of the Judeophobic "musical community," Khrennikov fell ill and had a nervous breakdown. Thus he did not participate in this anti-Semitic campaign. To some extent, this is perhaps the reason that not even one musician was declared a cosmopolitan, dismissed from the Union, or arrested. (See *Sovyetskaya kul'tura* [*Soviet Culture*], April 7, 1990.) As a matter of fact, the Union even hired people who had been kicked out of other organizations. For instance, the Union hired M.A. Grinberg, who had, on February 28, 1949, been removed as head of the Directorate on Music Broadcasting of the All-Union Radio Committee. The reason for his dismissal was that he, together with his friends Nestyev and Shimanovich, "tried to discredit and deny, in an organized manner, the criticisms of erroneous programs, and thus employed a non-Party method of opposing the exposure of instances of the manifestation of bourgeois cosmopolitanism and servility in broadcasting." (See RTsKhIDNI, f. 17, op. 132, d. 418, l. 210–214.)

72. GARF, f. 8131, op. 31, d. 16444, l. 23–24.

L.M. Subotskiĭ as far back as April 1945. He had been the USW board secretary and deputy secretary of the USW's Party Committee. Now he was dismissed from both positions for "troublemaking," for accusing the USW's publications of "RAPW-methods of criticism,"[73] and for "disparaging literary works under the demagogic slogan of the struggle against so-called 'jingoism'."[74]

The call to "smash the bourgeois cosmopolitans in the mition picture arts" brought forth an avalanche of articles. Vile abuse was heaped upon the leading film critics, film directors, and others in the film industry. Once again, most of the names were Jewish: L.Z. Trauberg, G.M. Kozintsev, Ye.I. Gabrilovich, M.Yu. Bleĭman, N.A. Kovarskiĭ, G.A. Avenarius, N.D. Otten, N.M. Tarabukin, and so forth.

The campaign of attacking the "cosmopolitans" transformed architects, philosophers, historians, journalists, state institution employees, industrial employees, social organization employees, professors, instructors, college students, and technical school students into game hunters. The campaign was all-encompassing. However, I would not like to tire readers by listing the names of all who were subjected to reprisals for cosmopolitan heresy. Indeed, to do so would be practically impossible, for they were legion. So let us return to the central topic of this chapter, theater critics, and examine the result of the Party meeting held in the USW on February 9 and 10.

THE GOAL IS ACHIEVED

The Party meeting unanimously passed a resolution declaring that it "fully associated itself with the *Pravda* and *Culture and Life* editorials."[75] At this time the USW Party Bureau was advised to "consider the question of the Party membership" of Altman, Subotskiĭ, Levin, and Danin.[76]

Many people were now forced to make a decisive choice. To retain a job, a position in society, welfare, and sometimes even life itself, one had to make sacrifices—often substantial sacrifices. Konstantin Simonov was also faced with a difficult choice. Sofronov, Surov, and their adherents at the USW accused him of sympathizing with "cosmopolitan critics." They wanted to deal with him not only

---

73. RAPW = Russian Association of Proletarian Writers.

74. RTsKhIDNI, f. 17, op. 132, d. 229, l. 44. The CC apparatus actively participated in dismissing Subotskiĭ as head of the USW. O. Reznik, I. Altman, D. Tamarchenko, F. Levin, and others had written denunciations to the CC, claiming that "Subotskiĭ's chorus" in the USW united literary men "exclusively of non-Russian nationality." To end the "Jewish domination," Sofronov was appointed the new USW board secretary on April 21, 1948. (See RTsKhIDNI, f. 17, op. 118, d. 39, l. 158–163.) This further confirms that the struggle against the cosmopolitan critics had begun to mature long before January 1949.

75. RTsKhIDNI, f. 17, op. 132, d. 229, l. 6.

76. All four were soon expelled from the Party. Aleksandr Borshchagovskiĭ, who was a member of the Central Red Army Theater's Party organization, also suffered the same fate.

because of his artistic views, but also to gain power and privileges in the USW. Others denounced him to gain favor with their superiors, hoping that, after having drowned somebody else, they would themselves remain afloat. One such person was V.G. Vdovichenko.

Vdovichenko was the editor-in-chief of *Soviet Art*. He came to this post from the army political organs, and he followed all directives from Agitprop, understanding them to be orders from a higher Party organ. However, Shepilov, the Agitprop head, upon being accused of patronizing theater critics, attempted to use the well-tested method of redirecting the anger to his subject, and even went so far as to draft a resolution for Vdovichenko's dismissal.[77] Vdovichenko now saw that he could only look to himself for salvation. On February 12 he sent Malenkov a verbose memo in which he, with soldierly straightforwardness and unconcealed anti-Semitism, represented the charge as a far-flung plot. The anti-Semitic character of his memo is obvious, for he enclosed a list of 83 theater critics, all of whom were Jewish. Apparently to prevent any possible doubts, he did not mention Leonid Malyugin, who, though officially branded as cosmopolitan, was a Russian.[78]

Vdovichenko devoted a considerable part of denunciatory memo to specifying in detail K. Simonov's numerous transgressions. He implied that it was no accident that Simonov found himself encircled by Jews. However, Vdovichenko did not tackle the topic immediately; he began from afar:

> At the Twelfth Plenum of the Union of Soviet Writers, K. Simonov, for completely incomprehensible reasons, did not express his attitude toward the questions of dramaturgy and critique that were under discussion; neither did he support Fadeyev. At the time of the important two-day Party meeting at the Union of Soviet Writers, which was called for the purpose of smashing the unpatriotic group of critics and their confederates, K. Simonov found nothing better to do than go to Leningrad. This happened in Fadeyev's absence. Simonov was Fadeyev's assistant, and as such he was responsible for carrying out the CPSU(b) CC policy on smashing the anti-patriotic group.
>
> The situation was in fact saved by Comrade Sofronov,[79] who

77. RTsKhIDNI, f. 17, op. 132, d. 237, l. 55–56.

78. RTsKhIDNI, f. 17, op. 132, d. 237, l. 25.

79. In his memoirs Simonov so characterized the "division of labor" between Fadeyev and Sofronov in starting the campaign against "stateless cosmopolitans." He wrote: "In the story of the unpatriotic critics (which Fadeyev himself initiated, not foreseeing its consequences, and which consequently horrified him), I was a man who from the very beginning did not share Fadeyev's embitterment at these critics. Attracted by Sofronov's remarkable energy, but failing to divine his humane nature, Fadeyev made him an initially obedient apprentice, who, availing himself of the first opportunity, became a full-fledged literary executioner." A.I. Simonov, "Glazami cheloveka moyego polokeniya" ("As Seen by a Man of My

took upon himself all responsibility for holding the meeting and adopting appropriate resolutions.

. . . The composition of the editorial board and editorial staff of *New World* magazine[80] is also worthy of consideration. Questions of Soviet art are handled by Borshchagovskií; Simonov's assistant is Krivitskií; important sections of work in the office are looked after by Leítes, Kholtsman, Kedrin, and other stateless people. Personal friends of Simonov: Erenburg[81] (whose jubilee celebration was arranged by Simonov by pushing it through the USW presidium in a covert way), Dykhovichnyí, Raskin, Laskin, Slobodskoí, and others. K. Simonov is in every possible way supporting cosmopolitans. He passionately spoke in defense of the defective plays *Taímyr is Calling*[82] by Galich[83] and Isayev, and *Combat Friends*[84] by Mass and Chervinskií.[85]

Generation"), *Znamya*, 1988, no. 4, p. 73.

80. Simonov was the editor-in-chief from the autumn of 1946 through March 1950.

81. Ilya Erenburg was also persecuted at that time. His works were no longer published, and his relatives and acquaintances feared to visit him and even to talk with him on the telephone. Many of the zealous movers and shakers in the campaign against "unpatriotic" critics craved his blood. Shepilov periodically sent Malenkov news clips and responses from public organizations to the "denunciation of the unpatriotic group of theater critics." One such response also contained information on the third session of the USSR Academy of Arts, and in particular it quoted from the speech given by A. Gerasimov, the Academy's president: "'To give Ilya Erenburg's publicist works during the war years their just deserts,' Gerasimov said, 'I simply cannot keep silent about the scurrilous things he permitted himself to say about Repin and about Russian painting in general. Where were our critics then? Why did they not raise an indignant protest against it?' Comrade Gerasimov pointed out the inadmissibility of I. Erenburg's systematic propaganda for Picasso's works." RTsKhIDNI, f. 17, op. 132, d. 237, l. 3.

Erenburg would not simply wait for the arrest that seemed inevitable. He wrote Stalin a letter, asking him to clearly spell out what was in store for him. As one would have expected, Stalin lent him a helping hand, for Erenburg was one of the most talented specialists in the ideological treatment of the West. Suddenly the demand for Erenburg's articles reappeared, his ill-wishers immediately all calmed down, and in April 1949 he was sent to the World Peace Congress in Paris. I.G. Erenburg, *Lyudi, gody, zhizn'* (*People, Years, Life*), pp. 572–574.

82. *Vyzyvayet Taímyr.*

83. Aleksandr Galich subsequently became a popular poet and a performer of his own songs. In the winter of 1971/1972 he was expelled from the Union of Soviet Writers, the Union of Soviet Composers, and the Literature Fund for nonconformity and civil rights activism. In 1974 he was forced to emigrate to the West. He died in an accident on December 15, 1977.

84. *Vernye druz'ya.*

85. RTsKhIDNI, f. 17, op. 132, d. 237, l. 13–15. Vdovichenko's zealous denunciatory efforts did not save him from dismissal. On March 30, 1949 Shepilov wrote to Malenkov: "Comrade Vdovichenko does not display a Bolshevik adherence to principles and a Party spirit on questions of Soviet art. He runs from one extreme to another. Until recently he favored unpatriotic critics and advertised them in his newspaper in any way possible; but after their denunciation he raised a clamorous ballyhoo in his paper, trying to represent the matter as though cosmopolitans had entrenched themselves everywhere . . . . " On April 7 the luckless editor was dismissed and sent to study at the Academy of Social Sciences (attached to the ACP(b) CC).

These invectives seriously alarmed Simonov. Realizing his imminent danger, he reluctantly, in the hope of salvation, resorted to lying. On February 15 he sent a short letter to Shepilov, declaring that the accusations that he supported the "unpatriotic group of theater critics," and in particular that he had edited Borshchagovskii's letter to the CC, were "slanderous and provocational."[86]

And on February 18, in order to eradicate the authorities' doubts about him once and for all, Simonov delivered a devastating report at the meeting of Muscovite playwrights and critics. He spoke of the critics who had been branded as cosmopolitans, calling their activity not only "harmful" but also "criminal work, hostile to Soviet dramaturgy." Apparently attempting to outdo his rivals in the USW leadership, he started denouncing cosmopolitanism as a global phenomenon:

> Speaking of cosmopolitanism, one cannot reduce its harmful activity only to the sphere of art or science; one must first of all decide what cosmopolitanism is from the political viewpoint. The propaganda of bourgeois cosmopolitanism is now beneficial to the world reactionaries, to the warmongers. Cosmopolitanism is the imperialists' policy. It is a striving for the simultaneous weakening of the patriotic feeling of independence in many countries; for the deliverance of the peoples of these countries (after having enfeebled them and bound them hand and foot) to American monopolies. Cosmopolitanism in art—this is a striving for sapping national roots, national pride, because people with their roots sapped are much more fit to be removed from the national soil and to be sold into slavery to American imperialism.[87]

Simonov was certain that his position at Stalin's court was enviable and that he could afford to waive his principles somewhat to maintain it. His romantic ideals of devotion to his literary peers disappeared under the grim prosaism of life, and together with it has last doubts vanished.[88] At a meeting of workers in the

86. RTsKhIDNI, f. 17, op. 132, d. 229, l. 17–23.

87. *Pravda*, February 28, 1949.

88. In his memoirs, "As Seen by a Man of My Generation" ("Glazami cheloveka moyevo pokoleniya," *Znamya*, 1988, Nos. 3–5), Simonov hardly even touched upon the events of early 1949. To explain this omission he wrote that he did not have at hand his diary notes relating to that period. However, it was possibly in hopes of justifying his participation in the substantially anti-Semitic campaign against so-called cosmopolitans that he wrote: "Problems of the assimilation or nonassimilation of Jews, which simply did not exist in our youth, when at school, and in the institute before the war, began to appear. Jews started dividing into those who thought their assimilation in the socialist society was naturally determined, and those who did not think so and resisted assimilation. In these postwar cataclysms, there appeared, in addition to unabashed anti-Semitism, also a concealed but stubborn Jewish nationalism, which sometimes was qualified in conversations as a sort of nationalism in the selection of personnel—all this was present in life as well as in consciousness" (*Znamya*, 1988, no. 4, p. 92).

motion picture arts he had already reproved the "bourgeois cosmopolitans and aesthetes" who were pursuing activity in films, scolding them for "propagating a shameful theory . . . of the Soviet motion picture art's forefather allegedly being American motion pictures, which began with decadence and finished with the Ku Klux Klan."[89] And on March 28 Simonov, together with Sofronov, signed a letter to Stalin and Malenkov that stated:

> In connection with the denunciation of the unpatriotic group of theater critics, the secretariat of the Union of Soviet Writers is raising the question of expelling from the ranks of the writers' union the following unpatriotic critics: Yuzovskií I.I., Gurvich A.S., Borshchagovskií A.M., Altman I.L., Malyugin L.A., Boyadzhiev G.N., Subotskií L.M., Levin F.M., Brovman G.A. as not conforming to Clause 2 of the Union of Soviet Writers Statutes . . . .[90]

The Kremlin bosses could now be satisfied. Simonov had formerly been a liberal and romantic. Sofronov was now a false patriot favoring the pogroms. And now they were fighting shoulder-to-shoulder on the ideological front carrying out the Party's will.

The clamorous anti-cosmopolitan propaganda campaign now began noticeably to subside. Stalin realized that it had already achieved its main objective; namely, to precipitate a sweeping postwar purge. And this new purge had by now spread from literary and artistic circles to other spheres of society, assuming a universal character. At first the bureaucratic machinery carried out the purge methodically and purposefully. This bureaucratic machinery was accustomed to doing its work in the tranquillity of its offices, and would resort to press ballyhoo only when unavoidable. It was no longer necessary to use propaganda as a cover for MGB actions intended to eliminate the "fifth column" of Zionism in the USSR. By April 1949 Jewish culture in the Soviet Union had, on the whole, been done away with, and all its prominent representatives were in Lubyanka. The assimilated Jews were so intimidated and demoralized that they could only dream of a national renascence, but they could not resist the greedy officials who had everywhere started forcing Jews out of prestigious positions. Fadeyev and his supporters among the leaders of the USW soon concluded that it was high time to wind up the campaign against cosmopolitans; for they had vanquished their opponents and could now celebrate victory.[91]

---

89. *Pravda*, March 4, 1949.

90. RTsKhIDNI, f. 17, op. 132, d. 229, l. 30. As it was in the case of the Jewish theaters, the Party leadership preferred to "wash its hands" of the question of expelling "unpatriotic" critics from the USW, and left the decision to the USW itself. As we have seen, the USW expelled only Altman.

91. On April 10, 1949 *Pravda* announced that the first-rank Stalin Prize had been awarded to

The process of deceleration began. Mikhail Suslov, Dmitrií Shepilov, Pyotr Pospelov, and Leonid Ilyichev insisted on putting a halt to the militant and excessively clamorous newspaper articles. They also attempted to get rid of zealous Vdovichenko-like editors who strove openly to propagate anti-Semitism, which the Stalinist regime, fearing for its international reputation, could not venture.

The last time *Pravda* mentioned the "unpatriotic" group of theater and literary critics was on April 10, 1949. The editorial was a kind of summation of the strange but predictable campaign, stating in an appeasing way that it "was a manifestation of the Party's anxiety for the steady and healthy development of Soviet literature and art on the path of socialist realism."

Nonetheless, the bourgeois cosmopolitans were seen as an arm of American expansion, and so the ideological attacks continued. Sometimes these attacks weakened; sometimes, during Stalin's fits of paranoia, they intensified sharply.

Sofronov for his play *Moscow Character*, and to A. Perventsev for his novel *Honor* (*Chest' smolodu*).

Five

Escalation of the Anti-Jewish Purges

The anti-Jewish purges in the various organizations that were predominantly under the propaganda apparatus's authority had been prepared as far back as the late 1930s, began during the war, gradually gained momentum, and expanded somewhat during the first few years after the war. However, their scale was limited. We have already seen some of the factors that restrained anti-Semitism. Until the autumn of 1948 the equilibrium between ideological and police control over society kept anti-Jewish sentiments in check, even if indirectly. The many branches of the propaganda apparatus were united by a single system; yet there was a rivalry between adherents of the moderate and extreme positions. Back when Zhdanov had held the ideological reins, "discussion" methods and "courts of honor" prevailed over arrests and exiles. (Examples of "discussion" methods were the mass media campaigns against formalism in music.) Stalin at that time took Zhdanov's opinion into consideration; but Zhdanov was superseded by Malenkov, a typical executive administrator devoid of any ideological pretensions whatsoever, who invariably relied on Stalin for his political orientation.

Being more of a pragmatist than a theoretician, Malenkov preferred punitive measures to persuasion or "re-education." He preferred eradicating "heresy" by administrative use of the ACP(b) and the MGB. Thus the period from 1946 to 1948 may be described as a relatively peaceful stage in postwar Stalinism; and propaganda campaigns, despite their extensive scale and hysterical character, were bloodless, so to speak, and resulted "merely" in the victims' dismissals from work and from the Party. This period was followed by the escalation of blatant political terror from 1949 through early 1953. The preference for resolving ideological problems by force helped strengthen the Party-police coalition that directed staff purges. With Malenkov at the helm, expulsion from the Party was often followed by arrest; and propaganda campaigns, such as the fabrication of political cases and the staging of closed-door trials, were now part of the MGB's "actions."

The chief organizer of such MGB "actions," together with the Department to Investigate Cases of Special Importance, was the Fifth Directorate, a political intelligence group that included a special force (the Sixth Department)[1] for the struggle with Zionism. The Fifth Directorate used blackmail, threats, and bribery to take advantage of people's weaknesses and vices. Capitalizing on the idea of patriotic duty, the Fifth Directorate steadily widened its base of secret agents, spinning an invisible web over offices, enterprises, art unions, and other organizations. The Fifth Directorate played a key role in carrying out various provocateur operations to fabricate "Jewish plots," upon which the watchful security "organs" demonstrated to the Kremlin authorities how timely and resolutely they could expose and counter the schemes of the "agents of American-Zionist special services." Such tactics brought the organs financial support and awards for their employees; further, they strengthened the organs' positions in the political system.

Colonel A.P. Volkov[2] headed the Fifth Directorate when Abakumov was minister of state security. However, once S.D. Ignatyev succeeded Abakumov, former MGB leaders who were now in prison (such as deputy ministers N.N. Selivanovskií and N.A. Korolyov, as well as the head of the Second Principal Bureau, Ye.P. Pitovranov) accused Volkov of being Abakumov's informer and minion. On December 22, 1951 Volkov was dismissed by decision of the ACP(b) and replaced by Major General A.P. Byzov.[3]

The postwar "chills" date back to 1947, when Suslov contributed by starting a semi-secret "combing" of the Party organizations—only a few of whose workers remembered the Party purges of the 1920s and 30s.[4] Thus the new purge had, at first, little publicity or mass indoctrination, but its results were no less impressive than those of previous campaigns. On July 25, 1947 a CC resolution "On the Further Growth of Party Ranks and the Political Education of Members and Candidate Members of the ACP(b)" was adopted and exploited to the hilt. This resolution sharply reduced admissions to the Party. In the first six months of 1947 Party membership had increased monthly by an average of 30 300 people; but by

1. I.V. Shumakov had headed the Sixth Department since 1946, and Lieutenant Colonel A.F. Rassypninskií headed it beginning in 1952.

2. Volkov was promoted to head of the Fifth Directorate in 1948 after having headed the work of reconsidering "groundlessly-shelved cases," i.e., cases against participants of the "right-wing Trotskyite underground," Social Revolutionaries (SRs), Mensheviks, anarchists, and so forth.

3. RTsKhIDNI, f. 17, op. 118, d. 20, l. 224; op. 119, d. 662, l. 108, 113–115.

4. As of July 1, 1947 there were 6 263 117 members and candidate members of the ACP(b), three-fourths of whom had become members during or after the war. RTsKhIDNI, f. 17, op. 118, d. 922, l. 93–94.

the latter half of 1948 the average increase was only 5 000. In 1947, 298 392 people had been admitted to the ACP(b), but in 1948 only 85 308 were admitted. Moreover, 146 181 people had been expelled from the Party in 1948. This was the first postwar year in which the number of people expelled far exceeded the number admitted.[5] This trend continued in 1949.

By the beginning of 1949 the incubation period of the "cleansing" was over, and it exceeded the limits of just Party "regulations." Gradually it spread to virtually all structures of the state apparatus, as well as to cultural, educational, scientific, and economic spheres. With the tumultuous "exposures" of "anti-patriots" among theater critics, the persecutions became overt. The campaign highlighted both the excellent coordination between the MGB and Suslov-Malenkov group in the ACP(b) CC, and the precision of their actions. Under the guise of anti-cosmopolitan propaganda, they together routed Jewish public organizations and culture. The campaign also demonstrated the bankruptcy of the "liberal" methods employed by Zhdanov and others, such as Agitprop head Shepilov. The campaign against "anti-patriots" made the purge assume an explicitly anti-Semitic character.

Journalism

From March 1 through 5, 1949 the Party staged an exhausting marathon meeting at which it selected its own ideological institutions, particularly *Pravda*'s editorial board, as the primary objectives of the purge. The Party declared that "the work collective had nestled a certain group of employers comprising S.R. Gershberg, L.K. Brontman, B.R. Izakov, A.E. Kornblyum, D.G. Kosov,[6] and others who had actively supported cosmopolitans." These employers were accused of factionalism, nationalist inclinations, and ties with JAC leaders. Gershberg, Brontman, and Ya.Z. Goldenberg (Viktorov) were criticized, among other things, for dragging materials onto the pages of *Pravda*—materials that actually advertised the Botkin hospital and its head at that time, B.A. Shimeliovich. The masterminds of the "Party trial" found out that *Pravda* had published 16 articles of a similar nature since 1939. International analyst Goldenberg now "repented" for not having rebuked the "nationalist" Mikhoels, who had called him an "assimilationist" for assuming the pen name Viktorov.[7]

Kornblyum was incriminated for his contacts with I.I. Yuzovskií, "the leader and ideologue of the bourgeois-cosmopolitan band." Kornblyum had also written

5. RTsKhIDNI, f. 17, op. 118, d. 922, l. 93–94.

6. Kosov is also sometimes referred to as Kossov.

7. RTsKhIDNI, f. 17, op. 118, d. 333, l. 97–129.

glowing reviews of Yuzovskiĭ's book, *The Image and the Epoch*,[8] which, incidentally, was never published. Kornblyum had also criticized *Pravda*'s literature department (i.e., V.M. Kozhevnikov and B.N. Polevoĭ), and this was the main reason he could not be pardoned.[9]

B.R. Izakov, an international analyst and deputy head of the Foreign Department, was severely disciplined for being among those who, back in 1948, had interceded for L.Z. Kopelev's release. And Kosov, the deputy head of the Economics Department, was related to Anna Louise Strong, an American journalist who had been accused of spying and was expelled from the USSR in February 1949.[10] Kosov had tried to conceal this relationship, and he was severely punished for this.

One of those who also "got it hot" was a grand master of Soviet Party journalism and Stalin's favorite, David I. Zaslavskiĭ.[11] Although his punishment was minimal, he did have to repent for his contacts with Mikhoels and Shimeliovich, and he did have to "plead guilty" of having bought a Jewish Theater season ticket and of being a JAC member (which meant "lack of political watchfulness").

To avoid suspicion of sympathizing with the accused, some Jewish *Pravda* workers tried to prove that they were uncompromisingly exposing cosmopolitanism. *Pravda*'s international analyst, Ya.S. Marinin (Khavinson), among others, made special efforts to do so when speaking at the Party meeting:

> Leaders of American imperialism among Jewish bourgeoisie use a variety of channels to inject the poison of national chauvinism into a certain stratum of the Jewish population of this country, exploiting here the influence exerted by family ties to a considerable number of American Jews of Russian origin, so that through these channels and these ties they could spread their ideology and install their agents. Influenced from the outside, the counterrevolutionary nationalist elements decided that it was time to raise their heads in order to try to implant their own agents of the external imperialist forces among the Jewish population here, within a certain Jewish stratum. A

---

8. *Obraz i epokha.*

9. RTsKhIDNI, f. 17, op. 118, d. 695, l. 21–22.

10. Vdovichenko (the editor of *Soviet Art*) had reported to the CC that Strong was Kosov's wife's sister-in-law.

11. Zaslavskiĭ was head of the Journalism Department at the Party School of the ACP(b) CC. On March 25, 1949 he was dismissed and Leonid F. Ilyichev was appointed in his place. Zaslavskiĭ had, among other things, published in *Pravda* in the mid-1930s an enthusiastic review of the Jewish Theater's production of *King Lear*, calling Mikhoels an actor of genius. Additionally, he had spoken so forcefully and emotionally at Mikhoels's memorial service in 1948 that he was even offered the chairmanship of the JAC. RTsKhIDNI, f. 17, op. 118, d. 345, l. 13–14.

> considerable group of well-known Jewish personalities from among cosmopolitan critics participates in these nationalist groupings. They are directly connected to each other and are nourished from the same sources.[12]

As a result of these Party debates (which dragged on for days), Gershberg, Brontman, Izakov, and Kornblyum were dismissed from *Pravda*'s editorial board on March 11, 1949.[13] Other journalists (Goldenberg, Mordkovich, and Zaslavskiĭ) who were criticized for their contacts with cosmopolitans were punished less harshly.[14] On May 19 G.Ye. Ryklin was dismissed as editor-in-chief of the satirical magazine *Crocodile*.[15] P.N. Pospelov was chief editor of *Pravda*, and as such he executed general control of *Crocodile*. It was he who proposed Ryklin's dismissal. Since Stalin did not think the results of the purge were sufficiently radical, Pospelov was accused of "liberalism" and was now considered too "lenient" to be *Pravda*'s editor-in-chief. He was then appointed director of the Marx-Engels-Lenin Research Institute at the ACP(b), and Stalin turned *Pravda* over to Suslov. Suslov, though, had his hands full as CC secretary, so L.F. Ilyichev was summoned to assist him as deputy editor. Ilyichev later became *Pravda*'s editor-in-chief.

Similar maneuvers, with some variations, occurred at other newspapers and magazines. Dismissals generally followed the pattern laid down by Agitprop, which was worried not so much by the monotonous purging process as by possible "amateurism," which was fraught with undesirable "distortions of the Party trend on the national question." This implied that the anti-Semitism resulting from the military journals' and newspapers' excessive zeal and industriousness had gone too far. Particularly chauvinistic was the Navy newspaper, *Red Fleet*.[16] Back in the autumn of 1947 I.V. Baru had criticized the rude and uncouth tone of the *Red*

---

12. RTsKhIDNI, f. 17, op. 118, d. 333, l. 106.

13. The MCSC had sentenced Kornblyum's brother-in-law, the playwright V.M. Kirshon, to be executed by firing squad in April 1938. Kornblyum would now not put up with being dismissed. He repeatedly applied to the CC, demanding reinstatement. As a result, he was charged with slandering the leadership of *Pravda*'s editorial board and was arrested. In particular, he was accused of criminal contacts with the nationalistic group at the Moscow Automobile Plant where he had earlier worked as a member of the editorial staff of the factory newspaper, and later as editor of *Pravda*'s roving editorial board.

14. RTsKhIDNI, f. 17, op. 118, d. 373, l. 131–135.

15. *Krokodil.* On September 6, 1948 Ryklin was charged with allowing himself to be led by a "handful" of Moscow satirists, namely L.S. Lench, E.Ya. German (Emil Krotkiĭ), B.S. Laskin, and M. Edel. Though he lost his post as editor-in-chief he remained on the editorial board until his final dismissal in May 1949. Among other things, he was charged with distributing Jewish Theater season tickets in his capacity as a JAC member. RTsKhIDNI, f. 17, op. 118, d. 397, l. 5; d. 143, l. 36–43; d. 153, l. 36.

16. *Krasnyĭ flot.*

Fleet's articles about the former Anglo-American allies; and traveling reporters G.S. Novogrudskií and M.B. Charnyí had come out against attacks by Stalin's authorities on A.A. Akhmatova and M.M. Zoshchenko. Now all three were "laid off due to staff reduction."[17] The campaign against theater critics stirred up even more anti-Semitic enthusiasm among the *Red Fleet* editors. Thus on March 16–19, 1949 there was a Party meeting devoted to the "struggle against bourgeois cosmopolitanism." In criticizing their colleagues, some of the speakers referred to them as "Jew Ponevezhskií," "Jew Rudnyí," "Jew Ivich," and so on. Captain Pashchenko, head of the Department of Party Life, went even further; he declared that "just as the whole German people is held responsible for Hitler's aggression, so the entire Jewish race must answer for the actions of bourgeois cosmopolitans."[18]

Indignant at this anti-Semitic escapade, S.A. Livshits, *Red Fleet's* deputy executive secretary, wrote Stalin about this incident. Stalin never saw his letter, which was forwarded to Malenkov and Poskrebyshev. The CC inspectors who were commissioned to investigate this case were quite satisfied that Pashchenko admitted that his words were "politically erroneous." The annoying incident was considered settled.[19] Later, after passions had subsided, the administration began to "squeeze" the Jewish troublemakers from the staff without much ado. In June 1949 Isaak D. Sakhnovskií was dismissed as executive secretary of *Red Fleet*.[20] In all probability the same happened to Semyon Livshits, who had sought justice from Stalin. Livshits was lucky not to have been arrested. Other staff members were not so fortunate, for instance Leonid Ivich, Solomon Zande (who afterwards was shot), I.D. Sakhnovskií, Arkadií Ponevezhskií, and Meri Umanskaya, who had supplied the JAC with information about Jews serving in the Navy.

The situation at the *Stalin's Falcon*[21] newspaper was somewhat different. This was published by the Political Department of the Air Forces, and its editor, B.P. Pavlov, "manifested a political recklessness" and "littered" the managerial staff with "hostile and dubious people." The MGB had to interfere. On September 9, 1949 MGB officers arrested B.L. Perelmuter,[22] a staff member who had carelessly mentioned to somebody that the struggle against cosmopolitanism resembled Yezhov's terror.[23] The Political Directorate of the Air Force later joined

17. RTsKhIDNI, f. 17, op. 125, d. 565, l. 138–140.

18. RTsKhIDNI, f. 17, op. 132, d. 118, l. 2.

19. RTsKhIDNI, f. 17, op. 132, d. 118, l. 6–7.

20. RTsKhIDNI, f. 17, op. 132, d. 118, l. 27–28.

21. *Stalinskií sokol.*

22. By a March 4, 1950 resolution of the Special Meeting, Perelmuter was sentenced to ten years of camp. He was released on December 31, 1954.

23. *Translator's note:* Yezhov was Beria's predecessor.

in, along with its major general, V.S. Shimko. This joint effort of political administrators and security men helped prove that Pavlov had been "manipulated" by a "friendly circle" composed almost entirely of Jews (among them Saksonov, Furmanov, and Fridlyanskiĭ). It is not difficult to guess what followed: Pavlov lost his position as head of the editorial board. All the members of the "Jewish group" were also fired.[24] The same happened to the staff of the *Frontier Guard*[25] magazine, a publication of the Political Department of Frontier Guard Troops at the Ministry of Internal Affairs. Its editor, G. Belykh, was dismissed for publishing the writings of—and for being on friendly terms with—such "stateless cosmopolitans" as D. Danin, L. Subotskiĭ, V. Shklovskiĭ, and B. Yakovlev (Kholtsman).[26]

The mass media's information on "cosmopolitan groups" inspired panic and paranoia among the ideological watchdogs at Old Square. If the cosmopolitan spirit could penetrate even the Army political body publications, then what on earth might be going on at other editorial boards where the proportion of Jews was considerably higher? Sweeping checks and double checks of journalistic cadres ensued, primarily among those entrusted with the important task of the "education of the young generation." In October 1949 the ACP(b) CC sent its inspectors to the *Komsomol Pravda*,[27] a newspaper for youth. The resulting report abounded in gloomy assessments and resolute measures to be taken. The commission stated that editor-in-chief A.Ya. Blatin had littered the editorial staff with such "politically dubious personalities" as Khesin, the head of the Information Department who had concealed his father's arrest; Yurovskiĭ, who had been fired from *Stalin's Falcon*; and Chekova, a literary associate who was the daughter of a man who had been a wealthy trader before the revolution. Further, among the non-staff contributors were Anatoliĭ A. Agranovskiĭ, whose father had earlier been subjected to repression by security bodies; Frida Vigdorova, who had relatives living in America; and others. The commission concluded that the staffing policy resulted in half of the employees being Russian and half being Jewish, with certain employees (such as Smirnova, Katsnevich, Kirklisova, Besfamilnaya, and others) trying to conceal their true nationality.[28]

The Politburo resolution of December 3, 1949 read:

> The proposal of the ALCUY Central Committee—to the effect that a) Comrade Blatin A.Ya. shall be relieved of his responsibilities as editor-in-chief and editorial board member of the *Komsomol Pravda*

---

24. RTsKhIDNI, f. 17, op. 132, d. 118, l. 41–47, 71.

25. *Pogranichnik.*

26. RTsKhIDNI, f. 17, op. 132, d. 339, l. 53–62.

27. *Komsomolskaya pravda* (literally, *The Komsomol Truth*).

28. RTsKhIDNI, f. 17, op. 118, d. 580, l. 76–79.

> newspaper; b) Comrade Goryunov D.P. shall be appointed editor-in-chief and editorial staff member of the *Komsomol Pravda* newspaper—is approved by the Central Committee.
>
> Secretary of the Central Committee, I. Stalin[29]

In July 1950 Blatin wrote to Stalin requesting exoneration from this groundless accusation. He explained that he had criticized the ALCUY CC secretary, N.A. Mikhaílov, at an ALCUY congress in the spring of 1949, and contended that he had now fallen victim to the schemes of Mikhaílov, who wanted to get even with him.[30]

As could be expected, Blatin did not achieve justice. Mikhaílov, who had dealt him the blow, was in Stalin's favor at the time. Powerfully climbing to the top of the apparatus hierarchy, he intuitively guessed that betting on anti-Semitism was the shortest way to the aging patriarch's heart. His calculation was as primitive as it was successful, and it led to *Komsomol Pravda* initiating, after the crucible of the anti-Jewish purge, an ambiguous discussion about pen names in the winter of 1950/1951. The February 27 issue featured an article by the writer Mikhail S. Bubennov who, under the pretext of combating "chameleon-like behavior," revealed a number of pen names of Jewish writers and journalists.[31] For appearance's sake Bubennov did list a few non-Jewish writers, but no one could doubt his anti-Semitic slant.

A new surge in the propagandistic hunt for "anti-patriots" seemed inevitable—and Bubennov attempted to instigate it when he wrote that "pen names were willingly used by cosmopolitans in their articles." However, his tactic failed. On March 6 the *Literary Gazette* featured a polemical article by K.M. Simonov, who declared that the use of a pen name was a writer's own business. The young Simonov could hardly have been guided by his own wishes in writing this. It is more likely that he had won Stalin's backing, having restored himself in the dictator's esteem after the theater critics scandal.[32] So Simonov

29. RTsKhIDNI, f. 17, op. 118, d. 615, l. 20.

30. RTsKhIDNI, f. 17, op. 118, d. 969, l. 69–71.

31. Yu. Ognetsvet went by the pen name of E.S. Kagan, L. Likhodeyev by Lides, and N. Grebnev by Rambakh. There were others also.

32. On May 11, 1950 Stalin signed a Politburo resolution of March appointing Simonov editor-in-chief of the *Literary Gazette*. Simonov's successor as head of *New World*, a literary magazine, was A.T. Tvardovskií. It was thanks to Fadeyev's support that these two liberal writers came to occupy the key posts. Fadeyev was beginning to fear the jingoistic faction in the Union of Soviet Writers. This faction was headed by A. Sofronov and was rapidly gaining strength after the defeat of cosmopolitan critics.

Simonov's predecessor as editor-in-chief was V.V. Yermilov, who had long been friends with Fadeyev, as both had been leading members of the Russian Association of Proletarian Writers in the late 1920s and early 1930s. Nonetheless Yermilov had begun to scheme, almost openly, against Fadeyev, and this was one reason for his replacement. Yermilov had to behave quietly for some time. However, in the

gained another opportunity to influence the patriarch's decision. Furthermore, Simonov was at that time frequently seeing Stalin at sessions of the Committee for the Stalin Literature and Art Award. However, though he was in the dictator's favor, he had to play the hypocrite and conform to the rules of the apparatus game; specifically, he had to emphasize indirect arguments rather than call a spade a spade with respect to the anti-Semitic attacks.

Next to join the discussion of pen names was M. Sholokhov, the author of *And Quiet Flows the Don.*[33] Sholokhov (who back in the autumn of 1941 was in Kuíbyshev and shocked I. Erenburg with his drunken anti-Semitic swearing), fully aware of Simonov's ambiguous position, accused him, in the pages of the *Komsomol Pravda*, of insincerity, and criticized his article for presupposing that readers would read between the lines. The grand master's article in support of M.S. Bubennov came out under the eloquent headline, "With the Visor Lowered."[34] Simonov parried the sketch with another article in the March 10 issue of his newspaper. This apparently closed the matter. This discussion never grew into a new anti-Jewish campaign. Stalin probably thought it too early to deal openly with bearers of pen names; he preferred to work quietly, utilizing secret arrests rather than propagandistic fanfare. This tactic, in the eyes of intellectuals, helped him retain the image of a just leader and an opponent of national intolerance. Simonov reminisced later that once, in March 1952, at one of the sessions of the Stalin Prize Committee, Stalin spoke in a deliberately harsh manner about disclosing pen names. "Last year enough was said on the subject," raged the patriarch with theatrical indignation. "We prohibited giving double surnames[35] when nominating for the Prize. What are you doing this for? Why instill anti-Semitism?"[36]

Thanks to Stalin's whim, fortune now smiled upon Simonov, not upon Mikhaílov, Bubennov, or Sholokhov. However, Simonov could hardly have felt like a winner, especially since his opponents could not be further from laying down their arms.

A certain V. Orlov, formerly employed with the *Literary Gazette*, wrote to Malenkov on June 15, 1951:

> The staff composition of many newspapers has improved considerably of late in terms of national proportions, and for this we ought heartily

---

early 1960s the Party leaders employed his services once again and he wrote a devastating article against Aleksandr I. Solzhenitsyn.

33. *Tikhii Don.*

34. "S opushchennym zabralom," *Komsomolskaya pravda*, March 8, 1951.

35. *Translator's note:* By "double surnames" Stalin is referring to the Russian names that Jews adopted and attached to their own names.

36. *Znamya*, 1944, no. 4, p. 85.

to thank the Central Committee.... At the same time we still have newspapers where the situation is lamentable. I have in mind two Moscow newspapers—*Labor*[37] and *Literary Gazette*. After Simonov came to work with the latter, the course for keeping Russians out, for strengthening and expanding the Zionist core... began to outline itself quite clearly in its staff policy.... Krivitskiĭ became Simonov's right-hand man, his foremost and constant advisor in all matters.[38] Besides Krivitskiĭ, a decisive role in the newspaper's life has been given to all sorts of Latsises, Chernyaks, Podlyashchuks, Rozentsveĭgs, and the like.[39] Thus Simonov started almost deliberately to follow a policy that was just the opposite to the one pursued at other newspapers at the time. It is extremely strange that this man, who calls himself a Russian (an outrageous lie, that!),[40] should gravitate so much to all sorts of Krivitskiĭs.... [He] almost openly declares himself their patron (just remember his polemics with Sholokhov); while they, in their turn, regard him as their leader and praise him to the heavens.... I left the staff of the *Literary Gazette* (one would never call it Russian, judging by its "letter and spirit"!) to work with *Labor*. Alas! Out of the frying pan and into the fire. The proportion of Russians among the staff was only 10% quite recently. 90% were made up of all sorts of Chershvelds, Livshitses, Miringofs, Litvaks, and Koffs. The predominance of this kind of people in all departments of the popular trade-union newspaper was absolute and complete. This undoubtedly prepared the fertile ground for the development of Zionist ideas and Zionist elements. It is no accident that a number of persons from among the staff, including Litvak and Ilyin (whose true surname is different), have been arrested of late. Practically no portraits of Party and state leaders were put up anywhere on the premises. This is a fact, however monstrous. The number of Russians working with the newspaper has increased lately (up to about 56% of the total), but the closely-knit group is still master of the situation; it acts as if on orders from a single center and pursues a single policy. The group includes Livshits (assistant secretary), Rossovskiĭ (editor of the

---

37. *Trud*.

38. Z.Yu. Krivitskiĭ was the editor of the "International Life" pages.

39. *Translator's note:* These are all typical Jewish names.

40. Simonov wrote in his memoirs about the time he had been invited to the Propaganda Department of the Central Committee and shown a similar letter accusing him of conniving with Jews at the *Literary Gazette*. The author of this letter maintained that Simonov's Jewish origin laid behind these sympathies. To support his theory, the author related a fantastic story about Simonov's father, an innkeeper named Simanovich. The CC ignored this letter. Yet in late January 1951 the CC found fault with a number of articles published in the *Literary Gazette* and so discharged its leading authors, A.A. Agranovskiĭ and B.I. Rozentsveĭg. *Znamya*, 1944, no. 4, pp. 103–104; RTsKhIDNI, f. 17, op. 119, d. 216, l. 1, 7–8.

> Propaganda Department), Manuilskiǐ (assistant editor), Vaǐnshteǐn (acting editor of the Foreign Department), Koff (assistant editor of the Economics Department), Yudkin (head of the Letters Department), Segalov, Raǐskiǐ, and many, many others . . . . This is, indeed, the limit. Indeed, our leadership resembles Shchedrin's "Sleepy Eye" that uses one eye only, while the other eye cannot see what is going on around it. Could we possibly get the "sleepy eye" to wake up at last, and could it replace the soft—I would even say flabby—policy with respect to these people with a hard and firm one.[41]

These reproaches against "poor" personnel work forced Suslov and his subordinates to defend themselves. They submitted a report to Malenkov with evidence that they had dismissed more than 40 employees from the *Labor* staff from April 1950 to August 1951. Among those sacked on political grounds were Gershfeld (assistant executive secretary of the editorial board); Khmelnitskaya (assistant editor of the Department for Cultural Work Among the Masses); feature writers Boǐm, Berkovskiǐ, Lelgant; reporters Vaǐntrub, Levin, Pitsyk; lawyers Shargorodskaya and Kronik; and personnel inspector Eǐdinova. Thus they had reduced the proportion of Jews from 50 percent of the staff in early 1950 to 20 percent by the autumn of 1951.[42]

Suslov and his subordinates presented these facts and figures to prove that the Party Ideological Agency did not at all deserve to be reproached for indecision, to say nothing of a lack of zeal. It was fairly easy for Suslov and his friends to fend off such a criticism "from below." It was not for nothing that they held their positions in the Central Committee. Besides, the CC apparatus acted secretly, methodically, and systematically. This was in contrast to their radical critics who went into hysterics over each instance of a "predominance of Jews" among this or that newspaper staff and who demanded immediate draconian measures "to promote a healthier atmosphere." In order to keep the staff of the propaganda sphere "regulated," Agitprop's "regulation" of personnel in propaganda institutions became omnipotent; it now kept not only the press and printing industry under careful control, but also those who delivered periodicals to the consumers.

In October 1950 Agitprop began to attend more closely to the Agency for Dispatch and Delivery of the Press (Soyuzpechat) which daily delivered to the Soviet population 4 638 national and local newspapers with a combined daily circulation of 28.6 million, as well as 436 magazines with a combined circulation of 8.6 million.[43]

---

41. RTsKhIDNI, f. 17, op. 119, d. 452, l. 4–12.
42. RTsKhIDNI, f. 17, op. 119, d. 452, l. 13–15.
43. RTsKhIDNI, f. 17, op. 119, d. 118, l. 230.

Agitprop discovered that among the 18 heads and assistant heads of the Soyuzpechat department and central offices, 10 were Jews. F.B. Ramsin, the head of Soyuzpechat, and Mlodik, the head of Soyuzpechat's Leningrad office, were held responsible and immediately dismissed "for inadequate supervision."[44]

Then Agitprop began an inspection of personnel at the country's main information center, the Telegraph Agency of the Soviet Union, which had long been under its and the MGB's careful control. From 1948 through 1949 the MGB arrested A. Gurevich, Emdin, and Kanter, who were all employees of the Telegraph Agency's Foreign Information editorial board. Then 66 people were discharged from TASS in 1949–1950, the greater portion of them Jewish. Under various pretexts the MGB got rid of S. Gurevich ("former Trotskyite" and brother of the arrested A. Gurevich); A.V. Lyubarskiı́; B.A. and A.M. Rabinovich (both on the Foreign Information editorial board); Dreı́tsen (the organizing manager); Baumshteı́n (head of the Local Press editorial board); and eight other employees: A.M. Teı́telbaum, L.O. Lempert, S.P. Meltser, N.E. Shapiro, D.Ye. Sherman, G.Yu. Shkarovskiı́, V.A. Bogorad, and G.Ye. Kunin, and others.[45]

The Radio-Telegraph Agency of the Ukraine (RATAU) was also turned upside-down. To begin with, on May 26, 1950 *Pravda* featured an article called "Fruit of Faulty Leadership,"[46] which sharply criticized RATAU's executive director, Lev Izrailevich Troskunov. The article alleged that "a group of dirty dealers" had "made a nest" in the agency with Troskunov's connivance. Among this group were Yeva Gorelik (Troskunov's "retainer") and other members of the press bureau, including Shteı́ngrob, Litvak, Aı́zenberg, and Lipavskiı́. Troskunov had started his career as a journalist in the town of Yuzovka in the Ukraine, where he met N.S. Khrushchev, who recommended him for the Party. Troskunov had been executive editor of the *Pravda Ukrainy* newspaper. Then Kaganovich briefly served as first secretary of the UCP(b) CC in 1947, and immediately started a decisive offensive against Jewish and Ukrainian nationalism. Troskunov was driven out of the newspaper.[47] When his persecutor was called back to Moscow Troskunov was appointed to RATAU with Khrushchev's assistance. But Troskunov encountered another difficult time, and Khrushchev, who was now far away in Moscow, could not protect his old friend. The Ukraine's new Communist leadership promptly reacted to *Pravda*'s May 26 article, and on the following day decided to remove Troskunov as head of the republic's information agency.[48]

---

44. RTsKhIDNI, f. 17, op. 119, d. 118, l. 235, 236.
45. RTsKhIDNI, f. 17, op. 118, d. 931, l. 133–150; 188–190.
46. "Plody porochnogo rukovodstva"
47. N.S. Khrushchev, "Vospominaniya" ("Memoirs"), *Voprosy istorii*, 1991, no. 11, p. 42.
48. RTsKhIDNI, f. 17, op. 118, d. 1003, l. 56–61; d. 959, l. 11.

Ousted from newspapers, journals, and institutes of higher education, Jews worked for subsistence wages at various public organizations, where Party control was then weaker. Many earned a living by going on lecture circuits (speaking chiefly on foreign policy) within the framework of the All-Union Society for Spreading Political and Scientific Knowledge. For example, in 1949 among the society's lecturers were Z.S. Sheínis, a journalist, and his colleague L.I. Eliovich, both of whom had been fired from the All-Union Radio Committee. Another lecturer at that time was E.G. Kutnik, who had worked as editor of the British Press Department at the Sovinformburo during Lozovskií's time. However, the CC began to receive numerous reports about "stateless cosmopolitans" earning good salaries by lecturing, and Agitprop reacted promptly by organizing the necessary checkups. As a result, in the society's Moscow Region branch alone, 98 lecturers, chiefly Jews, lost their jobs by early 1951.[49]

The persecution was increasing not only because the Jews were Jewish, but also because of what may be called state nationalism, which inevitably, and without the intention of the Russians, manifested itself as Russian nationalism. The nomenclatura was fearful because Jews accounted for a considerable proportion of the intellectual stratum. By the irony of fate, Jews were destined to be persecuted for the simple reason that intellectual elite, regardless of their national origin, were under special suspicion and control of Party, ideological, and state bodies. It was only natural under these circumstances that Glavlit would institute more severe censorship and staffing policies. Glavlit was then headed by K.K. Omelchenko, who was officially referred to as the USSR Soviet Ministers' authorized agent for guarding military and state secrets in the press. Omelchenko proudly called Glavlit "the state's highest control authority on the ideological front."[50] Glavlit began its massive attack on Jewish personnel after the CC received an anonymous letter signed "Well-Wisher" in September 1950. "Well-Wisher" was indignant that the censorship body had been "congested" with Jews, "directly" (by Dodzin, Pinsukhovich, Kaminskií, Tutantsev) or "indirectly" (by people who pretended to be Belorussians, Ukrainians, and Russians, such as Demchinskií and Mukha). "Well-Wisher" was especially annoyed that Dodzin was still working. For it was Dodzin, the assistant secretary of the Glavlit Party bureau, who had supervised forwarding the JAC materials abroad. The anonymous writer provocatively asked: "Could it possibly be that Glavlit is a masked affiliate of the Jewish Antifascist Committee—an entrenched nest of spies

49. RTsKhIDNI, f. 17, op. 118, d. 404, l. 65–73; d. 720, l. 71–80; d. 968, l. 142–149.

50. In 1949 Glavlit (by a resolution of June 6) withdrew from libraries many books written by Jewish literati, among which was L. Deích's *The Role of Jews in the Russian Revolutionary Movement* [*Rol' yevreyev v russkom revolyutsionnom dvizhenii*] (Moscow, 1925).

and traitors?"[51]

The supervising authority at Old Square could not help but be worried—and inspired—by such information. Old Square sent an Agitprop commission to Glavlit from late 1950 to early 1951. As could be expected, the watchful inspectors confirmed the discrediting report and succeeded in "exposing" many new facts. Glavlit's Foreign Literature Department was headed by a certain Dobroselskaya, a good acquaintance of M.M. Borodin (Gruzenberg), the former *Moscow News*[52] editor who had been arrested by security bodies. This the inspectors considered unacceptable. Further, the head of the Group for Censorship of Anglo-American Literature was Boleslavskií, who had lived in the USA from 1913 through 1917, had been a member of the American Socialist Party, and had, in conjunction with the exposed "Bund member" L.Ya. Aronshtam, handed uncensored books from abroad to the JAC. This was in violation of the CC resolution of September 14, 1946. As a result of this violation, "Bund member" David Pinskií's *Book of Travels* (published in New York in 1938) became available for general use, and in 1949 the censor Galperin[53] sanctioned open access to a Venezuelan Trotskyite newspaper published by Rudolfo Tintera. However, most suspicious were the contacts between S.A. Lozovskií and Glavlit employees prior to 1949. For instance, Glavlit's assistant head Balashov had worked as Lozovskií's assistant in the Sovinformburo and controlled the publications of the Supreme Party School at the ACP(b) CC, where Lozovskií was teaching. Omelchenko was consequently ordered to dismiss Dobroselskaya, Shteín-Kamenskií, Balashov, Boleslavskií, and other employees from Glavlit.[54]

Glavlit's peripheral bodies were also purged. For instance, Dadiomova, the head of the Belorussian Republic's Glavlit, was dismissed on July 29, 1950 at a session of the Belorussian Communist Party (Bolshevik) CC. The reason was that Minsk libraries freely lent out books by such "enemies of the people" as Bergelson, Markish, Fefer, Gikalo, and Gololed. In addition, Dadiomova's brother had been repressed as a Trotskyite; and Dadiomova herself was reported to have openly expressed indignation that there were no Jews among the nominees for the Supreme Soviet of the USSR, and to have attributed this to the anti-Semitic sentiments of certain Belorussian leaders.[55]

The two masters and guardians of Glavlit were the MGB and the CC. The MGB executed control over the non-betrayal of state and military secrets in the

---

51. The MGB had earlier presented the accusation about the loss of vigilance concerning the JAC materials to Glavlit's senior censor, Ya.M. Paĭkin. RTsKhIDNI, f. 17, op. 119, d. 66, l. 80–84.

52. *Moskovskiye novosti.*

53. The MGB arrested Galperin in 1950.

54. RTsKhIDNI, f. 17, op. 119, d. 216, l. 162–172, 179–182.

55. RTsKhIDNI, f. 17, op. 118, d. 750, l. 184–186.

mass media, and the CC carried out ideological control. Of these two, it was the CC that made the greatest contribution to reshuffling the staff. This may have been brought about by the Party's dissatisfaction with the censorship bureaucracy. Glavlit had felt uncomfortable, for it was given no clear-cut instructions about how to distinguish between what was allowed and what was forbidden for publication and reading. Glavlit was therefore overcautious and sluggish. The CC was besieged by those wishing to prove Glavlit officials guilty of insufficient political vigilance. For example. A. Fadeyev addressed Agitprop in August 1952 and complained that theaters, particularly in their variety shows, often presented works by 13 repressed authors, among them L. Sheínin, I. Maklyarskií, M. Ulitskií, and L. Rozner. If Glavlit and the Fine Arts Committee had shown greater initiative in banning the publication and public performances of works authored by those condemned for "counterrevolutionary activity," the Copyright Agency[56] would have stopped paying their relatives royalties.[57] Agitprop took this as indirect criticism of its activity and feared that these and similar reproofs may have reached Stalin. That is why censorship was escalated at publishing houses, radio stations, theaters, and elsewhere.

Arts

The Party and ideological agencies imposed a particularly strict censorship upon the Bolshoí Theater, for it was regarded as the prime "show case" Soviet art—and it was frequently attended by Stalin[58] and his comrades-in-arms. The Bolshoí celebrated its 175th anniversary in 1951 and Agitprop contributed to the preparations. In October 1950 the Bolshoí was preparing a new production of Camille Saint-Saëns's opera, *Samson and Delilah*. Agitprop demanded a copy of the libretto, and, after submitting it to ideological "expertise," the Art Section of Agitprop passed a resolution that today may seem merely amusing. At that time, however, it was taken as gospel truth and produced fear and trepidation:

> . . . The opera undoubtedly possesses messianic, biblical, and Zionist features . . . . The new text of the opera, though stylistically improved, is ideologically still rather dubious. Moreover, the main theme of persecuted and baited Jews who seek revenge for their destiny is

---

56. G. Khesin had long headed the All-Union Copyright Agency. The MGB arrested him in 1950.

57. RTsKhIDNI, f. 17, op. 119, d. 1061, l. 128–130.

58. On May 17, 1948 Stalin signed a Politburo resolution dismissing chief conductor and art director A.M. Pazovskií, and appointing N.S. Golovanov chief conductor. Professor D.R. Rogal-Levitskií of the Moscow Conservatory recalls that as early as 1944 Stalin remarked: "And still Golovanov is a real anti-Semite, an evil and dogmatic anti-Semite." *Nezavisimaya gazeta* (*Independent Gazette*), February 12, 1991.

> sometimes brought to the fore.... In the new libretto the two camps—Jews and Philistines—are contrasted more sharply. For example, Delilah has been "promoted" and acts in conjunction with the highest priest of the Philistines. Jews, with Samson as their leader, have been "demoted" to the position of slaves in the second half of the opera. However, this has only resulted in a greater emphasis on the "messianic" theme and on a Jewish elder's words addressed to Jews "as a sermon for the young"—"Eye for eye, tooth for tooth! *So be it till the end of the days!*"—acquire a definite symbolic meaning. A number of other examples from the libretto that produce similar associations could be given: the chorus of Jews, "Our time has come," which seems to be the chief theme at the end of the first act; the monologue of Samson speaking of the "Nazarite's mane"—a symbol of might among the ancient Jews; or, for example, Samson's "prophetic" words addressed to the Philistines: "*There are thousands and multitudes of us* and you will not count us all . . . . " There are many symbols from the Bible and ancient Jewish epics, for example, "Land of Canaan," "Nazarites," or, at the beginning of the second scene, "Rejoice, Israel, the sun is shining again. Your eternal enemy has fallen . . . . " It should be pointed out that though the word "Israel"—repeatedly used in the old text—has been replaced by "Adonai," this in most cases does not change anything, since Adonai is only a variant of the ancient Jewish word "Lord, master." Even the opera's finale itself is objectionable. If in the old text Samson spoke to God and asked to be given strength enough to destroy the temple to avenge him (God), in the new text Samson's concluding remarks sound symbolic and significant: "Time for revenge, you have come!" All these examples give one doubts as to the advisability of producing this opera, with a text like this, on the stage of the Bolshoí Theater. In the production of this opera, several episodes may play a negative role . . . as a stimulus for kindling Zionist sentiments among the Jewish portion of the population, especially if we take into account certain well-known facts of recent years.[59]

After such a negative assessment, the Fine Arts Committee gave instructions for all work on this opera production to be stopped.[60]

By this time, however, Agitprop had no say in the matter. Agitprop's

59. RTsKhIDNI, f. 17, op. 132, d. 419, l. 209–211.

60. RTsKhIDNI, f. 17, op. 132, d. 419, l. 212. Metropolitan of Krutitsy and Kolomna, Yuvenaliî (Poyarkov), relates another story that is as characteristic as it is absurd. At approximately the same time, the Council for the Affairs of the Russian Orthodox Church, by order of the ACP(b), sent a directive to its authorized agents in krais and regions prohibiting clergymen from pronouncing the words about the glory of the people of Israel in the canonical text of the funeral service prayer, "Lord, let Your slave now depart in peace . . . (Luke 2:29)."

activities of controlling art institutions were subjected to careful control by Suslov's apparatus. This control began in the spring of 1950, when the ACP(b) CC was flooded with collectively-signed letters (chiefly from the Moscow State Philharmonic Society) stating that there were "nationalist tendencies" in staffing.[61] These letters, usually initiated by the local Party committees, finally had their effect. In October 1950 Agitprop carried out what is officially called "an on-site inspection of the facts submitted." They sent Malenkov a memorandum on January 2, 1951 regarding the "situation with the staff" they saw upon arrival:

> The Moscow Philharmonic Society has long been housing a large group of former entrepreneurs and people banded together for mutual benefit,[62] in addition to implanting non-Soviet work methods. It includes Galanter, Kornblit, Dreízen, Ratner, Mikhaílov-Liberman, Yevelinov, Veksler, Edemskií, Mlenaris, Brozio, Barkova, Shapiro, and others. Many of the employees are not trustworthy politically. For example, the husband of society employee Brozio was subjected to repression; Barkova's husband was shot by a firing squad (as a close assistant of the enemy of the people Yagoda); Polekh's father was condemned in 1950; Tanayeva's husband was subjected to repression; Fibikh's family was subjected to repression . . . . Furer's sister lives in America. Such facts are not the exception . . . . For a number of years, especially during and after the war, the Philharmonic Society accumulated actors and heads of various concert departments predominantly of one and the same nationality. Of the 312 society employees, 111 are Jewish. Of the 33 executives in charge of concert arrangements, 17 are Russian, 14 are Jewish, 2 are of other nationalities. There are only 15 Russians among the 34 cashiers at local box offices, and only 5 Russians among the 13 concert administration managers.[63]

The provinces could not escape the ideological leadership's critical attention. The Fine Arts Committee submitted evidence to the CC that

> . . . the concert agencies were controlled by non-Russians: The Philharmonic Society of Molotov—director Veíkhman; that of the Ural Region—Vinnitskií; that of Voronezh—Ioffe; that of Khabarovsk—Freíd; that of Chkalovsk—Bronskií; that of Kemerovo—

---

61. RTsKhIDNI, f. 17, op. 132, d. 420, l. 35–36, 187–189.

62. *Translator's note:* The term *mutual benefit,* or *mutual guarantee,* (meaning "solidarity") had a negative connotation in the Soviet Union.

63. RTsKhIDNI, f. 17, op. 132, d. 420, l. 191.

Lifshits; that of Vladimir—Gurevich, etc.

In the same way Agitprop checked the composition of circus personnel. The hard-working inspectors collected statistics throughout the Soviet Union. It appeared that of 87 directors, chief directors, and administrators of Soviet circuses, 44 were Jewish, 38 were Russian, 4 were Ukrainian—and the list went on. In the Moscow Circus alone, the leading posts were occupied by Faíl (deputy director), M. Mestechkin (chief director), Gusso (chief administrator), and others.[64]

Agitprop went on to find that the personnel of the Union of Soviet Composers was no less "littered." P.A. Tarasov (head of Agitprop's Fine Arts Section) and V.S. Kruzhkov (assistant Agitprop head), in a memorandum dated October 25, 1950, reported to Suslov "that persons of non-principal nationality for the USSR were in the second place; namely 435 Russians, 239 Jews, 89 Armenians, etc." They also gave data for the Union's regional branches: in Moscow there were 174 Russians, 116 Jews, 16 Armenians; in Kazakhstan there were 6 Kazakhs and 6 Jews; in Moldavia there were 8 Jews, 5 Moldavians, 3 Russians; in Rostov there were 5 Russians and 5 Jews. T.N. Khrennikov[65] was blamed for this situation. Khrennikov, the general secretary of the Union of Composers, was accused of liberalism and leniency. He had not carried out the anti-Jewish lustrations among the personnel of the Union of Soviet Composers board, the Music Fund, the *Soviet Music* [66] magazine editorial staff, or the other central organizations of Soviet composers. On top of this, of the 50 musicians admitted to the union in 1949 and 1950, 14 happened to be Jewish. Among Khrennikov's close assistants, consultants, and deputies, the inspectors singled out I.B. Livshits (music critic), A.M. Veprik (composer), and M.A. Grinberg (music consultant), who had all been ousted from the Radiokomitet in early 1949; L.A. Veksler (assistant in matters of planning and finance), G.D. Bleíz (chief accountant of the board), and other Jews.[67]

---

64. RTsKhIDNI, f. 17, op. 119, d. 211, l. 83.

65. Khrennikov had been appointed to this post by a Politburo resolution of May 12, 1948. RTsKhIDNI, f. 17, op. 119, d. 211, l. 83.

66. *Sovyetskaya muzyka.*

67. RTsKhIDNI, f. 17, op. 132, d. 418, l. 201–209. In 1949 none of these Jewish composers was arrested. However, in February 1953 M.S. Vaínberg, Mikhoels's son-in-law, was taken to Lubyanka. Under the investigators' pressure he confessed that from 1944 he, at his father-in-law's order, propagated within the Union of Soviet Composers the idea of creating a Jewish republic in the Crimea. For this purpose, in 1945 and 1946 Vaínberg vainly insisted on creating a Jewish section within the composers' union, on the basis of which he planned to create a Jewish conservatory in the Crimea. He even asked A.M. Veprik for two volumes of synagogue music. Vaínberg was also accused of composing two cycles of Jewish songs employing lyrics by Isaac Leib Peretz and Samuil Galkin, as well as of giving Ya.A. Shaporin the idea of writing *Vokaliz*, based on a Jewish melody.

Faculty and students of the Moscow Conservatory also found themselves under Agitprop's anti-Semitic "x-ray examination." Agitprop's inspectors undertook scrupulously accurate calculations (to within 0.1 percent), and discovered that, in December 1950, 67.2 percent of the students were Russian, 15 percent were Jewish, 5.3 percent were Armenian, and 6.3 percent were of other nationalities. They went on to point out that

> . . . the group most littered with representatives of a single nationality is the violin section. Here the proportion of Jews has been the greatest for many years. This was preconditioned by the national composition of faculty and professors, as well as by the aforementioned composition of the ten-year school at the conservatory. Since professors' assistants A.I. Yampolskií and L.M. Tseítlin and others teach at the school, students "automatically" enter the conservatory to study in these professors' groups after finishing school.[68]

However, the most "blatant" bias was the predominance of Jews in the first violin section of the conservatory's Youth Symphony Orchestra. And these violinists were using about two-thirds of the state's collection of unique instruments made by old the Italian masters Stradivari, Guarneri, and Amati.[69]

Thus the Fine Arts Committee was ordered to start the offensive on a new front. New reports soon started to come to the CC: in early 1951 Edemskií (director of the Moscow State Philharmonic Society) and Dreízen, as we have already seen, were fired, along with V.P. Shirinskií, Burshteín, and others. Gusso, Faíl, and others were discharged from the Moscow Circus (in 1949 director A.M. Dankman was arrested), and Bernadt and Shteínberg were discharged from the *Soviet Music* editorial board. Directors were replaced at the State Hermitage (academician I.A. Orbeli was ousted), the Russian Museum, the Tretyakov Gallery, and other institutions.[70]

Humanities

Meanwhile it was primarily graduates from the Academy of Social Sciences and from the Supreme Party School who began intensively to fill the staff vacuum left by the purges. These two major institutions trained nomenclatura personnel attached to the ACP(b) CC, and the efforts by Agitprop had "vaccinated" these institutions against cosmopolitanism in the spring of 1949. On March 3 and 4 at the Academy of Social Sciences F.M. Golovenchenko addressed a general Party

68. RTsKhIDNI, f. 17, op. 132, d. 420, l. 205.
69. RTsKhIDNI, f. 17, op. 132, d. 420, l. 206.
70. RTsKhIDNI, f. 17, op. 119, d. 241, l. 138.

meeting with a speech on "The Goals of the Struggle Against Cosmopolitanism on the Ideological Front."[71] His call for a resolute eradication of sedition within the academy's walls started a discussion that named the future victims. However, the leadership of the Academy of Social Sciences—in the person of the rector, A.I. Kovalevskií—did not hasten to "set apart the sheep from the goats." Professors teaching at departments there usually had full-time jobs elsewhere, and the academy would not discharge those who had been declared cosmopolitans until their full-time employers had made the appropriate decisions. It is thusly that the academy dealt with the Jewish professor V.Ya. Kirpotin, who had first to be expelled from the Party at the Gorkií Institute of World Literature. It was not until afterwards, on July 1, 1949, that the Academy of Social Sciences discharged him from its Department of the Theory and History of Literature by a decision of the CC secretariat. All the meetings criticized Kirpotin for his book, *F.M. Dostoyevskií*, and for his "anti-patriotic" statement that Aleksandr Pushkin was a "child of the European Enlightenment who grew up on Russian soil," which he had dared to write in his new study, "Pushkin's Heritage and Communism" ("Naslediye Pushkina i kommunizm").[72]

On that same day the Academy of Social Sciences dismissed a lecturer, Professor S.S. Mokulskií, from that same department, accusing him of popularizing the German formalist school of dramatic art. Prior to this he had been taken through the Party purgatory at the Moscow Drama School, where he was dismissed as director in 1949. Now he was expelled from the Party as well.[73]

HISTORY

One by one, historians L.I. Zubok, I.S. Zvavich, and I.I. Mints were forced to quit the Supreme Party School. A closed Party meeting at the Moscow State University's Department of Soviet History on March 17, 1949 paved the way toward their resignations. Professor A.L. Sidorov,[74] the MSU vice provost, addressed the meeting, sharply criticizing academician Mints, the chair of the MSU Department of Soviet History. He also criticized two lecturers in Mints's department, Ye.N. Gorodetskií and M.M. Razgon, presenting all three as a group whose activities he described as "blatant anti-patriotism at the History Department." In addition to his work at the Moscow University, Mints also chaired the Department of Soviet History at

71. Professor Golovenchenko had long chaired the Russian Literature Department at the Moscow State Teacher Training College. He was most active in ideologically mobilizing the public against cosmopolitanism. He spoke on the subject at the Supreme Party School and the Lenin Political Military Academy and many other institutions. RTsKhIDNI, f. 17, op. 118, d. 333, l. 182–188.

72. RTsKhIDNI, f. 17, op. 118, d. 443, l. 98–104.

73. RTsKhIDNI, f. 17, op. 118, d. 443, l. 94–95.

74. After removing Mints from his post, the ACP(b) appointed Sidorov to fill his place on December 25, 1948. Sidorov endeavored to justify the Party's confidence to the best of his abilities.

the Supreme Party School of the ACP(b) CC as well as the Soviet Society Section at the History Institute of the USSR Academy of Sciences. He also supervised postgraduate research at the Academy of Social Sciences, acted as assistant secretary academician at the History and Philosophy Department of the Academy of Sciences, was an editorial board member of *Issues in History*,[75] was executive secretary of the chief editorial board of the voluminous *History of the Civil War in the USSR*,[76] and occupied some other posts as well. In view of this, the Party meeting incriminated his desire to monopolize historical science, and accused his "group" of de-emphasizing the role of the Russian people and their vanguard, the Russian proletariat, in Russian history.[77]

Mints immediately had to play the part of a repentant sinner at a Party meeting of the chief editorial board secretariat of the *History of the Civil War in the USSR*. The secretariat now added two other points to the list of his mistakes: (1) he had disrupted the preparation of the third and subsequent volumes of the book, and (2) one member of the group of Jewish historians that he had "thrown together" was his disciple, Professor E.B. Genkina. The Party organizations of the MSU History Department and the chief editorial board of the *History of the Civil War* predictably demanded that Mints and his supporters be dismissed. The demand was immediately met.

It was, naturally, Old Square that directed the persecution of the grand master of the Soviet historical school, a persecution that so resembled the routing of M.N. Pokrovskií's school in the mid-1930s. D.T. Shepilov and Yu.A. Zhdanov (head of Agitprop's Science Section) collected all the materials discrediting Mints, duly processed them, and forwarded them to Stalin and Malenkov on behalf of Agitprop. The collecting and processing of this information brought some data to light. For example, of the 28 research associates of the board secretariat of the *History of the Civil War in the USSR*, 8 were Russians, 14 were Jews, 1 was German, and 1 was Ukrainian.[78] Also, Mints had written an article on "Lenin and the Development of Soviet Historical Science"[79] stating that the foundations for studying the Soviet period of Russian history had been laid by his closest disciples Gorodetskií,[80] Genkina, Razgon, and others. Stalin was dissatisfied with this article, for Mints had ignored Stalin's *Brief Course of the History of the ACP(b)*. Such disregard of the leader's contribution to historical science could not go unpunished. So the information that Shepilov and Zhdanov had uncovered was

75. *Voprosy istorii.*

76. *Istoriya grazhdanskoí voíny v SSSR.*

77. RTsKhIDNI, f. 17, op. 132, d. 221, l. 41–42.

78. RTsKhIDNI, f. 17, op. 118, d. 425, l. 11.

79. "Lenin i razvitiye 'sovyetskoí istoricheskoí nauki'," *Voprosy istorii*, 1941, no. 1.

80. Stalin's dissatisfaction with Ye.N. Gorodetskií was so great that not even Zhdanov could defend him, though he had at one time assisted him in Agitprop.

exactly what he was after.

On April 4, 1949 the Politburo passed a resolution by which Stalin dealt a mortal blow to Mints's "school." The *Issues in History* editorial board, consisting of Mints, A.M. Pankratova,[81] and other historians who gravitated toward Leninist dogma, was disbanded. Replacing them was a new board headed by A.D. Udaltsov, a lecturer at the History and Material Culture Institute who came from the milieu of old Moscow professoriat.[82]

In addition to Mints, the "academic community" (directed by the authorities) also turned its wrath upon Professor N.L. Rubinshteín. Like Mints, Rubinshteín worked for the MSU Department of Soviet History. He authored a textbook, *Russian Historiography*,[83] which was criticized in 1948 and later banned. He was driven out of MSU in March 1949 and dismissed as research supervisor at the State History Museum.

The aforementioned closed Party meeting at the Moscow State University Department of Soviet History (March 17, 1949) reserved its most scathing criticism for Jewish professors who specialized in the modern and contemporary history of England and the USA. The attacks on Professor L.I. Zubok were particularly furious. His unusual personal history itself aroused the suspicions and annoyance of critics of cosmopolitanism. Zubok had been born in 1894 in the small Ukrainian town of Radomyshl, had worked in Philadelphia, Pennsylvania from 1913 through 1924, had been a member of the Socialist Party, and then joined the Communist Party. Xenophobia reigned supreme, and it seemed incredible that such a person could now be teaching at a Soviet establishment. His exhaustive monograph, "The USA's Imperialist Policy in the Caribbean Countries, 1900–1939,"[84] was criticized through and through. The officials at the Party meeting alleged that Zubok was inordinately appreciative of President Roosevelt's public activity and that he "glossed over" the expansionism of Roosevelt's "good neighbor" policy of 1933. The Party officials took particular

---

81. Pankratova had learned her lesson after the painful experience with the "great power" historians in 1944. This time she acted in the spirit of "conformist flexibility." Her popularly written book, *The Great Russian People* (*Velikií russkií narod*), came out in 1952. Stalin liked it and so accepted its author into the CPSU CC at the Nineteenth Congress.

82. A year later, on April 17, 1950, Udaltsov retired as editor-in-chief of *Issues in History* on account of his health. P.N. Tretyakov, a specialist in the field of ancient Russian history who had previously worked at Agitprop, filled Udaltsov's vacancy. That same year Molotov's son-in-law, A.D. Nikonov, "fortified" the editorial board. Nikonov was a specialist in modern history, and had served in the NKVD (People's Commissariat for Internal Affairs) as well as in the counterintelligence service Smersh. RTsKhIDNI, f. 17, op. 118, d. 328, l. 51–55.

83. *Russkaya istoriografiya* (Moscow, 1941).

84. "Imperialisticheskaya politika SShA v stranakh karibskogo basseína. 1900—1939" (Moscow, Leningrad, 1948).

exception to Zubok's description of US secretary of state Charles Evans Hughes[85] as a champion of independence for Mexico, whereas Stalin had called him "that gallows bird 'Ughes."[86] Zubok lost his position at the Moscow University and was soon left without any job at all. He expected to be arrested at any moment, but the worst did not happen. Svetlana Stalina was then a student at the History Department, and Zubok's family still believes that it was her intercession that warded off the trouble.[87] Actually, the credit should probably go to S. Lozovskií and I. Yuzefovich, who were then in prison, and who had known Zubok since the late 1920s when they worked together at Profintern. When they were questioned about Zubok, they denied that he was in any way involved in "anti-Soviet activity."

Another faculty member at the MSU Department of Soviet History was Professor I.S. Zvavich, who suffered a similar fate. Glavlit banned his booklet on *The Labour Party of England: Its Program and Policy*[88] because of the "social reformist" attitude of its author, who "failed to condemn the English Labour party as agents of Churchill's imperialism." Banished everywhere, Zvavich was left without any means of subsistence. He then left Moscow and moved to remote Tashkent, where he taught at the Middle-Asian University.[89]

Three years later it was B.Ye. Shteín's turn. Shteín was a historian and diplomat,[90] and, like Zubok and Zvavich, he was a lecturer at the Social Sciences Academy at the ACP(b) CC. The Academy of Sciences had published his book, *Bourgeois Falsifiers of History, 1919–1939,*[91] at the end of 1951. Then in April 1952 *Bolshevik* magazine featured a damning review, maintaining that Shteín's book was "pseudoscientifically objectivistic throughout."[92] It was probably not a coincidence that the review was abusive, for Shteín, virtually the last Jew still working at the USSR Foreign Ministry, was dismissed in March 1952. Among other reasons, one pretext for his dismissal was that he had been a Menshevik Party member from April 1918 through January 1919. On September 18, 1952, at the proposal of D.I. Nadtocheyev, the new provost of the Academy of Social Sciences, the CC secretariat discharged Shteín from the Party Academy. At about the same time he was expelled from the Party and lost his last job at the Supreme Diplomatic School of the Ministry of Foreign Affairs, where he had taught for

85. Hughes was secretary of state from 1921 to 1925, and chairman of the Supreme Court from 1930 to 1941.

86. RTsKhIDNI, f. 17, op. 118, d. 479, l. 96–104; d. 328, l. 57.

87. *Novaya i noveĭshaya istoriya* (*Modern and Current History*), 1992, no. 6, p. 160.

88. *Leĭboristskaya partiya anglii. Yeyo programma i politika* (Moscow, 1947).

89. RTsKhIDNI, f. 17, op. 118, d. 479, l. 100–101; d. 575, l. 143–149.

90. In the 1930s Shteín had been envoy to Finland, and later envoy plenipotentiary to Italy.

91. *Burzhuaznye fal'sifikatory istorii. 1919—1939.*

92. *Bolshevik*, 1952, no. 8, p. 78.

13 years.[93]

The organizers of the chauvinist hysteria labeled some historians "cosmopolitans," making them outcasts overnight. And they especially never forgot those who did not sever all ties with their ostracized colleagues, or who did not reproach them at meetings with sufficient zeal. The Jews were not alone, for the diminishing numbers of the prerevolutionary elite—Russian professors and their followers—were lumped into the same "category." They were not dismissed, but they were scolded at every opportunity and forced to "repent." Such was the fate of Professor A.S. Yerusalimskiĭ (the head of the German Philology Department at Moscow University), Professor R.Yu. Vipper (who delivered an "idealistic" course of lectures on the history of Christianity), Professor Ye.A. Kosminskiĭ (a specialist in medieval English history who suffered a heart attack in the autumn of 1949 as a result of the baiting), F.A. Kogan-Bernshteĭn (a research associate of the Medieval History Department headed by Kosminskiĭ), and to others as well. Even academician Ye.V. Tarle was open to attacks. Tarle, who was of Jewish origin, was a lecturer at the Supreme Diplomatic School and a three-time winner of the Stalin Prize (in the 1940s). His name—together with the names of his colleagues N.L. Rubinshteĭn, O.L. Vaĭnshteĭn. Z.K. Eggert, L.I. Zubok, V.I. Lan, and others—was mentioned in the November 19, 1949 CC secretariat resolution on shortcomings in the work of the Institute of History of the USSR Academy of Sciences. As the author of *Napoleon's Invasion of Russia*,[94] he felt particularly uncomfortable when M.A. Suslov[95] approved publication of an article by S. Kozhukhov[96] that criticized his book for its "anti-patriotic" assessment of Kutuzov's role in the War of 1812. It is important to note that Tarle's book had been published as far back as 1938. It seemed that earlier events were about to repeat themselves. In late January 1931 Tarle and other prominent historians had been arrested and accused of belonging to the nonexistent "National Union for the Revival of Free Russia" and of plotting to overthrow Soviet power through foreign intervention. He allegedly intended to become minister of foreign affairs in the new "bourgeois" government, and he supposedly "came into contact" with French prime minister R. Poincaré and Pope Pius XI. Tarle's case abounded in such "revelations," and in August 1931 he was exiled to Kazakhstan. Twenty years had passed since then, and now the scholar was again facing an ordeal. This time, however, all ended well; for Stalin defended the old academician and permitted him to parry his critics with an article in *Bolshevik*.[97]

---

93. RTsKhIDNI, f. 17, op. 119, d. 1093, l. 1–4.

94. *Nashestviye Napoleona na rossiyo.*

95. RTsKhIDNI, f. 17, op. 119, d. 441, l. 215.

96. *Bolshevik*, 1951, no. 15.

97. *Bolshevik*, 1951, no. 17.

The enthusiasm for purging the historical sciences of the "foulness" of cosmopolitanism knew no departmental barriers. Military historians participated in the campaign on a par with civil ones. From March 17 through 21, at the Lenin Political Military Academy, an expanded session of the Academic Council expressly castigated a book written by Professor G.A. Deborin, *International Relations During the Great Patriotic War*,[98] which had been published back in 1947. Deborin was head of the Department of International Relations and History of Soviet Foreign Policy, and was the son of the academician A.M. Deborin (Ioffe), whom Stalin had labeled a "Menshevist-like idealist" as far back as 1931. The officials at the Academic Council session now used this book as a pretext for their reprisals against Deborin, who represented the thin stratum of Jewry in the Soviet military sphere. With martinet-like straightforwardness they labeled the professor an "advocate of American imperialism."[99] This categorical accusation did not throw him off balance. During the war Deborin had served in the Soviet Embassy in London, where he had closely collaborated with security bodies. He knew what to do. On March 24 he forwarded a report to the Political Department of the Lenin Political Military Academy. Along with his self-flagellation was an accusation: he named professors I.S. Zvavich, L.I. Zubok, B.Ye. Shteín, A.A. Troyanovskií, N.L. Rubinshteín, and others, saying it was their cosmopolitanism that had caused him to go astray. He had suffered the greatest "harm," however, from the academician I.M. Maískií (Lyakhovetskií), the former ambassador to England who had acted as a consulting editor of the unfortunate book. It was Maískií who "had gone to great lengths in explaining the need for a maximum of objectivity and thoroughness in describing the USA and England." This, Deborin maintained, was in the long run conducive to his own whitewashing of the "worst enemies of the Soviet Union and progressive mankind." (Deborin reckoned President Roosevelt among the "worst enemies of the Soviet Union.")[100]

This was not Deborin's first attack upon the high-placed diplomat who had previously been his boss—in 1948 he had reported to the MGB that "Maískií's actions benefited England's imperialist interests." Maískií was arrested not long before Stalin's death and was brought before the Military Board of the Supreme Court on the charge of high treason in May 1955. Deborin acted as a witness and declared, with accusatory inspiration: " . . . closeness to Churchill, whose ties with the intelligence service are common knowledge, is unbecoming of a Soviet citizen."[101]

---

98. *Mezhdunarodnye otnosheniya v gody vtoroí mirovoí voíny.*

99. RTsKhIDNI, f. 17, op. 132, d. 237, l. 36.

100. RTsKhIDNI, f. 17, op. 132, d. 237, l. 47–49.

101. *Literaturnaya gazeta*, March 4, 1992.

Early in the summer of 1949 a feverish struggle against cosmopolitanism seized the Supreme Trade Union School, which was under the jurisdiction of the All-Union Central Soviet of Trade Unions. One of the first to be discharged was I.P. Shmidt (Goldshmidt), a professor at the Department of the History of the USSR. The reason for his dismissal was that "in his lectures he would praise Russian imperialism, showing that at certain stages of Russian history it played a positive role."[102]

The wave of dismissals spread from the capital to the provinces, where, at times, the persecution of "cosmopolitans" took even more severe forms. As a result of the growing "Leningrad case," that city's prestige had been seriously damaged in Stalin's eyes. V.M. Andrianov, the first secretary of Municipal and Regional Party Committees, headed Leningrad's new Party administration, which was trying its best to re-establish credibility. So the Leningrad authorities took the lead in implementing harsh methods of repressing intellectuals, including Jews.

The Leningrad State University suffered a devastating blow.[103] V.V. Mavrodin, dean of the History Department, was dismissed. He had formerly been chairman of the Scientific Board, in which capacity he had granted scientific degrees to V.Ya. Golant and Ye.I. Bernadskaya. But now Golant's and Bernadskaya's dissertations were seen to contain "gross political errors." In addition, Mavrodin was said to have allowed three lecturers to join his staff: L.Z. Trauberg (a famous film producer later condemned by the mass media as a cosmopolitan), B.Ya. Ramm, (who was described as "unworthy of political confidence"), and A.N. Vigdorchik. Further, Mavrodin was accused of protecting the "Trotskyite" N.A. Kornatovskií. The Leningrad State University fired all of these scholars and others as well. Those who remained at the MGB's Department for Leningrad and Its Regional Areas (or the "big house" on Liteínyí Avenue, as it was called) were doomed to still worse hardships. Among the Leningrad University professors who were arrested were historians M.A. Gukovskií, L.P. Peterson, O.L. Vanshteín, and M.B. Rabinovich. Rabinovich, a disciple of Ye.V. Tarle, was arrested for "divulgence of military secrets in the period of the Great Patriotic War." Also arrested were Political Economy Department head V.V. Reíkhardt and two lecturers from his department, Ya.S. Rozenfeld and the "Trotskyite" V.M. Shteín. Rozenfeld had authored *US Industry and War*,[104] which was later subjected to criticism; and Shteín had written *Essays on the*

102. RTsKhIDNI, f. 17, op. 118, d. 456, l. 140–141.

103. A.A. Voznesenskií was provost of the Leningrad State University from 1941 to 1948. His brother, N.A. Voznesenskií, was the chairman of the State Planning Commission (Gosplan). Both were reckoned among those involved in the "Leningrad case." On June 12, 1949 Stalin signed a Politburo resolution discharging A.A. Voznesenskií as RSFSR minister of education. He was later arrested, and the MCSC sentenced him to death.

104. *Promyshlennost' SShA i voína* (1946).

Development of Russian Socio-Economic Thought Through the Nineteenth and Twentieth Centuries,[105] which was described as "perverting the truthfulness of Marxist-Leninist theory."[106]

In the spring of 1949 the Kiev University dismissed L.Ye. Kertman, a specialist in modern English history and English current affairs. He found it almost impossible to obtain another post, but finally succeeded at Perm University. Also in the spring of 1949 the Latvian State University inquired into the formation and activities of the so-called "Jewish-Zionist group," which had, the university believed, united some of the faculty and students. This inquiry largely stemmed from a denunciation by a former student, A.L. Vitlin, a Jew baptized in the Orthodox Church. It was alleged that the organizers and most active participants in this group were S.A. Dudel (the dean of history and author of the 1930 text, *Readings for Higher Communistic Institutions*),[107] Gurvich[108] (an assistant professor of history accused of spreading "anti-Soviet rumors about anti-Semitism being indoctrinated from above, inspired by the Party and Soviet bodies, the CPSU Central Committee, and the Soviet government"), Niss (a senior lecturer on Modern History), Veínberg (a senior lecturer on medieval history), and others.[109]

PEDAGOGY

It was not only universities that carried out anti-Semitic campaigns; the pedagogical colleges, which were populated largely by humanities students, also participated. A new administration was appointed especially for mass dismissals. This, as a rule, contributed to the further strengthening of the purge. In April 1949 I.S. Zotov was discharged as director of the Moscow State Pedagogical Institute of Foreign Languages. Apparently he "did not manage to purge politically unreliable people from the staff."[110] The security bodies simultaneously arrested Ye.P. Shlossberg, the head of the Soviet History Department at the Minsk Pedagogical Institute.[111]

---

105. *Ocherki razbitiya russkoí obshchestvenno–ekonomicheskoí mysli v XIX—XX vekakh* (1948).

106. RTsKhIDNI, f. 17, op. 119, d. 668, l. 68–74; op. 118, d. 855, l. 82–86; d. 457, l. 2; d. 448, l. 84–92.

107. *Khrestomatiya dlya komvuzov.*

108. Vitlin defamed Gurvich. He told the MGB that Gurvich and some other Jews, during the Nazi occupation of Riga, were placed in the Institute of Race Hygiene, which cultivated typhus louses on their bodies to check the effectiveness of remedies for the Nazi army. Vitlin claimed that Gurvich had cooperated with Dr. Shtaíninger, the director of the Institute, and, in particular, that he may have written for Shtaíninger an article for the newspaper *Tevia* on the racial affiliation of the "Karaites." Thus, said Vitlin, Gurvich managed to survive, enjoying various benefits for his services. RTsKhIDNI, f. 17, op. 119, d. 78, l. 81.

109. RTsKhIDNI, f. 17, op. 119, d. 78, l. 75–98.

110. RTsKhIDNI, f. 17, op. 118, d. 356, l. 114–116.

111. RTsKhIDNI, f. 17, op. 118, d. 356, l. 142.

A month earlier the Kaliningrad State Pedagogical Institute dismissed N.G. Milyutin (the director) and Yurovskií (the secretary of the its Party committee), because "the fierce struggle against 'cosmopolitanism,' being in full swing throughout the country, has not received a proper response from within the Institute."[112] The Moscow Regional Pedagogical Institute suppressed some members of its Modern History Department, among them A.Z. Manfred,[113] S.D. Kunisskií, and E.V. Rubinovich. Rubinovich in particular was persecuted for his membership in Poalei Zion.[114] On July 26, 1951 D.A. Polikarpov[115] became the new director of the Moscow State Lenin Pedagogical Institute. He soon dismissed D.Yu. Elkina (assistant professor of Soviet History), L.K. Zakarzhevskií (head of the Marxism-Leninism Department), V.R. Granovskií, L.V. Neíman, and others.[116]

In January 1952 N.A. Mikhaílov, secretary of the Komsomol CC, informed the CPSU CC of some "disorder" at the V.P. Potyomkin Moscow City Pedagogical Institute. Some history students were accused of harboring "nationalistic views." At a Komsomol Bureau meeting in December 1951 four students—R.B. Genkina, L.M. Pukshanskaya, T.I. Dulkina, and L.A. Kaminskaya—"confessed" that for a number of years they had been discussing among themselves and with relatives and acquaintances the signs of anti-Semitism present in the country. Threatened and "persuaded," three of them acknowledged their faults. Lina Kaminskaya would not bend. She declared:

> In our country an improper national policy is being pursued. After the war a wave of anti-Semitism, as an expression of fascist ideology, hit our country. More fruitful than words at this bureau meeting would be two show trials against anti-Semites. My view is based on what I see and hear, and not on what you are saying here. Everything I am saying is my firm belief. These views are shared by my close intellectual acquaintances—doctors, engineers, lawyers, students.

---

112. RTsKhIDNI, f. 17, op. 118, d. 419, l. 32–40.

113. Manfred was also was on staff of the Institute of History at the USSR Academy of Sciences, which also unjustly criticized him.

114. RTsKhIDNI, f. 17, op. 118, d. 609, l. 47–87.

115. Polikarpov was an ideologue of the Stalinist school, both fanatical and cynical. His omnipresence and upward mobility became the talk of the town. He had also worked as the first deputy head of Agitprop under the CPSU CC (1940–1944) and simultaneously acted as chairman of the All-Union Radio Committee. Then he became secretary of the USSR Board of Soviet Writers (1944–1946) and director of the Gorkií Literary Institute (1949–1951). Under Khrushchev he reached the pinnacle of his career, heading the Section of Culture under the CPSU CC.

116. RTsKhIDNI, f. 17, op. 119, d. 459, l. 54–61; *Kentavr*, November/December 1992, pp. 69–70.

She refused to give any names, saying only that among them a few had been subjected to repression by security bodies.[117] Kaminskaya was dismissed from Komsomol and was expelled from the Institute.[118]

Leaders in pedagogical science also contributed to the struggle against cosmopolitanism. At a meeting of the Academy of Pedagogical Science (March 18–25, 1949) the president, I.A. Kairov, made a report criticizing two books by Professor S.L. Rubinshteín,[119] *Foundations of General Psychology*[120] and *Investigations into the Psychology of Perception.*[121] He demonstrated that Rubinshteín "does not value the priority of Russian scholars in the development of scientific issues." Kairov also called Professor Reznik (of the Kiev Pedagogical Institute) a bearer of the ideas of cosmopolitanism in pedagogics, and denounced him for having written most of his works in Yiddish. Others at the meeting recalled a passage from Reznik's autobiography: "My grandfather greatly influenced my intellectual development. He was an outstanding Talmudist and pedagogue . . . . To him I owe him my acquisition of the capability of logical thought and clear exposition." Reznik had also established a school for orphans similar to the so-called "new schools" in Europe and the United States. Some Americans had visited this school and praised it in the press. The participants of the Academy of Pedagogical Sciences meeting saw this as "servility" to the West, and this they could not forgive. They also found similar "sins" of servility to foreign culture and foreign schools of thought in the works of I.F. Svadkovskií, an acting member of the Academy of Pedagogical Science of the RSFSR and author of *Social Education in America.*[122] And they found more objectionable material in works by professors G.Ye. Zhuravskií and Ye.N. Medynskií.[123]

Kairov could not remain unnoticed, and in July 1949 the Party leadership appointed him to replace A.A. Voznesenskií as RSFSR minister of education. At his new post he quickly revealed himself as an advocate of an officially chauvinistic education policy. In 1952 his employees in the ministry went over his head and appealed to A.M. Puzanov, the chairman of the Soviet of Ministers of the RSFSR. They complained of difficulties connected with the mass dismissals of faculty suspected of a cosmopolitan bias. No sooner did this occur than the entire Higher

---

117. Among the repressed was the brave girl's father, who, prior to his May 1941 arrest, had worked at the People's Aviation Industry Committee.

118. RTsKhIDNI, f. 17, op. 119, d. 713, l. 69–74.

119. In the spring of 1949 S.L. Rubinshteín's brother, the historian N.L. Rubinshteín, was discharged as head of the MSU Psychology Department, as head of the Psychology Section of the Academy of Science's Philosophy Institute, and as deputy director of the Philosophy Institute.

120. *Osnovy obshcheí psikhologii* (1940).

121. *Issledovaniya psikhologii vospriyatiya* (1948).

122. *Sotsial'noye vospitaniye v amerike* (1929).

123. RTsKhIDNI, f. 17, op. 132, d. 205, l. 18–28.

Education Institutions Central Directorate administration find itself out of work. In contrast to his dealings with these employees, Kairov protected such blunt anti-Semites as his deputy, A.M. Arsenyev.[124]

PHILOSOPHY

The "nerve center" of anti-Jewish politics was situated in Old Square. In the spring of 1949 Agitprop and the Ministry of Higher Education focused their attention on 213 institutions of higher education in Moscow, Leningrad, Kiev, Kharkov, Rostov-na-Donu, Saratov, Kazan, and Sverdlovsk, and checked on the staff personnel of the departments of Marxism-Leninism, Political Economy, and Philosophy. Their major concern was the number of Jewish faculty in the sociopolitical departments. In the institutions they examined, Marxism-Leninism was taught by 720 Russian lecturers, 350 Jewish lecturers, and 318 lecturers of other nationalities;[125] political

---

124. A typical incident occurred in August 1950, when Arsenyev took a business trip to Chita. Upon arrival, and after a few stiff drinks, he decided to relax in his hotel room. Unfortunately there was a telephone in the corridor by the door of his room, and other lodgers, among them Ministry of Agriculture representatives Lugovskoí and Klyachko-Gurvich, were constantly talking on it. Lugovskoí's and Klyachko-Gurvich's calls, and especially their Jewish accent, made Arsenyev furious. He rushed out of his room, and made a violent anti-Semitic remark, calling the frightened culprits "dealers, selling Russia," and threatened them with physical reprisal. The two agricultural representatives cautioned him, saying they would call the MGB. Arsenyev responded that "The MGB is ours and calling it is of no use."

G.V. Kuznetsov, a CPSU CC inspector who was also then staying in Chita, reported on the incident, and the scandal became known in Moscow. The two victims sent a letter of complaint to the Commission of Party Control at the CPSU CC, but Kairov "blocked the issue" by conducting a closed board meeting of the Ministry of Education. Those at the meeting mildly reprimanded Arsenyev, but made no decision in the matter. On May 20, 1951 the Commission of Party Control considered Arsenyev's case, but washed its hands of it. Shkiryatov later reported to Malenkov that "since Arsenyev had acknowledged his fault, and since this was his first such incident, and taking into consideration that Kairov appreciated his achievements at work, the Commission of Party Control thought it possible to impose upon Arsenyev nothing more than reprimands, formulated by the ministry's board." RTsKhIDNI, f. 17, op. 119, d. 713, l. 69–74.

125. In March 1949 Professor Yudovskií, the head of the Department of Marxism-Leninism at the Moscow State University was persecuted. Also targeted were the lecturers Gurevich, Braínin, Atsarkin, Vinnitskaya, Kazachek, and others who worked under Yudovskií's guidance. Most of these people were later dismissed. According to materials at my disposal, in the late 1940s and early 1950s the same thing happened to Shames (the head of the of Marxism-Leninism at the Leningrad Library Institute) and to his colleagues Ya.L. Kharapinskií (Moscow Plekhanov Institute of the People's Economy), G.A. Levin (Minsk Law Institute), E.G. Fisher (Khabarovsk State Pedagogical Institute), and A.L. Ugryumyuv (Moscow Law Institute). It should be noted that Ugryumyuv (his adoptive parents' name) was dismissed for being one of a "group of cosmopolitans" who had been "unmasked" in the spring and summer of 1950. The group was also thought to have included B.Ya. Arsenyev (Leíbman) (a professor of criminal law and a past participant of the second RSDRP congress representing the "Mensheviks"), Ya.I. Pekker (head of the Political Economy Department), Assistant Professor I.B. Sternik, Assistant Professor S.M. Bertsinskií, Ye.U. Ziger (head of the Criminalistic Laboratory), and others.

economy was taught by 263 Russians, 157 Jews, and 85 of other nationalities; philosophy was taught by 25 Russians, 24 Jews, and 19 of other nationalities.[126]

The percentage of Jewish writers on philosophy was rather considerable, and this alarmed those in the CC bodies who were concerned about staff purity. They knew that Stalin (who had been proclaimed a brilliant theoretician of Marxism-Leninism) had been paying great attention to the "philosophical front" since the 1920s, for he believed it played a decisive role in asserting the new ideology. Thus from its very beginning the campaign against cosmopolitanism in philosophy was especially acute. The situation became more complicated when two apparatus groups each not only struggled against cosmopolitans but also spun intrigues in an attempt to gain the upper hand over the other.

As far back as the war, the philosophical circles close to the top authorities split into two hostile groupings led on the one hand by academician G.F. Aleksandrov (the head of Agitprop from 1940 to 1947), and on the other by academician M.B. Mitin, who grew to hate each other. Mitin had proved his personal loyalty to Stalin in the early 1930s by taking part in scathing attacks against the old Marxist guards (mostly followers of Plekhanov) who were centered around the journal *Under the Marxist Banner*,[127] which was edited by the "Menshevik idealist" A.M. Deborin (Ioffe). In fact, the dictator, who then was strengthening his power, gave Mitin the authority of an ideological inquisitor. We can see the extent to which Mitin carried out this role, for this until recently modest messenger from the provincial town of Zhitomir, who never defended his doctoral dissertation, in 1939 was given a title of member of the USSR Academy of Sciences.

Aleksandrov was typical of the young, greedy, and cynical generation of Soviet thinkers. As the head of the Department of Party Ideology he recruited and

---

The Commission of the Krasnopresnenskiĭ Regional Party Committee examined the Institute and reported to the CPSU CC on the "ominous" faculty structure: 74 Russian lecturers, 56 Jewish lecturers, and 12 of other nationalities. There were also data showing that out of the Moscow Law Institute's 2 240 students and 73 postgraduates, there were 1 685 Russians, 385 Jews, 55 Ukrainians, and so on. RTsKhIDNI, f. 17, op. 132, d. 221, l. 33, 35; op. 119, d. 284, l. 168; d. 300, l. 98; d. 102, l. 96, 101; op. 118, d. 342, l. 99–104; d. 785, l. 73–77; d. 768, l. 89–91.

The exclusion of Jews from the legal sphere influenced another individual destiny. In April 1950 Professor M.S. Strogovich was accused of servility before the Anglo-American legal system and jurisprudence and was discharged as head of the Department of the Theory of State and Law at the Academy of Social Sciences at the ACP(b) CC. Professor A.N. Traĭnin was "worked on" during the meeting in the Institute of Law of the USSR Academy of Sciences. He was not forgiven for having participated in the creation of the *Black Book*, and it was remembered that Mikhoels had sincerely liked him and used to say, "Our Aron behaves as a hero." Professor M.A. Arzhanov was then forced to leave the Institute of Law. RTsKhIDNI, f. 17, op. 118, d. 818, l. 29–32.

126. RTsKhIDNI, f. 17, op. 118, d. 420, l. 11–15.

127. *Pod znamenem marksizma.*

supported his proponents, who were personally obliged to him for their positions, scientific degrees, and salary bonuses. Aleksandrov's older and more eminent colleagues monopolized the exposition of scientific truth, but his adherents were gradually breaking this monopoly. His adherents were also breaking the monopoly on the perquisites and privileges provided to top-level authorities. Seriously concerned with this group's growing influence, Stalin, with Zhdanov's help, dealt Aleksandrov a heavy blow in 1947, demoting him to director of the Institute of Philosophy at the Academy of Sciences and ousting Aleksandrov's group from the CC. Yet Stalin was unable to change the situation.

By early 1949 Aleksandrov's influence had spread beyond the Institute of Philosophy to a number of ideological institutions, such as the editorial board of *Issues in Philosophy* (headed by the well-known philosopher of natural science, B.M. Kedrov) and *Bolshevik* magazine (edited by P.N. Fedoseyev).[128] The Academy of Social Sciences at the CC also felt his influence, for Fedoseyev ran its Department of Dialectical and Historical Materialism. And Aleksandrov's influence also spread to several departments within the MSU philosophy faculty, namely to the Department of History of Russian Philosophy (headed by I.Ya. Shchipanov) and to the Department of the History of Western European Philosophy (headed by T.I. Oízerman).[129]

What is more important, Aleksandrov maintained his reliable contacts in the CC where he enjoyed the protection of Malenkov and Suslov. Other top-ranking CC officials, who had worked for him before, also supported him, such as L.F. Ilyichev (the deputy head of Agitprop who had edited *Izvestiya* and *Pravda*), V.S. Kruzhkov (who had also been director of the Marx-Engels-Lenin Institute until 1948), and V.Ye. Yevgrafov (an Agitprop official). Further, Aleksandrov was on friendly terms with P.A. Sharia[130] (the former secretary of the Georgian Party

128. Until 1947 Fedoseyev had been Aleksandrov's deputy in the Department of Propaganda. This was concurrent with Aleksandrov's role on the *Bolshevik* editorial board.

129. T.I. Oízerman was the acting executive head of this department, as well as head of a similar department at the Institute of Philosophy.

130. In 1943 Sharia had written and published a book of religious and mystical poems, and so, on June 3, 1948 the Georgian CC Politburo approved a resolution to dismiss him as CC secretary responsible for propaganda. In 1951 he was arrested on a charge related to the so-called "Mingrel case," but in March 1953 Beria ordered his release. Sharia then worked in Beria's office as his deputy responsible for ideological issues until Beria's arrest.

Note: Beginning in November 1951 and over the next several months, a cleansing of personnel took place in Georgia at Stalin's order. As a result, hundreds of local Party and state functionaries lost their positions and were arrested. The reason behind this large-scale repressive action was the unmasking of a mythical "bourgeois-nationalistic center in Georgia," which allegedly fought, with the aid of foreign special services and Georgian emigration, for Georgia's disaffiliation from the USSR and affiliation with Turkey. Because the secretary of the CC CP(b) of Georgia and some other leaders born in Mingrelia (a national and historical region in Georgia) were the "ringleaders" of the "center," the MGB's fabricated "case"

CC), and he was close to L.P. Beria.

Unlike Aleksandrov, Mitin was not a candidate, but an equal member of the Party CC and took part in the Orgburo meetings when ideological issues were discussed. And he was backed by no less influential people and bodies. He also headed the Department of Dialectical Materialism at the CC Party School, and he was the first vice president of the All-Union Society that disseminated political and scientific knowledge. Fundamentalist Stalinist-Marxists, who had made their careers as philosophers of the early 1930s, were Mitin's closest supporters, and in many ways were similar to him. P.F. Yudin,[131] a fellow of the Academy of Sciences, was editor-in-chief of the Cominform newspaper, *For a Durable Peace, For a People's Democracy!*,[132] published in Bucharest. A.A. Maksimov,[133] a specialist in Marxist natural philosophy, was appointed head of the Department of the Philosophy of Natural Science at MSU; and Z.Ya. Beletskií had headed the Department of Dialectical and Historical Materialism at MSU since 1943. All three supported Mitin. Academician T.D. Lysenko, a colorful personality, was another of Mitin's supporters. Time and again, Mitin and Beletskií provided a philosophical foundation for the nonsensical treatment of biological processes ("transformation of plants," and so forth) that Lysenko, who was Stalin's favorite, advertised to the scientific world as a kind of revelation. S.F. Kaftanov, the minister of higher education, also supported Mitin. In October 1948 he asked

---

received the name of "Mingrelian." It was in this region that the most massive arrests took place.

131. Their mutual hatred of Aleksandrov drove Yudin and Mitin closer. In 1943 Aleksandrov, Mitin, and Yudin had edited and published the third volume of *The History of Philosophy*. In 1944 Zhdanov led the severe criticism of this work. Aleksandrov managed to escape the blow, and placed the burden of guilt on his coeditors. Yudin was dismissed from his top position at the Institute of Philosophy, and Mitin was dismissed from his similar position at the Marx-Engels-Lenin Institute.

132. *Za prochnyí mir, za narodnuyu demokratiyu!* Cominform (1947–1956) was an organization of the international Communist movement. It replaced Comintern, which disbanded in 1943. Its newspaper was published in Russian, Spanish, English, French, Romanian, Hungarian, German, and seven other languages.

133. In 1947 Zhdanov took part in a philosophical discussion, calling upon scientists to strengthen their struggle against "physical idealism." Since that time, Malenkov, whose basic knowledge of physics was seriously in doubt, had been constantly criticizing both professional physicists (in particular academician L.I. Mandelshtam, his disciple S.E. Khaíkin, academician V.A. Fok, and future academician Moiseí Markov) and philosophers (such as Kedrov and V.P. Yegorshin). He accused them of "departing from materialism" and "worship of the erroneous" quantum theory of Niels Bohr. Maksimov's newspaper article, "Against the Reactionary Einstein Theory in Physics" ("Protiv Reaktsionnogo Eínshteínianstva v fizike," *Krasnyí flot* [*Red Fleet*], June 14, 1952), proclaimed that "Einstein's theory of relativity undoubtedly propagates antiscientific views of fundamental issues of modern physics and science." Fok's article, "Against the Ignorant Criticism of Modern Theories of Physics" ("Protiv nevezhestvennoí kritiki sovremennykh fizicheskikh teorií," *Voprosy filosofii* [*Issues in Philosophy*], 1953, no. 1), was a severe rebuke to Maksimov. The CC secretariat approved Fok's article at its meeting of August 6, 1952. RTsKhIDNI, f. 17, op. 133, d. 256, l. 9.

Malenkov to approve a decision of the ministry's board to appoint Mitin head of the Department of the History of Philosophy at MSU, and Beletskiĭ dean of philosophy. He was unsuccessful in this endeavor. D.T. Shepilov (who worked in the CC as the head of Agitprop) and Yu.A. Zhdanov (A.A. Zhdanov's son and Stalin's son-in-law, and head of Agitprop's Scientific Department) were supporters as well. In early 1949, when the struggle against "stateless" cosmopolitanism swept through yet more ranks adjacent to ideology, Aleksandrov inflicted a blow on Mitin and his advocates (many of whom were Jews). However, preventive measures by Agitprop members considerably softened it.

Having mastered the rules of the apparatus game, Shepilov, in February, diverted his opponents' attention by writing to Stalin that it was necessary to dismiss Kedrov as editor-in-chief of *Issues in Philosophy*. He also mentioned Z.A. Kamenskiĭ, who worked in Aleksandrov's Institute of Philosophy; V.F. Asmus, head of the Department of Logic at MSU; and others as "supporters of cosmopolitanism." Shepilov simply believed that Kedrov was the most vulnerable of Aleksandrov's advocates.

Kedrov's father, M.S. Kedrov, had been one of Moscow's aristocracy, and had become a Bolshevik in 1901. After the revolution he became a notable statesman and high security official. In 1941 he was sentenced to be shot as "an enemy of the people." In 1947 B.M. Kedrov published in his magazine an article by well-known Russian biologist and academician I.I. Shmalgauzen, one of T.D. Lysenko's irreconcilable opponents. Kedrov continued to support "anti-Michurin" scientists, though they were everywhere victimized. As if this was not enough, and despite the chauvinistic hysteria incited by the top authorities, he called upon scientists not to exaggerate the success of Russian science in the past, and to appreciate the achievements of world philosophical thought. Shepilov noted this as a manifestation of Kedrov's cosmopolitan views. Worse, Kedrov had not published in his magazine enthusiastic remarks about the new volumes of Stalin's writings; he had not even informed his readers about them. This was his greatest sin.[134]

On February 25, the CC secretariat removed Kedrov as editor-in-chief of *Issues in Philosophy*. This was the second step in Agitprop's instruction. Afterwards, in late December 1948, I.A. Kryvelev, accused of holding cosmopolitan views, lost his position as executive secretary of the magazine's editorial board. At the same time, to "strengthen" the editorial board, three new members were brought in: Mitin, V.N. Stoletov (the director of the Timiryazev Agricultural Academy and a well-known advocate of Lysenko), and D.N. Chesnokov (Aleksandrov's deputy at the Institute of Philosophy). Stalin signed a Politburo decision of March 3 confirming Chesnokov's appointment as

134. RTsKhIDNI, f. 17, op. 118, d. 317, l. 115–124.

editor-in-chief.[135] It was Shepilov's protection that brought this rising star to the Moscow Party philosophical horizon. Earlier Chesnokov had been secretary of the Sverdlovsk Party Committee and was involved in propaganda. Then in November 1947 Shepilov appointed Chesnokov deputy head of a department in Agitprop. Shepilov came to regret this a few months later, for from Sverdlovsk came a stream of letters about his intimate dalliances. With Chesnokov's old sins unexpectedly brought to light, the CC found itself embroiled in a scandal. Chesnokov could no longer count on working in the CC, and in June 1948 he was sent to the Institute of Philosophy. Thus were two birds killed with one stone. Expelled from the sacred Party body, the "fallen angel" became its eyes and ears in the camp of those potentially dangerous to the regime.

Supporting the attack that Agitprop launched against Aleksandrov on March 2, 1949, the *Literary Gazette* published an article "Against Cosmopolitanism in Philosophy."[136] Mitin sat on the *Literary Gazette*'s editorial board and was responsible for its science section, and it was through his efforts that this article was published. The article told of the discussion by the Scientific Council of the Institute of Philosophy on the "anti-Marxist cosmopolitan works of Professor B. Kedrov." Seizing the initiative in unmasking the "anti-patriot" philosophers, Mitin on March 9 and 16 thundered forth with an extensive article in the *Literary Gazette*. Now he wrote of "a group of people who put forward cosmopolitan views and undermined the philosophical front." The "ideological inspiration" of this group, according to Mitin, was this very same Kedrov. Mitin went on to name the members who cooperated with Kedrov: I.A. Kryvelev, Ya.Z. Chernyak, Z.A. Kamenskiĭ, and M.Z. Selektor, as well as the literary critic V.Ts. Goffenshefer (who could hardly be reckoned as a philosopher, but whom Mitin mentioned most likely for the sake of assuring the necessary number of exotic Jewish surnames for such a case).

Aleksandrov's opponents spoke more and more of his cosmopolitan transgressions, which Zhdanov had revealed in the summer of 1947 and which Aleksandrov afterwards continued to commit. Feeling that his passivity only egged his opponents on, Aleksandrov could not sit idly by. He began to prepare a counteroffensive. On March 2, 1949, at the Academy of Social Sciences, he read a report on "The Main Tasks of the Struggle Against Cosmopolitanism in Philosophy." He admitted both his own mistakes and those of Kamenskiĭ and Selektor. He then accused of cosmopolitanism one of the most authoritative scientists from the philosophical group in opposition, Professor M.M. Rozental.[137]

---

135. RTsKhIDNI, f. 17, op. 118, d. 317, l. 113.

136. "Protiv kosmopolitizma v filosofii."

137. In October 1949 Rozental was dismissed as deputy head of the Department of Dialectical and

The opposing groups had exchanged blows, and some balance was re-established on the "philosophical front." The lead article in *Culture and Life*[138] (Shepilov's newspaper) reflected this. The Agitprop leaders were forced to compromise with Aleksandrov, and this could hardly be comforting to Mitin and his friends. On March 15 Malenkov received an indignant letter from P.F. Yudin. Yudin, who was at that time in distant Bucharest, declared that "the editorial staff of *Culture and Life* has acted too hastily in calling Rozental a cosmopolitan." He insisted that criticism be aimed against Aleksandrov, who inspired cosmopolitanism, advocated katyeder-socialism,[139] and "kowtows in obeisance before all the Western European philosophers."[140]

Malenkov expectedly took no heed of the accusations against his protégé. So Aleksandrov, feeling the support of the Party's (and state's) number two man, acted more and more resolutely, using his abundant experience to organize large-scale demagogic campaigns. As a preliminary measure he discharged all the researchers at his Institute who had been accused of cosmopolitanism: Kedrov (head of the Department of the Philosophy of Natural Science), S.L. Rubinshteín, Z.A. Kamenskií, M.Z. Selektor, V.S. Bibler, and Ye.M. Veítsman. In all, he dismissed 51 researchers between 1949 and 1950. He was now free to act as he pleased.[141]

At a general meeting of research workers and postgraduate and graduate students of the Institute of Philosophy on March 18, Aleksandrov and his adherents started a fight against "Mitin's" group. Aleksandrov leveled criticism at Beletskií and his department at the MSU. Public opinion had it that Beletskií thought highly of himself, that he thought himself the exponent of the truth of Marxist-Leninist philosophy. And it was Beletskií who, in 1944, had severely criticized the third volume of the *History of Philosophy*, which Aleksandrov had edited. Aleksandrov, the former head of Agitprop, had long dreamt of taking revenge on this incorrigible professor.

The time had come to settle accounts. Aleksandrov accused Beletskií of having opposed the "Leninist-Marxist" theory of Germany being Marxism's

---

Historical Materialism at the Academy of Social Sciences. Not long before he had been persecuted for his book, *Philosophical Views of N.G. Chernyshevskii* (*Filosofskiye vzglyady N.G. Chernyshevskogo*, 1948). He had imprudently written that the best features of this writer-democrat's world outlook were generalized from the Western European experience, and that his worst features derived from the social attitudes in Russia. RTsKhIDNI, f. 17, op. 118, d. 333, l. 185; d. 573, l. 174–179.

138. "Razoblachit' propovednikov kosmopolitizma v filosofii!" ("To Expose the Preachers of Cosmopolitanism in Philosophy!"), *Kul'tura i zhizn'*, March 10, 1949.

139. *Katyeder* is from the German *katheder* (a chair). This was a reformist—as opposed to revolutionary—trend in German political economy. It made its appearance in the 1870s, and was propagated mainly by the university professoriat (i.e., "from the chairs").

140. RTsKhIDNI, f. 17, op. 118, d. 339, l. 134–138.

141. RTsKhIDNI, f. 17, op. 119, d. 339, l. 108.

motherland. He also accused Beletskiĭ of denying "the relative independence of ideology" in socialist eras and for having "given shelter" in his department to S.S. Goldentrikht, "an enemy of the people" who was arrested in 1948. Chesnokov unexpectedly joined Aleksandrov in a united front. The chauvinistic state of public opinion was strong; Shepilov's situation, on the other hand, was tricky and uncertain—especially after Fadeyev had inflicted defeat upon him with the story of his "flirtation" with theater critics. So Chesnokov thought it necessary to side with the former Agitprop head.

At this meeting, the target of Chesnokov's criticism was the academician Mitin and those who worked with him (O.S. Voĭtinskaya, M.M. Rozental, and M.A. Lifshits) at the Higher Party School and at the Society for the Dissemination of Political and Scientific Knowledge. Participants of the meeting demanded from Mitin "detailed criticism of his cosmopolitan mistakes." The meeting's resolution stated that "it is intolerable that the struggle against stateless cosmopolitans, who acted with impunity in the sub-faculties, has not been yet carried out" at the Philosophy Department of MSU.[142] The concluding report of the meeting developed exactly the same idea. Aleksandrov, Chesnokov, and Konstantinov (the Party organizations' secretary of the Institute of Philosophy) sent this latter report to Stalin and Malenkov on March 21. This report referred to Professor Beletskiĭ:

> Taking a cosmopolitan position and supported by the biased selection of personnel (chiefly of Jewish origin), he himself is an obstacle to the utter defeat of cosmopolitans at the Philosophy Department.[143]

Aleksandrov and others who shared his ideas took advantage of the anti-Semitism of Stalin and his circle. And they knew that "the heightened concentration" of Jews at Beletskiĭ's department at MSU (7 out of 19 lecturers) had already been reported to the CC.

The seal of anti-Semitism was impressed during a six-day Party meeting at the MSU Philosophy Department. The meeting began on March 22. To all appearances Chesnokov, who had lectured at MSU, aspired to head the Sub-Faculty of Dialectical and Historical Materialism. He took the floor after the main report, and brought a grave accusation against Beletskiĭ, saying that an anti-Party faction had been created in his sub-faculty. Other speakers had been coached to present the same idea, so Chesnokov's statement was supported by concrete, provocative "evidence." For example, Nikitin (secretary of the Department of Philosophy's Party bureau) asserted that a Jewish group within the sub-faculty had

142. RTsKhIDNI, f. 17, op. 118, d. 340, l. 105–116.

143. RTsKhIDNI, f. 17, op. 132, d. 160, l. 51.

sought to include Beletskiĭ instead of Chesnokov in the CC, and had discussed this plan at "a special secret meeting." Nikitin maintained that Beletskiĭ had appealed to the unity and unification of the Jews "as a matter of course," that is, because of his Jewish origin.

Sh.M. German, V.Zh. Kelle, and other researchers at the Sub-Faculty of Dialectical and Historical Materialism endeavored to protect their academic advisor from these absurd accusations. The chauvinistic meeting dealt with them quickly. German was thrown from the platform and dismissed from the university on April 21 "in connection with organized cliquishness and serious misinterpretations of Marxist-Leninist theory." Kelle was dismissed from the Party Bureau the day after his speech.[144]

The vote to request the MSU administration and "higher organizations" to dismiss Beletskiĭ was taken on March 28.[145] However, though he seemed doomed, the professor did not think to give up. On April 9 he sent a long letter to Stalin and Malenkov, proving the accuracy of his philosophical views. He did not omit his defense of the view that relative independence of ideology in the USSR was an impossibility—a concept that Aleksandrov, Chesnokov, and their supporters described as a "vulgar theory." He went on to ask them to end the persecution and tyranny that the leaders of the MSU Philosophy Department imposed upon him and his collaborators.[146] Malenkov instructed Shepilov to examine Beletskiĭ's letter and to submit a report on his ideas to the CC secretariat ten days hence.[147] Nevertheless, the matter was dropped and Beletskiĭ's persecution continued. On June 12 Beletskiĭ again addressed Stalin, writing that a two-and-a-half-week investigation of his department had "cleared [it] as a nest of cosmopolitanism and of anti-Marxism."[148] This time his appeal was not in vain. On June 14 Shepilov summoned Beletskiĭ and told him that there was no longer any problem about his dismissal.[149] From that time on, the political sense of Beletskiĭ's criticism gradually came to naught; it acquired the characteristics of a protracted pseudoscientific argument, until it slowly disappeared on its own. In 1955 a plausible pretext was given to transfer the bothersome scholar to the less prestigious Moscow Institute of Engineering and Economy.[150]

There was no reprisal against Beletskiĭ, Mitin, and their supporters in 1949, for fear that such might lead to Aleksandrov's triumph. Stalin had ostracized

---

144. RTsKhIDNI, f. 17, op. 118, d. 369, l. 61–63; d. 451, l. 55–56.

145. RTsKhIDNI, f. 17, op. 132, d. 221, l. 49–50.

146. RTsKhIDNI, f. 17, op. 118, d. 369, l. 31–65.

147. RTsKhIDNI, f. 17, op. 118, d. 369, l. 30.

148. RTsKhIDNI, f. 17, op. 118, d. 451, l. 55–56.

149. RTsKhIDNI, f. 17, op. 132, d. 222, l. 35–38.

150. G. Batygin and I. Devyatko, "Delo professora Z.Ya. Beletskogo" ("Professor Beletskiĭ's Case"), *Svobodnaya mysl' (Free Thought)*, 1993, no. 11, p. 102.

Aleksandrov in 1947, so it was most unlikely that Stalin planned to have him accepted as the indisputable authority in the sphere of ideology two years later. The ongoing antagonism among the several factions of the "philosophical front" maintained an unstable equilibrium that the dictator found quite advantageous.[151] This situation guaranteed that he would obtain information from all the fighting parties, and that he could therefore act as arbitrator in all the scientific debates and the endless pseudoscientific conflicts and squabbles. Stalin kept the leaders of the opposing parties apart from one another, and decided to support a third party in the postwar philosophical establishment: Chesnokov. Chesnokov had originally gone over to Aleksandrov's side at the beginning of the anti-cosmopolitan campaign, but quickly realized that the former Agitprop head was no longer in Stalin's favor. After overcoming his provincial shyness and acquiring some independence as editor-in-chief of *Issues in Philosophy*, Chesnokov decided to play for high stakes. He boldly and insistently began to speak of his special mission as the bearer of Stalin's and the CC's official policy in philosophy. He sought to convince the Kremlin leaders that Mitin and Beletskiĭ were hopelessly obsolete, that their thinking had forever remained in the 1930s. He also maintained that Aleksandrov's time as the propagandist and philosopher of the 1940s had passed. Chesnokov himself, however, was most assuredly a promising ideologue and theorist whose potential would only be realized in the 1950s.

Chesnokov was not original in his means of struggle. He repeated the standard patterns: he criticized Mitin's circle for maintaining an orthodox dogmatism, and Aleksandrov's circle for academic "objectivism"—and he criticized both circles for having become "grandees having a fair opinion of themselves,"[152] who, in spite of having "received a high academic status from the Party, did not bring out for the people or the Party a single serious philosophical book since the mid-30s, nor elaborate a single major problem of Marxist-Leninist theory."[153]

The result of this tactic was that both sides attacked Chesnokov. On July 5, 1949 he wrote to Suslov:

> When I began to work in the editorial office of *Issues in Philosophy* I expected to become, to some extent, the object of attacks from some people, especially from the Aleksandrov and Beletskiĭ-Mitin factions.

---

151. Stalin sought to maintain this uneasy equilibrium. In September 1949 he rejected Yu. Zhdanov's proposal to dismiss Aleksandrov as head of the Institute of Philosophy. To ease the pressure at the "philosophical front," in April 1950 Stalin sent Mitin to Bucharest as editor-in-chief of *For a Durable Peace, For a People's Democracy!* RTsKhIDNI, f. 17, op. 132, d. 160, l. 98; op. 119, d. 446, l. 4.

152. This was an expression that Stalin coined at the Seventeenth ACP(b) Congress.

153. RTsKhIDNI, f. 17, op. 118, d. 494, l. 239.

> But I did not expect to face such unfair methods as biased information from the Party Central Committee. I am asking the Party Central Committee for protection from such methods.[154]

Chesnokov's was not a voice crying in the wilderness.[155] Stalin always defended those upon whom he counted in his political game. On September 13, 1949 *Pravda* published an article supporting *Issues in Philosophy*, and Chesnokov then began his ascent to the heights of the nomenclatura.

In July 1952 Chesnokov was appointed head of the newly formed CC Department of Economic and Historical Sciences. At the Nineteenth Congress in October he was chosen to be a member of the CC CPSU Presidium, and he was appointed editor-in-chief of *Kommunist* magazine (previously titled *Bolshevik*). Incidentally, in the summer of 1949 Stalin approved the decision concerning this magazine. This put a finish to the infighting among Soviet philosophers that had been provoked by the attacks on "stateless cosmopolitanism." Specifically, on July 13, 1949 he signed a Party Bureau resolution to reorganize the *Bolshevik* editorial board, dismiss Aleksandrov[156] and two of his supporters (editor-in-chief P.N. Fedoseyev and M.T. Iovchuk).[157] In October 1952 the *Bolshevik* was renamed *Kommunist*, and Chesnokov was appointed editor-in-chief. This forced Aleksandrov and his supporters to curtail their demands to dominate Soviet philosophy.

---

154. RTsKhIDNI, f. 17, op. 118, d. 494, l. 243.

155. It was no longer considered important that Chesnokov, with Aleksandrov's assistance, had been dismissed as deputy head of the Institute of Philosophy. The same had happened to another of Aleksandrov's deputies, F.V. Konstantinov (who supported Chesnokov), who was accused of "surrounding himself with a number of such unprincipled men as Kantorovich, Kucherskaya, Katsman, and Stempkovskaya."

156. The subsequent life of this fighter on the ideological front may remind the reader more of a story of an adventure novel hero. Aleksandrov came to the peak of political life again after Stalin's death, when Malenkov was prime minister, and in 1954 he was appointed minister of culture. Nevertheless, in 1955 the CC's private letter "On the Unworthy Behavior of G.F. Aleksandrov, A.M. Yegolin, Etc." found the minister for culture and the famous literary critic guilty of debauchery and of taking part in drunken orgies with young actresses, poets, and painters. It was said that the underground rendezvous house for the nomenclatura elite had been discovered at that time in a Moscow suburb. Since Malenkov had by then been dismissed as chairman of the Council of Ministers, no one could then support Aleksandrov. So Aleksandrov was dismissed as minister of culture and exiled to Minsk, where he worked at the local Institute of Philosophy of the Belorussian Academy of Sciences until his death in 1961.

157. Iovchuk was the propaganda secretary of the Belorussian CC, but in the summer of 1949 he was demoted to a post at the Department of Dialectical and Historical Materialism at the Urals State University in Sverdlovsk. At his new job a year later, in September 1950, Iovchuk was again severely criticized, this time for having protected a lecturer, L.N. Kogan, who had been accused of cosmopolitanism. RTsKhIDNI, f. 17, op. 119, d. 13, l. 44–45 obverse; 49–53.

ECONOMICS

This same decision also struck a blow to Zhdanov's group in the Soviet leadership. In the context of apparatus intrigue, this decision obviously had a tactical character rather than an educational one. V.M. Andrianov, the first secretary of the Leningrad City Committee and the Regional Committee, wrote an article in which he quoted N.A. Voznesenskiĭ's book, *Military Economy of the USSR in the Period of the Patriotic War.*[158] The book was banned at the time, and the editors inadvertently neglected to delete this quotation. The CC placed the lion's share of the responsibility for this on Shepilov, the Agitprop head.

Shepilov was also accused of having recommended, in Agitprop's newspaper, *Culture and Life*, Voznesenskiĭ's book as a work manual for the Party District Committee's secretaries and propaganda personnel. A Politburo resolution of July 13 pointed out to Shepilov in no uncertain terms that he had made an "egregious blunder."[159] In the autumn of 1949 he turned the Agitprop administration over to Suslov, and had to content himself with being a CC inspector—until he again won Stalin's favor and became editor-in-chief of *Pravda* in 1952.

A number of the former *Bolshevik* editorial staff were also suspected of sympathizing with Voznesenskiĭ. Among the suspects was Professor L.M. Gatovskiĭ, an economist of Jewish origin. He was dismissed immediately. From August through September 1949 Gatovskiĭ lost two jobs. The Higher Party School dismissed him as head of the Sub-Faculty of Soviet Economy, and the Academy of Social Sciences (attached to the ACP(b) CC) dismissed him as lecturer.[160] Yet he somehow managed to retain his position at the Institute of Economy of the Academy of Social Sciences. This latter institute was then widely using the factor of Jewish origin to square accounts with supporters of Voznesenskiĭ, who had fallen into disgrace.

It is significant that back in the autumn of 1947, when the all-powerful Zhdanov favored Voznesenskiĭ, this leader in Soviet economic science had rebuffed his main rival, the academician Ye.S. Varga. Voznesenskiĭ had accused Varga of propagandizing the "opportunistic theory" of "organized capitalism" as a continually evolving structure that naturally adopts the principles of socialist planned economy. On September 18 the World Economy and World Politics Institute was abolished and Varga was dismissed as its head. This institute was then combined with the Institute of Economy, thus forming the Institute of Economy of the Academy of Sciences of the USSR, and Voznesenskiĭ transformed two-thirds of this new institution into the Departmental Research Center

---

158. *Voyennaya ekonomika SSSR v period Otechestvennoĭ voĭny.*

159. RTsKhIDNI, f. 17, op. 118, d. 449, l. 4, 5.

160. RTsKhIDNI, f. 17, op. 118, d. 448, l. 54; d. 545, l. 65–66, 68.

(attached to the State Planning Commission).

No more than two years had passed when the oppressor fell prey himself, which caused a new wave or purges at the Institute of Economy. In March 1949 Shepilov, as publisher of *Issues in Economy*,[161] began to bombard Malenkov with notes on the necessity of "putting in order" the Institute of Economy and the editorial board of his magazine. The most detailed of these notes, dated July 7, 1949, contained an enormous amount of compromising material. In this note, Shepilov accused K.V. Ostrovityanov, a fellow of the Academy of Sciences and the administrative head of the new institute, of being unwilling and unable to abolish the "monopolistic" positions of certain scientists, most of whom were Jewish. Shepilov maintained that these scientists had seized power in the economic sciences and had obstructed promotions for new scientific personnel. That is why, he explained, "there is no sharp criticism of the bourgeois-reformist and cosmopolitan blunders" in the works on Western economy written by L.Ya. Eventov, V.I. Kaplan (Lan),[162] M. Bokshitskií, I.M. Lemin, S.A. Vygodskií, or the academician I.A. Trakhtenberg. Shepilov found that the writings of Gatovskií, A.I. Notkin, and G.A. Kozlov on socialist political economy utilized an "abstract-scholastic approach." Shepilov's conclusion was straightforward: "The research staff of the institute is still littered with descendants from enemy parties—former Trotskyites, Bund members, and those who have been expelled from the Party." All the remaining Jewish scientists were included on that list: I.M. Faíngar, L.A. Mendelson, D. Rozenfeld, and others.[163]

It was academician L.N. Ivanov who displayed the greatest zeal in carrying out the anti-Semitic CC directives on cleansing the research staff of the Institute of Economics. In 1949 he was appointed deputy secretary of the Department of Economics and Law at the Academy of Sciences, in which duty he was responsible for personnel. From the beginning of 1943 he had indefatigably fought for "purity of the ranks" among Soviet economists, constantly informing higher-ranking officials of "hostile ideological trends and opinions, and their bearers." The materials brought forth by Shepilov and his aid Ivanov were the basis for a July 15, 1949 resolution of the CC secretariat "Concerning the Institute of Economics of the Academy of Sciences of the USSR." This resolution was filled with political accusations against the Institute's administration. Similar resolutions of the CC Orgburo, signed on August 1 and 15, reinforced the criticism.[164]

---

161. *Voprosy ekonomiki.*

162. V.I. Kaplan (Lan) (1902–1989) authored lengthy monographs on the US economy. Dismissed from all his positions, he was forced to move to Soviet Middle Asia, where he lectured on political economy at the Frunze Medical Institute. On February 26, 1953 he was arrested as "an American spy."

163. RTsKhIDNI, f. 17, op. 118, d. 352, l. 17–18; d. 458, l. 261–272.

164. RTsKhIDNI, f. 17, op. 118, d. 458, l. 256.

Under the weight of accusations, K.V. Ostrovityanov, the director of the Institute of Economics, had to resort to self-flagellation. On July 25 he reported to Malenkov and Suslov, taking the blame for the nationalistic makeup of the Academy of Sciences fellows and scientists with doctoral degrees who were working at the Institute. Of the 34, 20 were Jews, only 12 were Russians, and 2 were of other nationalities. On the other hand, he also pointed out that of the 83 senior researchers at the Institute, 44 were Russians, 34 were Jews, and 5 were of other nationalities.[165] These statistics were a topic for discussion at the extended session of the Academy of Sciences presidium on August 25, 1949. The presidium decided that "among the employees of the Institute of Economics, scientists of Russian nationality are not properly represented."[166]

There then followed the so-called "conclusions of an organizational nature": the CC first considered the question of Ostrovityanov's resignation, but ultimately decided on blackballing him during the Academy of Sciences elections. Nevertheless, the Institute's deputy directors (G.A. Kozlov and V.A. Maslennikov) could not escape dismissal.[167]

Industry

MANAGEMENT

The criticism of "Jewish domination" at the Institute of Economics was acute and scandalous, yet it had a broader application. The Politburo had resolved on September 18, 1947 to have the State Planning Commission be responsible for the "scientific and organizational supervision" of the Institute of Economics. Therefore, in this particular case, the criticism served mainly to discredit the State Planning Commission's administration. The main target was Voznesenskií, the State Planning Commission's chairman. A resolution of the Council of Ministers, approved on March 5, 1949, forced him to leave his position. This latter resolution included a directive "to check scrupulously the staff composition of the State Planning Commission."[168] Stalin attached particular importance to this directive, and the job was entrusted to Ye.Ye. Andreyev, the head of the CC administrative department. A Politburo resolution of March stipulated Andreyev's transference to the State Planning Commission as a plenipotentiary CC representative for personnel. This was the first of many such appointments; new positions were established appointing CC representatives responsible for personnel in ministries, organs, and institutions mentioned in the Orgburo resolution of

165. RTsKhIDNI, f. 17, op. 118, d. 477, l. 77.
166. RTsKhIDNI, f. 17, op. 132, d. 158, l. 98.
167. RTsKhIDNI, f. 17, op. 118, d. 545, l. 47–48.
168. RTsKhIDNI, f. 17, op. 119, d. 383, l. 88.

March 23, 1949. The aging dictator was trying to install "new eyes and ears" in a state bureaucratic apparatus that was growing ever more autonomous. The Politburo resolution stated that, in central administrative bodies, "house discipline has become more important than state discipline; the employees choose methods of mutual benefit, but they do not help reveal and disclose evidence of dishonesty; and they do not diligently carry out and implement governmental directives." Therefore, to "strengthen Party control over the selection of personnel," the CC introduced the system of ("in some cases") appointing its representatives, "to work independently of the leaders of ministries and central union bodies."[169]

The strengthening of personnel politics was a reaction to the US policy of "loyalty checking" of state employees, which had been introduced in 1947. It also influenced the mass media. *Pravda* and *Bolshevik* were particularly active in inducing hysteria. They began publishing articles with such titles as "Bolshevist Methods of Leadership in Industrial Bodies," and "To Improve Personnel Recruitment Incessantly and Indefatigably." These articles were, for the most part, prepared by L.A. Slepov, the deputy head of the CC Department of Propaganda. In each article he explained, in his bureaucratic and extremely boring manner, "the Leninist-Stalinist principles on the selection of personnel according to their political and business abilities."[170]

In truth, these recurrent propagandistic movements camouflaged more serious tendencies—namely, the Soviet leadership's attempt to establish total control over personnel recruitment. The State Planning Commission became a touchstone of this allegedly new policy—a new policy that was essentially the old policy of Stalinist hyper-centralization.

Andreyev embarked on his mission with enthusiasm, pitilessly discharging those whose political or administrative capacity he, for whatever reason, did not trust. By May 1951 the State Planning Commission had fired 300 people. (However, it should be noted that 50 of them were transferred to other institutions.) Of Voznesenskii's 12 deputies, only 3 retained their positions. Of 72 department heads, 32 were replaced. Of 66 deputy department heads, 33 were replaced. And of 133 heads of various sections, 52 were replaced.[171]

Approximately one-forth of those ostracized were Jews. At first, in 1949, the so-called "fifth point" (nationality) did not, as a rule, matter considerably in the various economic bodies, the State Planning Commission, the ministries, or other enterprises. The "fifth point" only became operational in regard to expulsion from the Party, imprisonment, exile, having relatives who had been repressed or who had emigrated, personal membership (or a relative's membership) in "bourgeois"

---

169. RTsKhIDNI, f. 17, op. 118, d. 328, l. 72–73.

170. See for example *Bolshevik*, 1949, no. 18, pp. 27–40.

171. RTsKhIDNI, f. 17, op. 119, d. 383, l. 87–88.

parties, descent from the "exploiting" classes, and in other such cases. For instance, Ye.A. Shapiro (a Jew), the head of the Directorate of the Oil Industry Administration, was fired because his uncle had been exiled to Middle Asia[172] in 1927 for speculating on the rise and fall of prices, and also because all of his other relatives lived in the US. M.A. Kasperskiĭ (a Russian), the head of the Department of Industry in the Ukraine, was discharged for having served in General A.I. Denikin's army in the Ukraine in 1918–1919 and for having participated in Jewish pogroms.[173] In 1949 the Ministry of Geology, as well as affiliated research and regional organizations, underwent a large-scale purge similar to the State Planning Commission's. The outburst of paranoia here was not based totally on nationality, but was provoked by the latest exposure of a "saboteur organization" among Ministry of State Security employees. This "saboteur organization" included academician I.F. Grigoryev (director of the Institute of Geological Sciences at the Academy of Sciences and a well-known researcher of ore deposits), Professor V.M. Kreĭter (of the Moscow Geological Institute), A.V. Edelshteĭn (editor-in-chief of the *Soviet Geology*[174] journal), and others. In the spring of 1949 they were all arrested and charged with, among other things, the premeditated divulgence of state secrets. Grigoryev, who years earlier had served on A.B. Kolchak's[175] Geological Committee, was cruelly beaten as the "ringleader" of the saboteur organization until October 28, 1950 when the Special Meeting sentenced him to 25 years in a reform camp, where he soon died. The minister of geology, I.I. Malyshev, was forced to resign at this same time. All this took place against a background of mass firings. By November 1949, from the central apparatus of the Ministry of Geology alone, 149 employees had been fired, including 6 heads of directorates, 3 senior engineers from the directorates, and 3 department heads.[176]

A VICTIM OF APPARATUS INTRIGUE

A similar episode occurred with I.M. Zaltsman, the celebrated director of the Chelyabinsk Kirov plant and authoritative organizer of the tank industry. The reasons underlying this were far weightier than nationality. During the war Zaltsman had worked for a time as chairman of the People's Commissariat[177] of the Tank Industry; and now A. Zverev, the secretary

172. *Translator's note:* Middle Asia consisted of Kazakhstan, Uzbekistan, Tadzhikistan, Turkmenistan, and Kirghizia.

173. RTsKhIDNI, f. 17, op. 118, d. 467, l. 93, 95.

174. *Sovyetskaya geologiya.*

175. Kolchak was the leader of the "White Movement" at the time of the civil war (1918–1921).

176. RTsKhIDNI, f. 17, op. 118, d. 447, l. 213.

177. *Translator's note:* The precise term used for "chairman of the People's Commissariat" was "narkom."

of the Party Bureau of Zaltsman's plant, accused him of using vicious, authoritarian methods of administration, deceiving the state, contributing to the spending of state money without good reason, financial intrigues, and other economic offenses. This was all stated in a note to Stalin on February 21, 1949.[178] It is necessary to point out that almost half of the existing state enterprises registered such offenses, and that they quite often reported on these things to a higher body. Consequently the CC workers were at first indifferent to the information on Zaltsman. It was not until April 13 that the CC's administrative department prepared a note for Malenkov on the necessity of organizing a check. Finally, on May 21, the CC secretariat made a decision, selecting members for the commission and authorizing them to conduct a check at the Chelyabinsk tank plant.[179]

The delays were not accidental. Had it been just a question of Zaltsman, his case either would have been stopped and forgotten, or it would have been exaggerated with charges of "criminal activity" and quickly finished and swiftly punished, thus ending the career of yet one more economic leader "who failed to remain worthy of the Party's trust." However, Malenkov and his apparatchiks were engaged in fighting with their rivals, the so-called "Leningrad" group in the Kremlin administration. So it turned out that they had all along been considering the possibility of using Zaltsman's case in their own intrigue. Zaltsman had worked in Leningrad before the war, and he had known A.A. Kuznetsov and other now disgraced leaders of the city and the surrounding region quite well. Now he could serve as an important source of compromising information against them.

As Zaltsman recalled, in June 1949 the CC summoned him to a meeting of the bureau of the Commission of Party Control. Malenkov, Suslov, and Shkiryatov were present. Shkiryatov opened the meeting, declaring in the most straightforward manner: "There were enemies of the people in the former Leningrad administration. You know many of them. Therefore, you have to help us and put on record what you know about their criminal projects and actions." At the following meeting Zaltsman submitted evidence concerning his collaboration with the former Leningrad leaders. Shkiryatov quickly looked over the text and discontentedly commented: "It's no good at all." Malenkov concluded meaningfully: "You defend the leaders who went against the Party. This means that you share their position. Well then, we shall study your case."[180]

The veiled threats and psychological pressure quickly led to concrete actions and measures being taken against one of the most eminent directors of Soviet State enterprises. On June 24 the CC secretariat commissioned P.K.

---

178. RTsKhIDNI, f. 17, op. 118, d. 352, l. 146–161.

179. RTsKhIDNI, f. 17, op. 118, d. 352, l. 162; d. 448, l. 164.

180. *Trud*, October 13, 1988.

Ponomarenko (CC secretary), M.F. Shkiryatov (deputy chairman of the Commission of Party Control), V.A. Malyshev (deputy chairman of the Council of Ministers), and I.I. Nosenko (minister of the transportation industry) to prepare the CC draft resolution "On the Anti-Party Behavior of the Director of the Kirov Chelyabinsk Plant, Comrade Zaltsman." On June 30 these four officials sent Stalin a note presenting, in addition to previous accusations, new evidence regarding Zaltsman's Jewish descent. Among other things, they hinted that Zaltsman was protective of Jews. For instance, he had appointed Ya.Ye. Goldshteín ("who comes from a family of a big mining industrialist") as a senior metallurgist of the plant; and he appointed A.A. Belinkin ("comes from the family of a manufacturer . . . his brother, uncle, and two aunts live in the US") as deputy production manager. They also pointed out that Ya.T. Yudilovich ("Polish by descent . . . lived in Germany . . . his brother was arrested by NKVD organs, two uncles live in the US, one of them is a big capitalist") was the economist for the planning department; and the list went on.[181] On July 11 Stalin signed a Politburo resolution dismissing Zaltsman as director.

The Commission of Party Control was commissioned to "consider the materials concerning his Party behavior."[182] The Party prosecution machine gradually picked up speed, accusing Zaltsman of yet more offenses and crimes. On September 10 Shkiryatov reported to Malenkov that at the examination A.A. Kuznetsov (a former CC secretary who at that time was under arrest) declared that in 1945 Zaltsman had presented him with a saber, engraved with Kuznetsov's name and decorated with gold and precious stones, and also with a gold watch. (The saber was produced at the Zlatoust plant.) The same type of watch was also given to P.S. Popkov (secretary of Leningrad Regional Committee), and to Ya.F. Kapustin (secretary of Leningrad City Committee). In addition, the Commission of Party Control received information that Zaltsman had met Mikhoels in the spring of 1946 in Moscow, promising material aid for the Jewish Theater. Then in May 1946 the theater received five railway cars' worth of timber, three tons of iron, 800 kg of paint, and other items.[183]

On September 17 the CC secretariat confirmed the resolution of the Bureau of the Commission of Party Control concerning to Zaltsman's expulsion from the Party "for unworthy behavior."[184] Zaltsman was afterwards sent to Oryol as a foreman at Plant No. 537, which manufactured spare parts for tanks and tractors. As he later explained, he had once sent Stalin a gift—a desk-set shaped like a tank and artillery guns. The mere chance that Stalin greatly fancied this present saved

181. RTsKhIDNI, f. 17, op. 118, d. 448, l. 131–143.
182. RTsKhIDNI, f. 17, op. 118, d. 448, l. 126.
183. RTsKhIDNI, f. 17, op. 118, d. 536, l. 224–225.
184. RTsKhIDNI, f. 17, op. 118, d. 536, l. 223.

Zaltsman from a harsher fate.[185]

The Chelyabinsk Party leadership suffered together with Zaltsman. A.A. Beloborodov, the first secretary of the Regional Committee, along with some other secretaries of lower rank, were dismissed for having supported director Zaltsman.[186]

Later, as the purges in the economic sphere became increasingly regular, anti-Semitism played a greater role. Formerly it had been secondary and subservient, but now in some cases it became the primary factor. In part this was because the "experts" on "Jewish bourgeois nationalism," who had earlier worked in repressive structures, increased their activity. These institutions clearly perceived what the "social order" that emanated from the Stalinist leadership was all about.

THE ZIS CASE

The "Zionist danger" became of decisive importance to Soviet economics thanks to some events from late 1949 through early 1950. The events in question took place at some of the state enterprises of the Ministry of Automobile and Tractor Engineering, especially at the Stalin Automobile Plant (ZIS) in Moscow. In May 1948 Mark Leíkman, Boris Simkin, Girsh Leonov, Sarra Bortnik, and other workers and engineers at this plant sent to the Jewish Antifascist Committee a telegram that read in part: "From the bottom of our hearts we welcome and support the establishment of the state of Israel. The Jewish nation, on a par with all other peoples, has a full-fledged right to independence and free development."[187] Jewish social and cultural life at the plant had become noticeably animated after the war; and plant workers attended the Mikhoels Theater in groups. There were other activities as well. The organizer and the moving spirit of all those activities was Alekseí (Aron) Filippovich Eídinov (1908–1950), the director's aide. Eídinov was on the closest and friendliest terms with the leader of the Stalin Automobile Plant, I.A. Likhachyov. N.S. Khrushchev recalled that when he was still the first secretary of the Ukrainian CC CP(B), Likhachyov and Eídinov had visited him on vacation in Kiev soon after the war. Khrushchev could not have imagined then that sometime later, after he had become the first secretary of the Moscow Regional Committee, he would again meet his former guests Likhachyov and Eídinov ("a feeble, thinnish Jew") under such different and tragic circumstances.[188]

In February 1950 Stalin appointed Khrushchev chairman of the commission investigating the ZIS situation. The commission quickly carried out the

185. *Trud*, October 13, 1988.

186. RTsKhIDNI, f. 17, op. 118, d. 744, l. 222–227.

187. RTsKhIDNI, f. 17, op. 128, d. 608, l. 83.

188. N.S. Khrushchev, "Vospominaniya" ("Memoirs"), *Voprosy istorii*, 1991, no. 11, pp. 48–49.

investigation, and prepared a concluding note with some most radical and severe measures. Stalin then ordered the Ministry of State Security to act. On March 18, 1950 Eídinov was taken to Lubyanka (even though he had been working at a different enterprise since the spring of 1949). Within the next few months dozens of other plant employees were arrested, including M.M. Klyatskin (inspector to the director), G.E. Shmaglit (head of the Department of Main Constructions), P.M. Mostoslavskií (head of production), V.M. Lisovich (head of the Department of Labor and Wages), A.I. Shmidt (head of the department of production control), G.A. Sonkin (an eminent designer), B.M. Fitterman (senior plant designer), M.A. Kagan (deputy to the senior metallurgist), B.Yu. Persin (director of the plant's nutritional service), D.Ya. Samorodnitskií (head of the medical unit), and others.[189]

Sometime later Stalin ordered Khrushchev, Malenkov, and Beria to interrogate I.A. Likhachyov. They summoned him to the Kremlin and took him to the meeting hall of the Bureau of the Council of Ministers, where they accused him of a "loss of vigilance," which had led to complicity with the "anti-Soviet Jewish nationalistic sabotage group," established by his aide Eídinov. The imprisoned plant employees corroborated the accusation.[190] Likhachyov fainted. They brought him to his senses by pouring cold water over him and sent him home.[191] Upon being informed of this, Stalin decided that the untrustworthy industrialist had been taught his lesson, and simply dismissed Likhachyov as director. Likhachyov had suffered a heart attack during the purge of the plant; yet this tragic development ended more or less satisfactorily. On June 13, 1950 Stalin signed a Politburo resolution appointing him a director of Small Aircraft Plant No. 41 in Moscow.[192]

Even heavier ordeals befell the arrested ZIS employees. Interrogated in 1955, Sokolov, the former head of the Department to Investigate Cases of Special Importance to the MGB, testified that from the first Abakumov had issued an order for conducting interrogations of those arrested presuming their espionage, saboteur, and nationalistic activities. At the minister's order, Eídinov's first

---

189. In all, 48 people were arrested, 42 of whom were Jews. This is not counting the subservient departments and facilities not involved in production, such as the medical center club. (This information is provided by the Museum of the Moscow Likhachyov Plant.)

190. Testimony concerning American ambassador Walter B. Smith's visit to ZIS plant raised a peculiar suspicion. He had studied the governmental limousine ZIS-110, which was produced at the plant, had given Likhachyov a pen as a present, and had invited him to the embassy to show him the latest model Cadillac.

191. N.S. Khrushchev, "Vospominaniya," *Voprosy istorii*, 1991, no. 11, pp. 48–49.

192. After Stalin's death Likhachyov became minister of Automobile Transport and Highways. He died in June 1956. Khrushchev, possibly feeling guilty, then changed the name of the Stalin Automobile Plant to the Likhachyov Automobile Plant. RTsKhIDNI, f. 17, op. 118, d. 910, l. 32.

interrogation began with his being beaten with a rubber baton. This procedure was "explained" by the need of getting "frank confessions" from him. Klyatskin, Lisovich, Shmaglit, and others who were arrested were also subjected to physical coercion.

The investigation formulated the following main conclusion, which later became an accusation:

> It was established that the Jewish nationalistic underground, which functioned in the USSR under the protection of the JAC, tried to find support for their hostile work from the nationalists who lodged at the Moscow Automobile plant. The active participants of this hostile underground—Mikhoels, Person, Aízenshtadt—acting on America's direction, visited the plant, established the necessary contacts, and used them for criminal purposes.

The arrested were incriminated with political and clearly criminal activities, as well as with "wrecking saboteur work," i.e., intentionally decreasing the norms of the five-year production plans, producing deficient cars, constructing personal dachas at the plant's expense, stealing groceries provided for employees, and so forth.

Eídinov was declared the ringleader of the ZIS nationalists, and in addition was accused of conducting anti-Soviet meetings in his office, at which the national policy of the Party and Soviet state was criticized. As proof of this, the investigators cited, in particular, evidence earlier recorded from Ye.A. Sokolovskaya, who before her arrest worked as the plant's senior inspector. She had allegedly declared, in conversation with her accomplices ("the Zionists"), that "the Soviet Jews don't need the small and uncomfortable Birobidzhan . . . . It is humiliating for the Jewish people. A Jewish republic must be created in the Crimea or on the territory of the former German Republic of Volga."

The most serious accusation, however, ascribed to the former assistant to the ZIS director was that of "criminal" relations with "American spy" S.D. Persov, a journalist whom Eídinov had "helped collect espionage material about the plant." It was perhaps not a coincidence that they were both shot on the same day, November 23, 1950. Eídinov's Russian wife, R.G. Filippova, was also dealt with; she was at first criticized for "having gotten involved with a Jew," and was later sent to Kazakhstan for five years.

Of the plant employees who were arrested, Mostoslavskií, Shmidt, Persin, Samorodnitskií, Lisovich, A.Z. Finkelshteín, I.M. Blyumkin, and M.M. Klyatskin were shot. The rest for the most part were sentenced to the maximum number of years of imprisonment, including B.M. Fitterman, who was sentenced to 25 years at the MGB's special camp.

According to an October 1, 1955 decision of the MCSC, the November 23, 1950 sentence regarding Eídinov was annulled. At this time the other persecuted individuals in this case were also rehabilitated.

The automobile industry was the most popular manufacturing branch and its products, for many people, were not only a symbol of scientific and engineering progress, but were also visible testimony to the success of Party politics. The events at ZIS, therefore, were a sufficiently clear sign of Stalin's and his team's attitude toward the Soviet Jews. The ZIS massacre was just one episode; the purge of this industrial branch had started long before.

The first major victim of the anti-Jewish hysteria that raged throughout the entire automobile industry was A.M. Baranov, the director of the Moscow Small-Engine Automobile Plant. Early in 1948 he was fired and accused of concealing his Jewish nationality and of "illegally" changing his name from Abram Moiseyevich to Alekseí Mikhaílovich. Other Jewish workers at this plant were dismissed at about the same time. As a result of the Politburo resolution on the situation in the Ministry of Automobile and Tractor Engineering, E.L. Livshits (the head of the main administration of material and technical provision) lost his job on August 9, 1949.[193] The same happened to Aron Okun, who until January 3, 1950 headed the Carburetor Plant in Leningrad.[194] Then in February began the persecutions of personnel at the First State Kaganovich Bearing Plant, which was the leading enterprise within the Ministry of Automobile and Tractor Engineering system. Chief accountant Bronshteín, head of the Planning Department Sochinskií, and other employees were discharged. The plant director, P.G. Sukov, was also discharged; he was suspected of closing his eyes to the activity "of former Bund members."[195] In March 1950 the CC secretariat confirmed the ministry decree on the dismissal of A.M. Livshits, the chief engineer of the Yaroslavl Automobile Works, which produced automobiles and diesel engines. Until September 1945 Livshits had worked at the Ulyanovsk Automobile Works; now he was accused of having brought a number of specialists from the Ulyanovsk plant to the Yaroslavl plant—and these specialists were allegedly members of a bourgeois-nationalistic group who then launched a large-scale saboteur campaign in Yaroslavl. From October through December 1949 the regional bodies of the MGB arrested a number of these specialists (R.E. Kaplan, M.M. Rabinovich, M.Ya. Limoni, A.A. Bulatnikov, L.I. Kaplan, I.Ya. Koppel, and others). At the examinations some of these specialists testified that Livshits had taken part in their general discussions, and that they had concluded that the growing Russian nationalism led the government-controlled mass media

193. RTsKhIDNI, f. 17, op. 117, d. 1010, l. 158, 159; op. 118, d. 482, l. 88.

194. RTsKhIDNI, f. 17, op. 118, d. 668, l. 119–120 obverse.

195. RTsKhIDNI, f. 17, op. 118, d. 748, l. 45–54; d. 752, l. 153.

deliberately to emphasize the presence of Jews among cosmopolitans, thereby reviving and fostering anti-Semitism.[196] Similar such confessions made it impossible for Livshits to remain free. In May 1950 he was also imprisoned.[197]

Anti-Semitism, initiated and encouraged from on high, led some workers and employees to adopt a corresponding attitude. Looking forward to the prestigious and profitable vacancies, they demanded the brutalizing purges. Anonymous letters, calumny, disinformation, political and social demagogy grew common. Typical of such was a letter from the Ural Stalin Automobile Plant (UralZIS)[198] forwarded by "non-Party Bolsheviks" (as they called themselves) to the CC in April 1950. This unsigned letter appealed to patriotic feelings, adjuring the leaders:

> We have come to the conclusion that socialism is in danger, for all head positions are occupied by Jews who look to Wall Street and who will certainly betray us in the forthcoming struggle against capitalism. The people are filled with indignation. Our administration was turned into a Jewish administration with the help of Mr. Kil....[199] Common people are devoted to their government and hope that our voice will be heard.... You will never be able to find truth here in the lower classes, because the Jews have adjusted all Party and governmental laws to their own needs and mercilessly go on sucking our righteous blood, the blood that is needed to build the Communist society.... When will our glorious Russia, the motherland of socialism, get rid of the Jewish-nationalist-American hirelings?[200]

In answer to this letter, the Committee of Party Control sent one of its executive inspectors to the Urals. The regional Party authorities reported to him that they had already dismissed four specialists: E.A. Zaks, P.A. Fishbeín, N.Yu. Ganelin, and L.I. Geller. And after their visitor left, they discharged their director, I.F. Sinitsyn ("for loss of Bolshevik vigilance"), transferring him to a Stalingrad tractor plant; and they also discharged their chief designer, A.S. Aízenberg.[201]

The process of firing spread through the entire industrial branch in question. In accordance with a decision of the CC secretariat, Yakov S. Yusim, the director

---

196. RTsKhIDNI, f. 17, op. 118, d. 773, l. 178–194.

197. RTsKhIDNI, f. 17, op. 118, d. 773, l. 188.

198. This plant was located in the town of Miass in the Chelyabinsk Region.

199. In the 1940s M.Ya. Kil had been deputy head of the Central Administrative Body for All Automobile Plants at the Ministry of the Automobile and Tractor Industry. In 1950 he worked at ZIS.

200. RTsKhIDNI, f. 17, op. 118, d. 842, l. 74.

201. RTsKhIDNI, f. 17, op. 118, d. 842, l. 66–67; op. 119, d. 9, l. 119.

of the Kuíbyshev Bearing Plant, was dismissed on May 12, 1950.[202] This experienced industrialist had headed the First Kaganovich State Bearing Plant in Moscow in 1937. When he took it over in 1941 Yusim evacuated the Kaganovich plant and moved it to the town of Kuíbyshev, where he became its director. After the war the Kuíbyshev State Bearing Plant always fulfilled its five-year plans and was considered one of the leading state enterprises in all respects. In 1948 the Kuíbyshev plant published a book by A. Ivich (I.I. Bernshteín) entitled *Second Birth*,[203] which described the achievements of the Kuíbyshev plant under Yusim's leadership.[204] In the spring of 1949, when the campaign of the struggle against cosmopolitanism was in full swing, the CC's Department of Motor Engineering used information received from the local Party organs and security bodies to accuse Yusim of carelessness and of vicious recruitment policies. I.D. Serbin, the deputy head of the CC's Department of Motor Engineering, was undoubtedly one of those responsible for fanning the flames of anti-Semitism in economics,[205] and he was particularly active in his attempts to discredit Yusim. On April 14 he sent a memo to Malenkov blaming Yusim for the six Kuíbyshev Plant employees who had been arrested and convicted for political reasons. But his chief fault, however, was nepotistic recruitment, which led to the obstruction of management; specifically, he was accused of patronizing S.M. Broverman (deputy head of the Production Department), V.B. Boyarskií (deputy head of the Labor and Wages Department), and B.N. Perchik (head of the Design Bureau).[206] All three were dismissed; and though Yusim retained his position, he was officially reprimanded for his "non-Party attitude toward the selection and appointment of personnel."[207] Nevertheless, Serbin was not content with such an obscure solution. Stalin had appointed him head of the CC's Department of Motor Engineering for his special merits and achievements in disclosing the "Zionist conspiracy" at ZIS.[208] To justify Stalin's hopes, he sent Malenkov a list of people, including 17 Jews whom Yusim had appointed to leading positions at the Kuíbyshev Bearing Plant.[209] Serbin now succeeded in discharging Yusim as

---

202. RTsKhIDNI, f. 17, op. 118, d. 871, l. 107.

203. *Vtoroye rozhdeniye.*

204. Profizdat published a revised version of this book as *Road Up the Mountain* [*Put' v goru*] (Moscow: Profizdat, 1949). This book violated the main principle of survival in a totalitarian state: "Don't put your head above the parapet!" Soon afterwards the incautious Profizdat director suffered the consequences. In 1950 the book was banned.

205. I.D. Serbin (1910–1981) became deputy head of the CC's Department of Motor Engineering in 1948, and in 1950 he became head of that department. From 1958 through 1981 he headed the CC's Defense Industry Department.

206. RTsKhIDNI, f. 17, op. 118, d. 408, l. 221–225.

207. RTsKhIDNI, f. 17, op. 118, d. 408, l. 219.

208. RTsKhIDNI, f. 17, op. 118, d. 896, l. 126.

209. Yusim later worked at the Serpukhov Wheelchair Plant. Unable to withstand the undeserved

director; and at the end of 1950 he imposed a more severe punishment: a "strict reprimand with warnings of possible expulsion from the Party."[210] Others also lost their positions in 1950, among them I.B. Sheínman (head of the State Institute on the Motor and Tractor Industry), Ye.R. Meshuris (director of the Irbitsk Motorcycle Plant), and Ya.I. Nevyazhskií (chief engineer of the Kharkov Tractor Plant).[211]

Parallel with the industrial purge was a purge of the Party structures that supervised motor and tractor engineering. M.Z. Zelikson, head of the Department of Motor Engineering at the Moscow City Party Committee, resigned his position at the end of 1949. Later he was sent to Red October,[212] a machine-tool construction plant, as an ordinary worker of low rank.[213] In August 1950 the same thing happened to A.A. Pavlova, the head of the Automobile and Tractor Engineering Section of the Motor Engineering Department. Serbin got rid of her, having criticized her for her "improperly timed reaction to the Communists' signals concerning bad recruitment policy at the Ministry of Automobile and Tractor Engineering."[214] It is necessary to point out that considerable personnel transfers took place at the central administration of this branch as well.[215] Together with the mass arrests, the Jews who had not long before held high positions in the ministry were arrested, including B.S. Genkin (assistant to the minister), Yu.S. Kagan (deputy minister), E.L. Livshits (head of the Main Directorate of Material and Technical Supplies, who was later to be shot), B.S. Messen-Gisser (deputy director of the Directorate of Leading Personnel). They were all accused of being accomplices of the "saboteur-nationalists" unmasked at ZIS. In addition, Minister S.A. Akopov was dismissed and then appointed deputy minister of agricultural engineering. The deputy minister on personnel, P.D. Borodin, was sent to the periphery because he could not properly fulfill his duties.[216]

On May 5, 1950 the Politburo adopted a resolution "On Drawbacks and Mistakes in Working on Personnel at the Ministry of Automobile and Tractor Industry in the USSR." With this document, the Politburo directly accused the leaders of this industrial branch of "sloppy work on personnel at the Moscow

---

prosecution, accusations, and humiliations, he soon grew ill and died.

210. RTsKhIDNI, f. 17, op. 119, d. 290, l. 63–69.

211. RTsKhIDNI, f. 17, op. 118, d. 952, l. 71; d. 964, l. 177; op. 119, d. 173, l. 207, 208.

212. Krasnyí Oktyabr.

213. RTsKhIDNI, f. 17, op. 118, d. 617, l. 141.

214. RTsKhIDNI, f. 17, op. 119, d. 1, l. 63.

215. Dismissals at the bearing industry's main administrative body were particularly plentiful, as 12 of its 16 departments were headed by Jews.

216. Later, from 1963 through 1983, Borodin worked as general director of the Likhachyov Automobile Plant in Moscow.

Automobile Plant, into which a large group of saboteur elements managed to penetrate."[217] This was not the end of the matter. Stalin then demanded the CC secretariat to summarize all personnel inspections and purges starting from 1949 up through the "ZIS case," and to send a secret directive to all Party committees along with clarifications of Party policy in that respect.

Suslov and the Agitprop apparatus subordinate to him compiled the first draft of this directive, which contained numerous concrete facts about anti-Semitic purges in not only the Ministry of the Automobile and Tractor Industry, but also in the Committee of Arts, the Academy of Sciences, the All-Union Radio Committee, and the editorial boards of central newspapers and magazines.[218] Stalin did not approve of this draft as it was flagrantly anti-Semitic and revealed the reasons for staff rearrangements. He finally chose a draft that did not mention Jews or the "national feature" at all. This new draft was tailored after the best traditions of Soviet apparatus casuistry; it consisted of abstract slogans concerning the necessity of reinforcing Party control over "the selection, arrangement, and education of the staff." Stalin signed this Politburo resolution on June 21, 1950. Its title was "On Measures to Eliminate Drawbacks in the Selection and Education of Personnel, in Connection with Gross Errors Revealed in the Staff Routine of the Ministry of the Automobile and Tractor Industry," and it was strictly confidential. This resolution contained an outspoken concrete proposition, obliging ministers and other department heads to submit to the CC annual reports on their work on personnel at the central state machinery bodies as well as in lesser government bodies.[219] Outwardly this looked like bureaucratic formalism on an insignificant issue; yet in reality this resolution introduced a systematic and continual purge as a major attribute of state policy. The practice of conducting sporadic check-ups on the loyalty of state employees, along with check-ups on their national and ethnic background thus acquired an official, though hidden, sanction. The weeding out of personnel had actively begun in 1949, climaxed with the June 21 resolution, and reached its final stage with the sensational "doctors' plot" in late 1952 and early 1953.

STATUS OF THE JEWISH ELITE

Strangely, Jews among the upper stratum of the state and Party nomenclature remained almost intact through the course of the new purge. This was probably because there were so few Jews remaining in the uppermost Party elite. L.M. Kaganovich, who held the highest rank among the Party elite, left no doubt of his faithfulness to Stalin. Kaganovich had been a Politburo member since 1930,

217. RTsKhIDNI, f. 17, op. 118, d. 853, l. 130–131.

218. RTsKhIDNI, f. 17, op. 118, d. 897, l. 92–95.

219. RTsKhIDNI, f. 17, op. 118, d. 931, l. 126–130.

and was simultaneously deputy chairman of the Council of Ministers and head of the USSR State Supply Committee. His wife, Mariya Markovna, also retained her position as chair of the CC's Knitted Goods Industry Trade Unions, a position she had had since 1934. However, Kaganovich's elder brother, Yulií Moiseyevich (who from 1938 to 1945 had been deputy chairman of the Foreign Trade Committee), was dismissed in 1949 as head of the All-Union "International Book" Association. Among others who retained their positions were B.L. Vannikov, the head of the First Chief Directorate within the Council of Ministers (which supervised the design and production of nuclear weapons), and his deputy, Ye.P. Slavskií. These people, along with other Jews, were protected as they took an active role in strategic military projects; thus they belonged to a category of people that may be described by the Nazi term *WWJ* (*Wertvoller Wirtschaftsjude*, or *Economically Useful Jew*). L.P. Beria supervised the military industry, as he was not only chairman of the Council of Ministers, but also head of the Special Committee within the Council of Ministers that guided "all projects utilizing the atomic energy of uranium." As he was directly accountable to Stalin concerning the realization of the nuclear project, Beria could not allow anybody but himself to be in command of these peoples' lives, thus making them, in a sense, inviolable.

However, few people possessed that special status. Even L.Z. Mekhlis, who enjoyed Stalin's particular confidence, had to resign in 1950 "for reasons of health," thus leaving open the position of minister of state control.[220] He was succeeded by Beria's appointee, V.N. Merkulov, the former head of the Chief Directorate of Soviet Property Abroad at the Council of Ministers.

At the end of May 1950 S.Z. Ginzburg suffered some unpleasant changes in his life. He was minister of building materials production, but suddenly found himself out of work. Just as quickly, he was appointed deputy minister of mechanical engineering plants on June 28.[221] His successor at his previous position was P.A. Yudin, who promptly submitted proposals to the CC calling for an almost complete renewal the directorial staff. Ginzburg had been accused of nepotism and of appointing friends; now Yudin did everything possible firstly to get rid of the Jews. I.Z. Rykhletskií (deputy minister) was fired, along with N.I. Ferens, A.A. Lukatskií, and S.I. Danyushevskií (heads of the central administrative boards and directorates), and others.[222]

In the course of staff rearrangements, it was difficult to avoid some paradoxical incidents. For example, Yudin had previously been the minister of

220. In 1949, when the anti-Semitic campaign was in full swing, Mekhlis suffered a stroke and a heart attack at the same time. He was never able to get out of bed again and died on February 13, 1953.

221. RTsKhIDNI, f. 17, op. 118, d. 932, l. 35.

222. RTsKhIDNI, f. 17, op. 118, d. 919, l. 73; d. 952, l. 171; op. 119, d. 147, l. 111.

heavy industry plant construction. Yet when he left to fill Ginzburg's vacancy, his old position was given to D.Ya. Raízer. It might seem incomprehensible that Stalin would allow someone with such an undesirable nationality to attain such a high post. However, under the circumstances the appointment was not as arbitrary as it may seem. First, Stalin held I.F. Tevosyan (the minister of the metal industry) in high regard, and always considered his views and opinions. In 1949 Stalin promoted him to be deputy chairman of the Council of Ministers. It was Tevosyan who patronized Raízer, his former deputy. Second, the personnel status at the Ministry of Heavy Industry Plant Construction was taken under special control; and, as a preventive anti-Zionist measure, Lazar Z. Shub was dismissed as head of the ministry in October 1950 under the pretext of "the necessity of strengthening this position by employing a more efficient person."[223] At about the same time the Party instituted proceedings against V.E. Dymshits, the deputy minister of heavy industry plant construction.[224] The Party accused him of patronizing Jews from 1946 through 1950, when he was the Zaporozhstroí Trust manager, and of flooding the trust management apparatus with Jews during that time.[225]

The Crushing of the Synagogue in Stalinsk

Raízer's promotion was very timely for him. A revelation of a "nationalistic Zionist" organization caused much commotion at that time in the CC, in the MGB, and in the Metallurgy Ministry—where Raízer had worked as a deputy minister. This organization was in the town of Stalinsk[226] in the Kemerovo region, and consisted of workers at the Kuznetsk Metallurgical Enterprises The commotion all began with the discovery of an underground synagogue in the apartment of a certain Semyon Rapoport. Jews who had been evacuated from the western regions of the Ukraine, Belorussia, and the Baltic republics, Jewish refugees from Poland, and local Jews had established this synagogue as early as 1942 or 1943. After the Poles were repatriated and the evacuated Soviet Jews were returned to the European part of the USSR, and the leadership of the synagogue passed to those permanently residing in Stalinsk; that is, to Rapoport, Levenson, and Shildkraut.

It was established that, being Jews, many Kuznetsk Metallurgy Enterprise managers passed money to the synagogue via their wives and relatives. Ya.G. Mints (deputy director of the Kuznetsk Metallurgical Enterprise),

---

223. RTsKhIDNI, f. 17, op. 119, d. 107, l. 66.

224. Dymshits later became a prominent figure in Soviet economy under the Khrushchev and Brezhnev regimes.

225. RTsKhIDNI, f. 17, op. 119, d. 228, l. 137–142.

226. In 1961 Stalinsk was renamed Novokuznetsk.

S.A. Liberman (chief roller), S.Z. Arshavskií (head of the Financial Department), Nadot (head of the Supply Department), Uralskií-Trotskií (head of the Equipment Department), G.Sh. Zeltser (of the Planning Department), A.Ya. Dekhtyar (of the Technical Control Department), and others were all guilty of this. The donations were for rendering financial aid to Jews in need—first and foremost to those in camps, prisons, and exile. The Jewish community united around the town synagogue, in spite of its being underground, and was highly active. In 1948 it even sent a delegation to Moscow to see Golda Meir during her visit to the Soviet Union. In 1949 the community numbered over 70 active members.

Having learned that some leaders were being called upon for unregistered synagogue activities, the CC ordered the heads of the region to take immediate and stern measures. This was after the autumn of 1950, and as early as March 1951, 42 metallurgy enterprise managers, who were in one way or another involved with the dispersed Jewish community, were fired. Earlier, in December 1950, the regional Department of the MGB arrested Liberman (deputy chief engineer), Dekhtyar (head of the Technical Control Department), S.A. Leshchiner (deputy head of the production department), Zeltser (head of the planning department), Z.Kh. Epshteín (section head), Arshavskií (financial department head), and M.B. Rapoport (whose apartment, since 1947, had housed an underground synagogue). All were accused of conducting saboteur activity at the enterprise, of anti-Soviet propaganda, and of slandering the national policy of the Communist Party and the Soviet state. Moreover, Mints, Liberman, and Leshchiner were accused of having established, back in 1946, criminal connections with the JAC, and of passing to it secret information about the production capacity of the enterprise, which was later sent to the USA. These three persons, together with Dekhtyar were shot in accordance with the September 8, 1952 sentence of the MCSC. Zeltser, Epshteín, and Arshavskií then received 25 years in camp immediately followed by a five-year disfranchisement. The pensioner Rapoport was sentenced to ten years of camp.[227]

During that same time Jews were purged from the Central Board of the Metallurgical Industry as well as from other plants of this branch. For example, the managers of Glavmetalosbyt (Ye.S. Salit), of the Chief Refractory Industry Directorate (Ya.A. Goldin), and Chief Supply Directorate (G.A. Fridman) were removed from the ministry. A.L. Golubchik, the director of a coke plant in Makeyevka; P.I. Kogan, the director of the Zhdanov Metallurgical Plant; and M.S. Gendel, the director of the fire-clay factory in Chasov Yarsk, were also fired.[228]

---

227. RTsKhIDNI, f. 17, op. 119, d. 223, l. 2–12.

228. RTsKhIDNI, f. 17, op. 118, d. 860, l. 124; d. 918, l. 173; d. 942, l. 124–134; d. 955, l. 148;

The defeat of the Jewish synagogue in Stalinsk and the consequent reprisal over the workers at the Kuznetsk Metallurgy Enterprise, taken together, were the second significant step (after the Moscow Automobile Plant case) toward the policy of excluding Jews from the sphere of economic management—a policy that had begun in 1950. This process was even more characteristic in military industry branches where anti-Semitism was fanned allegedly in the interest of state security.

MILITARY PRODUCTION AND INVESTIGATIONS

The purging of Jews from the military defense industry began in the cradle of Soviet aircraft engineering, that is, in the N.E. Zhukovskií Central Aero-Hydrodynamic Institute.[229] During an inspection in May 1950, CC members concluded:

> In a number of extremely important departments of the Central Aero-Hydrodynamic Institute there are workers due to be substituted for political reasons. They gather around themselves people of the same nationality, impose the habit of praising one another (while making others erroneously believe that they are indispensable), and force their protégés through to high posts."[230]

Lest there be any doubt as to who was meant, the commission enclosed in its report to Malenkov a list of workers immediately due to be fired: 60 names (including research workers from different laboratories) such as A.S. Perelmuter, V.G. Galperin, L.A. Epshteín, B.K. Yavich, R.L. Kreps, I.I. Slezinger, I.I. Fayerberg, M.I. Nevelson, A.L. Rabinovich, and S.A. Tumarkin. All these workers had relatives abroad, mainly in the USA. For this the CC secretariat severely penalized S.I. Afanasyev, the deputy minister for personnel of the aircraft industry; and S.N. Shishkin, the director of the Central Aero-Hydrodynamic Institute. (Shishkin was finally expelled from the Institute in September 1950.[231]

The CC commission also made such proscription lists for other research institutes within the same aviation branch. For example, the list for the All-Union Institute of Aviation Materials consisted of 18 workers, including professors Mirkin and Fridlyander, who were heads of laboratories)[232]; and there were also lists for experimental design offices.[233]

---

op. 119, d. 155, l. 109; d. 119, l. 149–150; d. 960, l. 101–104.

229. Sporadic repressive actions preceded this. For example, on August 3, 1941 the director of the Moscow Aircraft Plant No. 339, I.I. Shteínberg, was arrested and ruthlessly tortured.

230. RTsKhIDNI, f. 17, op. 118, d. 908, l. 50–51.

231. RTsKhIDNI, f. 17, op. 118, d. 908, l. 45–47; op. 119, d. 75, l. 63.

232. RTsKhIDNI, f. 17, op. 119, d. 75, l. 81–91.

233. The most sophisticated staff inspection was conducted in Research Institute I, the highly secret

As usual, the MGB would not stand aloof, but tried to exaggerate the Central Board of Aircraft Industry Ministry sabotage case. The MGB grew tempted to fabricate one more Zionist plot as early as late 1949, when it conducted a preliminary "investigation" of Jewish saboteur groups at the Moscow Automobile Plant. The MGB viewed A.F. Eídinov as a "Zionist leader" at the plant, and now it turned out that Eídinov was a cousin of G.B. Eídinov, the former Belorussian CC secretary who had been dismissed in April 1947 as deputy chairman of the Belorussian Council of Ministers, and as a result suffered a heart attack.[234] And that was not all. A.F. Eídinov was also the cousin of S.M. Sandler, the deputy minister for supplies for the aircraft industry. On January 8, 1950 the MGB deputy minister, S.I. Ogoltsov, informed the CC that Sandler had deliberately littered the military industry ministry.[235]

Over a period of several months at Lubyanka, the CC studied the claims of direct connections between Jewish "saboteurs" (through kindred) within the automobile and aircraft branches of the industry. However, V.S. Abakumov and his loyal minions failed to make the case that Sandler was a Zionist leader, for Sandler had begun his career during the civil war in Baku (Transcaucasian region), where he communicated directly with Beria and I.F. Tevosyan[236] who admitted him to the Communist Party in 1920. In addition, Malenkov was familiar with Sandler, who supervised the aircraft industry during World War II. Further, for two months during the summer of 1948, Sandler was at the disposal of a Council of Ministers special committee that directed aluminum pipe production for the first industrial nuclear reactor, which was being constructed in the Chelyabinsk region. After a successful atomic bomb test on August 29, 1949, Sandler was awarded two orders, including the Lenin Order. With this background, Sandler could not be arrested. Nevertheless, on July 4, a Politburo resolution dismissed him as deputy minister for supplies for the aircraft industry and appointed him director of a branch of the All-Union Institute of Aircraft Materials.[237]

When Abakumov realized that Sandler could not be implicated, he chose another victim. On October 18, 1950 the head of the Financial Directorate of the Ministry of the Aircraft Industry, I.Ye. Khavin, was arrested. Since he was Jewish and had studied together with N.A. Voznesenskií at the Institute of Red Professors, he could be fitted into a scenario of a Zionist plot within the aircraft

---

branch for jet aircraft research, where G.N. Abramovich, the deputy director on scientific matters, and other managers of Jewish origin were purged.

234. In 1948 the MGB took pity upon G.B. Eídinov and appointed him deputy minister on general issues of the wood industry of the Russian Federation.

235. RTsKhIDNI, f. 17, op. 118, d. 952, l. 159.

236. Tevosyan later became a prominent leader in the state economy.

237. RTsKhIDNI, f. 17, op. 118, d. 952, l. 153–156.

industry headquarters. During the investigation, Khavin was stable and steadfast. To the investigator's question as to whether Sandler expressed nationalistic moods, he replied, "I have not had any nationalistic conversations with Sandler or heard nationalistic statements from him." On January 16, 1951 a Special Meeting of the MGB sentenced him to 10 years of camp for "having participated in an anti-Soviet organization and being a saboteur in the aircraft industry."[238]

So-called attestations helped along the intensive purges of Jews from the Ministry of the Aircraft Industry's Central Board. A ministry secret report "On Working with Personnel in 1951" presented an illustrative table:[239]

personnel alterations	employed	dismissed
according to nationality:		
Russian	187	179
Ukrainian	6	6
Jewish	–	13
other nationalities	1	2

As if by command, Jews began to be fired from high posts in this branch of industry. Few meetings of the CC secretariat during the summer and autumn of 1950 took place without a related resolution. During World War II the Saratov Plant No. 292 had produced fighter planes designed by A.S. Yakovlev under severe conditions.[240] I.S. Levin had headed this plant for 10 years, but on August 4 he was dismissed. Another expert of Jewish origin, M.S. Zhezlov, had been a director of various aircraft factories since 1937. Exactly a week after Zhezlov's dismissal, he too was dismissed as head of the oldest of the Soviet aircraft engine plants, Plant No. 24. He was reproached on such trivial accounts as "littering the staff" of that strategic factory by employing "politically dubious people" (M.I. Idelson, head of serial design department; S.K. Boyanovskií, chief metallurgist; Ya.S. Vishnevetskií, head of the branch factory; and others). More seriously, he was also accused of voting against signing the Brest Agreement in 1918—a most improbable allegation.[241] Two weeks later, on August 25, two more people were discharged: I.S. Vyshtynetskií (director of the Experimental Plant of Light Alloys No. 65), and I.D. Samoílovich (deputy director and chief

238. Document from the archives of the former KGB.

239. RTsKhIDNI, f. 17, op. 119, d. 1030, l. 112.

240. Nazi aircraft had almost completely demolished the Saratov Plant on June 23, 1943, thus damaging it to a greater extent than any other aircraft plant during the Great Patriotic War. Nevertheless, a mere three months after the bombing the plant achieved its pre-planned capacities. RTsKhIDNI, f. 17, op. 118, d. 1007, l. 126.

241. RTsKhIDNI, f. 17, op. 119, d. 1, l. 7–10.

engineer of Plant No. 456).[242] Then in September I.D. Solomonovich (director of Moscow Plant No. 315), lost his job, and in October N.A. Shapiro (chief engineer of the Aircraft Engineering Plant No. 30)[243] suffered the same fate. When Stalin received a report on the predominance of Jews at the plant, he became furious and ordered N.S. Khrushchev, who happened to be nearby at the moment: "One should inspire robust workers to take bludgeons and, after the working day ends, beat those Jews."[244] There was no mass slaughter, but the anti-Jewish purge conducted at the plant was radical. By the spring of 1951, 71 people were fired in all, including A.E. Shats (chief technologist), S.Ye. Levit (chief accountant), and R.L. Goldberg (superintendent).[245]

However, S.A. Lavochkin and M.I. Gurevich (aircraft designers), and M.L. Mil (chief of the Soviet First Helicopter Design Office) were deemed indispensable specialists, and continued to work in the field, though under reinforced surveillance. An exception was also made for A.E. Nudelman, a designer of aircraft cannons, whose office was subordinate to the USSR Armament Ministry, which had itself been sweepingly purged of Jews. In the late 1940s and early 1950s A.I. Bykhovskií, B.A. Khazanov, and B.A. Fradkin (directors of large artillery plants), M.Z. Olevskií (chief engineer), A.A. Forshter and D.F. Skarzhinskií (directors of Moscow Region Plants Nos. 304 and 353), M.M. Dunayevskií (director of the Íoshkar-Ola Plant No. 297), S.P. Rabinovich (chief designer of the Moscow Research Institute No. 20, which dealt with radar equipment design), and M.L. Sliozberg (deputy director of the Moscow Research Institute) all found themselves out of work.[246]

On July 14, in accordance with a CC secretariat resolution, L.R. Gonor was fired as director of Research Institute No. 88. His subordinates A.A. Umanskií (chief designer), B.Ye. Chertok (head of the Control Equipment Department), and other Jewish managing workers were also persecuted. Gonor was one of the most authoritative representatives of Soviet directors. He was a Hero of Socialist Labor and a Stalin Prize-winner; from 1939 to October 1942 he headed the Barrikady Plant No. 221 in Stalingrad; and during the Great Patriotic War he took active part in the defense of Stalingrad. D.F. Ustinov, the armament minister and head of the "Bolshevik" plant in Leningrad, had highly valued his deputy Gonor since the pre-war period. After the war, Ustinov entrusted Gonor with the most secret field unit, Research Institute No. 88, the code name for the Central

242. RTsKhIDNI, f. 17, op. 119, d. 34, l. 232; d. 35, l. 65–66.

243. This was the oldest such plant, presently known as the Moscow Dementyev Aircraft Production Group of Plants.

244. N.S. Khrushchev, "Vospominaniya," *Voprosy istorii*, 1991, no. 11, p. 56.

245. RTsKhIDNI, f. 17, op. 119, d. 124, l. 145; d. 56, l. 138–142.

246. RTsKhIDNI, f. 17, op. 118, d. 822, l. 164; d. 861, l. 177; op. 119, d. 50, l. 157; d. 90, l. 149; d. 192, l. 3.

Missile Equipment Research Institute.[247]

Located in Kaliningrad (Moscow Region), the Central Missile Equipment Research Institute represented an entire line of research, design, production, and experimental establishments that worked with all manner of missiles, including long-range missiles modeled after the German FAU-2 missile. It was here that the famous inventors of Soviet space equipment and future academicians S.P. Korolyov, M.K. Yangel, V.P. Mishin, N.A. Pilyugin, and others worked. Against a background of reinforced anti-Semitic paranoia, it seemed rather problematic that Gonor head such an important unit; and considering that until 1948 he had been an active member of the JAC and even of the JAC presidium, it seemed hardly possible at all. One can only wonder why he, who had been a few months without a job, was left alone. Obviously, Ustinov's intercession was decisive. In order to save the experienced production commander (as they called this position in those days), he sent Malenkov a message in 1950 asking him to appoint Gonor director of Plant No. 4 in the remote province of Krasnoyarsk.[248] However, after a while he was not so safe there either. On June 3, 1952 Gonor again found himself out of work.[249] This time the MGB was more persistent and found in the archives the testimonies of the journalist M.S. Aízenshtadt-Zheleznova (who had been shot for espionage in the autumn of 1950) and JAC secretary I.S. Fefer. They stated that Gonor, "a close acquaintance of Zheleznova," had helped her find a job at the *Stalingrad Pravda*[250] newspaper's editorial board. Later, after having established criminal connections with the JAC leader, Zheleznova was one of the first to write and export a feature story on the director of the Barrikady Defense Factory, L.R. Gonor. Based on this material, minister S.D. Ignatyev on February 6, 1953 addressed Malenkov, Beria, and N.A. Bulganin, insisting on Gonor's immediate arrest. In three days Malenkov, Beria, and Bulganin gave their sanction, and Gonor was put into the MGB's inner prison. Luckily for him, Stalin had little time to live. Hence, he was soon set free.

Jews were similarly ostracized in other military and civil branches of the economy, such as the construction of ships, the production of communication equipment, the agricultural machine industry (including plants producing ammunition), the chemical industry, the construction of machine tools, the electrical industry,[251] the production of heavy machinery,[252] the production of

---

247. The Central Missile Equipment Research Institute is now known as the Central Research Institute of Mechanical Engineering.

248. RTsKhIDNI, f. 17, op. 119, d. 124, l. 156.

249. RTsKhIDNI, f. 17, op. 116, d. 669, l. 27.

250. *Stalingradsakaya pravda*.

251. Concerning this field, the most severe purge took place at the Dinamo Electric Machine Construction Plant, where workers were dismissed en masse and some "enemies" were arrested. Among the latter, there were V.E. Kreíndel (deputy director), B.I. Kats (production manager), I.M. Ganopolskií

food and consumer goods, transport,[253] and communication and construction establishments, i.e., in all fields of state economy. However, it should be stressed that, as before, the "fifth point" could not formally serve as a reason for dismissal. The administration was strictly prohibited from officially referring to the point. The pretext of dismissal had to be more plausible, such as having relatives abroad, or not performing one's occupational duties, or actual or imaginary abuse. Should some directors decide not to play the hypocrite, and act as straightforward anti-Semites, the Moscow authorities would qualify their behavior as provocative and, as a rule, reprimand them. The Moscow bosses did not want to be accused of anti-Semitism. Thus, when in early 1952 the A. Marti Ship Repairing Plant in Odessa attempted to discharge 26 workers simultaneously for no plausible pretext except for being Jewish, the CC's Transport Department suggested that the director and secretary of the plant's Party organization, who inspired this move, themselves be fired.[254]

It would be worthwhile to dwell on another nuance. As mentioned above, those who dealt with the design and production of nuclear weapons held privileged positions, and most privileged were the physicists at the so-called

---

(head of the Planning and Production Department), and G.N. Fridman (head of the Technical Control Department). N.A. Orlovskiĭ (the director) was later expelled from the Party and arrested. RTsKhIDNI, f. 17, op. 119, d. 124, l. 162–163.

252. The greatest number of dismissals took place from 1950 to 1951 at the Ural Ordzhonikidze Heavy Machine Construction Plant (Uralmashzavod) in Sverdlovsk, which produced self-propelled oil drilling equipment, armored vehicles, and other military equipment. Among those discharged were chief designers Vernik and Gorlitskiĭ, production manager S.T. Livshits, and military representative G.I. Zukher. RTsKhIDNI, f. 17, op. 119, d. 119, l. 82–82 obverse; d. 275, l. 19–38.

253. As for anti-Semitism in transport units, the most sensational was the Metrostroĭ "case," in which 23 people were arrested, the majority of them Jews. They were accused of having concluded phony agreements, from 1945 to 1949, with artels and other research institutions dealing with the construction of a fourth metro line in Moscow. Thus they plundered more than 2 000 000 rubles of public money. The leaders of this "gang of plunderers" were E.Z. Yudovich, Ya.L. Kaplanskiĭ, and A.G. Tankilevich. RTsKhIDNI, f. 17, op. 119, d. 1024, l. 74–77.

Judging from the official documents, this may have been a big swindle indeed, though it differed little from other shady transactions typical of the Stalinist economy that favored patronizing one's friends and relatives—and not only among Jews! However, while unraveling ordinary economic cases, usually ending by punishing the criminals, the MGB widely used the Metrostroĭ case and others of the kind to justify and reinforce the global anti-Jewish purge. At the same time accusations of economic abuse served as an excellent camouflage for the state's anti-Semitism. Abram Tankilevich had actively attended JAC meetings beginning in 1945, and in 1947 he had gotten involved in the JAC presidium. For this he most likely paid with his freedom, being convicted in the Metrostroĭ case. After the Great Patriotic War he suggested the organization of a consulting technical body to sponsor Birobidzhan—and he suggested that this body employ Jews who had formerly worked in the various ministries of industry. Tankilevich had worked closely with Semyon Sinyavskiĭ, a representative of Birobidzhan in Moscow who was arranging groups of Jews due to be evacuated to the Far East region of the USSR.

254. RTsKhIDNI, f. 17, op. 119, d. 724, l. 127.

Design Office No. 11,[255] which was located in a town code-named Arzamas-16, in the Gorkií region, completely isolated from the rest of the world. There were quite a number Jews among these scientists, such as Yu.B. Khariton (the chief designer of the nuclear bomb), Ya.B. Zeldovich (who had made the basic theoretical calculations of the bomb), and I.K. Kikoin (Kushelevich) (the scientific director of the group of plants on diffusion emission of uranium-235). However, since they were under Beria's Special Committee, they were, to a great extent, protected. For example, after 1951 during the course of a regular periodic review, experimental physicist L.V. Altshuler dared criticize the doctrine of "people's" academician and destroyer of "formal" genetics, T.D. Lysenko. Altshuler was consequently accused of cosmopolitanism, and he was threatened with dismissal. Khariton's phone call to Beria saved him. As Altshuller later recalled, Beria asked Khariton only: "Do you really need him?" Khariton answered affirmatively, and no further questions were asked.[256]

Other physicists of Jewish origin, who were not protected by the umbrella of the nuclear project, suffered the same attacks as most of their fellow-tribesmen. The heaviest blow was dealt to the heads of research institutes. As early as 1946 P.L. Kapitsa, an academician who refused to work for Beria's Special Committee, ceased to be the director of the Academy of Science's Institute of Physical Problems, which institute he had founded.[257] In October of that same year the CC Directorate on Personnel checked, at CC secretary A.A. Kuznetsov's request, "the situation with working on personnel" in nine of the leading academic institutes—Organic Chemistry, Physical Problems, Physical Chemistry, Chemical Physics, Physical, Mechanics, Radium, Leningrad Physical Technical, and Geographic. The results showed that 208 of the 765 scientists at these institutes were Jews, as were 30 of the 110 laboratory heads. Later one more cardinal measure on "correcting the abnormal personnel situation" followed. The CC undertook a comprehensive investigation of all the institutions that worked within the USSR Academy of Sciences system—51 institutions, 3 special laboratories, the Central Botanical Garden, the Central Astronomical Laboratory, 6 branches, and 6 scientific stations. All the 14 577 persons, including 165 academicians, 271 Academy of Sciences fellows, 618 doctors of science, and 1 753 Ph.D. candidates who worked in these institutions were to be checked for loyalty to the regime. An Orgburo resolution of January 25, 1947 "On the Preparation, Arrangement, and Exploitation of Scientific Personnel in Institutions of the USSR

---

255. This later became the All-Union Research Institute of Experimental Physics.

256. *Literaturnaya gazeta*, June 6, 1990. In relation to this, the following episode comes to mind. It is said that when Reichsmarshal H. Göring was informed that one of his deputies in the Luftwaffe had Jewish blood and should be dealt with, Göring replied, "Let him continue working. I'll determine myself which of my subjects is Jewish."

257. *Ogonek* (*A Small Light*), 1989, no. 25, pp. 18–22.

Academy of Sciences" stated among other things that the presidium of the Academy permitted a number of institutions subject to it an excessive "littering" of Jews. All this paved the way for a massive campaign of anti-Jewish ostracism in the field of natural sciences, which was launched in early 1949.[258] On June 18, by a resolution of the CC secretariat, academician A.N. Frumkin was dismissed as director of the Academy of Science's Physical Chemistry Institute. He had served in the JAC presidium before its defeat, and was now fired on the grounds that he "had made errors on an anti-patriotic character," and that in employing personnel, he had "proceeded not in the interest of the country, but chose and arranged departments to patronize his relatives, littering the institute with alien people."[259] In November of the following year the academician A.F. Ioffe, founder and director of the Academy of Science's Leningrad Physical Technical Institute, one of the leading schools for Soviet physicists, was forced to retire.[260]

The CC concluded that the results of staff purification were flagrantly unsatisfactory, and laid the responsibility for this on the head of the board of the Academy of Sciences, P.A. Borisov, who was dismissed at the end of December 1950. V.S. Kruzhkov, the Agitprop deputy director, and Yu.A. Zhdanov, the head of Agitprop's Science Section, reported to Malenkov that "an exclusive group of theoretical physicists and physical chemists (L.D. Landau, M.A. Leontovich, A.N. Frumkin, Ya.I. Frenkel, V.L. Ginzburg, Ye.M. Lifshits, G.A. Grinberg, I.M. Frank, A.S. Kompaneyets, and N.S. Meíman) had flooded all theoretical departments of physical and physical-chemical institutes with its supporters, Jews by origin."[261]

The Lubyanka and Old Square authorities were most troubled by the activity of Landau and his circle. The omnipresent MGB secret agents reported:

> Landau is the center of a group of theoretical physicists from anti-Soviet and nationalist-oriented scientists of Jewish origin. The group comprises the disciples of the so-called "new Landau school" such as Ye.M. Lifshits and N.S. Meíman. Landau has founded and is head of the Theoretical Physics Seminar at the Institute of Physical Problems, which is attended mainly by people of Jewish nationality and closely connected with Landau.[262]

---

258. RTsKhIDNI, f. 17, op. 117, d. 664, l. 154–157, 161–176.

259. RTsKhIDNI, f. 17, op. 118, d. 433, l. 33–35, 40–41.

260. RTsKhIDNI, f. 17, op. 119, d. 138, l. 30, 34. The aged professor was so depressed by the growing anti-Semitic hysteria that beginning in 1948, when filling in forms, he would state his nationality as "Russian" instead of "Jew," which he had never done before.

261. RTsKhIDNI, f. 17, op. 119, d. 183, l. 184–185.

262. TsKhSD (Center for the Preservation of Modern Documents / Tsentr khraneniya sovremennoí dokumentatsii), f. 89, perechen' 18, dok. 42, l. 3.

Jews thus were forced from the leading positions in the physical sciences; and in addition, a directive was implemented that stressed the need of substantially reducing their percentage in the higher education system. V.F. Nozdryov was a senior lecturer the Moscow State University Physics Department as well as the elected secretary of the University Communist Party Bureau. As early as 1943–1945 he repeatedly tried to draw CC secretary A.S. Shcherbakov's attention to "a great danger of a monopoly" of Jews at the Physics Department. He supported his argument with figures:[263]

year	percentage of Jews to Russians graduated from the department
1938	46
1939	50
1940	58
1941	74
1942	98

Nozdryov made a predictably pessimistic conclusion, namely, that unless a national admissions quota were adopted immediately, "in just a year we will have to stop referring to the university as 'Russian,' for to do so would produce comic effect."[264]

Shcherbakov did not remain indifferent to this pleading from the University Party leadership. He gave Nozdryov "some personal instructions . . . aimed at strengthening the Moscow University as a major center of Russian science and culture." One can easily guess what these were. Nozdryov's anti-Semitic actions were so vast that he began to irritate the university's governing body.

After Shcherbakov's death, on April 20, 1946 the MSU provost, historian I.S. Galkin, sent a letter to Malenkov in which he complained that a small group of physicists (Nozdryov, N.S. Akulov, and others), headed by chairman A.S. Predvoditeltsev, were converting the Physics Department into their legacy. Under the banner of the struggle for the "originality" of Russian science they declared the academicians Kapitsa, Ioffe, Fok, Tamm, and Semyonov "idealists," "Westerners" who betrayed the interests of the motherland. "The university is in a fever; its activity is taking place in extremely abnormal conditions," wrote the provost.

At the end of May 1946 Nozdryov was relieved of his duties as secretary of the MSU Party organization, and professor Predvoditeltsev as chair of the Physics

263. RTsKhIDNI, f. 77, op. 1, d. 895, l. 120.

264. RTsKhIDNI, f. 77, op. 1, d. 895, l. 120.

Department.[265] This happened perhaps because a relatively liberal "Zhdanovite" grouping at that time strengthened its position in the Kremlin and because Stalin's anti-Jewish paranoia was not yet so strong. It should be noted that to neutralize somehow the intrigues of the chauvinist-reactionaries who took key positions in the Physics Department, on March 10, 1946 a new Physical-Technical Department was created at MSU on the initiative of Galkin and his allies and with the help of the influential military-industrial complex. This department was meant to prepare specialists in the areas of defensive equipment and nuclear weapons. S.A. Khristianovich (later to become the MSU vice provost) headed the department along with professor D.Yu. Panov, who acted as chair. Kapitsa, Landau, and Landsberg and others were enlisted as lecturers.

However, as the anti-Jewish cleansing of the country was becoming more widespread, the hysterical guardians of the national sterility of Soviet science once again lifted their heads. In late 1947 the liberal Galkin was replaced at his post as the MSU provost by A.N. Nesmeyanov, who was notorious for his adherence to a rigid personnel policy. At the beginning of 1950, when the anti-Jewish purge took on an all-inclusive nature. Then F.A. Korolyov, the acting chair of the Physics Department, inspired the persecution of S.E. Khaĭkin, who was teaching in the department. A specially-selected committee (containing the indefatigable V.F. Nozdryov) analyzed Khaĭkin's book, *Mechanics*, and qualified it as vicious and "not worthy of recommendation as a textbook or a manual."[266] At the same time academician P.L. Kapitsa was dismissed[267] from the Physical-Technical Department, and quite a few departments were closed. In 1951 the department was closed. Only after Beria and the leaders of the military-industrial complex that he supervised intervened in the affair did it become possible to convince Stalin that the chauvinistic scholars and personnel recruiters had gone too far and had severely damaged the defensive capacity of the country.

In 1952, at the leader's consent, the Moscow Physical-Technical Institute was established. Lieutenant General I.F. Petrov was appointed provost. The new institute initiated the preparation of scientific elite for the military and strategic needs of the country.[268] Thus, the pragmatic interest of assuring the defensive capacity of the country helped common sense win.

This was one of the many episodes that had a more or less happy ending. But

---

265. RTsKhIDNI, f. 17, op. 117, d. 606, l. 116, 119.

266. A. Sonin, "Trevozhnoye desyatiletiye sovyetskoĭ fiziki, 1947–1953" ("A Troubled Decade for Soviet Physics"), *Znaniye-sila* (*Knowledge-Power*), 1990, no. 5, pp. 83–84.

267. One reason for Kapitsa's dismissal was that he had had frequent meetings with S. Mikhoels after the Great Patriotic War, when Mikhoels visited Kapitsa's laboratory and observed experiments with liquid oxygen. Mikhoels was actively communicating with other scientists, including the academician B.I. Zbarskiĭ, the surgeon A.A. Vishnevskiĭ, and the academician biologist L.A. Orbeli.

268. I.F. Petrov, *Aviatsiya i vsya zhizn'* (Moscow: Izd-vo TsAGI, 1993), p. 92.

there is another aspect to it: the majority of similar collisions that resulted from the personnel cleansing of the last period of Stalin's leadership had tragic endings. It is remarkable that by getting rid of the Jews firstly in the administrative sphere, where they were numerous, the anti-Semitic functionaries were clever in directing against the Jews the hatred that the Soviet people had for many years reserved for the bureaucratic administration. It was this hatred that L.D. Trotskií, back in 1937, had qualified as the "main feature of Soviet life."[269]

---

269. L.D. Trotskií, *Prestupleniya Stalina* [*The Crimes of Stalin*] (Moscow, 1994), p. 217.

Six

"The Doctors' Plot"

The "doctors' plot" has gone down in history not merely as one of the many crimes committed by the Stalinist regime; these two words became a symbol of self-evident agony of the regime of Stalin's personal rule, capable of any extreme measures in order to survive, but already crippled under the burden of repressions and doomed. The doctors' plot was the apotheosis of the huge postwar purge that so unexpectedly turned against the dictator himself and, as we know, ended with his death. His closest associates in political leadership, now experts in intrigue, sensed that behind the propagandistic veil of the anti-Semitic hunt for "the murderers in white smocks" lay a fatal threat to themselves personally; and when the critical moment came, they got rid of the mad tyrant. It seems that this supposition has its right to exist together with the official version about the natural and nonviolent end of "the leader of the peoples"—if only the death of an insane person from his paranoia could be considered natural.

THE EARLY FORERUNNERS OF THE "DOCTORS' CASE"

The "doctors' plot," fabricated at Stalin's will, was preceded by a propagandistic attack initiated in 1949 against so-called stateless cosmopolitans, to which those who had the misfortune of having been born with Jewish names were automatically added. And since health care, along with art and literature, was considered a sphere of employment traditionally preferred by Jews, it was there that the persecution of Jewish professionals took on a mass and violent form. The victory of Trofim Lysenko over the biogeneticists[1] also aggravated the situation. Lysenko, an

1. Biogeneticists were treated with disdain as representatives of the Weismann-Mendel-Morgan

academician, was a charlatan and the author of the pseudoscientific "Michurin theory." It was the infamous August 1948 VASHNIL[2] session that marked his victory, after which many Jewish physicians of the biologist-geneticist school were persecuted on the grounds of their scientific beliefs.

For example, on February 16, 1949, by resolution of the CC secretariat, A.G. Gurvich was discharged as director of the Institute of Experimental Biology of the Academy of Medical Sciences. The report that accompanied the resolution stated that he had been "bored with his job" of late, and that after the August VASHNIL session he had submitted a written request for resignation.[3]

As the anti-Semitic mood grew, the main criterion for scientific credibility changed from expertise to nationality; and clearly, being a Jew had serious consequences. For instance, although Gurvich was criticized in early 1949 for his inability to conduct research "in the light of progressive materialistic study in biology," his outstanding contribution to that science was acknowledged and it was mentioned that he was a Stalin Prize-winner. Yet only a year later, his colleague from Leningrad, biology professor B.P. Tokin, numbered Gurvich among the founders of the "most reactionary idealistic" naturalistic philosophical teaching, and noted that when Gurvich had published his most important monographs in Germany in 1935, he had gathered about himself a school of scientists, including L.Ya. Blyakher, S.L. Braínes, and M.Ya. Baron. Tokin had an enviable memory, and further recalled that as far back as 1942 and 1943, the late academician A.A. Zavarzin had supposedly told him in private, "I'm convinced there is a Jewish Masonic lodge among the Leningrad scientists. Its honorable chairman is, without any doubt, Gurvich." Tokin continued, declaring that Professor V.Ya. Aleksandrov, the enigmatic aide of the "grand master" of the mythical Masonic lodge, had not ceased his activities and had, by the end of the 1940s, organized a Zionist group in the Leningrad All-Union Institute of Experimental Medicine at the USSR Academy of Medical Science. These "Zionists" included the director of the institute D.N. Nasonov, professors P.G. Svetlov, A.A. Braun, A.D. Braun, and other Jewish scientists.[4]

This denunciation soon led to a purge of the Leningrad All-Union Institute of Experimental Medicine. In order to convey its ferocity it is sufficient to mention one detail. On March 7, 1950 D.M. Popov (deputy chairman of Agitprop) and

---

"false demagogic" science that "served American racism." (August Weismann [1834–1914], German zoologist and founder of neo-Darwinism; Gregor Mendel [1822–1884], Austrian monk and discoverer of biological heredity; Thomas Morgan [1866–1945], American biologist and one of the founders of genetics, Nobel Prize-winner [1933], and president of the American National Academy of Sciences [1927–1931].)

2. The All-Union Lenin Academy of Agricultural Sciences.

3. RTsKhIDNI, f. 17, op. 118, d. 314, l. 6, 7.

4. RTsKhIDNI, f. 17, op. 118, d. 774, l. 120–126.

V.S. Yakovlev (deputy chairman of the CC's Department of Agriculture) stressed to Malenkov that Tokin's accusations deserved serious consideration.[5]

Aleksandrov's dismissal was not the end of the story. On October 24, 1942 Ye.Yu. Zelikson, the director of the Leningrad Institute of Scientific Research on Physical Training, was arrested. The previous March the *Komsomol Pravda*[6] and *Soviet Sport*[7] newspapers branded him a Weismannist and cosmopolitan who for many years had been conducting subversive activity in the field of physical training and sport.[8]

The anti-Semitic pressure was so strong that not even I.I. Prezent could tolerate it. This unprincipled adventurist and demagogue had made a phenomenal career by working with the academician M.B. Mitin to give a theoretical basis to T.D. Lysenko's "study." Mitin then promoted Prezent, making him an academician of VASHNIL. Mitin also made Prezent his right-hand man. However, beginning in late 1949 letters and complaints critical of Prezent flooded the Ministry of Higher Education, the Council of Ministers, and the CC ACP(b). One such message had this to say:

> He does nothing but deprave the youth in many ways . . . he dismissed from the Moscow University widely-known Russian scientists: academicians M.M. Zavadovskií, I.F. Shmalgauzen; professors D.A. Sabinin, A.A. Paramonov; and many others. They were replaced by ignorami of Jewish nationality, such as N.I. Feíginson, F.M. Kuperman, I.Ya. Pritsker, V.G. Likhovitser, B.A. Rubin, and others. These sorts of replacements are deeply subversive actions. The university that bears the name of the great Russian scientist Lomonosov has no room for the real Russian scientists; whereas the Jewish ignorami develop Russian science.[9]

Prezent's preferred method of defaming his colleague-opponents was demagogy, and his demagogy this time around had a chauvinistic and anti-Semitic

---

5. Other professors of the Institute of Experimental Medicine, S. Musaelyan and A. Smirnov, made denunciations similar to Tokin's. Consequently B. Andrianov (secretary of the Regional Party Committee) and the CC's Administrative Department insisted that Aleksandrov be dismissed from the institute. Aleksandrov, they argued, was a Jew who permitted himself a "scandalous nationalistic escapade": onto a mural at the institute he had drawn the Morphology Department's Party leader beheading the Jewish employees along with D.N. Nasonov (the director) and others. (Checking had revealed that Nasonov was not a Jew, but was of noble origins.) RTsKhIDNI, f. 17, op. 118, d. 774, l. 116–117; d. 703, l. 114–129.

6. *Komsomolskaya pravda.*

7. *Sovyetskií sport.*

8. RTsKhIDNI, f. 17, op. 118, d. 780, l. 41–43.

9. RTsKhIDNI, f. 17, op. 119, d. 993, l. 119.

character. Ironically, or maybe logically, his preferred method now turned against him. On May 26, 1950, by resolution of the CC secretariat, Prezent was dismissed as chairman of the MSU Biology Department.[10]

From late 1950 through early 1951 there were massive dismissals of Jews who worked at MSU's Moscow Society of Nature Research, which was headed by the academician N.D. Zelinskií. S.Yu. Lipshits (scientific secretary), G.M. Ginzburg (head of the publishing section), and G.N. Endelman (editor-in-chief of scientific publications) were now personae non gratae. Soon afterwards A.G. Chernov (vice president of the society) was arrested. In July 1952 the CC ordered a halt to the society's publication of the multivolume dictionary, *Russian Botanists.*[11] The CC justified this ban by explaining that the work allegedly abounded in personal articles about "persons who for the most part had not done anything notable in biology" (a list of mainly Jewish names followed). In addition, the editors were accused of promoting the scientific school of the biogeneticist and academician N.I. Vavilov, who had been repressed in 1940 (and who had died in the Saratov prison in 1943) and of kowtowing to the "Mendelists and Morganists."[12]

The so-called "Leningrad case" was gaining momentum, and though it appeared to have nothing to do with Jewish physicians, it had a strong negative effect on their situation. On May 5, 1949 V. Andrianov, the new secretary of the Leningrad Regional and City Committee of the ACP(b), forwarded to Malenkov a letter by an A. Makarov. Makarov's letter was openly anti-Semitic, and Andrianov claimed that the facts contained therein were true. Andrianov went on to ask that "the USSR minister of health, Comrade Smirnov, be given instructions to start restoring order to the medical institutions of Leningrad."[13] Makarov's letter was addressed to the Politburo of the CC and consisted merely of whining in the style of the Black Hundred:[14]

> Saint Petersburg, Petrograd, Leningrad—this has been a Russian city from time immemorial, built even upon the bones of solely Russian workers. Its population has always been mostly Russian. All sectors of the city's economy have always been managed by Russians. Presently the situation in certain sectors of the city's economy has become unbearable for Russians. Trade, local industry, institutes of various sorts, science, health care, etc., are increasingly controlled by Jews. And the situation in the health care system has become absolutely

10. RTsKhIDNI, f. 17, op. 118, d. 890, l. 60–70.

11. *Russkiye botaniki.*

12. RTsKhIDNI, f. 17, op. 119, d. 159, l. 84–88; op. 132, d. 968, l. 47–52.

13. RTsKhIDNI, f. 17, op. 118, d. 478, l. 245.

14. The Black Hundred was an extreme right-wing Russian chauvinist monarchical movement in 1905 through 1907, notorious for hostility toward Jews and participation in pogroms.

> unbearable for Russians: here everything Russian has been definitely forced out. It is so hard for Russians to work in health care organizations that they can no longer bear it. Jews hold all central positions in health care, keeping Russians beyond the reach of managing health care[15] in the city of Leningrad . . . .

Here Makarov lists 32 Jews holding leading positions in Leningrad's health care system and in the city's institutions of medical research. He then continues:

> Popkov,[16] the secretary of the ACP(b) City Committee, relying on the support of Kuznetsov, the CC ACP(b) secretary, went so far in selecting people useful for himself and only for himself, that they could not find a Russian in Leningrad to nominate as a candidate to the Supreme Soviet of the RSFSR, and so chose a figure hated by all Russians—Mashanskií,[17] a Jew.[18]

It is most likely that this letter was inspired by V. Andrianov himself. It is interesting that Malenkov kept this letter for nearly three months, waiting for the time when Stalin would be ready to make a final decision regarding the participants of the "Leningrad case."[19] It was hence on August 4, 1949 that Malenkov brought Makarov's letter up for discussion at the CC secretariat. He succeeded in making the secretariat send M. Ananyev, the deputy minister of health, to Leningrad "to help health care organs of the city and region of Leningrad in their work."[20] Stalin thus intertwined the "Leningrad" and "Zionist" cases, tying them up into a tight knot.

In those days many people took advantage of the fight against cosmopolitanism in medicine to make their careers. They would smear their Jewish colleagues in the hopes of having them dismissed from their jobs at prestigious central hospitals and institutes, and then take those jobs themselves. This primitive promotion tactic became rather widespread, especially among medical personnel in the provinces who lacked privileges—and who often lacked

---

15. *Translator's note:* Literally, "at gunshot range from managing health care . . . . "

16. P.S. Popkov had been dismissed as first secretary of the ACP(b) Leningrad Regional and City Committee by a February 15, 1949 decree of the Politburo.

17. F.I. Mashanskií was the head of the City Department of Health.

18. RTsKhIDNI, f. 17, op. 118, d. 478, l. 246–249.

19. On August 13, 1949 in Malenkov's office in Moscow, the following people were arrested without prosecutor's sanction: A.A. Kuznetsov (former CC ACP(b) secretary), P.S. Popkov (secretary of the Leningrad Regional Committee), M.I. Rodionov (chairman of the RSFSR Council of Ministers), P.G. Lazutin (chairman of the Leningrad City Committee), and N.V. Solovyev (first secretary of the Crimean Regional Committee).

20. RTsKhIDNI, f. 17, op. 118, d. 478, l. 244.

professional capabilities as well. For example, in September 1949 anonymous letters, presumably written by psychiatrists from the periphery, were sent to the CC. One such letter did not begin with a lengthy introduction, but got right to the point in the first line:

> This June there was a scientific session of the Institute of Psychiatry of the USSR Ministry of Health. About 300 people were present, among them many doctors who came from faraway places of the Soviet Union. We . . . could not help but notice that it was exclusively Jews who set the tone in neuropathology and psychiatry.[21]

Such an "alarming signal" was not left unheeded. On September 17 the CC secretariat decided to have the CC Administrative Department and the Commission of Party Control urgently carry out an inspection of the Moscow psychiatric institutions. The inspection sent a note about its conclusions to CC secretary P.K. Ponomarenko and deputy chairman of Commission of Party Control at CC ACP(b) M.F. Shkiryatov:

> 1. In Moscow, there are 3 psychiatric institutes, 4 clinics, and 5 neuropsychiatric hospitals. All but one of these institutions are headed by doctors of Jewish nationality. The scientific and medical staff of some of the scientific psychiatric and medical institutions is as follows: at the Central Institute of Psychiatry at the RSFSR Ministry of Health (director Posvyanskiĭ) there are 65 scientists, 43 of whom are Jews, 28 of whom hold the senior scientific worker position; at the Serbskiĭ Central Institute of Scientific Research on Criminal Psychiatry (director Faĭnberg) 52 of the 82 scientific workers are Jews, [and] all leading and administrative positions are also occupied by Jews; at the Gannushkin Clinical Psychiatric Hospital (senior doctor Posvyanskiĭ) 21 of the 35 doctors are Jews; at the Kashchenko Psychiatric Hospital 43 of the 79 doctors are Jews; at the Clinic of Neuropathology of the 1st Medical Institute 8 of the 10 employees are Jews; at the Clinic of Neuropathology of the 2nd Medical Institute (chair of the department professor Grinshteĭn) 4 of the 7 lectures are Jews.
>
> Also true is the statement of the author of the letter that the psychiatric divisions of the USSR Ministry of Health, the RSFSR Ministry of Health, and the Moscow Regional Health Care Department are headed by persons of Jewish nationality (Shmaryan, Karanovich, Barsuk) . . . .
>
> In order to improve this situation, which has formed in the psychiatric institutes and neuropsychiatric hospitals, we deem it

21. RTsKhIDNI, f. 17, op. 118, d. 530, l. 173.

> worthwhile to order the USSR Ministry of Health:
>
> 1. To conduct regular performance reviews of research staff in neuropsychiatric institutions, which would allow the dismissal of inactive research workers with no prospects. . . .
>
> 4. To strengthen the leadership at the Serbskiĭ Institute of Legal Psychiatry,[22] at the Institute of Psychiatry of the RSFSR Ministry of Health, and at the Second Moscow Suburban Mental Hospital.
>
> 5. To select for the posts of psychiatric division heads at the Ministries of Health of the Union of the SSR, the RSFSR, as well as for the post of head psychiatrist at the Moscow Region, people capable of heading the neuropsychiatric service and ensuring proper selection and training of personnel in psychiatry.[23]

Decisive actions followed this decisive document. Professor M.O. Gurevich was removed as deputy director of the Central Serbskiĭ Institute of Forensic Psychiatry; and head physician P.P. Posvyanskiĭ and his deputy M.D. Barzak were dismissed from the Gannushkin Clinical Hospital. However, the most intensive purge took place in the Central Institute of Forensic Psychiatry at the USSR Ministry of Health. From the second half of 1949 through February 1950 14 Jews were fired: T.P. Simson and I.I. Lukomskiĭ (deputy directors), Professors L.L. Rokhlin, M.A. Chalisov, I.A. Berger, and others. Officially, these dismissals were "voluntary," "due to staff reduction," "due to department liquidation," and so forth. The necessity of "the further strengthening of personnel" in psychiatric institutions of the provincial towns also served as a pretext for getting rid of the unwanted. Professor A.S. Shmaryan, the head psychiatrist of the USSR Ministry of Health, was sent to head the Psychiatry Sub-Faculty of the Yaroslavl Medical Institute. Professor A.R. Edelshteĭn, of the First Moscow Medical Institute, was sent to the Omsk Medical Institute. Professor L.L. Rokhlin was sent to the Kazan Institute of Advanced Medical Studies. M.A. Chalisov was sent to Azerbaijan Medical Institute. I.I. Lukomskiĭ was sent to Arkhangelsk Medical Institute. And

---

22. On October 16, 1950 the director of this institute, Ts.M. Faĭnberg, was replaced by Andreĭ Vladimirovich Snezhnevskiĭ, who had proved himself to be an active proponent of I.P. Pavlov's psychological studies. He was zealously critical of the "false scientific conception" of Professors Shmaryan and Gurevich, and this contributed to Shmaryan's dismissal as head psychiatrist of the USSR Ministry of Health and to Gurevich's dismissal as director of the Psychiatric Clinic of the First Medical Institute. During the time of Brezhnev's rule, Snezhnevskiĭ gained notoriety as the main theoretician of a repressive school of psychiatry that victimized many dissidents.

Nonetheless, it should be noted that Snezhnevskiĭ's medical beginnings were promising. He was an apprentice of the famous psychiatrist Mark Sereĭskiĭ, dreamt of a scientific career, and twice refused an appointment to the directorship of the Serbskiĭ Institute, despite strong pressure on the part of the CC's Administrative Department. However, his refusals were declined. RTsKhIDNI, f. 17, op. 119, d. 106, l. 66.

23. RTsKhIDNI, f. 17, op. 118, d. 530, l. 178–183.

the list went on.[24] Some of these people accepted an overt exile and were therefore simply dismissed.[25] The importance given to the expulsion of Jews from the Moscow psychiatry institutions is reflected in a resolution approved by the CC ACP(b) on January 27, 1950 demanding the USSR minister of health, Ye.I. Smirnov, make the personnel purge policy more strict.[26]

As the primary model for the realization of the directive—and also as its primary target—the USSR Ministry of Health chose its subordinate, the RSFSR Ministry of Health. In 1950 the almost all the Jews who held leading positions at the RSFSR Ministry of Health were dismissed. Among them were S.M. Reznikov (head of the Mobilization Department), I.L. Fayerman (head of the Law Department), and Ye.Ya. Khesin (head of the Directorate of Medical Institutions). In January L.M. Lemenev (Nemirovskiĭ), the head of the Directorate of Planning and Finance, was arrested. After a series of comprehensive checks and revisions, Stelmakh (head of the Central Department of the RSFSR Medical Supply), Ye.G. Uryashzon (deputy head of the Directorate of Pharmacies), Shpolyanskiĭ (head of the Directorate of Major Constructions), Gotlib (chief accountant), and others were accused of "major theft and machinations with valuables."[27]

On September 27, 1950 the CC secretariat approved a resolution "On the Cases of Serious Disorders and Abuse in the RSFSR Ministry of Health." This document placed responsibility for the "shortcoming in the work with personnel" on G.N. Beletskiĭ,[28] the minister of health, and on A.M. Sadovskiĭ, the Party Bureau secretary of the RSFSR Ministry of Health. Both were soon dismissed, along with G. Karanovich, the executive board secretary of the RSFSR Ministry of Health.[29]

As all this was happening, there was also an anti-Jewish purge in the clinics, scientific research, and educational institutions subordinate to the RSFSR Ministry of Health. The Moscow Dental School replaced almost entirely its Therapy Department faculty (headed by Professor Badylkes). On August 9, 1951 the Central Gelmgolts Scientific Research Institute of Ophthalmology removed its director, A.A. Kolen, for having committed a "number of fundamental mistakes in the selection, training, and arrangement of personnel."

---

24. RTsKhIDNI, f. 17, op. 118, d. 715, l. 64, 67, 176.

25. For the sake of objectivity, it should be noted that Jewish psychiatrists could have been dealt with much more cruelly had it not been for the restraining influence of CC personnel secretary P.K. Ponomarenko. After reading one of the notes that proposed a radical anti-Jewish purge of psychiatric institutions, he wrote on it, "Something that has been built over centuries cannot be changed in one year or one month." RTsKhIDNI, f. 17, op. 118, d. 530, l. 183.

26. RTsKhIDNI, f. 17, op. 118, d. 715, l. 59.

27. RTsKhIDNI, f. 17, op. 118, d. 713, l. 50–52; op. 119, d. 75, l. 160–164.

28. A Politburo resolution of December 2, 1950 replaced G.N. Beletskiĭ with M.D. Kovrigina.

29. RTsKhIDNI, f. 17, op. 119, d. 75, l. 156–157.

The Military Medical Department was also affected. On July 28, 1950, at the request of A.M. Vasilevskiĭ (the USSR minister of defense), the CC secretariat dismissed Major General A.M. Krupchitskiĭ as head of the Central N.N. Burdenko Military Hospital for having allegedly hired too many of his fellow Jewish tribesmen.[30]

A no less massive attack was undertaken against the staff of Jewish specialists who worked within the USSR Academy of Medical Sciences system. The Institute of Labor Hygiene and Professional Disease first expelled those who were "not trustworthy in a political sense" (former Trotskyites, Bund members, and their sympathizers). Among these were Professor D.I. Shatenshteĭn (head of the Laboratory of Physiology of Labor, who had also been a student of the academician L.S. Stern), Professors I.M. Neĭman, Z.B. Smelyanskiĭ, N.A. Bernshteĭn, and others.[31]

Despite its primitivism, the mechanism of anti-Semitic persecutions was not at all monotonous. Yet it did function according to a set pattern: (1) a denunciation (signed or anonymous) was sent to the CC; (2) the CC instructed the leadership of the corresponding CC department to check the facts set forth on the denunciation (if necessary, this would involve knowledgeable functionaries of the ministries, instructors, and inspectors of the Commission of Party Control); (3) this department reported the results of the investigations to the secretariat, and the secretariat usually decided to dismiss those who had been criticized in the denunciations from work and to expel them from the Party; and (4) the MGB organs carried out the arrests of the outcast, and then determined their future. It was often this last link in the chain, the MGB, that had initiated the mechanism. In such a case, the purge almost by definition became a pogrom.

There were similar happenings at the USSR Academy of Medical Science's Clinic of the Remedial Nutrition. On July 4, 1950 V.S. Abakumov sent a confidential typed letter to Malenkov in which he filled in by hand the "top secret" words. The secret words were the names of the suspected employees of the clinic and their nationalities.[32] (Abakumov's handwritten words are here underlined.)

> According to data at the MGB's disposal, a state of nepotism and cliquishness was created at the Clinic of Remedial Nutrition as a result

---

30. RTsKhIDNI, f. 17, op. 118, d. 713, l. 83–84; op. 119, d. 482, l. 81–85.

31. RTsKhIDNI, f. 17, op. 119, d. 136, l. 62–65.

32. This is one more example of how thoroughly the MGB concealed the anti-Semitic nature of its repressive action. Even more careful in this respect was the Party leadership. This is why historian R. Medvedev's claim that in the autumn of 1944 the CC allegedly sent the so-called "instruction from Malenkov' to all Party committees, thus marking the beginning of the methodical removal of Jewish staff, does not seem to be convincing. (See *Yunost* [*Youth*], 1988–1989, p. 73.)

> of a violation of the Bolshevik principle regarding the selection of personnel. For this reason 36 of the 43 leading and scientific positions are occupied by persons of Jewish nationality. In reality, the majority of people accepted to the clinic are of Jewish nationality, which is approved by its director Pevzner M.I., his deputy Gordon O.L., and head of the reception room Bremener S.M..
>
> According to the materials regarding the inspection of the clinic staff, it was established that there were compromising materials against 10 of the 43 leading and scientific employees.
>
> For instance, the head of the Department of the Clinic, Levitskií L.M., born in 1892 in the Kiev region, non-Party, Jew, was in February 1934 sent out of Kazakhstan for three years for his anti-Soviet activities. According to the testimonies given by Kogen B.Ye., arrested in 1949, Levitskií "in 1923 shared Trotskyite views and voted for the Trotskyite resolution" at the Kiev Medical Institute. . . .
>
> The head of the department, Limcher L.E., born in 1888, non-Party, Jew, is suspected of having connections with foreigners. In the notebook of American agent John Hazard, who from 1934 through 1937 studied at MSU and in 1939 visited the USSR as a tourist, was found a telephone number that belonged to Limcher.
>
> The MGB deems it necessary to propose that the USSR Ministry of Health take measures to bring the Clinic of Remedial Nutrition into a healthy state and to cleanse its staff.[33]

Having studied Abakumov's information, the CC secretariat decreed on August 11, 1950 that the Administrative Department, together with the USSR Ministry of Health, be entrusted with checking on the clinic's activities. The repressive machine was started up, and there soon followed the dismissals of the physicians and then their arrests. On January 27, 1952 Professor L.B. Berlin was arrested. Professor B.S. Levin found himself in the MGB prison along with G.L. Levin, assistant at the Sub-Faculty of Remedial Nutrition of the Central Institute of Advanced Medical Studies. Levin was the son of Professor L.G. Levin, who had been executed in March 1939 as the "poisoner" of V.V. Kuíbyshev, V.R. Menzhinskií, A.M. Gorkií, and of Gorkií's son, M.A. Peshkov.

On February 25, 1952 Abakumov's successor, S.D. Ignatyev, reported to Malenkov that at one of the interrogations G.L. Levin had testified that within the Clinic of Remedial Nutrition was a nationalistic group headed by the clinic's director, Professor M.I. Pevzner. Members of this group presumably "used defective methods of treatment that damaged the health of the patients . . . ."[34]

Unable to bear his ordeals, the aged professor M.I. Pevzner died in May

33. RTsKhIDNI, f. 17, op. 119, d. 12, l. 90–92.

34. Document from the archives of the former KGB.

1952. He had headed the Clinic of Remedial Nutrition since 1930. His wife, Leya Mironovna was arrested on December 6, 1952 in the "doctors' case." To get her to "confess" to her late husband's connections of with British intelligence services, she was tortured.

Professor L.B. Berlin, Dr. B.S. Levin, and G.L. Levin were sent to camp for 25 years according to a July 15, 1952 MCSC resolution. And at the end of that year all three were used by the investigation in the Kremlin "doctors' case."

The medical institutions were in a frenzy from the countless checkings and commissions that unmasked the enthusiasm of the meetings, and from the lava-like outflow of order that stemmed from staff dismissals on the basis of the "fifth item." The growing purges captured the largest educational and scientific medical center of Moscow—the Stalin Second Medical Institute.

Starting from early 1949 academician L.S. Shtern,[35] Professors E.M. Gelshteín, I.I. Feígel, A.M. Grinshteín, A.M. Geselevich, and others were forced to depart.[36] In 1950 the same fate befell Isaak Iosifovich Rogozin, who was dismissed as head of the Sub-Faculty of Epidemiology and head of the Central Sanitary and Anti-Epidemiological Directorate of the USSR Ministry of Health.[37] The direct organizers of this persecution were G.P. Zaítsev, the deputy director of the Institute in Charge of Research and Studies, and V.A. Ivanov, the secretary of the Institute's Party organization. Later in 1951 they arranged the ousting of Abram Borisovich Topchan, the director of the Institute. Topchan was dismissed as head of the First City Priogov Hospital as well.[38]

FABRICATING THE "DOCTORS' PLOT"

Endless personnel inspections, qualification exams, and Party meetings kept the scientific staff and faculty of the Second Medical Institute in a fever pitch until all who had irritated the administration with their "fifth item" were removed. Professor Ya.G. Etinger was no exception: in the autumn of 1949 he was relinquished to the post of department chair and dismissed on trumped-up charges. Not even the Kremlin hospital, which had earlier invited him to work as a consultant, wanted this general practitioner anymore. Etinger's involvement in treating members of the Kremlin leadership would later serve as a starting point and formal reason for fabricating the "doctors' plot."

Etinger had long been within the MGB's field of vision. From 1944 he had

35. Shtern was arrested on January 29, 1949 in connection with the JAC case. She headed the Sub-Faculty of Physiology at the Second Moscow Medical Institute.

36. All except for Geselevich were later arrested in connection with the "doctors' plot."

37. On January 16, 1951 M.I. Khazanov, the head of the Central Sanitary and Anti-Epidemiological Directorate of the USSR Ministry of Health, was dismissed as well. RTsKhIDNI, f. 17, op. 119, d. 206, l. 31–32.

38. RTsKhIDNI, f. 17, op. 119, d. 162, l. 123–124.

regularly visited the JAC and had read the international Jewish periodicals received there, including the *Jewish Chronicle*. He had also supported the creation of a Jewish republic in the Crimea. However, the organs started intensively to "work on" Etinger only after they received compromising material from the arrested JAC executive secretary, I.S. Fefer. During the interrogation, on April 22, 1949, Fefer characterized Etinger as one of the leaders of the bourgeois Jewish nationalists in medicine:

> His [Etinger's] nationalistic views were entirely shared by the academician B.I. Zbarskií, professor of the Second Moscow Medical Institute A.B. Topchan, director of the Clinic of Remedial Nutrition M.I. Pevzner, senior general practitioner of the Soviet Army M.S. Vovsi . . . . Etinger is quite displeased that the Soviet Union does not render aid to the state of Israel, and he accused the Soviet government of allegedly carrying out a hostile policy with respect to Jews. He said, "My friends," (referring to Zbarskií, Pevzner, and other persons whom I have mentioned above), "are simply surprised by this impossible situation. The Jews from all over the world help the Israeli fighters . . . but we don't have this opportunity. If the Soviet government does not want to help the Israeli Jews, let it allow us to do it."[39]

Collecting evidence against Etinger turned out to be a simple task for the MGB. According to his colleagues Etinger was courageous and talkative, and liked to discuss political matters, often even with people he did not know well.[40] As for speaking with relatives, Etinger did not take any precautions whatsoever. The MGB operation services took advantage of this. After bugging Etinger's apartment in 1949, they tape recorded one such tête-à-tête with his adopted son Yakov, a university student, in the first half of 1950. This conversation was filled with remarks critical of Stalin.[41] The minister of state security, Abakumov, soon informed Stalin of the "anti-Soviet conversations" between Etinger and his colleague Zbarskií.[42] Abakumov asked Stalin for a sanction to arrest Etinger, but

---

39. Document from the archives of the former KGB.

40. Rapoport, *Na rubezhe dvukh epokh. Delo vracheí 1953 goda*, p. 117.

41. K.A. Stolyarov, *Golgofa: Dokumental'naya povest'* [*Calvary: A Documentary History*] (Moscow: 1991), p. 9.

42. Boris Ilyich Zbarskií (1885–1954) was an academician of the USSR Academy of Medical Sciences and participated in the embalming of Lenin's body. In 1944 he published his reminiscences of the funeral and embalming in his brochure, *Lenin's Mausoleum* (*Mavzoleí Lenina*). The brochure went through several editions and sold out (330 000 copies). Zbarskií's brochure contained a number of documents and photographs from the CC ACP(b) Institute of Marx-Engels-Lenin. On May 6, 1952 Zbarskií was expelled from the Party, and the brochure was given as the formal reason. At the same time

Stalin would not yet grant it.[43]

Etinger was arrested on November 18, 1950. On the basis of agents' and other sources of information, he was incriminated with "slanderous inventions" about Shcherbakov and Malenkov, who he considered to be the main inspirers and guards of the policy of state anti-Semitism in the country. A month before, Etinger's step son Ya.Ya. Etinger (Siterman) had been forced to testify against his father. And on July 16, 1951 Ya.G. Etinger's wife, R.K. Viktorova, was taken to Lubyanka and was forced to confess that her husband and son listened to the BBC's anti-Soviet broadcasts and the Voice of America.[44] As we can see, Etinger's "medical sabotage" of the Communist Party and Soviet leaders was not brought up at the outset.

During the interrogation, Etinger denied the accusations made against him, and insisted that his statements about the repression of Jews were well grounded. Reluctant to "confess," the doctor was transferred to the Lefortovo prison on

---

the Commission of Party Control at the CC ACP(b) passed a resolution to expel the painter S.M. Telingater and the deputy editor of the State Political Publishing House, I.G. Verite, from the Party. In his painting, *At Lenin's Coffin in the Kollonyí Hall of the Union House in Moscow*, Telingater had allegedly "for hostile purposes" retouched the face of the person standing next to Lenin's coffin, giving him an overt resemblance to L. Trotskií. Verite had collaborated with Zbarskií in publishing the brochure and in "clogging up" the publishing house with Jewish personnel.

Formal reasons aside, Zbarskií was actually expelled from the Party because the MGB had arrested him back in March 1952. Shortly before the arrest, a CC ACP(b) commission inspected the lab that Zbarskií headed, for that lab was embalming the body of the Mongolian marshal Kh. Choíbalsan. The commission later accused Zbarskií of violating the secrecy of the lab's work, of nationalistically-biased selection of personnel, and of other crimes as well. The MGB investigators turned out to be even more resourceful. They incriminated the professor with his former membership in the SR (Social Revolutionaries) party, with his 1918 election to the Constituent Assembly, with his criticism of the Bolsheviks in regard to the Constituent Assembly's dismissal, with his espionage activities in the 1930s in favor of Germany, and with his relations with L. Trotskií, A. Rykov, N. Bukharin, G. Yagoda, and other "enemies of the people."

With the help of bugging devices and agents' information, extensive materials were collected on Zbarskií's "nationalistic conversations" with I.G. Verite, journalist G.Ye. Ryklin, and theater administrator I.V. Nezhnyí. The professor was reminded that he had been acquainted since 1940 with Mikhoels, and that back in 1944 he had been invited to Mikhoels's house for a family evening dedicated to the conferring of the Stalin Prize. And in 1948 Zbarskií embalmed the body of the great actor. It became known that Zbarskií had given an interview to *Einikeit*, had met with Fefer, Zuskin and other JAC leaders, that after Mikhoels's death he was named as one of his possible successors for the position of JAC president, and so forth. At almost the same time as Zbarskií's arrest, his wife, Ye.B. Perelman, whom he had met in 1926 in Germany at the painter L.O. Pasternak's house, was arrested, as well as S.M. Telingater and I.G. Verite. They were released only at the end of December 1953. The morally and physically broken professor did not live long afterwards. On October 7, 1954 he died while giving a lecture at the First Moscow Medical Institute. RTsKhIDNI, f. 17, op. 119, d. 940, l. 88–89.

43. Stolyarov, *Dokumental'naya povest'*, pp. 48–49.

44. Document from the archives of the former KGB.

January 5, 1951, where he was confined to a wet cell as cold air was being pumped in.[45]

It was Lieutenant Colonel M.D. Ryumin (senior investigator of the Department to Investigate Cases of Special Importance to the MGB) who conducted Etinger's case. Alluding to the "confession" allegedly given by his victim, Ryumin put forth accusations against a number of doctors as "Jewish nationalists who expressed their discontent with Soviet power and slandered the national policy of the ACP(b) and the Soviet state." Ryumin then drew up a list of Etinger's "accomplices who expressed hostile opinions," and sent it to Abakumov. The list included: B.I. Zbarskiĭ (chair of the Department of Medical Chemistry at the First Moscow Medical Institute), M.S. Vovsi (professor of the Central Institute for Advanced Medical Studies), V.S. Levit (chair of the Department of Surgery at the Second Moscow Medical Institute), I.L. Fayerman (chair of the Department of General Surgery at the RSFSR Medical Institute), Sh.D. Moshkovskiĭ (head of the Department of the Institute of Tropical Diseases), Ya.L. Rapoport (head of the laboratory of the Institute of Morphology of the USSR Academy of Medical Science), N.A. Shereshevskiĭ (director of the Endocrinology Institute), M.I. Pevzner (director of the Clinic of Remedial Nutrition), Ya.I. Mazel (assistant of the Clinic of the Second Moscow Medical Institute), N.L. Vilk (head of the Department of General Medicine at one of the Moscow hospitals), S.Ye. Nezlin (head of the Department of the Tuberculosis Institute), I.L. Braude (director of the Obstetrics and Gynecology Clinic), M.M. Averbakh (lecturer of the clinic of the Second Moscow Medical Institute), A.B. Topchan (senior doctor of the First City Hospital), and L.I. Fogelson, E.M. Gelshteĭn, and V.L. Eĭnis (directors of various clinics).[46] All of these people were later dismissed and some of them were arrested. On March 2, 1951 Etinger, unable to bear the pressure of the investigation, died suddenly in prison from—as the death certificate stated—"heart paralysis."

A few months later, on June 2, 1951, Ryumin, possessed of ambitious plans and dissatisfied with his role as a rank-and-file executor of his bosses' plans, sent a letter to Stalin accusing his chief Abakumov of allegedly concealing from the government "Jewish nationalist" Etinger's terrorist plans. Ryumin claimed that once Abakumov learned, from the doctor himself, of Etinger's sabotaged medical treatment of Soviet leaders and leaders of the international Communist movement, he forbade any further interrogations of Etinger regarding his participation in the undoubtedly real plot to murder Shcherbakov.[47] Abakumov

---

45. Document from the archives of the former KGB.

46. Document from the archives of the former KGB.

47. A.S. Shcherbakov suffered from a severe heart disease and died on May 10, 1945. At the Twentieth CPSU Congress, Khrushchev, as we know, debunked Stalin's myth about killer-doctors.

had also ordered Etinger's transfer to the Lefortovo prison, where he was deliberately brought to death. Ryumin concluded that Abakumov and his allies had "jumbled the case of the terrorist Etinger, thus seriously damaging the interests of the state."[48]

As noted above, the denunciation of this high-ranking person had an effect. Minister Abakumov found himself behind bars (together with all his protégés in the central state security apparatus). And according to a secret CC ACP(b) resolution "On the Unfavorable Situation within the MGB of the USSR" (approved on July 11, 1952), a directive was given to the new leaders of the organs to "unmask the group present among the doctors that perpetrated sabotage against the leaders of the Party and government." Soon after Stalin's death Ignatyev, the Party functionary who had replaced Abakumov as minister of state security, declared in his testimony on the "doctors' case" that when he had been appointed to this position, Stalin had ordered him to take "decisive measures to unveil the group of doctor-terrorists, the existence of which he had been for a long time convinced."[49]

It was from this moment that the essence of this pathetic sophistry and mystification became clear. The "doctors' plot" would soon be known to the whole world as a global plot by Western special services to disable the Soviet leaders by means of medical terrorism. Ryumin was now the head of the Department to Investigate Cases of Special Importance to the MGB,[50] and for him Abakumov's dismissal was a carte blanche to realize his initiative (luckily for him this coincided with the demand formulated by Stalin's leadership) on the further inquiry and re-examination of Etinger's case in line with the story about Shcherbakov's sabotaged treatment. Ryumin had first to obtain any kind of proof of the Kremlin doctors' malicious intrigues against high-ranking patients. Ryumin proceeded to get this information by hook or by crook.

Khrushchev later described the cause of the death of Shcherbakov, the secretary of the CC, the MC (Moscow Regional Committee), and MSC (Moscow City Committee) of the ACP(b): "He ended dismally. Beria was right when he said that Shcherbakov died because he drank awfully much. He overdrank and died. Stalin, however, was saying otherwise: that he was a fool—was just beginning to recover, but then ignored the doctors' warnings and died at night when he overindulged with his wife" (N.S. Khrushchev, "Vospominaniya," *Voprosy istorii*, 1991, no. 11, p. 54). However, according to the official version, Shcherbakov's death followed from a long and exhausting trip that he took on May 8 and 9, 1945 with his doctors' (R.I. Ryzhikov's and G.A. Kadzharduzov's) consent. He traveled from the Barvikha sanatorium to Moscow where he watched the light displays in honor of Victory Day.

48. Document from the archives of the former KGB.

49. Document from the archives of the former KGB.

50. It was perhaps by chance, but nevertheless true, that Stalin chose as inquisitors those who were not only in a state of mental decline, but were physically defective as well. Like Yezhov, Ryumin was short, and when, in the autumn of 1952, Stalin grew disappointed with the latter, he ordered Ignatyev to "remove this midget." K.A. Stolyarov, *Golgofa. Dokumental'naya povest'* (Moscow, 1991), p. 77.

RYUMIN'S "SYSTEM OF PROOF"

On September 1, 1951 Ya.G. Etinger's adoptive son Yakov was transferred from the Far East transit (i.e., interim) prison to the Lefortovo prison in Moscow. He was forced to testify to the existence of the doctors' plot.

By that time Dr. S.Ye. Karpaí had already been intensively interrogated for several months. She had been arrested on July 16, 1951 as a terrorist and became one of the characters of this prison/investigation drama.[51] As the person in charge of the Department of Functional Diagnostics at the Kremlin Hospital until 1950, in 1944 and 1945 she had monitored A.S. Shcherbakov's and A.A. Zhdanov's heart conditions via electrocardiograms. Despite the pressure placed on her, she was steadfast during the interrogation and denied having applied any manner of sabotaged treatments. She decisively refused to sign the falsified confession about acts of sabotage, thus dragging out the investigation. Thus were the arrests of other doctors postponed, which helped them survive past Stalin's death.

Ryumin also tried to accuse Karpaí of having desired to advance the death of Stalin's late comrade-in-arms, the All-Union elder M.I. Kalinin. But Ryumin did not manage this move. The uncompromising Karpaí made clear at the interrogation that she had been Kalinin's doctor from January 1940 to June 1942, i.e., long before June 10, 1944, when Professor A.D. Ochkin performed an operation on him that revealed intestinal cancer. Ochkin then diagnosed a malignant tumor of the sigmoid colon in a very neglected state. The tumor grew to be four or five centimeters, and the metastases penetrated the liver and lymphatic nodes. For this reason the surgeon decided against removing the tumor, and instead joined the unaffected parts of the intestine around it, thus preventing clogging. Kalinin lived for two more years and died in June 1946 when the growing tumor squeezed the intestinal artery.

However, Karpaí testified that in June 1942, when she had suggested that Kalinin be thoroughly examined (he was complaining of pain in his intestines), Professor V.N. Vinogradov, the senior general practitioner of the Medical and Sanitary Directorate of the Kremlin (LSUK), reduced the treatment to enemas, diets, and medicines.

This testimony, along with other testimony previously obtained, provided Ryumin with a loophole by which he hoped to get to the heart of the Kremlin doctors' "plot." The loophole was that Vinogradov was a most respected and experienced doctor who treated not only all Politburo members, but also Stalin himself. Thus, for example, as Stalin's personal doctor, he had accompanied the

---

51. In the 1940s Karpaí had been P.S. Zhemchuzhina's personal doctor. When in prison, Karpaí was put in a wet, cold cell and fell ill with asthma, from which she died a few years after her release.

dictator to Teheran in 1943 for the meeting of the "great troika."[52]

In early 1952, and not without Ryumin's effort, Vinogradov fell into disgrace. It was then that he examined Stalin for the last time. Having discovered a sharp decline in the leader's health (rapidly accelerating arteriosclerosis of the brain), he recommended that Stalin cease his political activity and retire. Naturally the decrepit dictator perceived this medical verdict as a disguised attempt by the enemy to deprive him of his supreme power. Thus he not only distanced the old professor from himself, but also decided to refuse any medical care.

In January 1952, while in a paroxysm of malicious suspicion, Stalin threatened Ignatyev, saying that if he did not "uncover the terrorists, the American agents among the doctors, he would follow Abakumov." The Kremlin boss raved, "I'm not a suppliant of the MGB! I can knock you out if you don't follow my orders . . . . We'll scatter your group."[53]

This is why the compromising materials Ryumin received on Vinogradov came at just the right moment. On February 15, 1952, to uncover Vinogradov's "criminal plans," Stalin ordered the arrest of Dr. R.I. Ryzhikov, the deputy to the director of the medical unit of the Barvikha governmental sanatorium. The senior investigator, a colonel with a soft sounding Ukrainian surname, Garkusha, threatening his new victim with the arrests of his wife and children, made Ryzhikov admit not only his guilt in shortening Shcherbakov's life (in May 1945 he had allowed him to undertake a tiring trip to Moscow), but also in his criminal negligence consisting of a tardy diagnosis of stomach cancer from which Party ideologist Ye.M. Yaroslavskiĭ died in December 1943.[54]

But most importantly, Ryumin was able finally to obtain the key evidence that "irrefutably" supported his story of the reality of the Kremlin doctors' plot, and he presented this in a letter to Stalin. He also noted that the state security minister Abakumov allegedly collaborated in this plot and even patronized it. On April 9, 1952 Likhachyov (formerly the deputy head of the Department to Investigate Cases of Special Importance to the MGB, but now arrested together with Abakumov), crushed by his swift fall from the heights of punitive power to the position of a pitiful prisoner devoid of all rights, said to Ryumin:

> The Jewish nationalist Etinger testified during Abakumov's interrogation that out of hatred toward Shcherbakov he had set himself the goal of shortening his life . . . as far as I can remember now, Etinger also declared that when treating Shcherbakov he used larger or smaller doses of medicines and intentionally altered the hours when

---

52. *Translator's note:* The "great troika" were Churchill, Roosevelt, and Stalin.

53. Document from the archives of the former KGB.

54. Document from the archives of the former KGB.

> those should be taken by the patient . . . . [55]

To expand upon his success and to offer grounds for the testimonies he had instigated, Ryumin on July 22 organized a confrontation between Abakumov and Likhachyov. At this session Likhachyov recalled the following details of investigations that the former MGB boss had "slurred over":

> . . . At the end of the interrogation Abakumov became interested in Etinger's involvement in Shcherbakov's murder. Etinger basically confirmed what he had said to Ryumin and me. But Abakumov apparently was not satisfied with this, and he interrupted Etinger while the latter was testifying and asked about certain persons who didn't have anything to do with the killing . . . . [56]

In order to present the conclusions of the investigation from a well-founded and professional medical point of view, the MGB invited a group of doctors who secretly cooperated with the "organs" to participate in the preliminary examination. Dr. L.F. Timashuk (1893–1983) was one of these experts who gained fame as the main initiator of the "doctor's case." In 1926 she graduated from the Samara University Medical Department and had since worked at the Kremlin Hospital. On July 24, 1952 she was called to Lubyanka and the very same Colonel Garkusha consulted her in regard to the investigation materials on Shcherbakov's "sabotaged" treatment.[57]

ZHDANOV'S TREATMENT AND DEATH

On August 11, at her next visit to the MGB, Timashuk gave investigator I. Yeliseyev information that considerably broadened the range of the investigation and provided it with a renewed spark of life. As the person in charge of the Electrocardiography Laboratory at the Kremlin Hospital, Timashuk was directly involved in Zhdanov's treatment during his final months. It was known that the main Party ideologist suffered from severe arteriosclerosis. As a result of the ever-growing stress that Zhdanov tried to counterbalance with heavy doses of alcohol, the disease started to develop in autumn of 1947 (upon which he underwent an unsuccessful treatment in Sochi) and became acute in summer of 1948, after he had been impelled to pass his position as second CC secretary[58] on to Malenkov.

---

55. Document from the archives of the former KGB.
56. Document from the archives of the former KGB.
57. Document from the archives of the former KGB.
58. This was not the official title of this position; rather, it was bureaucratic Party slang for the second highest ranking person in the Party and state.

On July 13, upset with what had occurred, he went to the south and then to the Valdaí sanatorium in the Russian mid-belt for rest. As the days passed he gradually calmed down, but Agitprop head Shepilov phoned him on July 23. (Apparently Shepilov realized that fortune had betrayed his former protector and so attempted to join the camp of the winner Malenkov.) According to the medical personnel, Zhdanov clearly found the conversation unpleasant; he shouted into the receiver and was extremely agitated. That night he had a severe heart attack. V.N. Vinogradov, V.Kh. Vasilenko, and P.I. Yegorov, all professors of the Kremlin Hospital, arrived from Moscow on July 25 and certified in the presence of the Zhdanov's doctor, G.I. Maíorov, and diagnostician S.Ye. Karpaí that nothing extraordinary had taken place and that the patient had overcome an acute bout of heart seizures. Cardiosclerosis was given as the main reason for the attack. The respected commission then left for Moscow without making any cardinal changes to Zhdanov's previously prescribed treatment.[59]

It should be noted that, under Stalin, the quality of the treatments given to the highest-ranking bureaucracy (who constituted the so-called "special group" with respect to medical care) was, to say the least, far from ideal. No matter how paradoxical it may seem, in the LSUK, where the cream of Soviet medicine worked, medical errors were not rare. Indeed, in an abnormally organized society all links are defective, and health care, even for the elite, is no exception. In the famous Kremlyevka (Kremlin Hospital), just as everywhere else, bureaucratic hierarchy, cooperativeness, and solidarity[60] hovered together, forming a death spirit that brought about all possible consequences. It is hard to describe as normal a situation in which each of the professors of the LSUK, burdened with several positions, was also in charge of sometimes dozens of high-ranking patients.[61] Not surprisingly, the treatments produced results contrary to those desired. For example, Professor P.I. Yegorov (the head of LSUK), who treated G.M. Dimitrov, Marshals A.M. Vasilevskií and S.M. Shtemenko, academician S.I. Vavilov, and many others, in summer of 1952 sent L.Z. Mekhlis (the former minister of state control), who had heart problems, to the Crimea to undergo a treatment that had been contra-indicated. Or to take another example, Professor M.S. Vovsi, who from 1941 through 1949 had been the senior general practitioner of the Main Military Medical Department, sent Ya.N. Fedorenko (marshal of the Armored

---

59. Document from the archives of the former KGB.

60. *Translator's note:* The Russian word here for "solidarity" can literally be translated "mutual guarantee," or "mutual benefit."

61. For example, before 1951 Vinogradov had been senior general practitioner of the Kremlin Hospital. Then he was staff professor-consultant and at the same time he chaired a department at the First Moscow Medical Institute. He was also editor-in-chief of the *General Practitioner's Archive* (*Terapevticheskií arkhiv*) magazine, head of the Electrocardiography Department at the Institute of Therapy of the Academy of Medical Science, and occupied a number of other positions.

Forces), who suffered from a chronic brain disease, for treatment in Sochi. In March 1946 Fedorenko died. It goes without saying that in none of these cases did the doctors pursue any manner of "sabotage." Rather, so-called socialist medical care, like the whole of society, was characterized by negligence, irresponsibility, and inhumanity. Stalin, however, with his perception of the world clearly marred by his declining faculties, considered this a crime. He saw a perfidious intent in something that was lawful, typical, and unavoidable within the bureaucratic system that he himself had created. The "organs" in their turn, due to their social functions, could not and did not wish to dispel the dictator's delusion, and thus acted in accordance with his orders, unmasking sedition where it never existed.

The health care system that treated the nomenclatura displayed its inefficiency in fighting Zhdanov's affliction. The severity of his disease required constant monitoring for three weeks beginning on August 7, 1948; nonetheless, instead of recording his cardiograms, the doctors regularly gave him arm and leg massages that did only harm. Instead of arranging for proper care and appropriate treatment, Dr. Maíorov entrusted this to the nurse and went fishing for hours. As a result, on August 27 Zhdanov suffered another heart attack. On the next day, Professors Yegorov, Vinogradov, and Vasilenko again arrived at Valdaí and brought with them Dr. Timashuk,[62] who was supposed to record the electrocardiograms. After conducting the examination, Timashuk established "a myocardial infarction in the area of the anterior wall of the left ventricle and interventricular septum." But Timashuk's opinion, which contradicted what the professor-consultants had stated earlier, was considered erroneous, and her colleagues insisted she rewrite her conclusion in accordance with the previously established vague diagnosis of a "dysfunction on the basis of sclerosis and hypertension." Zhdanov's personal doctor and Yegorov had allowed him to get out of bed and walk in the park, and on August 29 he thus suffered yet another heart attack.[63] Timashuk then decided to defend her point of view; to prevent a deadly outcome (which was shortly to come), she insisted that he be strictly confined to bed. That same day she wrote about all that had occurred to N.S. Vlasik, the head of the Main Security Directorate of the MGB, and dispatched her letter via Major A.M. Belov (the head of Zhdanov's personal bodyguard), who delivered it to Moscow within a few hours. Then on August 30 Abakumov handed it to Stalin, together with the electrocardiographs.[64]

---

62. Dr. Karpaí was then on holiday.

63. On August 28, Yegorov wrote in Zhdanov's medical history, "Recommended . . . move more, and from September 1 allow him to travel by car. On September 9, make the decision about the trip to Moscow."

64. Document from the archives of the President of the Russian Federation.

The next day Zhdanov died. On September 1, 1948 the newspapers and radio announced with "deep regret" the death of this "faithful pupil and comrade-in-arms of the great Stalin," which was caused by the "paralysis of an abnormally deformed heart accompanied by acute emphysema." But Timashuk's letter remained unexamined. Suspicious and usually prompt in dealing with people, Stalin for some reason did not conduct an investigation, though there were strong grounds to do so, and had the letter sent to the archives. It is possible that he considered Timashuk's facts insufficiently convincing, the more so because they differed from the opinions of well-respected doctors whom he then still trusted. However, four years later, this document was again brought to light and played a noticeable role in the events that took place during the dictator's last months.

Meanwhile, unaware of the terrible ordeals that the near future had in store for them, the Kremlin doctors who had treated Zhdanov carried out the routine work necessary after his death. On the evening of August 31, 1948 A.N. Fedorov, a Kremlin Hospital pathologist, performed the autopsy in the presence of CC secretary A.A. Kuznetsov.[65] This took place in a badly equipped washroom in one of the sanatorium houses, under dim light, and with Professor Yegorov (the head of the LSUK) rushing the events. Yegorov, who abided by LSUK interests, insisted that the final results of the autopsy correspond maximally to the clinical diagnosis. It was for this reason that Fedorov's description of old and fresh scars found on Zhdanov's heart, which testified to a number of myocardial infarctions, consisted of many unclear, vague, and ambiguous formulations (" . . . nidus," "necrosis foci," "nidus of miomaletion," etc.) intended to hide the earlier infarctions. The numerous infarctions also went unnoted by the participants of the so-called long-distance consultation that took place in Moscow on August 31 and included Professors V.N. Vinogradov, V.F. Zelenin, A.M. Markov, V.Ye. Nezlin, Ya.G. Etinger, and P.I. Yegorov. After examining the corresponding clinical and pathological documents, as well as the preparation of the formula to preserve the late Zhdanov's heart for postmortem study, these doctors, faithful to the principles of corporate solidarity, confirmed the validity of the conclusions drawn by the leaders of the Kremlin Hospital.[66]

To calm Timashuk, who continued to accuse the LSUK leaders of Zhdanov's faulty treatment and death, Yegorov on September 6 summoned a meeting in his office at which he branded Timashuk as an ignorant doctor and a "foreign" and "dangerous" person. V.Kh. Vasilenko, G.I. Maíorov, A.N. Fedorov, and V.N. Vinogradov supported Yegorov. Vinogradov felt a special hostility toward Timashuk, perhaps because he suspected her of having connections with

---

65. N.A. Voznesenskií and P.S. Popkov arrived at Valdaí that same day, as their intuition had told them it was better to get together on the threshold of heavy ordeals.

66. Document from the archives of the former KGB.

the MGB. In all likelihood her connections stemmed from her being a qualified doctor who considered it her civil duty to inform the "proper people" about everything that, in her opinion, threatened the health and lives of Kremlin Hospital patients. However, Vinogradov was a product of the old-school intelligentsia, and he considered even this kind of cooperation with the "organs" to be reprehensible. In addition, he could not forget an episode from back in the late 1930s, when he was often called to Lubyanka as a witness and an expert in the case of his teacher D.D. Pletnev. At one of these visits the "iron commissar of the people" Yezhov, who was drunk, frankly advised the professor, "You are a very good person, Vladimir Nikitovich, but you talk too much. Bear in mind that every third person is my person and informs me of everything. I recommend that you talk less."

It is easy to imagine the impression that such ominous "advice" had on him. Therefore when he encountered Timashuk he gave Ye.I. Smirnov (the USSR Minister of the Health Care) the following ultimatum: "I work at the Kremlin Hospital, or she does; but not both."[67] On September 7 Timashuk was summoned to the Personnel Department and read the order on her transfer from the Kremlin Hospital to one of its branches.

After Stalin's death the MGB's re-examination caused the "doctor's case" to collapse as little by little all the "evidence" collected by the investigation was deemed fabricated. Nevertheless, Professor Vinogradov stated in a March 27, 1953 letter to Beria:

> It is, however, necessary to admit that A.A. Zhdanov had an infarction; and it was erroneous of me, Professors Vasilenko and Yegorov, and Drs. Maíorov and Karpaí to negate it. We did not establish the diagnosis and the treatment methods with any malicious intent in mind.[68]

Thus the information that Timashuk had given to the investigation in 1952 concerning Zhdanov's disease and treatment had been quite well qualified and considerably well grounded. And on August 29, 1952 Professor P.Ye. Lukomskií (the senior general practitioner of the USSR Ministry of Health Care) had made a conclusion that supported Timashuk's diagnosis. Thus did the MGB's activities grow in significance in Stalin's eyes.

---

67. Document from the archives of the former KGB.

68. Document from the archives of the former KGB.

ANTI-SEMITISM GROWS STRONGER . . .

It was to the "organs'" benefit that, as if by command, letters of a clear anti-Semitic character started arriving at the CC ACP(b) with more and more reports on new facts about sabotage at the Kremlin Hospital. To give the reader an idea of what these were like, we cite one such letter. It was addressed to Malenkov and dated June 2, 1952:

> Look at all the disgrace going on at the Kremlin Medical Administration. The KMA director, P.I. Yegorov, is busy with his personal problems, with his family, leaving everything to his assistant—Vasilií Yakovlevich Braítsev, a Jew disguised as a Belorussian. Braítsev is not only his main assistant, but also the personnel manager. This is where he really shows himself, bringing together under his wing all Jews of the polyclinic, though many among them have lately turned out to be enemies of the people. Thus, at the First Kremlin Polyclinic Dr. Karpaí was arrested and exiled as a spy . . . . At Barvikha [a CC sanatorium] Ryzhikov, a Jew,[69] and his wife were arrested as spies. And all of a sudden the roof fell in . . . .[70]
>
> At the Second Polyclinic there are Jews all over the place. The pharmacy director there, Berta Borisovna Lyubman, has a brother abroad in America; he is a driver and he ran there with a car . . . . Lyubman has been involved in numerous cases of embezzlement, but Braítsev still keeps her and even gives her awards.[71] . . . At the Second Polyclinic all the pharmacy employees are Jews and they all have their Geschäft.[72] Of the 16 departments there, 14 are headed by Jews, who have grown moldy sitting there for so long . . . . While P.I. Yegorov, the director, after taking over from Busalov,[73] did not replace any of his assistants and accepted all this worn-out staff. It is time, it is time to refresh this bog, to purge out the long-standing thieves.[74]

The anti-Semitic refrain of the letters coming to the CC was not coincidental. Since early 1949 the propagandistic media were waging a wide-ranging campaign against "stateless" cosmopolitans, and they left no doubt as to who the primary targets were. In those days there was a saying: "Call a Jew a cosmopolitan—that

---

69. According to his questionnaire data, R.I. Ryzhikov was Russian.

70. Ironically, it was in this same room that the chairman of the Polish State Planning Commission, Hilary Mints, was receiving treatment.

71. Immediately after Malenkov received this letter, V.Ya. Braítsev (the Kremlin Medical Administration deputy director) and B.B. Lyubman were fired. RTsKhIDNI, f. 17, op. 136, d. 463, l. 69.

72. *Geschäft* is a German word that here means "dirty tricks."

73. A.A. Busalov was the former director of the Kremlin Medical Administration. He was later arrested in connection with the "doctors' plot."

74. RTsKhIDNI, f. 17, op. 136, d. 463, l. 66–67.

way you won't be an anti-Semite." In medicine, as in other fields, bureaucratic fighters against cosmopolitanism were acting chiefly in their own purely pragmatic and mercantilistic interests, which consisted mostly of improving their social status and their well-being by ousting Jews. In so doing there was a great temptation to disguise the real intentions by adopting a primitive national-Bolshevik rhetoric in the spirit of the prerevolutionary Black Hundred, with demogogic recollections of the historic roots of Jewish intrigue in the Party and the state. The favorite tool of the anti-Semites was the tried-and-true anonymous letter to top Party and state authorities. The letters had to be anonymous, for anti-Semitism was officially prohibited; there was even an article in the criminal code regarding this. A typical example of this epistolary art is the following letter from "a group of doctors from Moscow polyclinics, participants at the fronts of the Great Patriotic War," mailed in June 1952 to G. Malenkov (CC ACP(b) secretary), N. Mikhaĭlov (CC ALCUY secretary), Ye. Smirnov (minister of health of the USSR), M. Kovrigina (minister of health of the RSFSR), and to Ye. Vasyukova (executive secretary of the *Medical Worker*[75] newspaper). The letter criticized Vasyukova for her alleged pro-Jewish orientation. The letter opened in the denunciatory genre with high-flown words on civic spirit. Here are some fragments:

> It is the duty of a Soviet doctor-patriot, a Communist or a non-Party citizen, to write to you and point out to you that the *Medical Worker* newspaper, whether the editor notices it or not, systematically gives the floor to the same Butkeviches, Slutskiĭs, Lisitskiĭs, Malbergs, Rozenfelds, Glezers, Kopelzons . . . .
>
> Let's take, for instance, the newspaper's July 1, 1952 issue, number 44. On the first page we read: "In today's issue—A. Luganskiĭ, G. Speranskiĭ, L. Pruss, M. Slutskaya."
>
> The fourth page closes with *Z. Gidon*, Anatoliĭ Milyavskiĭ, Ye. Ostankovich, and a photo by A. Malmberg. These so-called representatives of medical science represent Moscow, the Moscow Region, Simferopol, Tashkent, Sochi, Anapa.
>
> *Polar regions* are represented by totally different names. On the fourth page of the "Beyond the Polar Circle" section we read: "The network of medical institutions is expanding . . . . Mainly young doctors and nurses work there. Nina Prokopenko, a young pediatrician and Komsomol member, came here after graduating from the Izhevsk Medical Institute . . . . Operations on the site are performed by surgeon Ivan Vasilyevich Anufriyev . . . . Medical workers and Komsomol members Tamara Simonova, Aleksandr Nesterov, and

75. *Meditsinskiĭ rabotnik.*

Nikolaí Zabolotskikh often go out to collective farms to lecture and organize discussions on medical issues . . . . Working in Tiksi, an Arctic village at the Laptevy Sea coast four thousand kilometers from the nearest railroad, are doctors Nadezhda Sergeyevna Kotelnikova, Nadezhda Nikolayevna Denisova . . . ."

Beyond the polar circle there are no doctor Rozenfelds, Altmans, Lifshitses, Butkeviches, Milyavskiís, or Slutskiís. It is here in the center where they occupy all key positions. The newspaper prints their names in large letters, advertises them.

Hasn't the time come to bring back to normal the upside-down trend in selecting and placing personnel in medicine? For 32 years—up to 1949—these Rozenfelds and Butkeviches were in command of medicine, fully occupying this field of science, bashing cadres of all other nationalities, Russians included . . . . Everyone knows this is the truth. Everyone knows that these Rozenfelds and Butkeviches committed evil deeds in medicine and caused our people innumerable sufferings. They killed Gorkií and his son; they killed Kuíbyshev, Shcherbakov, and Zhdanov. Just as their teachers—the Trotskiís, Kamenevs, Zinovyevs—they acted like swindlers and double-dealers. It is known that these despised enemies of the Party and the Soviet people, these Kamenevs and Zinovyevs, who took Russian names for themselves, together with Trotskií the Judas, had made it their aim to substitute Trotskyism for Leninism, to remove Stalin, to destroy Soviet rule. Zinovyev—the organizer and direct participant in the assassination of Sergeí Mironovich Kirov—the same Zinovyev, this political swindler and political double-dealer, writes an obituary on Kirov's death and goes to the newspaper *Pravda* to publish this obituary. They, these enemies and the like, also used the following dirty method: *they implanted those of their own category as wives and husbands for influential figures and officials.* This enemy practice persists among anti-patriots, cosmopolitans up to this day. We simply lacked a knowledge of Jewry, lacked practical experience in dealing with Jews, as was pointed out by G.V. Plekhanov in 1900.

V.I. Lenin cites Plekhanov's words in his article "How 'ISKRA' Nearly Died." But then, in the second and third editions of V.I. Lenin's works—which, as everyone knows, were edited by Trotskií's brother-in-law (married to his sister) L.B. Kamenev—these words of Plekhanov, cited by V.I. Lenin, were thrown out by Kamenev, by this Lev Borisovich—a stateless cosmopolitan, an enemy of Leninism. Only in the fourth edition of Lenin's works, published under the direct supervision and control of Comrade Stalin, was the article by V.I. Lenin restored in accordance with the original. On page 311, volume four of the fourth edition V.I. Lenin writes:

"On the issue of our attitude toward the Jewish Union [Bund]

G.V. [Georgiĭ Valentinovich Plekhanov] shows phenomenal intolerance, plainly declaring it not a social-democratic organization, but simply an exploiters' organization, exploiting Russians, saying that our aim is to knock this Bund out of the Party, that all Jews are chauvinists and nationalists, that the Russian Party should be Russian, not letting itself be 'captured' by 'the tribe of Gad,' etc."[76]

The Party of Lenin-Stalin knocked out this "Bund," did not surrender to "the tribe of Gad." But, unfortunately, we see that even in 1952 the *Medical Worker* newspaper is "captured" by this "tribe of Gad."

. . . It is time for the ministries of health and the *Medical Worker* newspaper to start a decisive, Party-style . . . restoration of order in personnel management, and to remove the inveterate schemers, the anti-patriotic cosmopolitans from leading posts as far as possible. The *Medical Worker* newspaper should organize and propagandize this fight for personnel cleansing in medicine and for promotion to high positions of worthy people, real patriots of our motherland, the hard-working, who love their people, whose primary concerns are the interests of the people, of guarding their health. [Emphases in the original].[77]

The hysteria regarding medical workers, especially the medical elite serving the government, grew stronger month after month. This went on until the autumn of 1952, when Stalin decided to reinforce the psychological pressure by more decisive actions.

THE ARRESTS OF THE MAIN PARTICIPANTS OF THE "PLOT"

Ryumin had by now become vice minister of state security, and he prepared a statement on the results of the investigation, medical reports, and so forth, stating with a great degree of certainty that Professors A.A. Busalov, P.I. Yegorov, V.Kh. Vasilenko, V.N. Vinogradov, G.F. Lang (1875–1948), Ya.G. Etinger, and others had deliberately killed Shcherbakov and Zhdanov. Ignatyev showed Stalin this statement in late September 1952, and thus did the MGB receive its long-awaited

76. It is true that the fourth volume of the fourth edition of Lenin's works was published in 1951 "under the direct supervision and control" of Stalin. It is true also that Lenin's notes on Plekhanov's attitude toward the Bund, which had been omitted in previous editions, were restored. However, the anonymous authors of this letter deliberately cut the quotation short. Further on Lenin wrote: "All our arguments against these ***obscene speeches*** had no effect and G.V. firmly held his own, saying that we simply lacked knowledge of Jewry, lacked practical experience in dealing with Jews." [Emphasis added.]

77. The USSR Ministry of Health's Commission for Testing Personnel Performance, after considering this letter, declared journalists Bluvshteĭn, Pishchik, Reĭsner, and others unfit for duty and fired them from the *Medical Worker*. RTsKhIDNI, f. 17, op. 136, d. 463, l. 71–76, 79.

sanction to arrest the first group of Kremlin doctors.

Having enlisted the leader's support, Ryumin meanwhile acted slowly and circumspectly. First he took into custody those whom neither rank, name, or nomenclatura connections could defend: Drs. G.I. Maĭorov, A.N. Fedorov, and the retired LSUK director A.A. Busalov. The latter was caught by the long arms of the "organs" on September 28 while on holiday in Alushta. On October 18 a group of sullen people in civilian dress came for Professor Yegorov, who since 1947 had been the director of the Kremlin Hospital. Because he possessed the greatest amount of information, Ryumin could therefore count on him in his attempt to succeed in his investigation venture. Moreover, he had arrested the professor's wife, Ye.Ya. Yegorova, as far back as September 27, and following this insidious tactic he obtained compromising material on her husband by threatening her.

Meanwhile the arrested doctors, despite exhausting interrogations and threats from the investigators, did not hurry to "confess" to having conducted sabotaged treatment of Party, state, and military leaders. Such "ineffective" work on the part of the inquirers made Stalin furious. On October 18, 1952 he allowed the MGB leaders to use methods of physical coercion with the doctors. In order not to lose time by transporting them to the Lefortovo prison, an improvised mini-room for tortures was created at the office of the head of Lubyanka's internal prison. To demoralize and intimidate the arrested, this room was furnished with screens and tables reminiscent of dissection and operating rooms. Ryumin felt more confident once all these inquisition-like props were installed. Busalov later said that Ryumin once went to one of the interrogations and shouted at him from the entrance: "You're acting like a whore! You are a bandit, an ignoble spy, a terrorist, a dangerous state criminal. We fussed over you. It's enough now. We will torture you with a red-hot iron. We have all the necessary equipment for that. It will be too late when your corpse will be thrown down there," he said, pointing at the floor. "We will transfer you to the military prison, and they will interrogate you there!"[78]

But when Ryumin left, B.N. Kuzmin, the investigator who was interrogating Busalov, "calmed" the noticeably excited professor: "Don't worry. We don't torture with red-hot irons. But flogging is possible." This was not an idle threat. On November 18, 1952 Busalov was put in handcuffs and he endured 52 days with his hands tied behind his back. On December 10 he was wildly beaten with sticks in the office of the prison director.[79]

P.I. Yegorov was treated in a similar way. The investigators insisted that he confess not only to his saboteur activity as a doctor, but also to his espionage

78. Document from the archives of the former KGB.

79. Document from the archives of the former KGB.

connections with A.A. Kuznetsov, the former CC secretary who, in May 1947, transferred him to Moscow from his position as senior general practitioner of the Leningrad military district. After the beating, and after Ryumin threatened to torture him with two torches at the same time, he stopped resisting and slandered himself, confessing to crimes he had never committed. Ryumin was present at that moment, and scornfully pointed at the victim who had been thrown to the floor, exclaiming, "And just think, this fellow was the director of the LSUK. What a shame!"[80]

Yegorov was accused of having "disabled" M. Thorez; of having "killed" G. Dimitrov, A. Zhdanov, and A. Shcherbakov; and of having deprived of life and of having damaged the health of many other Soviet and foreign Communist leaders; as well as of having plotted against the family of the "leader of the peoples." He had allegedly impaired the well-being of Vasilií Stalin, who suffered from alcoholism and who had been his patient from 1948 through 1950 for a "nervous disorder." Further, Yegorov was accused of having entrusted Professor A.M. Markov, in the spring of 1950, with observing Svetlana Stalina, who was then pregnant. Yegorov, it was alleged, was unable to prevent the development of her toxicosis. She had premature delivery, and her daughter Katya was born weak.

Ryumin not only coached his torturers; he also dealt with issues that required him to make use of his limited intellectual abilities. On October 20, 1952 he summoned M.A. Sokolov, V.F. Chervakov, S.A. Gilyarovskií (professors of the Kremlin Hospital), and N.N. Kupysheva (deputy head of the MGB Central Polyclinic and major of the medical troops) to Lubyanka, and suggested they conduct an official investigation into the effectiveness of Shcherbakov's and Zhdanov's treatments. The doctors realized perfectly what they were expected to do, and soon prepared the necessary conclusion for the investigation.[81]

Ignatyev informed Stalin that these experts confirmed the "criminal treatments" of Shcherbakov, Zhdanov, and other Kremlin leaders. This ended Stalin's hesitation. Stalin now decided to undertake a step he had long ago conceived; namely, he would give the MGB autonomy to act as it wished with regard to the leaders and leading professors of the LSUK. In November all the cream of the medical elite was taken to Lubyanka, namely Professors V.N. Vinogradov, V.Kh. Vasilenko, M.S. Vovsi, B.B. Kagan. In December, the arresting machine brought to Lubyanka Professors A.M. Grinshteín, A.I. Feldman, and Ya. S. Temkin.

---

80. Document from the archives of the former KGB.

81. These same people later participated in other medical investigations. In particular, on November 21, 1952 they signed a medical affidavit about the sabotaged treatment administered to Zhdanov. In late March 1953 they and other "experts" recanted their previous conclusions, thus implying that the invesitgators had forced them to accuse the arrested doctors.

On November 4, when the MGB went for Vinogradov, its agents were surprised by the furniture in his apartment, which looked like a museum. The professor had been born into the provincial family of a modest railway employee; but before the revolution he had become rich, possessed his own prize horses in the hippodrome, and collected paintings and antiques. Vinogradov's walls were now decorated with the paintings of such first-class Russian masters as I.Ye. Repin, I.I. Shishkin, K.P. Bryullov, and others. During the search, diamonds and other jewelry, as well as American currency, were found in this hiding place.

On December 15 F.F. Talyzin, the director of the First Moscow Medical Institute, issued a decree "To dismiss the deputy chair of the Department of General Medicine, Professor Vinogradov V.N., from his position, as of November 5, 1952, for not showing up to work." This was despite the celebration at this institute, on October 21, of Vinogradov's 70th birthday and 45th anniversary of medical and scientific activity.

THE NEW STAGE OF THE INVESTIGATION IS BASED ON AN OLD CONCEPT

Despite such radical measures, the investigation progressed slowly, and, most importantly, it did not follow the direction that Stalin wanted it to follow. He was irritated by the indecisive Ignatyev, chief of the MGB, and with his thinking, which was that of a coarsened Party functionary. The leader was especially indignant that this "safe player" Ignatyev's constant attempts to inform Malenkov and other patrons of the CC apparatus about his actions behind Stalin's back. None of these people was at all happy with Ignatyev's insane venture of arresting the Kremlin doctors, and justifiably feared that they themselves might become Stalin's next victims. Ryumin, who constantly ordered Ignatyev about, also restrained his official ardor, as he was becoming increasingly worried about his future. Having learned from the sad experiences of Yezhov and Abakumov,[82] he did not want to find himself in the situation of the Moor who had completed his task; therefore, whenever possible, he dragged out the investigation that had been entrusted to him. Further, Ryumin possessed a quite rich imagination, but so long as Stalin attached great political significance to this case he would not go beyond primitive accusations of sabotaged treatments. His sick imagination was in a state of constant reflection, and he invented all manner of perfidious intrigues in which his close but treacherous comrades-in-arms allegedly participated together with the

---

82. It is known that after Yezhov (the people's commissar of internal affairs) completed the Great Purge of 1937–1938 Stalin ordered him to be shot. Stalin likewise wished to get rid of Abakumov, who was a dangerous witness, and ordered his arrest after the conclusion of the "Leningrad case." Beria and Malenkov had also dreamt of being rid of him. Malenkov could not forget that in 1946 Abakumov had attacked him by fabricating the so-called "aviation case."

foreign intelligence services. He imagined court plots similar to the one he had overcome before the war in 1938, namely, the case of the so-called Anti-Soviet Right Trotskyite Bloc.

During the show trial, N.I. Bukharin and A.I. Rykov (formerly high-ranking Party and state leaders), G.G. Yagoda (the people's commissar of internal affairs), and others were made to appear as leaders of that mythical underground organization. Their goal allegedly was to overthrow, with the help of Western espionage services, the Soviet regime; to restore capitalism; and to break the country apart by having the republics declare independence. According to this scenario, Yagoda—with the help of "doctor-poisoner" L.G. Levin (who worked as a consultant at the Kremlin Hospital), I.N. Kazakov (the director of the Institute of Metabolism and Endocrine Disorders), and D.D. Pletnev (professor of the Institute of Functional Diagnostics)[83]—carried out a "malicious killing" of the writer Maksim Gorkiĭ, his son M.A. Peshkov, as well as of the eminent Soviet political figures V.R. Menzhinskiĭ and V.V. Kuĭbyshev.

The dictator's intellect, which had never bristled with original ideas, was increasingly drawn toward the old-fashioned schemes of the great terror of the late 1930s. Starting from January 13, 1953 Soviet propaganda intensively used such clichés as "right opportunists," "enemies of people," "our success brings about the aggravation rather then the extinction of class struggle," which were borrowed from the prewar pogrom-style ideological arsenal. New only was the rank anti-Semitism that emanated from newspapers, magazines, and radio.

Perhaps, Stalin did not want to invent anything new, preferring only to make use of primitive but tried-and-true criminal themes in a somehow modernized way. It was enough merely to perform a simple extrapolation and replace the shot doctors Levin, Pletnev, and Kazakov with the professors Vinogradov, Vovsi, Kogan, and others. The role previously performed by Yagoda (the former people's commissar of internal affairs) was now to be played by the arrested minister of

83. In an attempt to demoralize Professor Dmitriĭ Pletnev, *Pravda* published an unsigned article entitled "Professor—Rapist, Sadist" (June 8, 1937). The article alleged that three years earlier, while examining B., a woman who had consulted him after recovering from typhus, Pletnev bit her on the breast. As a result B. developed chronic mastitis and "lost the ability to work, [and] became disabled as a result of the wound and of the severe emotional shock." The article caused a flow of angry letters from working people and a series of protest rallies and meetings in the medical community, stigmatizing their colleague's "barbarian" act. Among those who castigated Pletnev were the prominent medical scientists V.F. Zelenin, B.B. Kogan, E.M. Gelshteĭn, M.S. Vovsi, and others who were later arrested in 1952 and 1953 in connection with the "doctors' plot." V.N. Vinogradov, Pletnev's pupil, also played an unseemly role in Pletnev's case, having confirmed, as an expert, the indictment against Pletnev on charges of "sabotaged treatment methods." In the early 1950s Vinogradov, following the trail of his teacher, also ended up in a cell in the Lubyanka prison as a participant in the "doctors' plot." Pletnev was sentenced to 25 years in prison; however, on September 11, 1941, during Hitler's advance on Moscow, he was shot in the basement of the prison in Oryol.

state security Abakumov, whose case Stalin personally supervised. Kuíbyshev and Menzhinskií, the victims of the "perfidious terror," would be replaced by Shcherbakov and Zhdanov. And Bukharin and Rykov, the ringleaders of the defeated opposition, would be succeeded by the newly-fledged "plotters" Molotov, Mikoyan, and other high-ranking officials whom Stalin suspected.[84]

Obviously, the "assistant" of the ingenious Lubyanka director did all he could to carry out his project. On November 15, 1952 the investigators knocked the following confession out of Professor V.Kh. Vasilenko:

> . . . the trial on Pletnev's case . . . revealed for me the technique of killing patients by administering incorrect treatments. From the materials on the case I understood . . . that the doctor could not only damage his patient's health, but also lead the patient to death by cunning methods. I thought about this many times during the years that followed, remembering Pletnev, whom I personally knew. In July 1948, when I visited the ill Zhdanov at his bedside, I unwittingly remembered again Pletnev and his killings . . . . And I decided to kill Zhdanov A.A."[85]

THE CZECHOSLOVAKIAN VERSION

By that time Stalin had gained valuable experience from having organized, in late November 1952, a show trial of "the anti-state conspiracy center" in Czechoslovakia. Brought to the court in Prague were those who not so long before had been the cream of Czechoslovakia's ruling elite: R. Slansky (former general secretary of the CC CPC),[86] J. Frank (Slanskií's deputy), V. Klementis (former foreign minister), A. Simon (former editor of the *Rudé Právo* newspaper), other former heads of ministries and agencies. Rudolf Slansky,[87] a Jew, was considered the leader of the "conspiracy." He was charged

84. The Nineteenth Party Congress abolished the Politburo and replaced it with the newly-formed Bureau of the Presidium of the CC CPSU. Stalin's old comrades-in-arms, V.M. Molotov and A.I. Mikoyan, were not included as members. Not even Beria could feel secure. After Stalin had engineered the disclosure of the so-called Mingrelian nationalist organization in late 1951 and early 1952, Beria had every reason to suspect that he would be next on the list of the dictator's victims.

85. Document from the archives of the former KGB.

86. Central Committee of the Communist Party of Czechoslovakia.

87. Slansky was a fanatical but (as it turned out) shortsighted politician. As far back as February 1951 he wrote an appeal: "To expose and neutralize enemy agents; to cleanse the Party of subversive, saboteur, and hostile elements; to educate Party members in a spirit of revolutionary vigilance necessary to uncover the class enemy; to raise the ideological level of the Communists to a height from which they would be able to recognize any bourgeois-nationalistic deviations, so that they may be ruthless toward any kind of divergence from the Marx-Lenin line—these are the tasks of our Party at this moment of aggravation of the class struggle" (*Bolshevik*, no. 4, pp. 39–40). But Rudolf Slansky expressed more than his ideological loyalty to the Soviet Union. In May 1951 a letter from A.Ya. Vyshinskií (the minister of

with supporting and encouraging "the subversive activities of Zionists, those reliable agents of American imperialism," and also with "taking active steps to cut short the life of the republic's president, Klement Gottwald" by selecting "for his medical care doctors from enemy circles and of dubious backgrounds, and establishing close ties with them, planning to use them for his hostile plans."[88] Most of those convicted in Prague were executed with unprecedented brutality. On December 3, 1952 eleven people were hanged, their bodies burned, and their ashes dispelled in the air.

STALIN'S SPECTACULAR OFFERS ESPIONAGE AND TERROR

After his "general rehearsal" in Czechoslovakia, Stalin began working on the final preparations for a similar auto-da-fé. Taking into account the Soviet Union's immense size, though, this time it would probably be even more bloody and horrible. Displeased with the pace, results, and most importantly the direction of the investigation into the "doctors' case," Stalin first routed the MGB staff. On November 14, 1952 Ryumin, without being given any reason, was removed as vice minister of state security and sent as senior controller to the Ministry of State Control. At the same time Ignatyev was summoned to the Kremlin where he endured a stormy session with the leader, after which he suffered a heart attack and took to his bed, staying away from business for some time. On November 15 a new person was appointed to lead the investigation of the "doctors' case": S.A. Goglidze, the vice minister of state security, who since the 1930s had been notorious as the initiator of the political repression.[89] Beria appointed him people's commissar of internal affairs of Georgia, and under Beria's protection Goglidze saw his career skyrocket. (The truth is that it later collapsed just as quickly and unexpectedly on December 23, 1953, when they both were shot as a result of another intrigue during the struggle for power among the Soviet upper strata.)

Goglidze, vested with Stalin's trust and according to Stalin's directions, was rebuilding the investigation, guiding it toward unmasking the terrorist espionage

---

foreign affairs) to Malenkov disclosed the other side of Slansky's cooperation with the Kremlin. Vyshinskií wrote that on May 14, 1951, during a reception in honor of the Czechoslovakian leadership, P.P. Razygrayev (the general consul of the USSR in Bratislava), being drunk, declared to V. Široký (the Czechoslovakian minister of foreign affairs), "Vilem, you're not a minister; you're Stalin's agent." Later the drunk diplomat, amidst his foul language, told Široký about those in the Czechoslovakian leadership who were informants for the Soviet Embassy in Prague: R. Slansky, B. Geminder (the head of the International Department of the CC secretariat of the Communist Party of Czechoslovakia), and others. After this incident, Razygrayev was immediately recalled to Moscow.

88. *Pravda*, November 21, 1952.

89. Document from the archives of the former KGB.

organization that the Western special services had allegedly established in the USSR by involving the Kremlin doctors. The employees of the Department to Investigate Cases of Special Importance to the MGB were given hints that Stalin expected decisive actions from them directed toward the unmasking of the enemy's plans—and that their methods of attaining this goal were not important, but that their results would be. On behalf of the "instance"[90] it was directly declared that it was not possible to work in the MGB organs "wearing white gloves, and remaining clean." Goglidze insisted his subjects stop "fussing over" the arrested and act as "truly revolutionary investigators."[91]

Stalin, however, did not limit himself to studying only the general directions. The daily minutes of the doctors' interrogations were delivered to him, and he read them attentively. He now not only determined the design of the investigation, but also undertook concrete steps to redirect it to the necessary course. Thus in the November 18, 1952 minutes concerning Professor V.N. Vinogradov, accused in regard to the "doctor's case," appeared the following "statement of the investigation":[92]

> We have received an instruction from the leadership to inform you that you could be hanged for the crimes you have committed, but that you may save your life and be given a chance to continue working if you tell us the truth about the origins of your crimes, about who directed you, who your bosses were, and who your allies were. We are also committed to let you know that if you decide to confess everything, you may address your testimony to the leader, who promises to save your life should you sincerely confess all your crimes and unmask your allies. The whole world knows that our leader has always kept his promises.[93]

G.Ye. Zinovyev, L.B. Kamenev, and other leaders of the former opposition had experienced the worth of such promises. They believed Stalin's promise to save their lives in exchange for confessions of guilt in mythical anti-Soviet crimes. They were shot in 1936.

But this old perfidious method did not work with Vinogratov. Having lived a life full of tragic trials, he did not have any naïve illusions with respect to the Bolshevik leaders' loyalty to their promises. Shocked by the statement read to him, the old professor kept silent. "Why are you silent?" asked Colonel Sokolov, who

---

90. *Translator's note:* In other words, on behalf of Stalin.

91. Document from the archives of the former KGB.

92. This "statement of the investigation" was shown to Professor Vasilenko on November 16, 1952. Document from the archives of the former KGB.

93. *Pravda*, November 21, 1952.

was conducting the investigation. "My situation is tragic; I have nothing to say," replied Vinogradov. He then added firmly, "I never served foreigners, nobody ever directed me to commit a crime, and I never involved anyone in any crimes."[94]

Such stubbornness did not ruffle the investigator, especially as he had prepared for his interlocutor a quite unpleasant surprise. Dr. G.I. Maíorov, broken by threats and tortures, was waiting next door, and he was ready to accuse his teacher of all manner of deadly sins. Immediately as he was escorted into the entrance of the room, he robotically delivered a phrase he had rehearsed the day before: "Professor Vinogradov involved me in the crimes." "And who did Vinogradov work for?" Sokolov asked. "For the Americans, undoubtedly," came the reply.

The investigator looked searchingly at Vinogradov, anticipating the result of this provocation. But Vinogradov, not without malicious irony, said, "Maíorov slanders me, declaring that I worked for the Americans. He should rather call me a German spy, because I sympathized with Germans, was an adherent of the German school, visited Germany, where the scholars gave me a warm reception . . . ."[95]

Driven into a fury by such insolence, the investigator ordered that the professor immediately be taken to the office of the head of the internal prison. There the unfortunate wretch was viciously beaten and cursed. The beatings continued for three days, and were so refined and terrible that they caused a severe bout of stenocardia, and the traces from the beatings persisted for six weeks. Vinogradov was put in handcuffs for several days and told that his legs would be shackled if he resisted. Professors Vasilenko, Vovsi, Kogan, and other arrested doctors were also beaten, handcuffed for several days, and subjected to other humiliations.[96] Vinogradov, finding himself on the edge of life and death, yielded to the importunities of the torturer and signed the prepared "confession" about his terrorist espionage activity.

According to the investigator's vulgar and clumsy story, Vinogradov, who, unlike his Kremlin colleagues, had enjoyed the confidence of the highest Soviet leadership and had treated Stalin himself, was the key figure in the doctor's plot, upon whom the realization of the main plans of the foreign special services depended. Later, during the investigation of Vinogradov and other arrested doctors, this premise was coated with a whimsical symbiosis of fabrications and jumbled facts. On the basis of "proofs" thus obtained, the MGB claimed that Vinogradov had been recruited, as far back as late 1936, by the "English spy" M.B. Kogan, who worked at the LSUK from 1934 as a consulting professor. It

94. Document from the archives of the former KGB.

95. Document from the archives of the former KGB.

96. Document from the archives of the former KGB.

became known that this "old-time intelligence-service agent" had in 1917 been a member of the Jewish Socialist Labor Party, and that he had known Mikhoels, Fefer, Shimeliovich and other JAC leaders quite well. Further, he had treated V.M. Molotov; and since 1944 had been P.S. Zhemchuzhina's personal physician, accompanying her in the autumn of 1948 on her trip to the Karlovy Vary resort. After being tortured at several interrogations, Vinogradov "confessed" that M.B. Kogan, up to his death from cancer on November 26, 1951, had insisted that Vinogradov inform him of the health and circumstances of Stalin's family and the families of other leaders whom he treated.

According to the primitive conjecture of the investigation, the duties of Vinogradov's "curator" were over the next few years passed on to Professor M.I. Pevzner, the director of the Clinic of Remedial Nutrition of the USSR Academy of Medical Sciences. This was allegedly done on the basis of a "secret order from London." Apparently Pevzner, during a trip to Karlsbad in the early 1930s, was ensnared by an espionage trap skillfully placed by his relative, a certain Mendel Berlin, a British citizen born in Russia. Later, according to the same scenario (retrospectively written in Lubyanka), M. Berlin's brother was "placed" in Pevzner's clinic in order to control the latter directly, and to serve as a liaison with the British intelligence agent resident in Moscow. Thus did the medical professor L.B. Berlin, a Soviet citizen, begin his work there as a department head. In December 1945 L.B. Berlin had met his brother Mendel's son, Isaí, who had moved to Moscow as second secretary of the British embassy. Through Isaí, L.B. Berlin established a regular delivery of classified information abroad. Thus was the channel of espionage communication begun. During its first phase, the chain was V.N. Vinogradov to M.B. Kogan to M.I. Pevzner to L.B. Berlin to Isaí Berlin. Upon the death of M.B. Kogan in 1951, Vinogradov contacted Pevzner directly. This was even more convenient, as Pevzner was a member of the *General Medical Archives*[97] journal's editorial board, which Vinogradov headed.[98]

In order at least somehow to support this myth, L.B. Berlin was on December 10, 1952 moved from the Taíshetsk camp to Moscow. On December 14, at the first interrogation there, the investigators Sokolov and Panteleyev accused him of having concealed from the previous investigation his espionage activity, and declared in plain terms that they would take physical measures if he did not confess to transmitting information from Vinogradov to his nephew Isaí.

Berlin refused to slander himself and Vinogradov. Consequently he was taken to the office of the director of the internal prison, where people were subjected to four-day beatings. But this did not help. Berlin courageously continued to undergo tortures. He was then transferred to the Lefortovo prison, to be "worked

97. *Terapevticheskiĭ arkhiv.*

98. Document from the archives of the former KGB.

on" more seriously. There he was subjected to tortures so refined that he several times attempted suicide. He was then placed in handcuffs for several days. His resistance finally broke and he testified to his cooperation with British intelligence, starting from the day of recruitment in 1926 up through his arrest in 1952. Berlin was in prison for over one year. He was released on February 4, 1954 according to a resolution of the minister of internal affairs, S.N. Kruglov.

Apart from Vinogradov, the investigation also classified Kremlin Hospital professors P.I. Yegorov, V.Kh. Vasilenko, A.A. Busalov, V.F. Zelenin, and others as British intelligence agents. Zelenin, arrested on January 25, 1953, testified that from 1925 up through the beginning of the war he had been a devoted agent of German intelligence. He received his espionage tasks directly from the "Jewish nationalist" professor M.S. Vovsi.[99]

When the investigation confronted Vovsi, the "ringleader of Zionists who entrenched themselves in the Soviet medicine," with this absurd accusation of spying in favor of Nazi Germany, he noted with bitterness, "You have made me a agent of two intelligence services, but don't ascribe the German one; my father and brother's family were killed by the fascists in Dvinsk during the war." "Don't speculate on the blood of your relatives," came the cynical reply.[100]

Since Vovsi, whom the Jews called "wise Meyer," was S.M. Mikhoels's cousin, he was also accused of postwar cooperation with the American intelligence services. On the night of November 11, 1952, immediately after his arrest, Vovsi, the former senior general practitioner of the Red Army and editor-in-chief of the *Clinical Medicine* journal,[101] was required to confess how he received orders from his "bosses overseas." No stone was left unturned, and an exhausting and extensive interrogation, handcuffs, and threats (such as "We'll quarter you, hang you, impale you") followed.[102]

From November 21, 1952 the professor was left powerless, and like an automaton he obediently started to sign all the minutes fabricated by the investigation. All these minutes contained a persistent and paranoid idea about the leading and guiding role of American (i.e., Zionist) organizations and intelligence services in creating the doctors' plot. The first item of overseas influence on this story was Mikhoels's return from his propagandistic tour of the USA. In the autumn of 1946 he called Vovsi to his apartment on Tverskoí Boulevard and allegedly asked him to fight to keep key positions in science, technology, and arts

---

99. Document from the archives of the former KGB.

100. *Moskovskiye novosti* (*Moscow News*), February 7, 1988

101. Vovsi remained as editor-in-chief until May 1952. Afterwards and until his arrest he held only one staff position: chair of a department at the Central Institute of Advanced Medical Studies.

102. Document from the archives of the former KGB; A.N. Yakovlev, ed., *Reabilitatsiya. Politicheskiye protsessy 30—50-x godov* [*Rehabilitation: Political Processes of the 1930s through the 1950s*] (Moscow: Politizdat, 1991), p. 513.

in the hands of Jews. Mikhoels also allegedly gave Vovsi the concrete task of agitating in favor of Jewish personnel in Soviet medicine. As this primitive story had it, Vovsi was then forced to "recall" that at the Botkin Hospital in 1947 he had met with Professor B.A. Shimeliovich, who told him about the directive from Joint in the USA regarding a large-scale operation to damage the health of executive Soviet and Party workers. Vovsi was also forced to say that Shimeliovich had acted not as a mere individual, but as a JAC representative.

According to the investigation, Professor B.B. Kogan (M.B. Kogan's brother) and Professor Ya.S. Temkin became Vovsi's close allies. They testified that as far back as 1946 they had organized, with Vovsi's approval, a criminal group and deemed it necessary to form a solidarity with American and world Jewry, and discussed the possibility of using foreign Jewish assistance for their purposes. The "truth" was that they at first decided to act carefully and to observe cautiously the rule of security, damaging their nomenclatura patients gradually, mainly by establishing incorrect diagnoses and treatments. A heart-rending story was invented to verify this mythical plan. Vovsi and B.B. Kogan at different times treated G.M. Dimitrov, who suffered from a number of chronic illnesses (such as diabetes, emphysema, and arteriosclerosis). In this story, the two doctors deliberately, and in cahoots with other "doctor-saboteurs," concealed the rapid development of a more severe disease, cirrhosis, from which Dimitrov died in 1949.[103] The investigation fabricated many similar "facts."

Until 1949 Vovsi had been senior general practitioner of the Military Ministry of the USSR, and as such consulted such Soviet military commanders as F.I. Tolbukhin, I.S. Konev, L.A. Govorov, A.M. Vasilevskiĭ, G.I. Levchenko, Ya.N. Fedorenko, and others. Now he was depicted as a saboteur in a white coat who, in performing his task, undermined from within the intellectual capacity of the Soviet Armed Forces. The MGB ascribed to him an outstanding organizational ability, alleging that under his supervision Professors A.M. Grinshtein, A.I. Feldman, and B.S. Preobrazhenskiĭ, Dr. G.I. Maĭorov, and others who treated A.A. Andreyev "had deliberately disabled" this high-ranking Party figure and agricultural expert. Further, because of his severe headaches and insomnia, these doctors had, since 1947, permitted Andreyev to take, along with large dosages of sleeping pills, cocaine. Thus there was nothing to prove; "the sabotaged" treatment was self-evident. The investigation ignored one detail: in 1951 Andreyev's condition improved and he stopped taking the drug.

The investigators' imaginations grew from interrogation to interrogation. In time they grew bored with fabrications and could no longer relish the terrifying details of the doctors' intrigues regarding G. Dimitrov, A. Andreyev and other Party and state nomenclatura. The rules of the detective genre required that the

---

103. Document from the archives of the former KGB.

Lubyanka authors each time produce an even greater unmasking and ever more provocative facts. The minutes of the interrogations were sent to the "nearby" dacha[104] of the main inspirer of this creation. In these minutes Vovsi and B.B. Kogan claimed that in July 1952, already expelled from the Kremlin Hospital, they agreed to direct all their efforts to killing Stalin, Beria, and especially Malenkov, whom they considered the main inspiration of the anti-Semitic policies. The main executor of this "devil's" plot was Vinogradov, who continued working at the LSUK. However, the cunning plan of the doctor-terrorists was not to be carried out. According to the investigation's primitive and naïve story, it was firstly the inability of the "plotters" fully to agree among themselves that foiled the plan. In August Vovsi had gone on holiday. Upon returning to Moscow he could not meet with Vinogradov, who by then had gone on holiday himself, and was soon to be arrested. The document emphasized that this unexpected turn of events, coupled with decisive moves by the Chekas, put Vovsi and his allies into a hysterical rage. In response, they allegedly decided to plan an armed attack on government cars in the Arbat area. But here again, the vigilant organs were on their toes and at the most critical moment arrested the criminals, thus eliminating the threat to the security of the leader and his comrades-in-arms.[105]

THE OLD COMRADES-IN-ARMS UNDER SUSPICION

It is difficult to say today whether Stalin himself believed all these ravings. However, there is no doubt that he trusted his closest circles less and less all the time. So when he was shown, together with the materials mentioned above, L.F. Timashuk's testimony concerning Major General N.S. Vlasik's indifference in 1948 toward evidence of the incorrect treatments prescribed for Zhdanov, the dictator felt seriously threatened. Advancing arteriosclerosis dulled his memory, and he apparently did not remember that he had already read Timashuk's letter four years earlier and had sent it to the archives. Stalin was indignant that someone he trusted completely, and who for more than 20 years had served as his personal body guard, was now demoralized by unbridled drunkenness and debauchery, and that this person, having lost his flair for vigilance against the enemy, had embarked upon the path of betrayal.

But if Vlasik could reprimand himself at all, it would be for his lack of initiative in not having personally undertaken an inquiry into the facts Timashuk

104. Stalin had a number of houses in the Moscow suburbs, as well as a large number of luxurious mansions in the Crimea and the Caucasus; but he spent most of his time in this so-called "nearby" dacha, in Kuntsevo, where he actually lived and later died.

105. Document from the archives of the former KGB.

had supplied. He trusted entirely the opinion of Kremlin Hospital director P.I. Yegorov, whom he knew quite well as their families were on friendly terms. The truth is that when Abakumov was arrested in summer of 1951 and the investigation on the "doctors' plot" started, Vlasik sensed the danger and confiscated from Yegorov all the documents relating to the examination of Timashuk's letter. However, the old guard was not able this time to come out unscathed. Later, upon his arrest, Yegorov was forced to confess:

> There is no doubt that if Abakumov and Vlasik had conducted the necessary inspection of Timashuk's statement right after its reception, then we, the enemies guilty of Zhdanov's death, would have been unmasked back in 1948.[106]

Stalin then ordered A.N. Poskrebyshev to investigate Vlasik's role in relation to Timashuk's letter and, first of all, to locate her letter in the archives.

Meanwhile, the dictator's feverish brain continued to create ominous pictures of a global terrorist plot for his physical elimination. Those who inspired and initiated the plot were, of course, imperialist intelligence services that used nationalistically-minded Jews to penetrate all the vital spheres of Soviet society—including the medical institutions that provided care for the highest echelons—to carry out their goals. Having subjected to their influence the most authoritative Russian doctors—firstly those who were of bourgeois origin and hostile to Soviet power—the Western special services began to eliminate Party and state leaders, each time getting closer to the very "leader of the peoples." But the "killer-doctors," according to Stalin, were just one tentacle of the giant espionage octopus, whose head consisted of yet-to-be unmasked high-ranking traitors who were firmly entrenched in the CC apparatus, the USSR Council of Ministers, and the MGB. By "cleansing" the power structure of so-called Leningraders, and by arresting Abakumov and his creature at Lubyanka, the "plotters" suffered a noticeable blow. But the dictator would not rush to celebrate his victory.

Some of those whom Stalin had not long before considered his comrades-in-arms (Molotov, suspected of espionage in favor of Americas; and Mikoyan, allegedly recruited by the British) were not yet defeated in the government. In October 1952, after the Nineteenth Party Congress, Stalin did not include them in the Bureau of the Presidium of the CC of the CPSU (the successor to the old Politburo). Thus distancing himself from them he prepared to deal with them when convenient. And now on top of this there suddenly arose the suspicious story about Vlasik.

Poskrebyshev finally found Timashuk's letter in one of the archive folders and

---

106. Document from the archives of the former KGB.

showed it to Stalin. The dictator was somehow bewildered when he saw on it a statement he himself had written: "Send to archives." However, he quickly recovered himself, ordered his assistant to hold his tongue, and decided that he would carry out his preconceived plan all the same. As had happened many times in the past, the Kremlin schemer was once again going to place the responsibility on one of the scapegoats and, by shuffling the facts, gain the maximum benefit from the situation.

Stalin summoned a meeting of the Bureau of the CC Presidium on December 1, 1952, and there declared that in 1948 Abakumov and Vlasik had concealed from the Soviet leadership, and from him personally, an important document that exposed the plot to kill Zhdanov. Exerting an influence upon his audience as a boa would upon a rabbit, the dictator began to frighten it: it was not only Zhdanov but all the Soviet leadership (excepting perhaps Molotov and Mikoyan, who were suspected of espionage) that were to have died at the hands of "the killers in white coats." Supporting this revelation were the confessions from the arrested doctors who, on Stalin's orders, had beforehand been sent to those who were not yet "victims of the medical terror," i.e. to Malenkov, Khrushchev, and other high-ranking leaders. Assuming the role of the rescuer of his careless and foolish comrades-in-arms, Stalin concluded with a feeling of triumphant superiority: "You are blind, kitties. What will happen without me is that the country will die, because you can't recognize your enemies."[107]

As a result of the provocative action he so skillfully carried out, on December 4 a CC CPSU resolution, aimed at exterminating the "sabateur activity in the medicine," was approved. As could be expected, the main responsibility for the extensive and unpunished activity of the "doctor-poisoners" fell upon Abakumov and Vlasik, who by relaxing their vigilance had indulged the saboteurs. The resolution also removed Ye.I. Smirnov from his post as USSR minister of health care, as he had allegedly pandered to his criminal colleagues and "joined them on the basis of alcoholism . . . . " In February 1953 he was replaced by A.F. Tretyakov.

As had been planned long before, Vlasik, already dismissed from work, was arrested on December 15, 1954. His trial was held on January 17, 1955. As the "doctor-saboteurs" had been rehabilitated by that time, he could not be accused of concealing their criminal intentions. Nonetheless, the trial revealed other sins of this bon vivant (plunder, official abuse as a result of immoral behavior, divulging secret documents, etc.). This was enough for the investigation to sentence him to five years of exile.

---

107. Document from the archives of the former KGB.

THE "CASE" GROWS INTO A POLITICAL ACTION

To make the CC equally responsible for the consequences of his adventurist course, Stalin even sacrificed his beloved child, the MGB, preparing for it the role of the scapegoat. It was most likely no coincidence that on December 4, 1952, along with a resolution "On the Saboteur Activity in Medicine," the CC also approved a resolution "On the Situation in the MGB," which pointed out the necessity of "decisively putting a halt to the lack of control in the work of the MGB organs, and placing its work in the central and local organizations under systematic and constant Party control."[108] Thus assuring himself of support from the Party's upper strata, Stalin elevated "the doctors' case" into a large political action and began to prepare the entire country's involvement in it.

On January 9, 1953 the Bureau of the CC CPSU Presidium met to discuss a draft of the TASS announcement about the arrest of the "saboteur-doctors." Bureau members L.P. Beria, N.A. Bulganin, K.Ye. Voroshilov, L.M. Kaganovich, G.M. Malenkov, M.G. Pervukhin, M.Z. Saburov, and N.S. Khrushchev were present. Along with them were CC secretaries A.B. Aristov, L.I. Brezhnev, N.G. Ignatov, N.A. Mikhaílov, N.M. Pegov, P.K. Ponomarenko, M.A. Suslov, as well as M.F. Shkiryatov (the head of the CC CPSU Committee of Party Control), D.T. Shepilov (now the editor of *Pravda*), and S.I. Ogoltsov and S.A. Goglidze (the deputy ministers of state security).[109] It is interesting that among those invited we do not see S.D. Ignatyev, the minister of state security. Stalin was dissatisfied with him and often openly castigated him for his "failures" regarding the "doctors' case." (Ignatyev was at the time so upset that he fell ill.) Even more remarkable is that Stalin unexpectedly backed out of participating in this meeting himself,[110] even though he had gathered his Kremlin coworkers just one day earlier to read them Timashuk's 1948 letter.[111] Judging from his insidious nature, one may suspect that he not only wanted to avoid any responsibility for engineering the "doctors' case," but that he also wanted, if necessary, to blame it on those who participated at the meeting.[112]

---

108. *Izvestiya TsK KPSS*, 1991, no, 2, p. 204.

109. Document from the archives of the president of the Russian Federation.

110. Stalin's name stood first among the original list of participants in this meeting, but later his name was crossed out and next to it, in brackets, appeared a note: "Did not attend" (Document from the archives of the president of the Russian Federation).

111. N.S. Khrushchev, "Vospominaniya," *Voprosy istorii*, 1991, no. 12, pp. 69–70.

112. The Bureau of the CC Presidium passed a resolution on January 9, 1953, protocol number 7 of which read: "To approve the draft of the announcement in press about the arrest of the group of saboteur-doctors and to publish it together with *Pravda*'s article on this matter." This resolution was signed "Bureau of the Presidium of the CC CPSU" instead of the usual "Secretary of the CC, I. Stalin." This further speaks in favor of this hypothesis (Document from the archives of the president of the Russian Federation).

PROPAGANDISTIC ACCOMPANIMENT

In view of the upcoming court hearings on the "doctors' case" there immediately began a vigorous preparation for a large-scale propagandistic campaign to brainwash the public. M.A. Suslov, D.T. Shepilov (editor-in-chief of *Pravda*), D.I. Chesnokov (head of the Department of the CC),[113] and N.A. Mikhaílov (appointed secretary of the CC CPSU and head of Agitprop at the Nineteenth Party Congress) played the leading roles in this endeavor, which was carried out in the spirit of political trials of the 1930s. Even among the Party hierarchy, with its generally low intellectual level, Mikhaílov was distinguished for his narrow-mindedness, made worse by an almost pathological ambition and arrogance. (This was characteristic, by the way, of many functionaries who came to Old Square from the CC of the Komsomol, the most amoral school of Soviet careerism.) Mikhaílov's promotion came after the Nineteenth Congress, as Stalin, who was then fighting against his old guard, gambled on the new generation for the political leadership. The most important landmarks in Mikhaílov's career were his appointments, in the midst of the bloody purges of the 1930s, as editor-in-chief of the *Komsomol Pravda* (1937)[114] and as the first secretary of the CC ALCUY (1938). After the war he actively joined the fight against "stateless" cosmopolitans and took an extremely firm stand on it. The documents he signed and submitted to the CC ACP(b) were openly anti-Semitic in nature. It is most likely because of this, rather than his mediocre talents, that Mikhaílov won Stalin's sympathy and belonged for several months, until the dictator's death, to

113. According to rumors that circulate among Jews to this day, Chesnokov authored at Stalin's request a document that theoretically grounded the necessity of forcibly deporting the Soviet Jews to the east. The first edition of this book was supposedly printed in February 1953 and stored in the basements of Lubyanka, awaiting the "X" day. At the appointed moment this literature would be quickly distributed throughout the country. (See for example Z.S. Sheínis, *Provokatsiya veka* [*Provocation of the Century*] (Moscow: PIK Independent Publishing House, 1992), pp. 106–107.)

How true this rumor was is difficult to say now. Chesnokov published his dull article on Stalin's speech at the Nineteenth Congress in the second January 1953 issue of *Kommunist*. In it he sharply attacked "the professor-physicians, hirelings of the imperialist investigation, cannibals who masked, with the honorable word *physician*, their loathsome faces of killers and spies" (p. 20). It was possibly an aberration here as well that made the author of this article appear to be the creator of a mythical brochure that justified the deportation of Jews.

114. Mikhaílov replaced in this post V.M. Bubekin, who was arrested as an "old Trotskyite." At about the same time, Mikhaílov proposed that Jews take Russian pen names. For example, Perets Markish would sign his poems "Pyotr Markov." Markish's brother-in-law, A.E. Lazebnikov, who then worked at the *Komsomol Pravda* (he was arrested in May 1938), remembered that in early September 1937 the CC sent a secret instruction on this matter to the editorial boards of the central periodicals. As Pevzner, who was then the head of *Pravda*'s Party Department, explained to Lazebnikov, Stalin and his circle had decided on this in reaction to Hitler's claim at one of the Nuremberg rallies that several high-ranking Soviet politicians demonstrated that Soviet Bolshevism was of a "Jewish nature." E. Markish, *Stol' dolgoye vozvrashcheniye*... (Tel-Aviv: 1989), p. 99; *Sovyetskaya kul'tura*, June 16, 1988.

the top level of the Party nomenclatura.

On January 13, 1953 TASS published its announcement under the title "The Arrest of the Group of Saboteur-Doctors":[115]

> Some time ago state security agencies discovered a terrorist group of doctors who had made it their aim to cut short the lives of active public figures of the Soviet Union through sabotaging medical treatment.
>
> Among the participants in this terrorist group there proved to be: M.S. Vovsi, general practitioner; Professor V.N. Vinogradov, general practitioner; Professor M.B. Kogan, general practitioner; Professor B.B. Kogan, general practitioner; Professor P.I. Yegorov, general practitioner; Professor A.I. Feldman, otolaryngologist; Professor Ya.G. Etinger, general practitioner; Professor A.M. Grinshteín, neuropathologist; G.I. Maíorov, general practitioner.
>
> Documentary evidence, investigations, conclusions of medical experts, and the confessions of those arrested have established that the criminals, who were secret enemies of the people, sabotaged the treatment of patients, undermining their health.
>
> Investigation established that the participants of the terrorist group, taking advantage of their positions as doctors and abusing the trust of patients, by deliberately evil intent undermined their health, knowingly ignored the data of objective medical examinations, made incorrect diagnoses that did not correspond to the true nature of their illnesses, and then doomed them by incorrect treatments.
>
> The criminals confessed that, taking advantage of Comrade A.A. Zhdanov's ailment, incorrectly diagnosing his illness, and concealing his myocardial infarction, they prescribed a regimen counter-indicated for this serious illness and thereby killed Comrade A.A. Zhdanov. Investigation established that the criminals likewise cut short the life of Comrade A.S. Shcherbakov by incorrectly employing strong drugs in his treatment, prescribing a damaging regimen, and thus causing his death.
>
> The criminal doctors sought above all to undermine the health of top Soviet military personnel, to put them out of action, thus weakening the country's defense. They sought to put out of action Marshal A.M. Vasilevskií, Marshal L.A. Govorov, Marshal I.S. Konev, Army General S.M. Shtemenko, Admiral G.I. Levchenko, and others; but arrest disrupted their evil plans and the criminals did not succeed in attaining their aim.
>
> It has been established that all these killer-doctors—these monsters in human form, trampling the holy banner of science and

115. "Arest gruppy vracheí-vreditelií."

> desecrating the honor of the man of science—were hired agents of foreign intelligence services.
>
> Most of the participants in the terrorist group (M.S. Vovsi, B.B. Kogan, A.I. Feldman, A.M. Grinshteĭn, Ya.G. Etinger, and others) had ties with the international Jewish bourgeois nationalist organization Joint, established by American intelligence services for the alleged purpose of providing material aid to Jews in other countries. The true purpose of this organization is to conduct extensive terrorist and other subversive activities in a number of countries, including the Soviet Union, under the guidance of American intelligence services. The arrested Vovsi told investigators that he had received instructions "to exterminate the leading cadres of the USSR" from the USA through the Joint organization, via Shimeliovich, a doctor in Moscow, and the notorious Jewish bourgeois nationalist Mikhoels.
>
> Other participants in the terrorist group (V.N. Vinogradov, M.B. Kogan, P.I. Yegorov) proved to be longtime agents of the English intelligence service.
>
> The investigation will be completed in the nearest future.
>
> —(TASS).[116]

Simultaneously, the central newspapers *Pravda* and *Izvestiya* published front-page articles commenting (if one can call their hysteric cries comments) on the TASS announcement; other newspapers soon followed suit. Newspaper offices had received orders to prepare these articles beforehand, and accompanying these orders were corresponding materials with especially persistent instructions to utilize the documents of the Great Purge of 1937 and 1938. Stalin directed and participated in the writing of a *Pravda* editorial entitled "Ignoble Spies and Killers Under the Mask of Professor-Doctors." Here Stalin made use of the old prewar demagogic rhetoric about the intrigues of external and internal enemies of the Soviet state growing as the construction of socialism progressed. He attacked the MGB organs and the Ministry of Health leaders who "became scatterbrained" and were unable to neutralize the terrorist-doctors' organization in time. Khrushchev's son-in-law, Alekseĭ Adzhubeĭ, who was then working for the *Komsomol Pravda*, later said that his front-page article, "To Be Clear-Sighted and Vigilant,"[117] was based on precisely these sorts of materials.[118] The Glavlit leaders soon found themselves also mired in the situation. On January 13 they approached Old Square with a request for a sanction to withdraw from libraries and bookstores the works of the "doctor-saboteurs," as well as M. Zagorskiĭ's book on *Mikhoels*.[119]

---

116. *Pravda*, January 13, 1953.

117. "Byt' zorkim i bditel'nym," *Komsomolskaya pravda*, January 15, 1953.

118. A. Adzhubeĭ, "Te desyat' let" ("Those Ten Years"), *Znamya* (*Flag*), 1988, no. 6, pp. 105, 106.

119. GARF: f. 9425 sch., op. 1, d. 830, l. 1.

All this indicated that Mikhaĭlov's Agitprop conducted a thorough and methodical preparation for the campaign of badgering "saboteur doctors." Taking advantage of the opportunity that life—or rather Stalin—had given him to strengthen his position at the Kremlin Olympus, he did not miss a single chance to proclaim his pogrom-like stand. Speaking at an annual V.I. Lenin memorial meeting on January 21, Mikhaĭlov cited, from a *Pravda* editorial, words that were certainly authored by Stalin:

> But there still survived in our midst remnants of bourgeois ideology, remnants of the psychology and morals of private owners—*living people,* hidden enemies of our people. These hidden enemies, supported by the imperialist world, have been involved in sabotage and will in the future be involved in sabotage against us. Convincing evidence of this is the case of the saboteur-doctors—foul spies and murderers, disguised as doctors, who have sold themselves to the slave-owner-cannibals from the USA and England. [Emphasis in the original.][120]

It seems likely that Stalin, via Mikhaĭlov's Agitprop, decided to make extensive propagandistic use of Lidiya Timashuk. She was summoned to the Kremlin on January 20, 1953 where Malenkov personally told her that Stalin offered her his official thanks for the "great courage" she had shown in 1948 when she had "stood against the prominent professors who treated A.A. Zhdanov . . . defending her opinion as a doctor regarding the patient."[121] The next day the newspapers printed the decree of the Presidium of the Supreme Soviet: "For helping the government disclose the killer-doctors, Dr. Lidiya Fedoseyevna Timashuk is awarded the Order of Lenin."[122] Within a few days the name of this humble doctor from the Kremlin Hospital became known throughout the country.

The regime demanded that the press and radio implant in the people's minds the image of a national heroine, a new Joan of Arc, who shattered the cabal of evil forces and thus saved the country and its leaders from impending doom. The journalist who approached this project with the greatest fervor was Olga Chechetkina. She had formerly worked under N. Mikhaĭlov at the CC ALCUY and then at the *Komsomol Pravda.* Finally, in March 1949, she worked at *Pravda* as an editor in the Foreign Information Department. As she often went abroad, the Soviet secret service monitored her and knew everything about her, right down to her friendship with Jean L., a Frenchman and member of the National

---

120. *Pravda,* January 22, 1953.

121. Document from the archives of the president of the Russian Federation.

122. *Pravda,* January 21, 1953.

Bureau of the Union of Youth of the French Republic. Chechetkina had met him in 1946 when visiting Paris as representative of the Soviet Youth Antifascist Committee at the editorial offices of the World Federation of Democratic Youth.[123]

On February 20, 1953 *Pravda* published Chechetkina's article on "Lidiya Timashuk's Mail," where glorification of the latter reached its highest point:

> Until recently we did not know this woman . . . now Dr. Lidiya Fedoseyevna Timashuk's name has become the symbol of Soviet patriotism, of the utmost vigilance, of the relentless and courageous struggle against the enemies of our motherland. She helped tear the mask off the American hirelings, the monsters who used the doctor's white smock to medically murder Soviet people. The news that L.F. Timashuk was granted the highest award, the Order of Lenin, for helping to unmask the thrice-cursed killer-doctors spread all over our country. Lidiya Fedoseyevna became near and dear to millions of Soviet people.

The propagandistic hysteria caused a two-fold reaction among everyday people: On the one hand it caused aggressiveness, the urge to punish the "murderers" in white smocks; on the other hand it caused a panicky fear, an animal fear of them. Combined with anti-Semitism this was a truly explosive mixture, arousing vulgar destructive instincts among the ignorant "Philistine" masses. Persecution of Jews, whom propaganda labeled "monsters in human form" like Hollywood's Dr. Frankenstein, was on the rise everywhere, not only in medicine.

THE REACTION TO THE PERSECUTION

As a result of the persecution, the consciousness of those who were persecuted brimmed over with all manner of gloomy presentiments. Here, for instance, is well known theater administrator I.V. Nezhnyi's evaluation of the events, and in particular of the January 13, 1953 TASS announcement:

---

123. The romance between the young Soviet journalist and the son of the French miner was so passionate that rumors of it reached the ears of the high officers at Old Square. The truth is that Chechetkina made little effort to conceal her ardor. The administration was terrified by her license when she openly declared that she wanted to marry Jean L. In September 1947 she wrote in a letter to Moscow that: "I love this man as one can love only once." However, there was an insuperable obstacle in her way, namely, Stalin's 1947 decree prohibiting marriages between Soviet and foreign citizens. Despite her numerous requests to extend her stay abroad, Chechetkina was urgently recalled to the Soviet Union and transferred to a different place of work. To underscore this sad story, one regrets that the state not only prohibited its citizens from loving, but forced them to hate.

> . . . The initiators of the pogrom, who steer all over the place, will make use of it and lead the ship to its destruction . . . . They need to ruin the Jews, and they will do it . . . . In Romania an anti-Semitic trial is quickly being prepared! There Anna Pauker[124] happened to be a Zionist, she helped the Romanian Jews immigrate to Israel . . . . The trial will be in Romania, and the procurator will come from here. Everything starts here. Later, it will be in Bulgaria, then in Albania, and then all the Zhids will be lumped together and sent to hell, to Siberia . . . ."[125]

Nezhnyí was not forgiven for his words. Although he had worked from 1947 through 1951 as a secret informant for state security (under the name Chaíkovskií), he was suspected of double dealing and of being "insincere with the organs." (For example, the MGB learned that in 1951 Nezhnyí had informed the famous circus artist E.T. Kio (Girshfeld-Renard) that the "organs" were "working on" him as nationalist and spy.) On March 6, 1953 he was arrested for anti-Soviet nationalistic propaganda."[126]

Under these circumstances, according to a number of different testimonies (unconfirmed by documentary sources), certain Jews close to Kremlin circles decided to write and sign a collective declaration of loyalty, in which, for the sake of self-preservation, they would dissociate themselves once and for all from the Jewish doctors accused of participating in the antigovernment plot. This declaration would appear in *Pravda* as an open letter. The most active participants in preparing the text and collecting signatures were *Pravda* staff members David Zaslavskií and Yakov Marinin (Khavinson), historian Isaak Mints, and philosopher Mark Mitin. There is evidence that the letter was signed by General David Dragunskií, composer Matveí Blanter, writer Vasilií Grossman, and some other prominent scientists, literati, and artists of Jewish origin.[127] But there were others who, for various plausible excuses, refused to take part, among them singer Mark

---

124. Anna Pauker (1893–1960) was a daughter of a rabbi and the wife of Comintern member Marsel Pauker (who had been shot by Stalin in 1937). From November 1947 she had been minister of foreign affairs of Romania. In May 1952 she was dismissed from the Romanian CC of the CP and expelled from the Party. She was later placed under house arrest.

125. Document from the archives of the former KGB.

126. Document from the archives of the former KGB. On April 30, 1953 Nezhnyí's case was closed and he was released Over the following years and until his death in the early 1970s he continued to spread widely his understanding of Stalin's plan with respect to Jews in early 1953. See, for example, E. Markish *Stol' dolgoye vozvrashcheniye . . . [A Long Way Back . . . A Memoir]* (Tel Aviv, 1989), p. 306-307. This perhaps is the reason why many people were led to believe, in time, that Stalin's actual intention was to prepare a migration of Jews to Siberia.

127. Rapoport, *Na rubezhe dvukh epokh. Delo vracheí 1953 goda*, p. 68; Vaksberg, "Stalin protiv yevreyev," *Detektiv i politika*, 1992, no. 3, p. 203.

Reízen, composer Isaak Dunayevskií, and General Yakov Kreízer.[128]

Ilya Erenburg also declined to sign this letter, which, by the way, was never published. Moreover, he wrote to Stalin that such a publication would be a severe blow to the pro-Communist international peace movement and would cause an outburst of anti-Sovietism in the West.[129] The regime needed Erenburg, who was an advocate of Jewish assimilation and a skillful defender of Stalin's diplomacy. Erenburg could feel secure for his personal safety and confident in his future. On January 27, 1953 he was awarded the International Stalin Prize for strengthening peace and friendship among nations; he was called "a prominent Soviet writer, a famous fighter for peace." In his speech of gratitude to the Soviet government he ventured a phrase with an implication:

> No matter what the ethnic origin of a Soviet man may be, he is first of all a patriot of his motherland and a genuine internationalist opposed to racial or ethnic discrimination, a zealot of brotherhood, a fearless guardian of peace.[130]

However, neither Erenburg's prestige nor his phenomenal talents could in any was mitigate the West's negative reaction to the "doctors' case." Speaking nationally on radio US president D. Eisenhower declared that the American secret services had never approached the arrested Soviet medical scientists and had never given them any instructions.[131] Leading British politicians made similar statements. Nor did the international Jewish community stay aloof: world-famous scientist Albert Einstein sent the USSR foreign minister Andreí Vyshinskií (who was then in New York for a UN General Assembly session) a telegram expressing his protest and outrage. But, as one could expect, the most bitter reaction to the persecution of Jews in the USSR came from the government and people of Israel. Emotions grew so strong there that, as popular Soviet journalist Yuríí Zhukov reported in *Pravda* on February 9, 1953, a bomb exploded on the property of USSR diplomatic mission in Tel Aviv. Several mission employees and their family members were injured. Although the Foreign Ministry and the president of Israel offered their apologies to the Soviets for this terrorist act, the latter accused the Israeli government of waging "an unruly campaign of slander." According to Zhukov, this campaign "turned especially fierce" after "state security organs

---

128. Vaksberg, , "Stalin protiv yevreyev," *Detektiv i politika*, 1992, no. 3, p. 203.

129. Ibid., pp. 203–204.

130. *Pravda*, January 28, 1953.

131. In addition to official statements by the Soviet authorities that American secret services had recruited the "saboteur-doctors" (through the humanitarian organization Joint), there were also reports in the Soviet press that the US government had allocated $100 million for subversive activities against the USSR and its allies. *Pravda*, January 13, 1953.

of the USSR and of a number of countries of people's democracy[132] had chopped off the bloody tentacles of the international Jewish bourgeois nationalist organization Joint, established by the American intelligence service to conduct espionage, sabotage, and terrorist activities against peace-loving states."[133] The article ended by stating that it was impossible to continue diplomatic relations with Israel and by giving the traditional call to "bring vigilance to a yet higher level."[134]

THE FINAL CHORD IN THE "CASE" IS PLAYED

In January and early February 1953 the MGB activated "operative investigatory measures" on the "doctors' case" with a warlike propagandistic accompaniment. A new wave of arrests spread over Moscow, and as a result the number of doctors in Lubyanka's cells increased considerably. Professors V.F. Zelenin and E.M. Gelshtein (general practitioners), Professor Ya.L. Rapoport (pathologist), Professors N.A. Shreshevskií, M.N. Yegorov, B.S. Preobrazhenskií, and others were put behind bars. All in all, a total of 37 people had by now been arrested in relation to the "doctors' case." Of them, 28 were doctors. The rest were their family members, mainly their wives. The majority of these doctors were consulting professors and other specialists who worked in the LSUK system, namely P.I. Yegorov, V.N. Vinogradov, V.Kh. Vasilenko, B.B. Kogan, A.M. Grinshteín, A.N. Fedorov, V.F. Zelenin, A.A. Busalov, B.S. Preobrazhenskií, N.A. Popova, G.I. Maíorov, S.Ye. Karpaí, R.I. Ryzhikov, Ya.S. Temkin, M.N. Yegorov (the scientific advisor of the Second Hospital of LSUK), B.A. Yegorov[135] (consulting professor at the Central Polyclinic of LSUK), G.A. Kadzharduzov, and T.S. Zharkovskaya. The rest were employees of other medical institutions, and the majority had worked at the LSUK, either previously or had been used at the LSUK as untenured consultants. These were M.S. Vovsi (Central Institute of Advanced Medical Studies, or CIAMS), N.A. Shereshevskií (CIAMS), V.Ye. Nezlin (CIAMS), S.Ye. Nezlin

---

132. *Translator's note:* "Countries of people's democracy" were socialist countries.

133. *Pravda*, February 14, 1953.

134. Ibid.

135. B.A. Yegorov, who was of noble origin and a pupil of Professor D.D. Pletnev, had been arrested back in January 26, 1952 for conducting anti-Soviet conversations. In part, somebody squealed that, in late 1949, he had declared at a family gathering that "Stalin will die soon, and all the rest of the leaders will fight for power. Then the foreigners will intervene, and we will see Kirill Vladimirovich Romanov as the tsar of the Russian throne." Additionally, Yegorov was incriminated with having "malicious terroristic intentions toward the leaders of the ACP(b) and of the Soviet government." This latter accusation arose when someone reported that Yegorov, upon seeing a newspaper report on the celebration at the Bolshoí Theater of Stalin's seventieth birthday, allegedly said, "Too bad that nobody threw a bomb during the celebration. The head of the government and all the government would have been killed. Life would have become easier."

(consulting professor at Moscow Polyclinic No. 63), Ya.L. Rapoport (Central Control Institute of Serums and Vaccines), E.M. Gelshteín (Botkin Hospital), Ya.G. Etinger (consultant at the Polyclinic of the Ministry of Petrol Industry), R.A. Zasosov (Leningrad Military Medical Academy), V.V. Zakusov[136] (First I.P. Pavlov Leningrad Medical Institute), A.I. Feldman (director of the Moscow Clinic of the Moscow Clinical Institute of Scientific Research).[137]

Although, the majority of the Kremlin doctors were Russians, the case more and more acquired a distinct anti-Semitic character as the investigation developed. Thus was Professor M.S. Vovsi accused in February of 1953 not only of sabotaging treatments administered to the Soviet Party and state elite and of terrorist activity, but also of heading an alleged network of groups of "Jewish bourgeois nationalists" that were situated in a number of Moscow's medical institutions. The following institutions and people were named: Ya.G. Etinger, V.Ye. Nezlin, O.B. Makarevich, N.P. Rabinovich, and others from the Second Moscow Medical Institute; A.B. Topchan, Ya.L Rapoport, Ya.I. Mazel, N.L. Vilk, E.M. Gelshteín, A.M. Grinshteín, Sh.D. Moshkovskií, V.S. Levit, and others from the First Moscow Hospital; director S.A. Reínberg, I.L. Tager, and others from the Molotov Central X-Ray Institute; and L.B. Berlin, M.I. Pevzner, B.S. Levin, G.L. Levin, and others from the Clinic of Remedial Nutrition. But the most numerous group allegedly functioned at the Central Institute of Advanced Medical Studies (Vovsi's main working place). Professors B.B. Kogan, Ya.S. Temkin, G.F. Blagman, I.S. Shnitser, and the doctor S.M. Khaskin, and others were supposed to be members.

Vovsi was forced to "confess"[138] that he had given the leaders of all these groups, except for Pevzner, directives to conduct propagandistic work. The investigation obtained evidence that M.S. Vovsi had deliberately sent Ya.G. Etinger to work at the First Moscow Hospital, and thus carried out Mikhoels's directive to transform this hospital into a focal point of Jewish nationalism. To enhance this image of the doctor's feverish nationalistic activity, the investigation squeezed from him one more "picturesque" detail: to exchange opinions within the circle of his closest accomplices, he in 1951 and 1952 organized several "nationalistic meetings" at his suburban dacha (near Moscow), which were regularly attended by Professors Ya.L. Rapoport, Ye.Ya. Gertsenberg,

136. Leningrad professors Zasosov and Zakusov were also arrested for "anti-Soviet conversations." In addition, Zakusov had been abroad, and from 1947 through 1952 had been the Soviet representative at the UN Drug Commission.

137. Document from the archives of the former KGB.

138. To make Vovsi more "talkative," the MGB arrested his wife, Vera Lvovna, on January 14, 1953 and forced her, with the most refined methods, to slander her husband. For example, the professor had once allegedly been unfaithful to his wife, and this the investigation relished and turned to its advantage. The investigation further threatened to arrest her daughter and son-in-law.

B.B. Kogan, M.S. Vovsi's relatives Kh.M. Vovsi and S.M. Itin, and some others.[139]

As a result of such approaches, together with the fabrication of the main case "of the Kremlin doctor-poisoners," the investigation initiated a parallel and large-scale criminal persecution of other doctors, mainly Jews, who were accused of bourgeois nationalism. The MGB leaders were truly tireless and did not take cognizance of anything in their zealous desire to please their leader who was going insane from his miasma.

On February 9 S.I. Ogoltsov issued an order to arrest M.Ye. Veítsman, who worked as a doctor at the GOSSTRAKH (State Insurance Agency). She might possibly have been spared, except that the all-knowing state security organs learned that she was the sister of Chaim Weizmann, the first president of Israel. Before arresting the humble GOSSTRAKH doctor, the MGB leadership sent Malenkov the following note:

> . . . The MGB of the USSR is working on the sister of the former president of the state of Israel, C.A. Weizmann—Mariya Yevzorovna Veítsman,[140] born in 1893 in the town of Pinsk; a Jew, not a Party member . . . .
>
> Through agents and by means of covert bugging it has been established that M.Ye. Veítsman for several years conducted Zionist agitation in her circles, criticizing Soviet life from a hostile point of view, heaping heinous calumny upon the Party leaders and the Soviet government, and displaying extreme animosity toward the head of the Soviet government.
>
> V.M. Savitskií—M.Ye. Veítsman's husband, arrested by the MGB of the USSR in 1949 for anti-Soviet activities—testified in the course of the investigation that they had both systematically, in an evil manner, heaped heinous calumny upon the leaders of the Party.
>
> Because of her adversarial beliefs, M.Ye. Veítsman steadfastly cherishes the thought of leaving the Soviet Union and going to Palestine.
>
> . . . As for M.Ye. Veítsman's brother, Chaim Weizmann, the former president of the state of Israel: it is known that during World War I he was director of the laboratory of the British Admiralty; from 1921 through 1946 he was president of the reactionary World Zionist Organization and leader of the General Zionist Party; from 1929 through 1946 he held the post of president of the Jewish Agency for Palestine.
>
> Through C. Weizmann the English intelligence service used

139. Document from the archives of the former KGB.

140. *Editor's note:* Weizmann and Veítsman are exactly the same name, transliterated differently.

> Zionists for their own purpose. Because of the weakening of England's status he reoriented the Zionists to serve American imperialism.
>
> . . . Another brother of Weizmann, Samuil Yevzorovich, a former member of the Jewish United Social-Democratic Party, was deputy chairman of the Central Board of the OZET (the Company for Settling Jewish Toilers in Agriculture). In 1930 he was repressed for sabotage, and in 1939 he was executed by shooting as an English spy.
>
> M.Ye. Veítsman's three sisters have at different times emigrated abroad and are now living in Palestine.
>
> Delegates from the state of Israel in Moscow for the period of 1949–1952 had made numerous attempts to establish secret contact with M.Ye. Veítsman.
>
> Of late, fearing arrest, M.Ye. Veítsman speaks of her intention to turn to the Israeli diplomatic mission, hoping to find protection there.

The investigation was interested in literally everything. The arrested woman was interrogated about all the details of her six sisters and four brothers. What happened to them in the past? Which of them are dead? Those who are alive, what do they do? In 1926 Mariya Veítsman spent three and a half months in Palestine to see her mother, and during that time she had also met with someone else. The investigators questioned her about the identity of this person. They also insisted that she recount Chaim Weizmann's relationship with Vladimir Zhabotinskií, the leader of Zionist-Revisionists whom she had met in 1912 in St. Petersburg, where he published *Dawn*[141] magazine. But the investigators hoped to determine, by the majority of their questions, Mariya Veítsman's "criminal connection" with her late brother Chaim, the first president of Israel. The investigators' preoccupation was to prove that she and her brother had had secret contacts lasting through his death in November 1952. Exhausted from the nighttime interrogations, the old woman declared that the last time she had seen Chaim was forty years earlier in Berlin, when she graduated from Zurich University and was returning to Moscow. The investigators did not believe her.

"The investigation knows everything," said Major Ivanov, who was conducting the interrogation. "During his visit to the USA in 1943, Mikhoels, who was well known to you, deliberately met with your brother. We know that he received from him hostile directives, which he transmitted to you in the USSR. Tell us what those directives were?" After Stalin's death on March 20, 1953, M. Veítsman was forced to confess that "[my] bitterness toward Soviet power and its leaders reached such a state that I rejoiced in Zhdanov's death and . . . expressed my desire for Stalin's death."

The leader's death led to the gradual reduction and finally to the closing of

141. *Rassvet.*

Veítsman's case. The Special Meeting at the Ministry of Internal Affairs on August 12, 1953 accused this sister of the first president of Israel of anti-Soviet agitation and sentenced her to five years in reform camps. Yet at the same time, the USSR Presidium of the Supreme Soviet's March 27, 1953 decree on amnesty deemed it necessary to release her from her punishment and from her imprisonment.

Only half a year earlier the imprisoned doctors could not have dreamt of such a happy ending. As recently as January and February 1953 the orgy of terror had been growing at a constant rate. And although this terror was accompanied by the weight of anti-Semitic propaganda, it can be supposed that cruel punishments were being prepared not only for the Jews.

Stalin's repressive actions were becoming increasingly wild and sinister, and their anti-Jewish bias was a sure sign that the behind-the-scenes political struggle at the highest levels of the Kremlin leadership had further intensified. Stalin did not abandon his idea of radically purging and renewing his closest entourage, and of discarding some old comrades-in-arms. On the contrary, feeling that the outcome was rapidly approaching, he pressed even harder, playing the Jewish card. In late January 1953 he ordered that Polina Zhemchuzhina be brought to Moscow from her exile in Kustanaí. (Her code name in the operation documents was "object-12.") Zhemchuzhina (Molotov's wife) was interrogated in connection with testimony given by the arrested physicians V.N. Vinogradov, B.B. Kogan, and M.S. Vovsi, who had exposed her as a "Jewish nationalist." Stalin apparently hoped for evidence against his former foreign minister, whom he had severely criticized shortly after the Nineteenth Party Congress, suspecting him of ties with American intelligence services.[142]

The interrogations of Zhemchuzhina lasted through February. Her final summons to see an investigation officer was on March 2, 1953. Then suddenly everything stopped. And there was nothing strange in this. On the previous night, March 1, Stalin suffered a brain hemorrhage. The dictator was in agony. His apparatchik entourage (which some historians believe[143] had done much to

---

142. As Molotov later recalled: "She suffered because of me . . . . They tried to find a way to bear down on me, and tortured her in order to find something to accuse me of." F.I. Chuyev, *Sto sorok besed s molotovym*, Moscow, 1991, p. 466. Published in English as *Molotov Remembers: Inside Kremlin Politics. Conversations with Felix Chuev*, Chicago: I.R. Dee, 1993.

To support Stalin's suspicion of Molotov's "espionage activities," the MGB arrested I.M. Maískií on February 19, 1953. Maískií was the former Soviet ambassador to the UK, and from 1943 through 1946 he was Molotov's deputy at the Narkomat [People's Commissariat] of Foreign Affairs. On the basis of his testimony, the MGB arrested three diplomats who had worked with him in London on March 5, 1953. (S.N. Rostovskií, also known as Ernest Henry, was among the three.) Maískií would subsequently say in an interview: "I am sure that preparations were then being made against Molotov, and only because of Stalin's death were we saved" (*Druzhba narodov*, 1988, no. 3, p. 239).

143. A. Avtorkhanov, *Zagadka smerti Stalina (zagovor Beria)* [*The Mystery of Stalin's Death (Beria's*

expedite the death of "the Father of the Peoples") awaited the outcome with fear and anticipation.

The Death of the Dictator and the Release of the Doctors

On March 6 TASS announced that the heart of the brilliant disciple of Lenin's cause had stopped beating on March 5 at 9:50 p.m. Stalin's funeral, accompanied by a massive throng that crushed nearly four hundred people to death, took place on March 9. The next day Beria, who had been appointed minister of internal affairs, issued a special order for Zhemchuzhina's release. By a CC CPSU resolution, she was re-established in the Party on March 21, and M.F. Shkiryatov issued her a new Party ID card two days later. By an irony of fate, four years later Shkiryatov was to draw up a resolution on Zhemchuzhina's dismissal from the Party. The doctors under investigation remained in prison, but their release was now a matter of time.

In mid-March the new minister of internal affairs organized a thorough inspection of the investigation on "the doctors' case." He never hid his conviction that the entire case had been falsified and was unlawful. Most likely he thought such a liberal and humanistic facade was necessary to strengthen his popularity firstly among the intelligentsia, who had suffered more than anyone during the last years of Stalin's terror. Beria also hoped to have a positive effect on public opinion, just as he had enjoyed in 1938 when he replaced the pathologically cruel Yezhov as people's commissar of internal affairs. Moreover, having unmasked the MGB's unlawful acts, Beria hoped to discredit Yezhov's former leadership, primarily his potential rival Ignatyev, and clear a path to establish his own people in the ministry.

The arrested doctors were given the opportunity to state in writing their experiences. All of them referred to physical and psychological coercion and denied their previous confessions in which they had accused themselves and their colleagues of serious crimes. Notably, some of them not only criticized the unlawful methods used by the investigation, but also expressed their quite sincere opinions of Soviet state policy toward the Jews. Professor Ya.L. Rapoport then expressed his credo. This intellectual, who harbored deep and original thoughts, was the author of interesting memoirs on the "doctors' case." In hope of a better future (though with certain caution about the regime's unalterable essence), he wrote on March 15, 1953:

> In all sincerity and frankness I state the circumstances of the case such as they actually were . . . . I personally never allowed a thought that the

---

Plot)], (Moscow, 1992), pp. 83–96.

> policy (whose existence I recognized) of restriction with regard to Jews was grounded on racist, anti-Semitic motives. I claimed that it was caused by a lack of trust toward the Jews as a result of their extensive relations with the capitalist world abroad (especially the USA and Israel); [and] that this policy to a known extent was justified by reasons related to the defense of USSR state security, especially considering the large number of persons of Jewish nationality in a number of institutions, particularly medical institutions. I also believed that the staff of some of the institutions, particularly scientific and medical institutions, testified to the existence of nationalistic tendencies in the selection of personnel, which constitute an abnormal phenomenon. However, these considerations did not remove the feeling of dissatisfaction and offense, especially among the youth who have no contacts with Jewry and who are allegedly subjected to all manner of restrictions merely because of their Jewish origins . . . . During the formation of the state of Israel those who shared my views showed great interest in all the stages and manifestations of this state's struggle for its independence; we followed this struggle with a feeling of great sympathy, and we experienced a feeling of enormous gratitude to the Soviet government for that support it rendered for the organization of this state. However, no one with whom I spoke (not even Etinger) expressed the view that Israel was the new motherland. And later it became perfectly obvious to me and to my close friends (Sh.D. Moshkovskiĭ, etc.) that Israel in its current mode was a lifeless puppet of the American imperialists, serving their purposes and making the situation of Jews in the USSR more difficult . . . .[144]

With such trump cards in his hands, Beria on March 31, 1953 approved a resolution concerning the criminal persecution and release of those arrested in "the case of the Kremlin doctors."[145] And on April 3, at the initiative of this new minister of internal affairs of the Presidium of the CC CPSU, a new resolution was approved on rehabilitation of those arrested in the "doctor-saboteurs case."[146]

WHO IS GUILTY?

On the next day an "Announcement of the Ministry of Internal Affairs of the USSR" appeared in the press, stating that the arrested doctors had been released. This announcement especially emphasized that "the persons guilty of the improperly conducted investigation have been arrested and called to criminal accountability." At the same time, Beria signed a decree prohibiting any manner of coercion, including physical coercion, toward

144. Document from the archives of the former KGB.

145. Document from the archives of the former KGB.

146. Document from the archives of the President of the Russian Federation.

the arrested; and purging prisons of areas for and instruments of tortures. The decree, using the nonspecific word *persons*, alluded to Ryumin, the former vice minister of state security. This main torturer of the defamed doctors was arrested on March 16, 1953. In essence, he had only been king for a day, a pitiful but dangerous toy in the dictator's hands. Nonetheless he was deemed to be the main initiator and executor of the crimes committed by the regime. Ryumin, who enjoyed no support in the Party and state structure, thus had to pay for his own sins as well as for the sins of others. The decree did not take into account his dismissal from the state security organs two months before the culmination of the "doctors' case," i.e. two months before the infamous TASS announcement of January 13, 1953. Ryumin was not merely accused of having deceived the government and of having inspired the falsified case; he was also made politically responsible for the fanning of state anti-Semitism in the country. On April 6, 1953 *Pravda* wrote:

> Despicable adventurers of Ryumin's kind attempted, with the help of cases they themselves had fabricated, to ignite within Soviet society—which is welded together morally and politically, unified by the ideas of proletarian internationalism—a feeling of national hostility, which is profoundly alien to socialist ideology. Pursuing these provocative goals, they employed unbridled slander of the Soviet people. The thorough inspection established that, for example, the honest public figure, people's artist of the USSR Mikhoels, was thus slandered.

Ryumin persistently denied his guilt at first, but he finally surrendered after the investigator grew weary of arguing with him in vain and employed more effective methods, such as solitary confinement. He then provided the necessary testimony. On July 7, 1954 the Military Collegium of the USSR Supreme Court sentenced Ryumin to death. The sentence was carried out on July 22.

In comparison, those who were truly and directly responsible for the semi-official, implicit policy of anti-Semitic propaganda—Suslov, Mikhaílov, and Chesnokov—escaped with a mere slap on the wrists. Suslov was deprived of membership in the CC Presidium (he was re-established in July 1955), but he remained as CC secretary. Mikhaílov was punished more severely; he was dismissed from the Central Party apparatus. But as compensation he was for some time permitted to head the Moscow Party organization. In actuality he did not long remain in the Moscow CPSU Committee, and in 1954 was sent as ambassador to Poland. In March 1953 Chesnokov was sent to the periphery (i.e., to the Gorkií Regional Party Committee) as head of a department. In 1957 he was again returned to Moscow as head of the State Television and Radio

(Gosteleradio) Enterprise, and later he worked as a professor at MSU. Immediately after Stalin's death—and with Malenkov's help—Ignatyev (Ryumin's direct head of the Ministry of State Security) dramatically climbed the ladder, becoming the CC secretary. Then on April 5, 1953, at Beria's insistence, he was removed from this post "due to his political blindness and for being a scatterbrain"; and on April 28 he was dismissed from the CC altogether. But this alumnus of the Party apparatus would not long remain in disgrace. His principal enemy, Beria, was arrested on June 26; and Ignatyev became a CC member on July 7. Thus in December Ignatyev was appointed first secretary of the Bashkir Regional Committee.

Suslov, Mikhaílov, Chesnokov, and Ignatyev lived the remainder of their lives in prosperity and honor. They experienced no remorse over having organized and conducted their inhuman action back in 1953.

In contrast, Beria, the main initiator of the release of the unlawfully-arrested doctors, died a tragic and shameful death. The conservative Party apparatus members would not forgive him for having taken the liberty to make a number of independent and courageous decision and actions, including his intention to re-open both the Jewish Theater in Moscow and the central Jewish newspaper. A session of the CC in early July 1953 was in fact a Party trial of Beria. N.N. Shatalin, the CC secretary, delivered a most harsh tirade. This orthodox high-ranking Party official (who looked like a misanthrope suffering from stomach disorders) proved himself to be an uncompromising fighter against bourgeois nationalism. Beria had published, on April 4, 1953, a Ministry of Internal Affairs special communication on the rehabilitation of the doctors. Shatalin now castigated him for this, saying that it made a "painful impression" (?!) on public opinion.[147] On December 23, 1953 Beria was shot according to the sentence of the Special Court Presence of the Supreme Court of the USSR.

Party intellectual Shepilov survived the scandalous "doctors' case" unscathed. Though *Pravda* had shaped, in early 1953, the pogrom-like tone of all Soviet propaganda, he continued as its editor-in-chief for another three years. From 1955 Shepilov's political influence grew noticeably, mainly because he had written, at Khruschev's order, an article entitled "The General Party Line and the Vulgarization of Marxism,"[148] which implicitly criticized Malenkov. As a result, the next day a CC CPSU session released Malenkov from his duties as head of the Council of Ministers of the USSR. Thus Shepilov, who had been promoted by Zhdanov, took vengeance, although belatedly, against the enemy of his late benefactor. The grateful Khruschev made Shepilov first the CC secretary and later the minister of foreign affairs. However, Shepilov's political career soon collapsed.

---

147. *Izvestiya TsK KPSS*, 1991, no. 3, p. 99.

148. "General'naya liniya partii i vul'garizatsiya marksizma," *Pravda*, January 24, 1955.

This master of apparatus intrigues ultimately outwitted himself, moving again to the camp of Malenkov his allies—Molotov and Kaganovich. In June 1957, Khruschev and his allies in the CC declared that those three constituted an "anti-Party group," and stigmatized Shepilov for "joining" them. Shepilov consequently found himself in Kirghizia, practically in exile. He later faded into obscurity in the Archives Administration in Moscow.

It was with all these troubles and consequences that Stalin's last criminal operation, "the saboteur-doctors case," came to an end. This case is still fraught with many mysterious details. Was Stalin fully committed to his decision to put the doctors on trial, or did he intend ultimately to void it? What would the consequences of such a process have been—a massive deportation of Jews to Siberia, as some of the investigators claim? Or would the leader have dealt with his close comrades-in-arms by a political decree, as others say? Perhaps both events would have occurred. Let us hope that we shall someday receive a clear response to these and other questions.

Epilogue

The End and the Exodus

Romain Rolland, after visiting the USSR in 1935, wrote in his diary about "the Russia of the pharaohs," where "people sang while erecting pyramids for them." One might suggest that had he visited a few years later, the French writer would have used the singular. For very soon it became evident that there was only one red pharaoh—Stalin. In the internecine war among the Bolsheviks, Stalin's power was enhanced not only by the pyramids erected in his honor—that is, by the innumerable monuments, paintings, books, and articles of praise—but also by the constantly growing number of prisons and detention camps built by people who were by no means singing songs and dancing with joy. The whole country was transformed into a giant stockaded village, and its people were transformed into its prisoners. And even in servitude there exists a certain hierarchy. Stalin, in his last decade of rule, exerted much effort to place Jews at the lowest rung. Subjected to mass repressions and forced assimilation, the Jews were deprived of national status within the framework of the Communist totalitarian state. To preserve their culture and national ethnic background under these circumstances, and not to become dispersed among other peoples, the Soviet Jews had no alternative but an exodus (in tune with the Zionist idea) from the empire that had been oppressing them, and to secure a new home in the land of their ancestors, the state of Israel.

The first ray of hope for freedom glimmered when the tyrant died and the granite, prison-like stronghold of power he had created began to crack. In 1955, when Ilya Erenburg finished his symbolic story, "The Thaw,"[1] Stalin's old comrades who had inherited his power had at first tacitly refused to acknowledge the most odious sins of the recent past, but gradually they began to concede them.

---

1. "Ottepel'."

In the autumn of 1955 the CC CPSU commissioned the Office of the Public Prosecutor of the USSR to review the case of S.A. Lozovskiĭ, I.S. Fefer, P.D. Markish, and other Jewish Antifascist Committee leaders who had been shot in August 1952. On October 1 R.A. Rudenko, the USSR prosecutor general, dispatched a strictly confidential note to Old Square reporting that the case had been "forged upon the instructions of the denounced enemies Abakumov and Ryumin."[2]

Also acknowledged as falsified were the "expert" conclusions that the information JAC members sent for publication abroad was confidential, and that their literary works were of a "nationalistic nature." The invalidity of the expertise was obvious, for the MGB investigators' influence on the experts "was so strong that the latter arrived at conclusions that in no way followed from the documents under study."[3]

Yet at the same time, three years after the execution of the JAC leaders, the CC CPSU and, of course, the Office of Public Prosecutor of the USSR were still insisting that the letter to Stalin about establishing a Jewish Republic in the Crimea was of a "nationalistic nature." Later, though, they expressed the reservation that "sending such a letter to the head of the Soviet State cannot be regarded as a juridically punishable deed."[4] And that was not all. On August 29, 1956 Khrushchev met with T. Buck, J.B. Salsberg, and other delegates from the Progressive Labor Party of Canada during their visit to the USSR. Misrepresenting his former anti-Semitic escapades, Khrushchev adopted the old falsification that "when the Tartars were expelled from the Crimea, some of the Jews began to develop an idea about having Jews migrate there in order to create a Jewish state in the Crimea . . . . It would have been an American base in the south of our country. I was entirely against this idea and agreed on this issue with Stalin."[5]

The JAC leaders were again accused of "nationalistic motives," as it were, for having had the committee engage in unrelated functions, for having sought to speak and act on the behalf of all Soviet Jewry, and also for having allowed statements of a nationalistic character to appear in their literary works. "These wrong deeds, as has been emphasized in the prosecutor general's note, intentionally promoted Jewish nationalists' rallying around the Jewish Antifascist Committee."

These arguments proved that Stalin's policy of state anti-Semitism survived even his death. However, another era had begun. The new Soviet government clearly saw that it could not use absurd accusations as a cover, for such accusations

2. RTsKhIDNI, f. 589, op. 3, d. 15624, l. 364–370.
3. RTsKhIDNI, f. 589, op. 3, d. 15624, l. 366.
4. RTsKhIDNI, f. 589, op. 3, d. 15624, l. 365.
5. RTsKhIDNI, f. 589, op. 3, d. 15624, l. 365; *Istochnik* (*The Source*), 1994, no. 3, p. 99.

could not mask their appalling crimes. That is why the Office of Public Prosecutor could do nothing other than enter a protest to the Supreme Court of the USSR proposing that the sentence of July 11–18, 1952 be repealed.

By a resolution by the Office of Public Prosecutor of the USSR, and considering "some newly disclosed details of the case," the MCSC on November 22, 1955 rescinded the sentence given to S.A. Lozovskiı́, I.S. Fefer, and others that the closed court session in 1952 had condemned. The Military Collegium now dismissed the case for absence of the corpus delicti.[6]

The victims of Stalin's anti-Semitism began to be rehabilitated, especially after the Twentieth Party Congress. From Kazakhstan, Middle Asia, and other remote places, the exiled wives, children, and other relatives of JAC members and Jewish writers repatriated. Probably the first to see Moscow again was academician L.S. Shtern, who returned from her exile in Dzhambul (Kazakhstan) in June 1953. In 1956, at a detention camp in the Irkutsk region, I. Fefer's wife, R.Kh. Kalish, whose mother had been shot by the fascists in Babiı́ Yar near Kiev, was set free.

Nonetheless, hopes of a better life and future proved ephemeral. Khrushchev's rehabilitation could not fully render historical justice. On the one hand, the gesture was effective propaganda (though the regime still retained its oppressive nature); on the other hand, the newly-emerging public opinion compelled the regime to make this concession in order to camouflage its still unchanged policy of forcibly assimilating the Jews.

That is why, beginning in the mid-1960s, Jews took the most active part in the dissident movement that was then gaining momentum. The aim and purpose of their public activity, especially after Israel's victorious Six-Day War of 1967, was to struggle for repatriation. For, under the circumstances, leaving for their ancestral motherland was their only hope of survival as a nation.

It should be noted that the liberalization of the emigration policy was to a certain extent promoted by US president Richard Nixon's visit to Moscow in the early 1970s and the resulting détente that soon followed. In 1972 the USSR permitted 29 800 Jews to leave, and in 1973 another 33 500 were granted permission.[7] Among these were quite a few who had suffered the Stalinist persecutions of the 1940s and early 1950s, as well as their families, including S. Mikhoels's daughters and poet P. Markish's widow and children.

For all its efforts, the West, after World War II, was unable, even minimally, to break through Stalin's hermetic "iron curtain"; thus it could not organize a

6. RTsKhIDNI, f. 589, op. 3, d. 15624, l. 318.

7. This is according to the "Information given to the fraternal parties regarding the inventions of anti-Soviet propaganda about the violation of human rights that allegedly took place in the USSR," approved by the Politburo of the CC CPSU in January 1976 (Minutes #201).

considerable emigration of Soviet Jews to Israel. The first break in this seal was made during Brezhnev's gerontological regime, a regime that devoted the major part of its life potential to suppressing the 1968 "Prague spring" and then fell into stagnation.

Israel's long-standing patron, the USA, launched in the 1970s (especially under Jimmy Carter's presidency) a concentrated and, it should be admitted, quite successful propagandistic attack on the Soviets under the slogan of defending human rights. The primary purpose of this campaign was to facilitate the emigration of Soviet Jews. The Communist counterpropaganda revealed its total inefficiency, being unable to resist this skillful but cruel attack. Since then hundreds of thousands of Soviet Jews have left for their historical motherland. Having lost this and other invisible battles (as well as visible ones, such as in Afghanistan) of the "Cold War," the Red empire collapsed, prompting a new stage of international crises (including the crisis related to the Jewish problem) in the country.

Taking advantage of the vulnerability and numerous defects of the newly-fledged Russian democracy, its most irreconcilable enemies started actively to use rather moth-eaten anti-Semitic slogans in their political struggle. However, I think it unfruitful and dishonorable for even self-respecting ultra-patriots today to talk seriously about the *Protocols of the Elders of Zion* and other such literature that is being widely spread at present. It seems that Winston Churchill once said, "We have few anti-Semites in England, because Englishmen don't consider themselves inferior to Jews." Our country has yet to rid itself of the inferiority complex that nurtures anti-Semitism. But the problem is in part solving itself as many Jews leave for Israel and others are caught up in the process of natural assimilation. The Jewish influence in Russia, which so irritates the chauvinists, is constantly decreasing. Now, as opposed to the situation in the early postrevolutionary period, Jews occupy much more modest positions in the key spheres of public life. To see what lies behind this tendency, we must take into account the aggressive nationalisms of the peripheral and contiguous territories of the former Soviet empire, which express themselves more loudly and more decisively each time. Yet we must also consider that each time the provocative bugaboo of the notorious "Jewish danger" seems to be more the result of sick minds than political intent.

The creation of an open society in our country, the consolidation of contacts with the outside world, and the conversion of Russia into a stable legal state are necessary if our people are finally to recover entirely from the Stalinist fear of "international Zionism" and become a civilized partner of other nations. It is quite obvious that such cooperation—including cooperation with Israel, where more than half a million Russian Jews now live—will, in its turn, help establish and strengthen the new politics, economics, and ideology of the new, yet at the same time eternal, Russia, and enhance its prestige throughout the world.

Select Bibliography

Adzhubeí, A.I., "Te desyat' let" ["Those Ten Years"], *Znamya* [*Flag*], 1988, nos. 6, 7.

Aleksandrovich, M., *Ya pomniu . . .* [*I Remember . . .*]. Moscow: Progress-Akademiya, 1992.

Alliluyeva, S.I., *Dvadtsat' pisem k drugu* [*Twenty Letters to a Friend*]. Moscow: Izvestiya, 1990.

Alliluyeva, S.I., *Tol'ko odin god* [*Only One Year*]. Moscow: Kniga, 1990.

Altshuler, M. and S. Ycikas, "Were There Two Black Books About the Holocaust in the Soviet Union?" *Jews and Jewish Topics in the Soviet Union and Eastern Europe*, Spring 1992, pp. 37–55.

Andrew, Christopher M. and Oleg Gordievsky, *KGB: History of Foreign Policy Operations from Lenin to Gorbachev*. London: Hodder & Stoughton, 1990.

Avtorkhanov, A., *Tekhnologiya vlasti* [*Technology of Power*]. Moscow: Slovo / New World Center, 1991.

Avtorkhanov, A., *Zagadka smerti Stalina (zagovor Berii)* [*The Mystery of Stalin's Death (Beria's Plot)*]. Moscow: Slovo, 1992.

Beladi, L. and T. Kraus, *Stalin*. Translated from the Hungarian. Moscow: Politizdat, 1989.

Beria, S.L., *Moí otets—Lavrentií Beriya* [*My Father—Lavrentii Beria*]. Moscow: Sovremennik, 1994.

Boffa, Giuseppe, *Istoriya Sovyetskogo Soyuza* [*History of the Soviet Union*]. Trans. from the Italian. Moscow: Mezhdunarodnye otnosheniya, 1994, vol. 2.

Borshchagovskií, A.M., *Obvinyayetsya krov'* [*Blood on Trial*]. Moscow: Progress-Kul'tura, 1994.

Borshchagovskií, A.M., *Zapiski balovnya sud'by* [*Notes of a Favorite of Fortune*]. Moscow: Sovyetskií pisatel, 1991.

Bugaí, N.F., "20—50–ye gody: pereseleniya i deportatsii yevreískogo naceleniya v SSSR" ["From the 20s Through the 50s: Migrations and Deportations of the Jewish Population in the USSR"], *Otechestvennaya istoriya* [*History of the Native Land*], 1993, no. 3, pp. 175–185.

Chuyev, F.I., *Sto sorok besed s Molotovym // Iz dnevnikov F. Chuyeva.* Moscow: Terra, 1991. Published in English as *Molotov Remembers: Inside Kremlin Politics. Conversations with Felix Chuev.* Edited with an introduction and notes by Albert Resis. Chicago: I.R. Dee, 1993.

Conquest, Robert, *Power and Policy in the U.S.S.R.: The Struggle for Stalin's Succession, 1945–1960.* New York: Harper & Row, 1967.

Djilas, Milovan, *Litso totalitarizma* [*The Face of Totalitarianism*]. Translated from the Serbo-Croatian. Moscow: Novosti, 1992.

Dubson, V., "The Archive of the Jewish Antifascist Committee," *Jews and Jewish Topics in the Soviet Union and Eastern Europe,* Winter 1991, pp. 64–77.

Erenburg, I.G., *Lyudi, gody, zhizn'* [*People, Years, Life*], in *Sobr. soch.* [*Collected Works*], vol. 9. Moscow: Khudozhestvennaya Literatura, 1967.

Etinger, Ya.Ya., "'Delo vracheí' i sud'ba" ["The Doctors' Case and Fate"], *Nauka i zhizn'* [*Science and Life*], 1990, no. 1, pp. 126–129.

Etinger, Ya.Ya., "Kogda nachalos' 'delo vracheí'?" ["When Did the 'Doctors' Case' Begin?"], in *Zven'ya: Istoricheskií al'manakh* [*Links: A Historical Miscellany*], Part 1. Moscow: Progress/Feniks/Atheneum, 1991, pp. 555–559.

Fedotov, G.P., *Tyazhba po Rossii* [*Competition Over Russia*], vol. 3. Paris: YMCA Press, 1982.

Gaí, D.I., "Konets 'dela vracheí'" ["The End of the 'Doctors' Case'"], *Nedelya* [*English translation?*] 1988, no. 6.

Geízer, M.M., *Solomon Mikhoels.* Moscow: Prometeí, 1990.

Gilboa, Yehoshua A., *The Black Years of Soviet Jewry, 1939–1953.* Translated from the Hebrew by Yosef Shachter and Dov Ben-Abba. Boston: Little, Brown, and Company, 1971.

Gitelman, Zvi Y., *The Jews of Russia and the Soviet Union—1881 to the Present.* New York, 1981.

Kahan, Stuart, *The Wolf of the Kremlin.* New York: W. Morrow, 1987.

Khrushchev, N.S., "Vospominaniya" ["Memoirs"], *Voprosy istorii* [*Issues in History*], 1991, nos. 11, 12; 1992, no. 1.

Kolesnik, A.N., *Khronika zhizni semyi Stalina* [*The Chronicle of the Life of Stalin's Family*]. Moscow: All-Union House of Political Education, TSENDSI Commercial Center, 1990.

Kutafina, O.Ye., comp. and ed., *Inkvizitor. Stalinskií prokuror Vyshinskií* [*The Inquisitor: Stalin's Prosecutor Vyshinskií*]. Moscow: Respublika, 1992.

Lenin, V.I., "Kriticheskiye zametki po natsional'nomu voprosu" ["Critical Notes on the Nationality Problem"], in *Polnoye sobrachenieye sochinenií* [*Collected Works*]. Moscow: Institute of Marxism-Leninism, 1961, vol. 24, pp. 113–150.

Malenkov, A.G., *O moyom ottse Georgií Malenkove* [*About My Father, Georgií Malenkov*]. Moscow: NTTs "Tekhnoekos," 1992.

Markish, Ester, *Stol' dolgoye vozvrashcheniye . . . Vospominaniya* [*A Long Way Back . . . A Memoir*] Tel Aviv, 1989.

Medvedev, R.A., *Oni okruzhali Stalina* [*They Were Stalin's Entourage*]. Moscow: Politizdat, 1990.

Nekrasov, V.F., comp. and ed., *Beriya: konets kar'yery* [*Beria: End of a Career*]. Moscow: Politizdat, 1991.

Ortenberg, D.I., *Sorok tretií: rasskaz-khronika* [*The Forty-Third: A Story-Chronicle*]. Moscow: Politizdat, 1991.

Pinkus, Benjamin, *The Jews of the Soviet Union: The History of a National Minority.* Cambridgeshire: Cambridge University Press, 1988.

Popov, N.V., compiler, *Arkhivy raskryvayut taíny . . . Mezhdunarodnye voprosy: sobytiya i lyudi* [*Archives Open Secrets . . . International Issues: Events and People*]. Moscow: Politizdat, 1991.

Rapoport, Ya.L., *Na rubezhe dvukh epokh. Delo vracheií 1953 goda* [*At the Boundary of Two Epochs: The Doctors' Case of 1953*]. Moscow: Kniga, 1988.

Redlich, Shimon, *Propaganda and Nationalism in Wartime Russia: The Jewish Antifascist Committee in the USSR, 1941–1948.* Boulder, Colorado: East European Quarterly, 1982.

Shatunovskaya, Lidiya A., *Zhizn' v Kremle* [*Life in the Kremlin*]. New York: Chalidze Publications, 1982.

Sheínis, Z.S., *Provokatsiya veka* [*Provocation of the Century*]. Moscow: PIK Independent Publishing House, 1992.

Simonov, A.I., "Glazami cheloveka moyego pokoleniya" ["As Seen by a Man of My Generation"], *Znamya* [*Flag*], 1988, nos. 3–5.

Solzhenitsyn, A.I., *Arkhipelag GULAG, 1918—1956. Opyt khudozhestvennogo issledovaniya,* Parts 1 and 2, in "Maloye sobraniye sochineníí" ["The Shorter Collected Works"], vol. 5 Moscow: INCOM NB, 1991. Published in English as *The GULAG Archipelago, 1918–1956: An Experiment in Literary Investigation.* Translated from the Russian by Thomas P. Whitney. New York: Harper & Row, 1974–1978.

Stalin, I.V., "Natsionalnyí vopros u Leninizm. Otvet tovarishcham Meshkovu, Lovalchuku i drugim" ["Leninism and the National Question: A Reply to Comrades Meshkov and Kovalchuk and Others"], *Sochineniya* [*Collected Works*]. Moscow: Gospolitizdat, 1949, vol. 11, pp. 333–355.

Stalin, Iosif V., *Marksizm i natsional'no-kolonial'nyí vopros. Sbornik izbrannykh stateí i recheí* [*Marxism and the National-Colonial Question: Collected Articles and Speeches*]. Moscow: Gospolitizdat, 1939.

Stalin, Iosif V., "Ob Antisemitizme. Otvet na zapros Yevreiskogo telegrafnogo agenstva iz Ameriki" ["On Anti-Semitism: A Reply to a Question of the Jewish Telegraph Agency from America"], *Sochineniya* [*Collected Works*]. Moscow: Gospolitizdat, 1951, vol. 13, p. 28.

Stolyarov, K.A., *Golgofa. Dokumental'naya povest'* [*Calvary: A Documentary History*]. Moscow, 1991.

Trotskií, Lev D., *Moya zhizn'. Opyt avtobiografii.* Moscow: Kniga, 1990, 2 vols. Published in English as *My Life: An Attempt at an Autobiography.* New York: Scribner's Sons, 1930.

Trotskií, Lev D., *Prestupleniya Stalina* [*The Crimes of Stalin*], ed. by Yu.G. Felshtinskií. Moscow: Izdatel'stvo gumanitarnoí literatury, 1994.

Trotskií, Lev D., *Stalin,* vol. 2, ed. by Yu.G. Felshtinskií. Moscow: TERRA, 1990.

Vaksberg, A.I., "Stalin protiv yevreyev" ["Stalin Against the Jews"], *Detektiv i politika* [*Detective Stories and Politics*], 1992, no. 3, pp. 150–208.

Vasilyeva, L.N., *Kremlevskiye zheny* [*The Kremlin Wives*]. Moscow: Vagrius, 1992.

Vovsi-Mikhoels, Nataliya, *Moí otets Solomon Mikhoels: vospominaniya o zhizn' i gibeli* [*My Father, Solomon Mikhoels: Memoirs of His Life and Death*]. Tel Aviv: Iakov Press, 1984.

Werth, Nicolas, *Istoriya sovyetskogo gosudarstva. 1900—1991* [*History of the Soviet State: 1990–1991*]. Translated from the French. Moscow: Progress-Akademiya, 1992.

Volkogonov, D.A., *Triumf i tragediya / Politicheskií portret I.V. Stalina.* 2 vols. Moscow: Izd-vo APN, 1989. Published in English as *Stalin: Triumph and Tragedy.* London: Weidenfeld and Nicholson, 1991.

Volkov, F.D., *Vzlet i padeniye Stalina* [*The Rise and Fall of Stalin*]. Moscow: Spektr, 1992.

Yakovlev, A.N., ed., *Reabilitatsiya. Politicheskiye protsessy 30—50-kh godov* [*Rehabilitation: Political Processes of the 1930s through the 1950s*]. Moscow: Politizdat, 1991.

Index of Names

Gennadi V. Kostyrchenko was born in 1954 and graduated from Moscow State Historic Archives Institute, obtaining his Ph.D. in history. His 1988 dissertation on *Soviet Aircraft Industry During World War II* was included in a two-volume work entitled *Aircraft Industry in the USSR: 1917–1945* [*Samoletostroyeniye v SSSR: 1917–1945 gg.*] (Moscow: TsAGI, 1993–1994). He was director of the Central Archives of Ministry of Aircraft Industry through 1989, when he became senior researcher at the Institute of Marxism-Leninism of the Communist Party of the Soviet Union Central Committee. As a member of Dmitry A. Volkogonov's research group, he worked on the preparation of the multivolume *History of World War II* [*Istoriya Velikoí Otechestvennoí Voí Sovyetskogo Naroda*]. Since 1992 Dr. Kostyrchenko has been a senior researcher at the Russian Center for the Preservation and Study of Modern History Documents (the former Central Party Archives). His basic field of interest is Soviet Jewry during post-war Stalinism. He has published various papers on this topic in Russian and Israeli periodicals.